REPRESENTING ZION

The prophetic books of the Old Testament offer a fascinating collection of oracles, poetic images and theological ideas. Among the most prominent themes are those of judgement and salvation, especially concerning the fate of Zion. This place, where the people of God dwell, is alternately presented as either the object of divine wrath or the image of a salvific ideal.

Representing Zion provides a thorough and critical study of the images of Zion in the entire prophetic literature of the Old Testament. The book challenges traditional interpretations of Zion and offers a fresh exploration of the literary and theological nature of the biblical writings. Zion has largely been treated by scholars as an image of the inviolable city consistently and unambiguously used by Old Testament authors. *Representing Zion* reveals the Zion motif to be a much more contested, complex and profoundly theological, a reflection of the ambiguous role of YHWH as judge and saviour.

Frederik Poulsen teaches in the Department of Biblical Studies, University of Copenhagen.

COPENHAGEN INTERNATIONAL SEMINAR

Available:

JAPHETH BEN ALI'S BOOK OF JEREMIAH
Joshua A. Sabih

THE EMERGENCE OF ISRAEL IN ANCIENT PALESTINE
Emanuel Pfoh

ORIGIN MYTHS AND HOLY PLACES IN THE OLD TESTAMENT
Lukasz Niesiowski-Spanò

CHANGING PERSPECTIVES I
John Van Seters

ARGONAUTS OF THE DESERT
Philippe Wajdenbaum

THE EXPRESSION 'SON OF MAN' AND THE DEVELOPMENT OF
CHRISTOLOGY
Mogens Müller

BIBLICAL STUDIES AND THE FAILURE OF HISTORY
Niels Peter Lemche

BIBLICAL NARRATIVE AND PALESTINE'S HISTORY
Thomas L. Thompson

'IS THIS NOT THE CARPENTER?'
Edited by Thomas L. Thompson and Thomas S. Verenna

THE BIBLE AND HELLENISM
Edited by Thomas L. Thompson and Philippe Wajdenbaum

RETHINKING BIBLICAL SCHOLARSHIP
Philip R. Davies

REPRESENTING ZION
Frederik Poulsen

Forthcoming:

THE JUDAEO-KARAITE RECEPTION OF THE HEBREW BIBLE
Joshua A. Sabih

SYRIA-PALESTINE IN THE LATE BRONZE AGE
Emanuel Pfoh

REPRESENTING ZION

Judgement and Salvation
in the Old Testament

Frederik Poulsen

LONDON AND NEW YORK

First published 2015
by Routledge
2 Park Square, Milton Park, Abingdon, Oxon, OX14 4RN

and by Routledge
711 Third Ave., New York City, NY 10017

Routledge is an imprint of the Taylor & Francis Group, an informa business

© 2015 Frederik Poulsen

The right of Frederik Poulsen to be identified as author has been asserted in accordance with sections 77 and 78 of the Copyright, Designs and Patents Act 1988.

All rights reserved. No part of this book may be reprinted or reproduced or utilised in any form or by any electronic, mechanical, or other means, now known or hereafter invented, including photocopying and recording, or in any information storage or retrieval system, without permission in writing from the publishers.

Trademark notice: Product or corporate names may be trademarks or registered trademarks, and are used only for identification and explanation without intent to infringe.

British Library Cataloguing in Publication Data
A catalogue record for this book is available from the British Library

Library of Congress Cataloging in Publication Data
A catalog record for this book has been requested

ISBN: 978-1-844-65811-4 (hbk)
ISBN: 978-1-315-74421-6 (ebk)

Typeset in Sabon
by Graphicraft Limited, Hong Kong

Printed and bound by CPI Group (UK) Ltd, Croydon, CR0 4YY

CONTENTS

List of abbreviations	vi
Preface	vii
Introduction	1

PART I
Zion in the Old Testament — 23

1 Isaiah	25
2 Jeremiah	36
3 Ezekiel	44
4 The Book of the Twelve	52
5 The remaining books	64

PART II
The Zion Motifs: Between Judgement and Salvation — 77

6 The enemy attack on Zion	79
7 The deliverance of Zion	88
8 The defeat of Zion and the exile	122
9 The return to Zion	144
10 The New Zion	164
Conclusion	189

Bibliography	193
Index of scripture	203
Index of names	207
Index of subjects	209

ABBREVIATIONS

BHS   Biblia Hebraica Stuttgartensia
ET   English Translation
LXX   Septuagint
NRSV   New Revised Standard Version

PREFACE

This book is a completely revised edition of my Danish prize essay *En redegørelse for Zionmotivet i profetlitteraturen*, which was awarded the University of Copenhagen gold medal in 2009 and published in Danish in 2011.[1] The revision was completed in the spring of 2013, thanks to a beneficial research stay at Oriel College, Oxford.

I express my sincere gratitude to Jesper Høgenhagen, who supervised the rough draft of the thesis and first encouraged me to undertake an English version, and to the editor of the series, Ingrid Hjelm, for including this volume and for her many valuable comments on the manuscript. Thanks also go to Jim West for linguistic corrections, to Juliet Gardner for careful copyediting and to the people at Acumen and Routledge for much help in the process.

Family, friends and colleagues at the Faculty of Theology in Copenhagen have offered me kindness and assistance in so many ways, especially the gentlemen of Borchs Kollegium, where the original draft of the thesis was written. I also wish to thank my wife Maren and our sons Johan and Samuel for their love and encouragement during the work on this book. Without their support, the revision would never have been completed.

Finally, my parents Helle and Niels Jørgen Poulsen have provided a loving and intellectually stimulating home for me and my siblings. I dedicate this book to them in gratitude.

Frederik Poulsen
Vordingborg, Denmark, May 2014

Note

1 Poulsen 2011.

INTRODUCTION

The prophetic books of the Old Testament contain a fascinating collection of oracles, poetic images and theological ideas. Among the most prominent themes are those of judgement and salvation. Yet peculiar and even seemingly contradictory features stand side by side: divine words of harsh judgement and glorious salvation. Especially concerning the fate of Zion – the place where the people of YHWH dwell – the prophets constantly switch back and forth between scenarios of judgement and scenarios of deliverance.[1] Zion will be destroyed! Zion will be saved! In particular in Isaiah 29:1–8 and Micah 3:9–4:4, divine justice and divine mercy are portrayed in the starkest contrast.[2] Due to God's justice, sinful Zion must fall. However, due to his mercy, he will protect his city despite the sins of its inhabitants.

The common historical-critical answer to these tensions in the prophetic books has been to distinguish between different layers within the redactional process of shaping, that is, later redactions have tried to replace the 'pessimistic' picture of judgement with an 'optimistic' vision of hope.[3] However, this answer is unsatisfactory. First, the theological structure of the passages indicates that the themes of judgement and salvation have a logical connection rather than just being contradictory.[4] Second, the complexity at stake is not just literary, but indeed theological: God both judges and saves, kills and brings to life.[5]

As we shall see below, scholarly works on Zion have focused on other areas than the Old Testament prophets as such. First, attention has been given to Zion as the cosmic and inviolable mountain of YHWH rather than it being an object of divine judgement. The origin and dating of this mythological motif has been the primary subject of discussion, rather than exploring the variety of Zion images within the Old Testament. Second, scholars have regarded the mythology of Zion as it is revealed in the Psalms as the earliest and, therefore, *primary* source of a Zion theology, whereas the prophets have been regarded as later and, therefore, *secondary* interpretations of this mythology. These circumstances partly explain why specialized studies on Zion in the entire prophetic literature have been

1

almost completely lacking. Instead, many studies take their point of departure in either the Psalms or the historical books, and compare these with the prophets.

In her recent and stimulating work *Images of Zion*, Lois Dow notices another lack of scholarly attention: 'not enough emphasis is given to the fact that Jerusalem/Zion has the dual role in the Old Testament of being *both* inviolable cosmic mountain of God *and* capital city of sinful people vulnerable to God's judgement.'[6] Also, or perhaps in particular, in the prophetic literature, Zion appears, on the one hand, as God's holy mountain and as a place of protection and prosperity and, on the other hand, as a sinful city liable to divine judgement. As Dow observes, 'there is a tension between the security of God's dwelling-place and the vulnerability of the sinful human community.'[7] Because of that, the images of Zion in the prophets are apparently stretched out between a present and actual Zion as the object of divine wrath and a future Zion as transformed into a salvific ideal – in a word, Zion exists between judgement and salvation.[8] The present book explores this variety of Zion images in the entire prophetic literature of the Old Testament.

Survey of scholarly literature on Zion and the Zion tradition

As indicated above, Zion has gained a lot of attention because of mythological events associated with this place. Rather than being purely a mundane place, Zion is highlighted as YHWH's special dwelling: 'YHWH has chosen Zion' (Ps 132:13), 'YHWH is great in Zion' (Ps 99:2) and 'YHWH Sebaoth dwells on Mount Zion' (Isa. 8:18). Especially German scholarship within the twentieth century has treated these mythological ideas as a fixed concept of theological motifs, referred to as the 'Zion tradition'. To speak about a Zion tradition is a sign of a historical approach. To be sure, tradition reflects the idea that a certain literary motif – the inviolable mountain of God – has emerged out of a certain historical or cultic context, and developed through time when taken up and reworked by new generations and cultures. The Zion motif is here regarded as having a simple and clearly defined content: the highest mountain of the world from which a life-giving river springs and which offers protection against chaos and hostile nations.[9] This perspective has dominated large parts of the scholarly interest throughout the past century, roughly until the mid-1980s, and is reflected in the articles on Zion in famous German theological dictionaries.[10]

In his early 1919 *Der Gottesberg*, Johannes Jeremias examines all the mountains that appear in the Old Testament, with special regard to the mythic character of the mountain.[11] In his *Psalmenstudien II* from 1922, Sigmund Mowinckel develops his thesis of the New Year festival in Jerusalem. Accordingly, many of the psalms were part of a cultic ritual or drama

INTRODUCTION

depicting YHWH's enthronement. The battle against the nations on Zion (Pss 46; 48; 76) has never historically taken place, but rather derives from the cultic myth of the battle of creation and from the myth of the crossing of the Red Sea. Essentially, the myth is a 'Projizierung der kultischen Wirklichkeiten in die Urzeit'.[12] The Psalms testify to this mythological reality. The ethical preaching of the prophets, however, marks a shift in the perception of reality, namely from the cult's actualization of the mythic creative victories to the eschatological hope in future realization.[13] Concerning Zion, the prophetic description of the battle of the nations draws upon the mythological psalms; the New Jerusalem is a reinterpretation of the mythic mountain of God from where the world was created; and the image of God's worldwide kingdom builds on the pilgrim myth. In sum, Mowinckel claims that whereas the Psalms regard the inviolability of Zion as a past and mythological event actualized in the cultic ritual, the prophets regard Zion as an eschatological reality.

In his 1950 article 'Jerusalem und die israelitische Tradition', Martin Noth stresses the religious importance of Jerusalem within the faith of Israel, especially the significance applied to the city in David's move of the ark thereto (cf. 2 Sam. 6).[14] In his 1955 article 'Jahwe und die Kulttraditionen von Jerusalem', Herbert Schmid explores the pre-Israelite cult in Jerusalem and observes the many parallels in the Old Testament accounts to the material from Ugarit (see below). Of special importance, Schmid argues, is the fact that Jerusalem was already known as the divine mountain of El Elyon before David's conquest.[15] In his Heidelberg dissertation *Die Bedeutung der Erwählungstraditionen Israels für die Eschatologie der alttestamentlichen Propheten* from 1956, Edzard Rohland introduces the idea of what he designates as the 'Zion tradition', by which the proclamation of the prophets was shaped.[16] He defines the tradition as having four basic elements (see below). In his 1957 article 'Die Völkerwallfahrt zum Zion', Hans Wildberger adds the pilgrimage motif as a fifth element.[17]

In his seminal *Theologie des Alten Testaments* from 1957 to 1960 (published in English in 1962 and 1965), Gerhard von Rad refines his thesis of the different theologies within the Old Testament, of which the Zion tradition is one.[18] As such, the Zion tradition is an independent election tradition ('Erwählungstradition') alongside other traditions such as the Patriarchal tradition, the Exodus tradition and the David tradition.[19] To von Rad, especially Isaiah of Jerusalem in the eighth century draws upon the ancient tradition of the special protection of Zion (probably Pss 46; 48; 76) and readdresses this to his own time of the Assyrian crisis. Apparently, the historical prophet in general builds upon the two traditions that are dominant in the Psalms: the Zion psalms (God has chosen Zion) and the royal psalms (God has chosen David). However, like Mowinckel, von Rad argues that, whereas the Psalms depict this election in terms of myths (*has* chosen), Isaiah changes the tradition into an eschatological reality: God *will* choose (again).

3

INTRODUCTION

The contributions from the 1960s and early 1970s are massive. In his 1961 Festschrift contribution 'Jerusalem Zion: the Growth of a Symbol', Norman W. Porteous focuses on the idea of peace and its development within the poetic and prophetic texts.[20] In his 1962 inaugural speech in Tübingen, 'Der Davidsbund und die Zionserwählung', Hartmut Gese attempts to demonstrate the inner unity of the election of Zion and the promise to David.[21] In his 1963 *Sion-Jerusalem Jahwes Königssitz*, Josef Schreiner offers a thorough study of the growth of Zion/Jerusalem theology, building on critical reconstructions of the biblical texts and their theology.[22] In his 1963 article 'The Tradition of Zion's Inviolability', John H. Hayes asserts that the election of Jerusalem happened due to David's move of the ark-traditions to Jerusalem. Here these traditions were fused with the existing Canaanite traditions of the city's inviolability (cf. 2 Sam. 5:6).[23] Psalms 46, 48 and 76 especially bear witness to Canaanite material and must be understood as myths. For instance, there is no river of the nature described in Ps 46:5[4], and Ps 48 cannot possibly refer to the physical Jerusalem. As Hayes states, 'This material in Ps 48 must have originally been applied to another city and only secondarily to Zion or else have been purely mythological from the beginning with no relation to a geographical place.'[24] To Hayes, Isaiah radically changed this cultic tradition in two ways. First, Isaiah called for faith in YHWH as a condition for the special protection (cf. Isa. 7:9); second, he placed the enemy attack within the realm of God's work as an instrument of divine wrath (cf. Isa. 29:1–4).[25]

Remarkably, in his *Die Zionstheologie der Korachiten* from 1966, Gunther Wanke argues that the central Zion psalms and their theology (Pss 46; 48; 76; 87) belong to the post-exilic period, not a pre-exilic Jerusalemite cult tradition.[26] In his *Jahwe, Jerusalem und die Völker* from 1968, Hanns-Martin Lutz focuses on the motif of the battle of the nations and, like Hayes and in opposition to Wanke, concludes that this motif stems from the pre-Israelite, Jerusalemite El Elyon cult.[27] Likewise, in his 1970 *Strukturen und Figuren im Kult von Jerusalem*, which thoroughly reconstructs the content of the alleged pre-Israelite cult of Jerusalem, Fritz Stolz sees this motif as a Jebusite heritage.[28] In his 1971 article 'Lade und Zion', Jörg Jeremias stresses that the David tradition is closely connected to the move of the ark to Jerusalem and that the Zion tradition is an updating of the ancient Israelite ark-traditions (in contrast to Hayes, Lutz, Wanke and Stolz).[29]

An important religio-historical study appears with Richard J. Clifford's *The Cosmic Mountain in Canaan and the Old Testament* from 1972.[30] His approach seems similar to that of J. Jeremias, yet, unlike the latter, with access to the findings of Ugarit in 1929. After a survey of possible parallels to the Old Testament motif in Mesopotamian, Egyptian, Hurrian and Hittite cultures, Clifford concludes that we should expect 'a lively interchange among Canaanite, Hittite, and Hurrian religions', and that the

INTRODUCTION

concept of the cosmic mountain is central to these religions. Importantly, however, motifs associated with the mountains of El and Baal, which are strictly separated within Canaanite religion, appear to be fused in the Old Testament portrait of Zion. Furthermore, whereas there are 'striking similarities' between the mountains of Baal and YHWH, the figure of YHWH seems to adopt the characteristics of El.[31]

In his 1980 *Isaiah and the Deliverance of Jerusalem*, Ronald E. Clements analyses the narratives about the Assyrians' unsuccessful siege of Jerusalem in 701 BCE and asserts that the doctrine of the city's inviolability emerged as a theological interpretation of this historical event.[32] Through a series of articles, J. J. M. Roberts has for more than four decades attempted to show that the Davidic and Solomonic era is the proper *Sitz-im-Leben* of the origin of the Zion tradition.[33] To him, when David conquered Jerusalem and made it the capital of Israel, the act lacked religious justification. However, by a transmission of the ark-traditions, YHWH chose Zion as his dwelling-place and David as his king. In short, the Zion tradition is best understood as 'a product of Zion's most glorious day, the golden age of David and Solomon'.[34]

Despite the richness and variety of these manifold historical studies, some kind of consensus seems to have emerged concerning the religio-historical background of the content of the alleged Zion tradition. As we have seen, historical-critical scholars generally agree that the biblical motif of the holy mountain, on which the supreme god dwells, is well-known from ancient Mediterranean and Near Eastern cultures, for instance, Egypt, Greece and Mesopotamia.[35] Nevertheless, the biblical motif clearly draws upon ancient themes and ideas of Canaanite mythology, as is expressed in the tablets from Ugarit, dated to the fourteenth century BCE. For instance, in Ps 48, God's mountain Zion is identified with Zaphon, which in Canaanite religion is the name of the warrior god Baal's mountain. Just as Baal battles against his enemies on Zaphon, YHWH battles against the hostile nations on Zion. In addition, YHWH and Baal are both storm gods and warriors; they fight against the Sea and other cosmic enemies; and they dwell on holy mountains.[36] In short, the mythological features of Mount Zion derive from a set of common West-Semitic concepts and images.

In his influential study, Rohland lists these four characteristics of the alleged Zion tradition based on the most important Zion psalms (Pss 46; 48; 76):[37]

(a) Zion is the highest mountain.
(b) A river flows from Zion.
(c) YHWH defeats the chaos waters on Zion.
(d) YHWH defeats the kings and nations on Zion.
[(e) The pilgrimage of nations to Zion.][38]

5

INTRODUCTION

Concerning the first three, there are obvious parallels in the portrait of the divine mountain(s) in the sources from Ugarit.[39] However, the fourth characteristic – often referred to as the *Völkerkampf*-motif ('war of the nations') and regarded by Rohland as the most central one – divides the scholarly guild. Some argue for a parallel in Canaanite mythology, which the Old Testament psalms adopt.[40] Others argue that the defeat of the foreign nations is a genuine Israelite motif, which did not derive from the Canaanite motif of the defeat of the chaotic floods, and which does not have parallels outside the Old Testament.[41]

Nevertheless, it remains certain that the Old Testament portrait of Mount Zion employs common West-Semitic material. However, a question remains: when was the myth of the divine and inviolable mountain historically applied to the ridge surrounding Jerusalem? As we have seen, several proposals have been offered. Significantly, all of them build on the account of the history of Jerusalem that the Bible offers:[42]

(a) The most widespread hypothesis argues that the tradition of the inviolability of Zion goes back to Jerusalem's pre-Israelite citizens, the Jebusites, whose local religion is thought to have been Canaanite.[43] In other words, due to the Jebusite cult, the tradition was already there when King David besieged the city (c. 1,000 BCE). Eventually, the tradition was adopted by the Israelites and lived on as part of their temple ideology.

(b) Scholars criticize this hypothesis by pointing out that the pre-Israelite Jerusalem hardly had political and religious significance sufficient to be identified with 'the holy Zaphon' and 'the cosmic world mountain'. The application of the ancient myth to Jerusalem cannot have happened before David's conquest, the move of the ark and the founding of Solomon's temple. These crucial events during the Davidic-Solomonic 'golden age' undergird the idea that YHWH has chosen Zion. As mentioned earlier, J. J. M. Roberts especially has argued in favour of this view for at least four decades.[44] A slight variant of this opinion sees the mythology of Mount Zion as a combination of the Canaanite traditions and the Israelite ark-traditions (YHWH's presence and protection). To an even higher degree, this position emphasizes that the Zion tradition is a genuine Israelite tradition, whose origin is inseparably linked with the move of the ark and the traditions associated with it to Jerusalem.[45]

(c) An alternative hypothesis argues that the concept of Zion's inviolability did not emerge from a cultic setting, but from a historical experience – that is, the failed Assyrian siege of Jerusalem in 701 BCE. Rather than being an adaption of an ancient cultic myth, the Zion tradition is an *interpretation* of a specific historical event.[46] Against this claim, proponents of the above-mentioned views will contend that the biblical account of Sennacherib's unsuccessful conquest was *interpreted* in light of the cultic myths.[47]

INTRODUCTION

(d) Particularly isolated and controversial is Gunther Wanke's assertion that the Canaanite motifs were applied to Jerusalem very late in connection with the loss of political independence.[48] To Wanke, the ideology expressed in central Zion psalms such as Pss 46, 48 and 76 derives from the exilic or post-exilic period (after 587 BCE).

As was mentioned, all of these proposals are mainly based upon the biblical material's own account of Israel's history and religion. However, within past decades, scholars have become highly sceptical of the historical reliability of the biblical version of ancient history.[49] We now know that the historical narratives of the Bible, rather than being historically accurate accounts, are literary constructions reflecting a much later time (Persian or Hellenistic period). In that way, the Bible contains a set of different *histories*, or rather a set of different theological reflections. Interestingly, scholars have no problem seeing Chronicles as an expression of a later ideology, whereas the accounts in Kings are deemed as reliable historical sources. However, as literary constructions, *all* the biblical narratives have only little to do with the findings and theses of Syro-Palestinian archaeology.[50] Historically, the nation Israel hardly originated as a result of Israelite intruders' invasion of the land of Canaan. Likewise, it is by no means certain that there was a King David in Iron Age Palestine; therefore, in the case of the alleged Zion tradition, a dating before or after David's conquest is meaningless.[51]

A similar criticism concerns the above-mentioned proposals' sharp distinction and alleged conflict between 'Israelite' and 'Canaanite'. We know of this distinction from the Bible; the Canaanites are the arch-enemy. However, this distinction is determined by the ideological interest of a later time.[52] The historical Israelites themselves were 'Canaanites', and their religion has emerged from a common West-Semitic culture. Unfortunately, the lack of reliable evidence outside the Old Testament material implies that an exact historical setting for the application of the myth of the inviolable mountain to the ridge surrounding Jerusalem fades into mist.

Recently, major criticism has been launched against the concept of a Zion tradition as a 'fixed' concept of ideas. As Gordon McConville states, 'if a "Zion-tradition" [as defined by Rohland and von Rad] ever actually existed, it was never in fact openly propounded or advocated either in the Psalms or in Isaiah, or indeed anywhere in the Old Testament'.[53] More crucially, Ingrid Hjelm observes that

> based on the Bible's own chronology and course of events, the Zion ideology has been separated from the narrative structure of the texts in which it occurs, as if it were an established ideology behind the texts. However, if the ideology is not merely creative, but created by the texts, then we need to look for some other historical context for its origin and development.[54]

An analogous problem is at stake concerning in what manner this alleged tradition was taken up and altered by the Old Testament authors. As mentioned above, the classical proposal of Sigmund Mowinckel and Gerhard von Rad argues that YHWH's defeat of the enemies was originally part of the ritual of the primordial cult as expressed in the temple psalms.[55] In a later period, the prophets 'reinterpreted' the motif as an eschatological event and actualized it into their distinctive historical contexts.[56] In short, Mowinckel and von Rad distinguish between a mythological use in the psalms and an eschatological use by the prophets. I, however, see a major problem concerning this basic distinction. Both search for a historical *Sitz-im-Leben* of the imagery of the inviolable Zion: Mowinckel by means of form criticism, von Rad by means of tradition criticism. Doing so, they presuppose that the psalms as part of the Jerusalem cult are older than the prophetic literature. Furthermore, they deem the 'eschatologization' by the prophets as a *secondary* interpretation of an already known (and collected?) tradition. In other words, they regard the psalms as the earliest and *primary* witness to an Old Testament adoption, which *secondarily* has been employed and actualized by the prophets. However, Wanke indirectly questions this idea by dating the central Zion psalms to the exilic or post-exilic period and thereby later than important prophets such as Isaiah.[57] Within past decades, this way of dating has been seriously challenged; therefore the sharp distinction between the early dating of the Zion psalms and the later dating of the prophets cannot be sustained. Because the Psalms have been – and often still are – viewed as the oldest and primary source of the Zion tradition/theology, the prophets' sayings about Zion have mostly been studied in light of these, rather than in their own right. Taking its point of departure in analyses of Zion in the prophetic literature, this study will seek to add a more nuanced view of the Zion ideology in the Old Testament.

The entire uncertainty about origins and dating of the Old Testament material, and interrelations of different parts of it (the Psalms vis-à-vis the prophets), as well as the literary turn within biblical studies have pushed the scholarly work into new directions. 1985 marks a new era with Jon D. Levenson's *Sinai and Zion*. Here, the essential approach is 'synchronic and literary', although the work also includes the rich history of rabbinic interpretations.[58] Levenson shows how the Jewish Bible contains two distinctive theologies centring on Sinai as the mountain of YHWH's law and covenant, and Zion as the mountain of his temple. He lists a series of valuable comparisons between the two. Whereas Sinai is located outside Israel, Zion forms the centre of the land. What is unthinkable in the Sinai (and Deuteronomistic) tradition – that God promises his support to the Davidic monarchy – constitutes a basic element of the Zion tradition. Here, temple and royal court are closely connected. Whereas the central matter of the Sinai covenant is history and morality, the covenant with David is a covenant of grace, which undergirds the Davidic kingdom of Jerusalem.

INTRODUCTION

Furthermore, whereas God's activity in the Sinai covenant and in history is concealed, God's activity on Zion is a visible sign of his faithfulness. Concerning Zion, Levenson argues that the Zion theology primarily exists as a *protological* reality (i.e. the mythic and founding acts, which order reality) in the cult (cf. Mowinckel) and that Zion – even after the Roman destruction of the temple in 70 CE – continues both as a protological and eschatological reality within rabbinic tradition.

Likewise, in his 1987 monograph *Zion, the City of the Great King*, Ben C. Ollenburger treats Zion as a symbol within a specific theological tradition, rather than speaking of a Zion tradition or Zion theology;[59] crucially, the origin and dating of such a tradition is not part of his investigation. Nevertheless, he argues that the basic feature of Zion – that YHWH dwells here – derives from the ark-traditions and their transmission to Jerusalem. The overall aim is to analyse the symbol of Zion within its primary context, which is the Jerusalemite cult as witnessed especially in the Psalms. Zion is related to YHWH's enthronement at the autumnal New Year festival and as such part of the rituals of the cult (cf. Mowinckel). Ollenburger's main thesis is that 'Zion symbolized security because the divine king who resided there exercised his royalty in his dual activity as creator and defender'.[60] In other words, because YHWH is king, creator and protector of Zion, it is a place of security and refuge. Ollenburger does look for the origin of this motif – he calls it 'Yahweh's exclusive prerogative' – and finds it, surprisingly, in the cultic tradition of Jerusalem!

Antti Laato, in his 1998 book *About Zion I Will Not Be Silent*, searches for an overall ideology that undergirds the composition of the final form of Isaiah.[61] Interestingly, he sees the fate of Zion as a dominant theme and finds the proper context of this in the Persian, if not Hellenistic, period. To him, the failed Assyrian siege of Jerusalem in Isaiah 1–39 forms an ideological-historical paradigm of YHWH's saving act that points forward to the post-exilic situation of Isaiah 56–66.[62] In his easy-to-read 2000 book *The Holy City*, Leslie Hoppe traces the growth and development of the theology of Jerusalem within the Old Testament and apocryphal material.[63] In her 2004 book *Jerusalem's Rise to Sovereignty*, Ingrid Hjelm, like Laato, argues in favour of a late dating of Isaiah and sees the (in her view) late Zion theology as a means to undergird the special status of the Jerusalemite sanctuary on behalf of Samaritan Gerizim.[64] Rather than repeating a tradition-historical analysis of the Zion tradition, Corinna Körting, in her 2006 habilitation *Zion in den Psalmen*, focuses on all psalms referring to Zion.[65] Her attempt includes a detection of all the concepts and images connected to Zion. Through a series of close readings, she concludes that Zion functions as a magnet of different motifs and traditions. In his 2007 book *Zion's Rock-Solid Foundations*, Jaap Dekker addresses the interpretation of Isaiah 28:16 in its Old Testament contexts and beyond.[66] As Laato does, he stresses the importance of Zion and Zion imagery for the preaching of Isaiah.

INTRODUCTION

Finally, in her 2011 *Images of Zion*, through a biblical theological investigation, Lois Dow demonstrates that the picture of the New Jerusalem in Revelation draws upon antecedent theologies of Jerusalem/Zion to provide a meaningful depiction of the final state of believers in Jesus as both communion with God and life as a community.[67] Besides these important monographs, there is a series of recent articles focusing on the Zion motif within discrete books or parts of the Old Testament.[68]

Methodological issues

As the review of recent literature has demonstrated, the scholarly engagement with Zion has centred on a variety of questions, concerns and methods. In the 1950s, 1960s and 1970s, the turning point was in particular on the origin and dating of an alleged Zion tradition, including the adoption and transformation of it within the Old Testament writings. Concerning the work of these decades, it is striking that the proposals for dating the application of the mythology of the cosmic mountain to Jerusalem range from the pre-Davidic to the post-exilic period, without achieving of any consensus. After the break with classical historical criticism, the tendencies of the late dating of the biblical material (Persian and Hellenistic periods) and the emergence of literary, narrative, structuralist, canonical and *rezeptionsgeschichtliche* approaches mark a decisive change within the field of biblical studies. The question of dating has not become entirely irrelevant; however, its importance has been downplayed over against other approaches and questions to the texts. In this study, we shall not deal with the dating of the discrete text passages, and redaction-critical considerations will only be taken up when deemed necessary (especially concerning the Book of Amos; see chapter 4). The intention of the study is neither to explore issues concerning Zion/Jerusalem of a purely historical or topographical nature,[69] nor to include extra-biblical material from the Ancient Near East to shed light upon the biblical material (cf. the religio-comparative approach).

Rather, the approach taken in the present study is synchronic, in so far as the biblical texts are read as a whole, without any intention to follow the literary development of them or to search for the historical events behind them.[70] Although the biblical material frequently contains references to historical persons and events, we shall work within the compositional structures provided by the final form and thereby seek to understand how these events and persons interact within the present form of the Bible. The approach can be deemed canonical, in so far as we treat the textual material and its theological assertions according to their canonical form and order.[71] Accordingly, the prophetic literature here is defined as the text, scope and order of the fifteen books of the Hebrew Bible[72] – Isaiah, Jeremiah, Ezekiel and the Book of the Twelve – as is common in recent introductions.[73]

10

INTRODUCTION

The present work falls into two main sections: descriptive and constructive.[74] The descriptive part contains a survey of Zion in discrete passages and books with attention to their overall narratives and compositions. The constructive part, however, roughly sets aside the structures of the discrete books. Creating a synthesis, this part compares, puts together and integrates several discrete text passages, displayed from their historical and literary context. By doing so, we shall construct two main Zion motifs. Moving beyond strictly historical questions about the origin and development of the Zion tradition makes it possible to investigate the place of Zion within theological structures of the prophetic literature, that is, Zion between judgement and salvation.[75]

Defining the Zion motif

According to its general occurrences in the Old Testament, 'Zion' mostly refers to a place, including a fortress, a city, a mountain, a temple and the people dwelling here.[76] As we have seen, the alleged Zion tradition has been presented as having a simple and clearly defined content, expressed in four motifs centring on this mythopoetic place: a high mountain, a paradisical river, the battle of chaos and the battle of the nations (Rohland, von Rad and others); eventually, the pilgrimage motif has been added (Wildberger). God's kingdom and election of Zion as his dwelling-place have been stressed as main motifs (Roberts, Ollenburger).[77] Besides Rohland's four-motifs-definition, Roberts and Levenson have presented their own definitions of the Zion tradition.[78] Nevertheless, Tan has recently asserted that we should indeed speak of Zion traditions in the plural, since historically there was no set understanding of Zion.[79] Likewise, Körting has stressed that Zion is not a fixed concept of ideas; rather it is a theological motif with variable emphases determined by its concrete literary setting.[80] Finally, as was mentioned, Hjelm proposes that the Zion ideology as contained in the idea of a Zion tradition may very likely have been created by the biblical texts, rather than being a historically independent ideology behind the texts.

In line with this recent criticism of the narrow motif of the Zion tradition, I see primarily two dangers in first defining a distinctive motif – on the basis of other scholars' work – and then searching for this motif in the prophetic literature of the Bible. First, as we have seen, the Zion motif has traditionally been defined from a limited number of psalms (in particular, Pss 46; 48; 76).[81] However, since our investigation focuses on the prophets, it would be rather odd to try to apply a motif based on these psalms to the prophets; in addition, historically, we have no certainty that the prophets knew these psalms (cf. Wanke's criticism). A thorough comparison of the Zion motif in the Psalms and that in the prophets would be illuminating; this task, however, lies outside the scope of the present work. Second, and

INTRODUCTION

more crucially, it is always a risky business first defining a motif from a group of texts, before looking for this motif in the same group of texts. A similar circularity is found in the historical-critical attempt first to reconstruct the history and theology of the eighth century BCE by using the Book of Amos, and then to show how the message of Amos fits this reconstruction. In other words, if solely searching for historical traces of an alleged Zion tradition as defined by Rohland and von Rad in the 1950s, we shall easily overlook the variety and richness of images of Zion within the Old Testament as a whole. As Körting asserts concerning the Psalms,

> Nimmt man andere Belege des Psalters für Zion hinzu, erweisen sich die spezifischen Vorstellungsgehalte zum Teil jedoch als *spannungsreich*, zuweilen sogar *widersprüchlich*. Zion kann zum Inbegriff zerstörter (Ps 102) und beheimateter Existenz (Ps 84) werden.[82]

Because of this, we shall begin by regarding 'Zion' very broadly as a *main motif* – a magnet – to which a range of sub-motifs are attracted: YHWH as king, the battle of nations, the pilgrimage, the place of creation, Zion as the last bastion and so on. Here, Ollenburger presents a good point of departure for his own work on the Zion symbol:

> Interpretation of the Zion symbol cannot be restricted only to those texts that display the principal motifs of what has been identified as the 'Zion tradition', nor can it be restricted to those texts which explicitly mention Zion or Jerusalem. It must rather be expanded to a range of texts which form the network of relationships within which Zion functions as the central symbol.[83]

Of relevance to our study, the proper point of departure demands a cursory reading of the *entire* prophetic literature to look for texts and motifs centring on Zion, either explicitly due to the occurrence of the term or implicitly as a sub-motif within a larger 'network of relationships'. As Körting likewise states, 'Wer etwas über Zion sagen will, darf nicht mit einer auf geringer Textbasis gewonnenen Vorstellung von Zionstheologie beginnen und sie auf andere Texte applizieren, sondern er muß bei den Texten anfangen, und zwar bei allen.'[84] Whereas Körting's pregnant study focuses on the Book of Psalms, our intention is to explore Zion as a theological motif within the prophetic literature of the Bible.

Two questions concerning terminology need to be addressed; the first regards the term 'Zion' in relation to 'Jerusalem'; and the second regards the term 'daughter Zion'. Especially the older scholarly literature or literature offering a general survey tends to see the terms 'Zion' and 'Jerusalem' as virtually synonymous.[85] Hans Wildberger asserts that 'Isaiah uses "Zion" and "Jerusalem" without distinguishing them in any way'.[86] A variation of

12

INTRODUCTION

this view contends that the two terms are not synonymous, but complementary.[87] However, recent studies with a narrower focus often present a
more nuanced view. Concerning the Psalms, for instance, Körting concludes
that 'Zion und Jerusalem werden nur in wenigen Fällen bedeutungsgleich
verwendet'.[88] Concerning Isaiah, Hjelm asserts that

> While Jerusalem is the name of a mundane city, partaking in mundane
> affairs and therefore liable to judgement (5.3), Zion is an ideal, a
> divine abode, a holy mountain (4.5; 8.18; 12.6; 16.1), which can
> be abandoned by its god (64:9–10), but not accused.[89]

My own survey will display a variety of usages and meanings of 'Zion'
within the Old Testament material. In some books, such as Isaiah, there
may very likely be a subtle play on the use of different terms (cf. Hjelm).
Likewise, the historical books know the term, but hardly use it, and only
in relation to salvific themes. In Micah, however, Zion and Jerusalem
definitely appear to be used as poetic synonyms (e.g. Mic. 3:10, 12; 4:2).
Furthermore, whereas Isaiah 'protects' the term by not depicting the defeat
of the city (except from the allusions in Isa. 6:11–13; 64:9–10), Jeremiah
and Micah state that YHWH will destroy daughter Zion and that Zion
will be ploughed like a field. Apparently, Ezekiel deliberately avoids the
term, even though he, on the one hand, employs material from the alleged
Zion tradition and, on the other hand, portrays the same events as Jeremiah.
However, being aware of this subtlety concerning the term 'Zion', I will
not deal with this issue as such. As we shall see, Zion stands in relation
to Jerusalem, Judah, the temple mount and even the people of Israel.[90]
Therefore, in the present study, we shall use 'Zion' very broadly as designating *the place where the people of YHWH dwell – or wish to dwell.*[91]

Second, although 'Bat Zion' (בת ציון) frequently is rendered as 'the
daughter of Zion', I will maintain that it – in accordance with the NRSV
– should be rendered as 'daughter Zion'. This idiom refers to the place
itself, personified as a daughter.[92] In *Lamentations*, for instance, Adele
Berlin has convincingly mounted the case that 'Bat Zion' should be understood as an appositional genitive, or a genitive of association: Zion herself
is classified as 'daughter';[93] cf. all the allusions to Israel as a daughter in
the prophets.

The structure of the study

Drawing upon these methodological considerations, part I offers a
descriptive survey of Zion motifs in the prophetic literature. Chapters 1–4
provide a cursory reading of all of the prophetic books to register material
and sub-motifs connected to Zion. First, we shall list the occurrences or
non-occurrences of the term; then, we shall look for events, motifs and

13

INTRODUCTION

characteristics associated with Zion; and finally, we shall consider how Zion and the Zion motif function within each book. As was indicated, this overview sets aside questions of dating and authorship in order to sketch the overall message of the prophets. These initial observations and listings of motifs will come into play in part II. To complete our survey, chapter 5 cursorily looks at Zion motifs in the remaining books of the Old Testament.

Part II offers a fresh attempt to put together the number of sub-motifs centring on Zion that have been detected in part I. As a constructive proposal, this part provides a systematic description of what I consider to be *two main perceptions of Zion*, existing side by side in the prophetic literature. This part will analyse passages portraying the enemy attack on Zion, the deliverance of Zion or of its defeat and exile, the return to Zion and the New Zion. Finally, an overall conclusion will be offered.

Notes

1 Dow 2011: 103.
2 Levenson 1985: 164; Marrs 2004: 82–3.
3 Childs 2001: 218.
4 Dow 2011: 103.
5 Childs 2001: 218.
6 Dow 2011: 27.
7 Dow 2011: 104–5.
8 Dow 2011: 110.
9 Cf. Jaap Dekker's definition: 'The Zion tradition is that group of Israel's traditions related to the unique place and significance of Zion on the journey God has made with his people'; Dekker 2007: 317; see further below.
10 For instance, Georg Fohrer's article in *Theological Dictionary of the New Testament* (Fohrer 1971), Fritz Stolz's article in *Theologisches Handwörterbuch zum Alten Testament* (Stolz 1976) and Eckart Otto's article in *Theological Dictionary of the Old Testament* (Otto 2003). Fohrer offers a chronological presentation of the meaning of 'Zion' beginning with the pre-Israelite and early Israelite period, the period of the Davidic monarchy to Josiah and the period of the last kings of Judah and the exile before turning to the post-exilic period (Fohrer 1971: 300–7). Likewise, by means of redaction-critical observations, Otto places all text passages and motifs concerning Zion within a chronological framework. To him, the *pre-exilic* Zion theology forms a sub-theology of the Jerusalemite temple theology and is further developed during the Assyrian crisis in the eighth century BCE to support the faith in the city's strength. The experience of *exile* challenges the idea of God's special protection, and the temple, rather than the city, becomes the centre of the nation. The *post-exilic* Zion theology stresses that God dwells in heaven and that his presence and holiness in the temple is an expression of his protection (Otto 2003: 348–63). For other studies employing a similar chronological framework, see McConville 1992; Hoppe 2000; Riesner & Kreuzer 2000; Rudnig 2007. It remains questionable, however, if such a clear chronological development of the concept is really discernible at all; cf. the criticism in Dow 2011: 22.
11 Jeremias 1919. He sees the mountain as a symbol, a mythic meeting place between God and man, mediated through language, myths and art. Drawing

INTRODUCTION

upon Sumerian and Babylonian material, he argues that such 'mountain cults' were common in ancient Mesopotamia and stresses the fascinating nature of the mountain: 'Der Berg ragt in den Himmel, der Berg ist in ein Paradies von rotglühenden Wolken morgens und abends eingehüllt, der Berg ist umgrollt von den Donnern des Ewigen, er empfängt den Morgenkuß der Sonne und ist des Nachts von Myriaden himmlischer Welten umleuchtet' (Jeremias 1919: 33). The earthly mountain reflects the divine reality: God dwells in heaven, yet the mountain provides an earthly symbol of this dwelling. In short, the mountain mediates between the three parts of the universe: the heavens, the earth and the sea.

12 Mowinckel 1922: 64.

13 For instance, instead of being a cultic experience, YHWH's enthronement is pushed into the future, where it becomes the Day of YHWH. The eschatological reorientation thereby takes up the ancient motifs and changes them into future events: the New Creation and the New Jerusalem. Isa. 40–55 interprets YHWH's return to Jerusalem by means of the myth of YHWH's advent as king.

14 Noth 1950. For an excellent review of especially the German contributions from which I have benefitted a lot, see Dekker 2007: 283–318.

15 Schmid 1955: 187–92.

16 Rohland 1956. For a review of Rohland's antecedents, including K. Galling, H. Gunkel, G. von Rad, M. Noth, O. Eißfeldt, H.-J. Kraus and H. Schmid, see Dekker 283–92. Kraus, in particular, has criticized Rohland's designation of the Zion tradition as an election tradition ('Erwählungstradition'). According to Kraus 1988: 91, 'we must distinguish strictly between the (pre-Israelite) cultic traditions . . . and the genuinely Israelitic act of the "election of Zion".' For Kraus' own treatment, see the section 'The Zion Theology' in Kraus 1986: 78–84; cf. also 1988: 68–9, 89–92.

17 Wildberger 1957.

18 von Rad 1962; 1965. Already in his 1949 article 'Die Stadt auf dem Berge', von Rad argues that the image of the holy mountain originates from common oriental mythology (von Rad 1958: 214–24).

19 Among the prophets, von Rad finds that Isa. 1–39 employs the David and Zion traditions, whereas Hosea, Jeremiah, Ezekiel and Isa. 40–55 employ the Exodus tradition; Isa. 40–55, however, is a mixture of several traditions (von Rad 1965: 117). von Rad argues that after the exile, there is a renewed interest in Zion as it becomes an image of the New Jerusalem; cf. Isa. 56–66, Haggai, Zechariah and Ezek. 40–8. To this eschatological reorientation belongs also the idea of the nations going up to Zion, expressed in two contrasting ways: as a battle on Zion (Joel 4[3]; Zech. 12; 14; Ezek. 38–9) and as a peaceful pilgrimage (Isa. 2; 49; 60; Hag. 2).

20 Porteous 1961.

21 Gese 1974. Analysing Ps 132, Gese concludes that by David's transmission of the ark to Zion YHWH *answers* by offering his support to the Davidic monarchy: 'Die Dynastieverheißung ist der politisch-religiöse Ausdruck der kultisch-religiösen Bindung Jahwes an Zion' (Gese 1974: 121).

22 Schreiner 1963. This monograph was planned as the first of three volumes providing a complete theology of the holy city in the Old Testament. The first volume focuses on the mythological or idealized image of Zion testified to in the historical material concerning the time of David and Solomon (1 Sam. 4–6; 2 Sam. 6; 7; 24), in the Psalms and in the alleged eighth-century Isaiah of Jerusalem. Unfortunately, the second volume on 'Die Heilige Stadt und Israel' and the third volume on 'Die Eschatologie der Heiligen Stadt' never appeared.

INTRODUCTION

23 Hayes 1963.
24 Hayes 1963: 424.
25 Hayes 1963: 425–6.
26 Wanke 1966. Although the psalms adopt material from Canaanite and Meso-potamian religion, their application of it to Jerusalem does not occur before the end of exile: 'Vor allem die Verbindung Zion-Jerusalem mit Bildern aus den außerisraelitischen Mythen gehört ausschließlich der exilisch-nachexilischen Zeit an' (Wanke 1966: 108). In general, he contends that the motifs employed in the Korah psalms (Pss 42–9; 84–5; 87–8) are close to those of the late eschato-logical prophets, including Zech. 12; 14; Joel; and Mic. 4:11–13: 'An diesen vier Stellen im Alten Testament finden wir nun das Völkerkampfmotiv in einer Ausgestaltung, die der in den Psalmen einigermaßen entspricht' (Wanke 1966: 83). As a final argument for his thesis, Wanke argues that the motif of the battle of nations has no parallels outside the Israelite literature and that it could not have developed from the battle of chaos-motif.
27 Lutz 1968. Lutz's work searches for the prehistory of Zech. 12:1–8 and 14:1–5. Focusing on the battle-motif in the Old Testament, he finds three main motifs: the nations' battle against Jerusalem, YHWH's battle against the nations and YHWH's battle against Jerusalem. To him, the nations' battle against Jerusalem is clearly at stake in Pss 46, 48 and 76 as ancient testimonies to the Canaanite El Elyon cult. Eventually, however, this tradition is mixed with others and, in Zechariah, it appears as only a meagre formularized phrase.
28 Stolz 1970: 89: 'Das Völkerkampfmotiv hat in Israel also seinen Ort seit der frühesten Königszeit. Wie das Chaoskampfmotiv ist es als jebusitisches Erbe anzusprechen.'
29 Jeremias 1971: 185–6: 'Vor allem aber hängt die Dynastieverheißung, die im Zentrum der Davidstradition steht, engsten mit der Überführung der Lade nach Jerusalem zusammen.' And further in 1971: 195–7: 'Der Völkerkampf in den Zionpsalmen ist letztlich wiederum nichts anderes als eine Explikation dessen, *was das Handeln des mit der Lade verbundenen Kriegers Jahwe bedeutet* . . . Die gesamte Ziontradition ist in ihrer ältesten Gestalt für das damalige Israel nicht anders gewesen als eine moderne, mit Hilfe kanaanäischer Motive vollzogene Eksegese der Lade und ihrer Tradition.'
30 Clifford 1972. For another important study of the city and temple as religious and political centre against the background of ideologies from other Ancient Near Eastern cultures, see Weinfeld 1983.
31 Clifford 1972: 131.
32 Clements 1980: 84: 'The doctrine of the inviolability of Jerusalem . . . which several scholars have come to regard as a central feature of the so-called "Zion tradition", must rather be understood as a particular adaptation of the inter-pretation placed upon what happened in 701 . . . the doctrine of inviolability associated with the city stemmed from what was believed to have happened in 701 and the divine purpose that was believed to be revealed in this . . . The doctrine of Jerusalem's inviolability . . . emerged, not as an adaption of an ancient myth, but as an interpretation of a series of historical events, and focused most directly upon Hezekiah's confrontation with Sennacherib.' Recently, Clements has maintained his view; cf. Clements 2011: 141, 236: 'As a consequence of being spared the fate of Lachish in 701 BCE Jerusalem was elevated into an ideal, supernaturally endowed, and ultimately eschatological, city. The historical and logistical factors which led to this outcome have certainly been exaggerated in the narratives, but the broader point remains of importance that, as a result of its occurrence Jerusalem obtained considerable advantage in its long-standing

INTRODUCTION

rivalry among its neighbours . . . The belief that a miracle of divine intervention saved Jerusalem in 701 BCE was later enlarged upon and expanded in the Psalter to express a wider belief that Jerusalem-Zion was a unique place of refuge – a city of supernatural majesty that offered peace to its citizens and to the world. Such a belief gave rise to the unique "Zion tradition".'

33 Roberts 1973; 1982; 2003. For a full list of his numerous contributions on this topic, see Roberts 2003: 163, n. 1. In his 1973 article, Roberts rejects both the attempts to derive the Zion tradition from the pre-Israelite cult of Jerusalem (cf. von Rad, Hayes, Lutz and Clifford) and late exilic or post-exilic dating of the tradition (cf. Wanke). In 1973, Roberts relies on Rohland's sketch of the motif; in 1982, however, he makes his own attempt to describe the content of the motif (see below). In 2003, facing the recent trends of late-dating the biblical and archaeological material, he remains convinced 'that the Zion tradition was formulated by the Israelite court theologians in the period of the Davidic-Solomonic empire and that its creation is in part a reflection of Israel's, and thus Yahweh's, rise to imperial power' (Roberts 2003: 165).

34 Roberts 1973: 344. Among the many critics of Roberts' thesis, Ingrid Hjelm has intriguingly pointed out that Roberts wrongly presupposes that the narratives about David and Solomon contain a clear Zion theology; cf. Hjelm 2004: 254: 'Seemingly unaware that "Deuteronomistic" and "Chronistic" authors of these narratives do not present any explicit Zion or mountain ideology, modern interpreters [read Roberts] have linked the Zion ideology in the prophets and the Psalms with the biblical David-Solomon kingdom. Interpreting their biblical colleagues' projection of ideal kingship in the prophets and Psalms as descriptions of an ephemeral Davidic kingdom "known" from prose literature, modern scholars have created historical scenarios of a tenth-century BCE golden age by synthesizing these forms. Biblical projections, however, which appear as paraphrastic forms of such prose descriptions, can hardly count as source material for historical reconstruction.' According to Hjelm, a Zion ideology is related to the Deuteronomistic composition, but by no means at its base; see Hjelm 2004: 303 and further in chapter 5 of the present book.

35 Clifford 1972: 9–29.

36 Clifford 1972: 131; Smith 1995: 2036.

37 Rohland 1956: 141–2; cf. Dekker 2007: 294.

38 As mentioned above, this element was later added by Hans Wildberger (Wildberger 1957). However, Ollenburger 1987: 15–16 critically asserts: 'the "Völkerwallfahrt" motif was a later combination of the pre-exilic motifs of pilgrimage to a shrine and the "pilgrimage" of kings and/or nations to the kings of Jerusalem.'

39 Cf. Wanke 1966: 64: 'Alle diese Motive sind sowohl im mesopotamischen wie im nordsyrischen Raum nachweisbar.' According to the Ugarit sources, El – the sovereign god and creator of the world – dwells in his abode on a mountain, from where he reigns and from where two life-giving rivers flow. Baal's mountain Zaphon is centre of the war between life and death and of a subsequent celebration of the defeat of the enemies; see further in Clifford 1972: 35–79; Weinfeld 1983; Smith 1995.

40 See, for instance, Rohland 1956: 137; Schreiner 1963: 226, 235; Lutz 1968: 171–2; Stolz 1970: 89; Kraus 1986: 78–9.

41 See, for instance, Wanke 1966: 77: 'das Völkerkampfmotiv [aufweist] erstens keine entsprechenden Parallelen in außerisraelitischer Literatur und [kann] zweitens nicht als aus dem Chaoskampfmotiv abgeleitet gelten, obwohl es durchaus mit Zügen desselben versehen worden ist'; see also Clements 1980: 84.

42 For a short, yet rather precise review of these positions, see Conroy 1983: 258–9.

INTRODUCTION

43 von Rad 1962: 46–8; Albrektson 1963: 220; Hayes 1963: 422; Schreiner 1963: 308; Stolz 1970: 89; Kraus 1986: 78–9.

44 Roberts 1973; 1982; 2003; Wessel 2006: 731. Although Roberts recognizes that the Zion tradition contains pre-Israelite material, he maintains that 'its crystallization point must still be sought in the Davidic-Solomonic era' (Roberts 1982: 105).

45 Jeremias 1971: 195–7; Ollenburger 1987: 62–3; Dekker 2007: 318.

46 Jeremias 1919: 138: 'Das Dogma von der Unvergänglichkeit Zions mag seinen Ursprung in der geschichtlichen Tatsache haben, daß im Jahre 701 die Macht des assyrischen Großkönigs Sanherib an dem Felsen Zion zerschellt. Es entsteht der Glaube, daß menschliche Macht nichts gegen den heiligen Berg vermag'; see also Fohrer 1971: 304; Clements 1980: 84; McConville 1992: 23–4, 33; Otto 2003: 356.

47 Mowinckel 1922: 65: 'Der im großen Ganzen ungeschichtliche Bericht über eine über Nacht eingetroffenen vernichtenden Katastrophe, die Sanheribs Heer von Jerusalem getroffen habe, II Kg. 18, 17–19, 37, ist nichts anderes als eine Übertragung unserer Kultlegende auf geschichtliche Personen und Ereignisse.'

48 Wanke 1966: 108: 'die aus alten kanaanäischen oder mesopotamischen Mythen übernommenen Motive im Alten Testament [wurden] erst in sehr später Zeit zur literarischen Ausgestaltung gewisser Sachverhalte verwendet. Vor allem die Verbindung Zion-Jerusalem mit Bildern aus den außerisraelitischen Mythen gehört ausschließlich der exilisch-nachexilischen Zeit an.' See the criticism of Wanke in Lutz 1968: 213–16; Kraus 1986: 83–4; 1988: 91–2.

49 Whitelam 1996; Thompson 1999; Hjelm 2004; Davies 2008; Lemche 2008 and other scholars associated with the Copenhagen School.

50 Cf. Hjelm 2004: 10: 'Taking the Bible's own chronology as a point of departure for its composition and redaction has not proven to be a valid working hypothesis.'

51 However, even if we follow the Bible's own literary construction, 'it was not David's moving the ark to Jerusalem (2 Sam. 6) that gave the city and its temple their special status. The struggle for sovereignty had only begun. It was not until much later – half a century after Yahweh's election of the city during the reign of Hezekiah (2 Kgs 18–20) – that competing cult places were finally destroyed and Jerusalem appears as the only place fit for the worship of Yahweh' (Hjelm 2004: 30).

52 Cf. Lemche 2008: 295–6; see further in Lemche 1991 for a seminal study of the Canaanites in ancient history and tradition.

53 McConville 1992: 28.

54 Hjelm 2004: 6.

55 Mowinckel 1922: 191–2; von Rad 1962: 46–8.

56 Mowinckel 1922: 315–16; von Rad 1965: 174–5.

57 Despite this late dating of Pss 46, 48 and 76, however, von Rad would maintain his view; cf. von Rad 1965: 157: 'These psalms probably date from before the time of Isaiah: but their date is in fact of little importance; for their tradition of an unsuccessful attack on Jerusalem is quite certainly of very much earlier origin.'

58 Levenson 1985: 46.

59 Ollenburger 1987: 14.

60 Ollenburger 1987: 74.

61 Concerning Isaiah, see also the important contributions by Webb 1990; Berges 2012.

62 Cf. Laato 1998: 169–75: 'The Assyrian invasion in Isaiah 1–39 is an historical paradigm which is a typos for the purifying operation which Yhwh will realize among his people in the post-exilic period . . . The destruction of the Assyrian

INTRODUCTION

army before Zion is a paradigm in the Book of Isaiah which demonstrates that Yhwh has power to make Zion the center of the whole world ... a paradigm illustrating how Yhwh will save his faithful in Zion ... Just as Yhwh saved the loyal remnant in the time of Hezekiah and Isaiah so he will do again.'

63 Hoppe 2000.

64 Hjelm seeks to demonstrate that the third- to second-century discussions between Judeans and Samaritans about the proper place for YHWH's dwelling form the proper *Sitz-im-Leben* for the accounts in the Deuteronomistic Histories about the conflicts between the northern and southern kingdoms; cf. Hjelm 2004: 303: 'Its implied historical context is not the Iron Age kingdoms of Israel and Judah, but the competition over cult places, such as we know from the third-second century BCE onwards. Based on characters and events related to the "Hasmonaean" struggle for Judaean hegemony, our author(s) completed a work in which imperial unity is mirrored against devastating factionalism.' According to these Judean accounts, Jerusalem (and Zion) is highlighted over the Samaritan Gerizim.

65 Körting 2006: 6.

66 Dekker 2007.

67 Dow 2011: 19, 235–40. For other recent studies focusing on Zion theology in the New Testament, see Tan 1997; Son 2005.

68 See, for instance, Meyers & Meyers 1992; Renz 1999; Berges 2000; Bolin 2003; Dobbs-Allsopp 2004; Marrs 2004; Willis 2004; Wessel 2006; Rudnig 2007; de Jong 2011.

69 See, for instance, Scharling 1890; Simons 1952; Levine 2002; Strange 2007.

70 Cf. the approach taken in Webb 1990: 65; Dow 2011.

71 Cf. Dow 2011: 5–14.

72 See BHS. Most of my quotations from the Old Testament are based upon the NRSV, occasionally with slight variations, to stress certain aspects of a particular phrase.

73 See Childs 1979: 303–498; Petersen 2002; Sweeney 2012: 265–368.

74 See also Dow 2011: 13.

75 Cf. the similar considerations in Ollenburger 1987: 145.

76 The term 'Zion' occurs 154 times in BHS: ninety-four times in the prophets, fifty-four times in the poetic writings (Psalms, Song of Songs and Lamentations) and six times in the historical writings (2 Samuel; 1 and 2 Kings = 1 and 2 Chronicles). Importantly, the term neither occurs in Genesis through 1 Samuel nor in famous prophetic books such as Ezekiel and Hosea. 'Zion' is related to the topographical designation 'mountain' (הר) twenty times, a few times to 'the city of David' (e.g. 2 Sam. 5:7) and more than forty times to the name 'Jerusalem'. In general, Zion appears to cover at least four different things: (a) a fortress, ridge of hill or a quarter in Jerusalem; (b) a temple, sanctuary or a temple mount; (c) the entire capital city (parallel to Jerusalem); and (d) the people of YHWH, the community worshipping here and Israel; cf. Fohrer 1971: 293–300; Otto 2003: 343–4; see further in part I of the present study.

77 Cf. also Tan 1997: 30: 'The important organising concept of the Zion traditions is that Yahweh has chosen to dwell in Jerusalem and exercise his kingship in and through the city. From this important bipolar concept many strands of these traditions ... receive their impetus and origin: the inviolability of Zion; Zion as a place of refuge, security and salvation; Zion as a place of blessing; Zion as the place of pilgrimage of the nations; Zion as the place of the universal dominion of Yahweh.'

INTRODUCTION

78 Roberts finds two main motifs in the Zion tradition: (1) YHWH is king; and (2) he has chosen Jerusalem for his dwelling-place. YHWH's choice of Jerusalem has three implications: (a) concerning *topography*, Zion is a high mountain and there is a life-giving river; (b) concerning *security*, YHWH defeats the enemies of Zion, who then recognize his sovereignty; and (c) concerning the *inhabitants*, they live from the blessings of YHWH's presence, but must be fit to do that; cf. the schematic representation in Roberts 1982: 94. Levenson's Zion motif draws upon the features of the cosmic mountain: Zion is (a) the meeting place of gods; (b) the battle place of conflicting natural powers; (c) a meeting place of heaven and earth; (d) an administrative centre of the cosmos; and (e) the location of the streams of water; Levenson 1985: 111–37; cf. Dekker 2007: 315.

79 Cf. his definition of Zion traditions as designating 'the use of Zion or Jerusalem as a focus and symbol of Jewish national and eschatological thought . . . The plural of the term is used to indicate that there was no set understanding regarding Zion or Jerusalem' (Tan 1997: 24).

80 Cf. Körting 2006: 227: 'Zion ist kein systematisierbares Vorstellungssyndrom, sondern oszillierendes Zentrum fortschreitender Theologiebildung mit eigens zu nennenden Konstanten und Variablen, je nach den Erfordernissen von Kontexten und den Herausforderungen der Zeit.' See also Ollenburger 1987: 18: 'The significant point for us is that it is inappropriate in a consideration of the meaning of Zion as a symbol to restrict ourselves to one motif associated with it (e.g. "Völkerkampf") and one theological theme derived from it (e.g. inviolability). Like any other central symbol Zion was capable of being placed in designs of more than one configuration, and was capable of evoking more than one response.'

81 Cf. Körting's review of recent literature: 'Aus dem präsentierten Zugang zum Thema "Zion" ergibt sich jedoch das Problem, daß man den Schwerpunkt dessen, was Zionstradition und Zionstheologie ausmacht, bei einigen wenigen Psalmen sucht' (Körting 2006: 4); cf. Dow 2011: 76: 'The Psalms are the main source for ideas that are usually known as "Zion Theology" or the "Zion tradition".'

82 Körting 2006: 4; emphasis added.

83 Ollenburger 1987: 20.

84 Körting 2006: 5.

85 See, for instance, McConville 1992: 26, n. 8: 'indeed in many Biblical writings there *is* virtual synonymity between "Zion" and "Jerusalem"'; and Tan 1997: 24–5: '"Jerusalem" and "Zion" are used synonymically in the OT.'

86 Wildberger 1991: 30; Webb 1990: 68, n. 1: 'Functionally, . . . the two terms [Zion and Jerusalem] are synonymous and the variation in their usage is not, in itself, semantically significant.'

87 Cf. Hoppe 2000: 24: 'While in the psalms Jerusalem and Zion are often equivalent terms referring to the place where God reigns on earth, the two words do have distinct but complementary connotations. Jerusalem is more comprehensive of the two. It refers to the royal city of the Judahite monarchy, which includes the Temple. Zion is the mountain of God's temple. Together they delineate the city's role as the political and religious center of Judah'; see also Meyers & Meyers 2010: 120: 'the two words may more appropriately be taken as distinct and complementary entities rather than as synonymous expressions. That is, Jerusalem is a broader term, representing the monarchic holdings of the Judean kings; and Zion is the mountain of God's temple.'

88 Körting 2006: 84, 227: 'Es sind verschiedene theologische Konzepte mit Zion und Jerusalem verbunden. Grundsätzlich läßt sich festhalten, daß Jerusalem

INTRODUCTION

stärker national, Zion hingegen stärker universal ausgerichtet ist. Treten beide nebeneinander, so können Charakterzüge Jerusalems auf Zion übertragen werden und umgekehrt. Es ist möglich von Zion als zerstörter und aufzubauender Stadt zu sprechen, wenn er parallel zu Jerusalem genannt wird. Jerusalem hingegen erhält die universalen Züge Zions in der Vision der zum Zion und nach Jerusalem pilgernden Völker (Ps 102,22f.).'

89 Hjelm 2004: 257.

90 Cf. Hoppe 2000: 40: 'Although it was originally a name for a portion of the city, Zion came to be a synonym for the whole of Jerusalem, then for the entire land of Israel, and eventually for the people of Israel as well.' See also Dekker's first sub-group of the independent use of Zion in Isa. 1–39, that is, 'those [texts] in which Zion stands for the city of Jerusalem, with or without its inhabitants' (Dekker 2007: 271).

91 This geographical place is, however, mostly the place we today know as Jerusalem; cf. Levenson 1985: 92: 'It is not clear that "Zion" always referred to the same spot in ancient time. In any event, most of the biblical references to Zion have in mind what is today known as the Temple mount, on which sits the spectacular mosque, the Dome of the Rock.'

92 Cf. Meyers & Meyers 2009: 121; Hoppe 2000: 91, n. 14: 'The singular form, "daughter Zion", is a poetic personification of Jerusalem'; Follis 1992: 1103: 'Bat Zion' is 'an image of the unity between place and people within which divine favor and civilization create a setting of stability and home'.

93 Berlin 2002: 10–12; see also Hillers 1992: 30–1.

Part I

ZION IN THE OLD TESTAMENT

1

ISAIAH

The Zion motif in the Book of Isaiah: where to begin? Apparently, Zion forms a leitmotif throughout the entire book. The appearance of the term 'Zion' – forty-seven times – indicates the centrality of this theme in Isaiah. Recently, Ulrich Berges has asserted that 'the book of Isaiah is a "Drama of Zion" in which the readers or hearers witness the transformation of Jerusalem from a place of judgement into a place of eschatological salvation for both the people of God and the nations'.[1] In addition, Antti Laato has convincingly demonstrated that the destiny of Zion divides Isaiah on formal grounds: Isaiah 1–39 concerns the danger of invasion; Isaiah 40–55 concerns the return from exile and the rebuilding of the city and its temple; and Isaiah 55–66 concerns the future of Jerusalem.[2] As we shall see, Zion indeed serves a multifaceted role in Isaiah.

The term 'Zion'

The term 'Zion' (ציון) occurs forty-seven times in Isaiah: twenty-six times independently[3] and twenty-one times as part of a construct relation: eight times as 'Mount Zion' (הר ציון),[4] four times as 'daughter Zion' (בת ציון),[5] three times as 'the daughters of Zion' (בנות ציון),[6] two times as 'the mount of daughter Zion' (הר בת ציון),[7] once as 'inhabitant of Zion' (יושבת ציון) in 12:6,[8] once as 'the fight for Zion' (ריב ציון) in 34:8,[9] once as 'the herald of good tidings to Zion' (מבשרת ציון) in 40:9[10] and once as 'those who mourn in Zion' (אבלי ציון) in 61:3. In four cases, the name is associated with the terms for 'city' (קריה/עיר);[11] fifteen times it stands next to the name 'Jerusalem';[12] and twice it stands next to the name 'Israel' (46:13; 60:14).

Zion is called 'the City of YHWH' (60:14) and is a holy city (52:1). YHWH has founded Zion (14:32); he will reign on Mount Zion (24:23; 52:7); and Mount Zion is the place of his name (18:7). YHWH will fight for Zion and bring her salvation (29:8; 34:8; 46:13); here YHWH will finish his work (10:12). The word of YHWH goes forth from Zion (2:3), and here is his fire (31:9). Zion is a place to which YHWH returns (40:9; 52:8; 62:11); he dwells on this mountain (8:18), although he in another

25

passage dwells 'on high' from where he fills Zion with justice and righteousness (33:5; cf. 1:27). His chosen people live on Zion (10:24; 14:32; 30:19); again, it is a place to which one returns (35:10; 41:27; 51:11). Zion is even identified with the people of YHWH (51:16). Zion is the last bastion (1:8), where the remnant of Israel will be saved (4:3; 37:32), while Zion at the same time is depicted as the place to which the foreign nations will come (2:3; 18:7). Zion is also portrayed as a woman, who thinks YHWH has forsaken and forgotten her (40:27; 49:14); yet he comforts her (51:3) and she gives birth to children (66:8). Finally, YHWH comes down to fight *against* Mount Zion (31:4),[13] and we are told that Zion has become a wilderness and is left desolate (64:9). In sum, Zion plays a significant yet ambiguous role in the Book of Isaiah.[14]

Motifs, events and characteristics associated with Zion

As argued in the introduction, scholarly works on Zion have mostly focused on the motif of Zion as the last bastion against aggressive nations. Such a view, for example, determines Gerhard von Rad's examination of Isaiah.[15] The concept of YHWH's special protection of Zion indeed forms a main line of thought in Isaiah, in particular in the first thirty-nine chapters. Since we shall return in the following to many of the passages listed, the present examination is only meant to be an initial sketch of texts and motifs; see chapter 7 for a more careful treatment.

Already in the initial chapter of the book, Zion is left as a besieged city while the land and cities surrounding her lie desolate (1:7–9). If YHWH had not spared some survivors (a remnant), the city would have suffered the fate of Sodom and Gomorrah, that is, total annihilation. In 14:28–32, Zion is depicted as a highly protected place. YHWH has founded her, and the weak, poor and helpless among the people will find refuge here. The initial depiction of the enemy army that approaches to invade the city is found in Isaiah 5:25–30. It is YHWH himself who summons it, and its nature is almost superhuman: none of the soldiers is weary; their weapons, horses and chariots are prepared for battle; their cry is like that of a lion and their roaring like that of the sea. By the presence of the army, darkness covers all the land. In 8:6–8, we hear that the enemies are like mighty waters, which sweep into Judah and pour over her until they reach up to the neck. Furthermore, in 17:12, the noise of the attackers is likened to the thunder of the sea and the roaring of the mighty waters. On the one hand, YHWH clearly urges the hostile nations to come. On the other hand, YHWH shows mercy, for he will protect his city (30:18–19). The foreign peoples flee far away (8:9–10; 17:13–14), and YHWH tramples the Assyrian army on his holy mountain (14:24–7). In a tremendous manner, 30:27–33 portrays the appearance of the burning wrath of YHWH and the annihilation of the enemies by his breath of fire.

ISAIAH

A subtle ambivalence undergirds the texts just mentioned. On the one hand, the Assyrian army and the hostile nations are in YHWH's service and fulfil – as an instrument of his wrath – divine judgement against the chosen people because of their sins. On the other hand, the enemies are exactly those YHWH needs to defeat in order to manifest himself as the saviour of his city. An illustration of such ambivalence is expressed in the song of Ariel in 29:1–8.[16] In vv. 1–6, YHWH mourns the arrogant city and besieges it in order to destroy it. In vv. 7–8, however, YHWH makes it abundantly clear that all peoples who fight against Ariel are deemed to fail. In addition, 31:4–5 literally seems to express a paradox: v. 4 states that YHWH will come down to do battle against his city; v. 5, on the contrary, states that YHWH will protect and rescue Jerusalem.[17] In Isaiah, this ambivalence may be summed up by the notion in 14:26 of 'the plan that is planned' (זאת העצה היעוצה). First, YHWH *judges* his city by calling the enemies; then, YHWH *saves* his city by defeating the attacking nations; cf. 10:12: 'When YHWH has finished all his work on Mount Zion and on Jerusalem [i.e. judging his people], he will punish the arrogant king of Assyria and his haughty pride [i.e. saving his people].'

The ambivalence in YHWH's relation to his people as both their judge and saviour is part of a larger theological framework, which we – in the words of Otto Kaiser – should refer to as 'a theology of decision' (*Entscheidungstheologie*).[18] Within this framework, faith and trust in YHWH play a significant role, for instance, as in the famous verse about Zion as a foundation stone, a tested stone that will test the faith of the rulers of Jerusalem (28:16).[19] The approaching enemies in 5:25–30 will place great pressure on the inhabitants of the city so that they – in fear of the imminent invasion – must decide what to put their trust in. Do they rely on their weapons and support from foreign military powers (e.g. Egypt, cf. 30:1–5; 31:1–3)? Or do they solely rely on YHWH's salvific intervention?

Concerning this issue, Isaiah contains two crucial narratives which stand in serious opposition: the account of the unfaithful King Ahaz (Isa. 7) and the account of the faithful King Hezekiah (Isa. 36–7).[20] Significantly, these narratives are related on formal grounds.[21] First, they are introduced by dating formulae (cf. 7:1; 36:1). Second, the events portrayed in the narratives take place on the same spot: 'at the end of the conduit of the upper pool on the highway to the Fuller's Field' (cf. 7:3; 36:2).[22] Third, both events end with a similar phrase: 'the zeal of YHWH will do this' (cf. 9:7[6]; 37:32). Fourth, and most importantly, Ahaz and Hezekiah react differently to the imminent danger of invasion: Ahaz is seized with panic and refuses to put his trust in YHWH, whereas Hezekiah keeps calm and turns to YHWH in the temple.[23] In sum, in the phrase of Kaiser, Ahaz's decision leads to divine judgement, whereas Hezekiah's decision leads to divine salvation. In sharp contrast to Ahaz's unbelief, Hezekiah's attitude provides a model of faith.[24]

In the Ahaz narrative it is initially stated that the city cannot be conquered (7:1). YHWH tells the prophet Isaiah that Ahaz and the people will not fear the approaching army (7:4). As long as they stand firm in faith, the army will not succeed (7:7, 9). Nevertheless, Ahaz fails to do so by not asking for a sign (7:12).[25] The punishment for this unfaithful deed is harsh: YHWH will bring terrible days upon them, in which the Assyrian super-power will come and ravage the land (7:17).[26]

In the Hezekiah narrative the army of the Assyrian King Sennacherib stands at the walls of Jerusalem after having captured all the fortified cities of Judah. The king's Rabshaqeh (chief messenger) scornfully asks on what Hezekiah relies (36:4). Through the polemical statements of the Rabshaqeh, we are indirectly informed that Hezekiah reigns in the belief that YHWH will rescue them and that the city will not be given into the hands of the Assyrian king (36:7, 15, 18). The Rabshaqeh continues his taunt: when other countries' gods could not protect their countries against the mighty king of Assyria, how could YHWH do it?[27] Despite these threats, Hezekiah stays calm, goes into the temple and asks Isaiah to pray for the remnant of survivors that is left in Jerusalem (37:1–5). Answering Hezekiah's confession to God as the creator of heaven and earth and king over all kingdoms (37:16–20), YHWH promises that he will rescue them and save the city (37:30–5). During the night, the angel of YHWH kills 185,000 in the camp of the Assyrians. Because of this slaughter, King Sennacherib leaves and the city has been rescued – by YHWH's salvific intervention! In sum, the Hezekiah narrative displays two central features of the Zion theology. First, it is stressed that – due to the faithfulness of King Hezekiah – YHWH will save his city. Second, it adopts the dramatic element of the *Völkerkampf* that salvation occurs in the very last moment at the very last bastion, Zion (see also 8:4–10; 10:27b–34; 14:24–7; 17:12–14).

The Hezekiah narrative contains another important Isaianic theme, namely the concept of a surviving remnant on Zion.[28] Initially, 1:9 states that YHWH only leaves a few survivors. 10:20–3 likewise points out that although the people of Israel are numerous like the sand of the sea, only a remnant will return (cf. the first of the three symbolic names in Isa. 7–8: 'Shearjashub'; a remnant will return). In 30:12–17, YHWH punishes the majority of the inhabitants of the city, because they were unfaithful to his word; only a small remnant will be saved. According to 37:30–2, however, this remnant will again be turned into a people of prosperity. The vision in 4:2–6 informs readers that those who are left in Zion will be called holy and their sins will be washed away. Mount Zion will serve as a pavilion which will offer shade from the heat and shelter from storm and rain.

To sum up: these characteristics, which we have listed above, recall what the scholars in the 1950s, 1960s and 1970s defined as *the Zion tradition*. In short, it is the motif of a place that YHWH protects against foreign nations, expanded in Isaiah's version with faith as a condition of salvation ('the theology of decision') and with an emphasis on a surviving remnant.[29] Yet the Book of Isaiah has a lot more to say about Zion. First, all the passages referred to above stem from Isaiah 1–39 and, in particular, from passages which historical-critical scholars have regarded to be – or at least to contain – authentic words of the historical prophet Isaiah.[30] Second, there are an abundance of passages and images about Zion in the rest of Isaiah that do not fit the motif of Zion as the last bastion. We shall now turn to these passages.

Unlike, for instance, Jeremiah and Ezekiel, Isaiah does not offer an extensive account of the Babylonian invasion of Jerusalem.[31] However, 6:11–13 contains a general announcement that the cities will lie waste without people, that the land will be utterly desolate and that YHWH will send everyone surviving far away. Furthermore, in Isaiah 39, Hezekiah shows the Babylonian envoys his treasure-house, his armoury and his store-houses.[32] Nevertheless, a proper account of the fall of Jerusalem such as that in 2 Kings 25 is lacking.[33] On the one hand, its absence constitutes a 'hole' in the overall narrative of the Book of Isaiah between chapters 39 and 40.[34] On the other hand – and this may be a crucial point – it protects the inviolability of Zion, so to speak, that we *do not* hear about the burning of the temple and the destruction of its walls.[35] Yet the peculiar break between Isaiah 39 and 40 remains. Apparently, it is presumed that the reader knows that Jerusalem has fallen and that its inhabitants have gone into exile. In any case, that is where Isaiah 40–55 begins. The central topic of these chapters is God's forgiveness of sin[36] and the proclamation of a way out of exile, from Babylon to Zion.[37] After a long period of silence, YHWH will act again (42:13–16). Already in 40:3–5, we hear that the way of YHWH will be prepared in the wilderness and that the glory of YHWH will be revealed to all peoples.[38] Isaiah 35 has adumbrated this holy way by which the wilderness and desert are turned into prosperity when the ransomed of YHWH return with joy and gladness.[39] However, not only the people of YHWH return. Also God returns in full strength, gathers his flock and returns to Zion (40:9–11; 52:8; 66:10–12). Further-more, YHWH promises that he will restore Jerusalem (44:26–8; 45:13) and put salvation in Zion (46:13).

Whereas Isaiah 40–8 focuses on the redemption of the people Jacob/Israel, with a few references to Zion as the ideal goal of the journey from Babylon, Isaiah 49–55 focuses on the restoration of Zion/Jerusalem.[40] Isaiah 49:14–23 depicts Zion as a mourning woman who is being restored and repopulated,[41] and 51:1–4 subsequently states that YHWH comforts her and turns her wilderness into the Garden of Eden. This motif is of great significance, because elsewhere we hear that Zion has become a wilder-ness and a desolation (cf. 64:9–10). This is an entirely different image of Zion than that of her as the last bastion. Furthermore, 51:11 recalls the joy of the ransomed returning to Zion (cf. 35:10), and in 51:16, YHWH addresses Zion as his people (cf. 'You are my people'). In 52:1–2, Zion must shake the dust from herself, put on beautiful garments, and is, along with Jerusalem, called the holy city (cf. 48:2). Isaiah 54 contains a magnificent vision of the new glory of Zion/Jerusalem, in which the abandoned cities are being repopulated (54:3); the walls and the foundations are ornamented with precious stones (54:11–12); everyone is taught by YHWH (54:13–14); and all who attack the city will fall (54:15–17).

While Isaiah 49–55 mostly concerns the restoration of the city, Isaiah 56–66 describes the restoration of the temple and its service, introduced by the famous description of the new house of prayer in 56:1–8.[42] Very interestingly, YHWH will also bring foreigners who keep his covenant to his holy mountain and make them joyful in his house (56:6–7). This kind of universalism – 'a house of prayer for all the peoples' – appears as a central theme throughout the rest of the book, although it also points backward to the previous chapters (see further below). Isaiah 60 stands monumentally in the heart of this section.[43] The light rises upon Zion and all the nations come to see its glory (60:1–3); they bring treasures to the temple (60:4–9); and the foreigners and their kings will restore the walls of Zion, adorn this holy place and honour it as the city of YHWH (60:10–17). Here, there will be peace and eternal light, and all in the land will be righteous (60:18–22).

Isaiah 62 continues the line of thought from chapter 60: Zion will be the bride of the king, since YHWH will take her as wife (62:1–6); in addition, the image of the way, for instance, in Isaiah 35 recurs in 62:10–12.[44] Finally, besides the visions in chapters 60 and 62, a third great vision on Zion appears in 65:17–66:24: YHWH will create a new heaven and a new earth, and he will create Jerusalem as joy (65:17–19); there will be peace in Zion (65:25).[45] Furthermore, Zion is portrayed as a woman giving birth (66:7–9); there is joy in Jerusalem (66:10–11); YHWH takes care of her and extends prosperity to her (66:7–9); and YHWH will punish her enemies (66:15–16). Finally, 66:18–21, 23 underlines the universalistic perspective, in so far as YHWH gathers the nations and brings them to his holy mountain, where all peoples will come and worship him.

This universalism, which is clearly revealed within Isaiah 56–66 as a frame and centre of the entire composition, is manifested in other parts of Isaiah as well. Frequently, 2:2–4 is highlighted as the most important passage in which the nations do not come as enemies, but as pilgrims seeking to hear the word and teaching flowing from Zion. Verse 4, in particular, expresses the hope for worldwide peace. The weapons are beaten into working tools and no one learns war any more. We also find this positive view of the foreign nations both in 18:1–7, where Nubia will bring gifts to Zion, and in 19:22–5, where Egypt and Assyria will return to YHWH and along with Israel be a blessing in the midst of the earth (cf. Isaiah 45:18). Furthermore, 25:6–8 accounts for YHWH's great feast for all the nations. Interestingly, in 14:1–4a, we encounter the idea that the foreign peoples will join the house of Jacob and become its male and female slaves. Likewise, in 49:22–3, the foreign kings and queens will be the foster-fathers and nursing-mothers of the children of Zion. In addition, Zion is the place to which foreign rulers come to seek counsel (16:1–5).

In sum, we have not only discovered that there are numerous examples of a more 'peaceful' view of the foreign nations in Isaiah, but also that Zion appears as a central and unifying symbol for the whole world. Peace and prosperity rule here. By means of a utopian imagery, 11:6–9 depicts how peace dominates the divine mountain: the wolf lives with the lamb, the leopard with the kid and the nursing child with the asp (cf. 65:25). On his holy mountain, YHWH swallows up death and wipes away the tears from all faces (25:6–8).

Summing up: Isaiah

Zion constitutes a central, yet multifaceted motif in the Book of Isaiah. There are but a few chapters that do not contain images or concepts related to Zion. Crucially, the images are different and even diverse. In general, it appears that there is *a conflict between two main perceptions of Zion*: on the one hand, Zion as the last bastion in the battle against foreign nations; on the other hand, Zion as the ruined city (desert) that will be restored and repopulated. It seems of great importance, however, that an account of the fall of the city is absent (apart from allusions in Isa. 6:11–13; 39). The image of Zion enjoying special status and protection remains intact, and the indications that the city has been destroyed are but a few (cf. 54:1–4; 64:9–10).

Isaiah is often referred to as a prophet of judgement, since the proclamation of the judgement of YHWH constitutes a prominent element of the message of the book. There are clear signs, however, that the Book of Isaiah in general establishes a tension between judgement and salvation: first, the proclamation of judgement; then, the proclamation of salvation.[46] The main thesis is therefore as follows: against the background of a broken relationship with God, judgement is proclaimed to the people and their leaders, followed by a message of salvation for those who return. The harsh words about judgement form a decisive basis for the comforting words about salvation. Now, how does this observation correlate with the two main perceptions of Zion throughout the book? In the first case, the judgement consists of YHWH's calling of the enemies to ravage and threaten the city. Salvation, then, is that YHWH rescues the righteous remnant in Zion, while all others perish. In the second case, the judgement entails the destruction of the city and deportation of the people (although only indicated in Isaiah). Salvation, then, is the way that leads from captivity to the restored Zion.

In the following study of the Zion motif, we shall focus on this twofold perception of Zion. As we have seen, we should actually talk about two main Zion motifs that structurally correspond to each other. A comparative analysis between these two motifs has appeared fruitful. The first motif, which we from now on will call the classical Zion motif, contains the static image of Zion as the last bastion: despite enemy attacks, the city remains intact but only with a remnant of survivors. In contrast, Zion as the goal of the journey out of exile is indeed an entirely different and dynamic image, which we shall call the dynamic Zion motif: the city is completely destroyed by the enemy attack and left desolate. Yet out of this desolation, a new city will be created to which those who have survived in exile will return; eventually also the foreign nations will come and worship YHWH there.

Notes

1 Berges 2012: 24.
2 Laato 1998: 45–50, 63–4. Also Barry Webb notices the general movement from apostate Jerusalem to the New Jerusalem. As he contends, 'the transformation of Zion is the key to both the formal and thematic structure of the book as a whole' (Webb 1990: 67); cf. Dow 2011: 84–5. For a recent study of how the concept of Zion has shaped the growth of Isaiah, see de Jong 2011: 37–47.
3 Isa. 1:27; 2:3; 4:3; 10:24; 14:32; 28:16; 30:19; 31:9; 33:5; 33:14; 33:20; 35:10; 41:27; 46:13; 49:14; 51:3; 51:11; 51:16; 52:1; 52:7; 52:8; 59:20; 60:14; 62:1; 64:9; 66:8.
4 Isa. 4:5; 8:18; 10:12; 18:7; 24:23; 29:8; 31:4; 37:32.
5 Isa. 1:8; 37:22; 52:2; 62:11.
6 Isa. 3:16; 3:17; 4:4.
7 Isa. 10:32; 16:1. Isa. 10:32, however, constitutes a special problem, because MT actually has 'the temple mount of Zion' (הר בית ציון), cf. Isa. 2:2? NRSV as many other translations follows the Masoretic qere by reading בת (cf. 1QIsaᵃ, LXX, Vulgate and Peshitta).
8 NRSV has 'royal Zion'.
9 NRSV has 'Zion's cause' (or 'Zion's defender'; cf. footnote in NRSV).
10 For the adequate translation of this verse, see chapter 9.
11 Isa. 1:8; 33:20; 52:1; 60:14.
12 Isa. 2:3; 4:3; 10:12; 10:32; 24:23; 30:19; 31:9; 37:22; 37:32; 40:9; 41:27; 52:1; 52:2; 62:1; 64:9.
13 Against NRSV, which has 'to fight upon Mount Zion'; see further in chapter 7.
14 See the review in Dekker 2007: 266–75.
15 von Rad 1965: 155–69.
16 Cf. von Rad 1965: 164: 'Jahweh's work for Zion is here given a remarkable theological ambivalence: it judges and saves at one and the same time.'
17 See further in my exegesis of these verses in chapter 7.
18 Kaiser 1983: 114.
19 Cf. Hoppe 2000: 60: 'A basic assumption of [Isaiah's] message is that Jerusalem can secure its future by faith in the God who calls for the creation of a just society.'

ISAIAH

20 Cf. Childs 2001: 272: 'in the recounting of the ensuing events there is a clearly antithetical typology developed between the response of Ahaz in 734 and Hezekiah in 701 to threat of a hostile siege.'

21 For a careful comparison of these figures, which also takes the portraits in Chronicles into account, see Hjelm 2004: 115–20, 128.

22 Cf. Laato 1998: 103: 'It is hardly a coincidence that the Assyrian army under RabSaqe were deployed exactly where Ahaz refused to take refuge in the Lord.' See also Berges 2012: 43. However, Hjelm 2004: 128 rightly states that 'Ahaz's presence at the "conduit of the upper pool" is contrasted to Hezekiah's absence from this place (Isa. 36.3).'

23 See Ferry 2008: 88–90.

24 See further in chapter 7.

25 Intriguingly, Ingrid Hjelm has argued for a different interpretation: 'The clue does not lie in Ahaz' refusal to accept a sign, but in Isaiah's offensive suggestion that Ahaz should seek an answer from Yahweh his god either in "the valley" or on "the mountain" (Isa. 7.11) . . . With the implied accusation of not seeking Yahweh, but of offering at the high places, on the hills and under every green tree . . . of burning incense (to Moloch) in the valley of the son of Hinnom and burning his children in fire . . . of placing altars on the roof of the temple in Jerusalem . . . Isaiah is referring to circumstances well known from tradition' (Hjelm 2004: 126–7).

26 However, 'The prophet's ambiguity in explicitly ascribing Judaea's disaster to Ahaz, but rather conferring the guilt on his people (. . . 8.6) and the Assyrian king (10.7–11), leaves open the possibility of condemning Judah, while retaining goodwill for the royal house, the city and its saved remnant . . . Ahaz might not have been Isaiah's favourite king, but condemning him, as Kings and Chronicles do, would have led to insurmountable inconsistencies regarding Isaiah's theological agenda as set out in Isa. 7.9' (Hjelm 2004: 128).

27 Cf. Hjelm 2004: 35: 'The *hubris* of the Assyrian commander, who himself relies on the powers of this world – gods made by men's hands, of wood and of stone – marks the Assyrian attack as a theological contest rather than a political one.'

28 Cf. Clements 2011: 207: 'The divine protection of Jerusalem made possible through God's presence on the holy mountain has become the basis for an assurance that a "band of survivors" will remain, and will flourish again in Jerusalem.'

29 Cf. the review of Gerhard von Rad, John H. Hayes and J. J. M. Roberts in the introduction; see further in chapter 7.

30 See, for instance, Schreiner 1963: 243–70; von Rad 1965: 155–69; Childs 1967: 20–68; Barth 1977: 17–202; Høgenhaven 1988: 77–189; Wildberger 2002: 579–85. However, due to his form-critical concerns, Childs rejects any attempts to fuse the different oracles into a coherent theological pattern (as we have just attempted to); cf. Childs 1967: 68: 'The message of Isaiah is cast within a limited number of stereotyped forms. Within these traditional structures certain major emphases of the prophet have emerged with clarity: a threat of judgement is directed to unfaithful Israel, a message of failure and defeat is hurled against proud Assyria, Zion as God's abode is proclaimed inviolable against the fiercest attacks of its enemies, the response of faith as quiet trust is assured the safety of Yahweh. However, *these recurrent themes do not build a complete system of political or theological thought*. There are no Isaianic principles which let themselves be extrapolated from the particular form of the oracle as it was delivered in a specific situation' (emphasis added).

31 Nevertheless, Laato has argued that, within Isaiah as a whole, Assyria functions as a typos of Babylonia: 'the Assyrian invasion is described in Isaiah 36–7

33

according to the pattern of the historical events in Judah in the reign of Zedekiah when the Babylonian army was forced to abandon the siege of Jerusalem because of the invasion of the Egyptian/Ethiopian army (Jeremiah 37–39) . . . These parallels constitute evidence that Assyria is a typos for Babylonia in the Book of Isaiah' (Laato 1998: 94).

32 Cf. Laato 1998: 63: '[The] destruction and exile are also implicit in Isaiah 39'; see also Clements 2011: 122–3.

33 The oracle against Babylon in Isa. 13–14 lacks clear allusions to any historical event (except perhaps from 13:17, 19) and thereby 'describes the annihilation of Babylonia as an event which concerns the future' (Laato 1998: 126).

34 This hole or gap also exists in terms of different genres in Isa. 1–39 and 40–66, in terms of headings (many in 1–39, none in 40–66) and in terms of characters (Hezekiah and Isaiah only appear in 1–39). The fate of Zion, however, offers continuity between the two parts. See further in van Wieringen 2011: 81–2.

35 Cf. Berges 2012: 47: 'One of the greatest peculiarities of the book of Isaiah is that the events of exile are not portrayed . . . This silence concerning the events of exile in the book of Isaiah cannot, therefore, be accidental; it must be an intentional part of the message of the authors. It was the concept of Jerusalem as an unconquerable refuge for all those who trust in Yhwh (28.16) that prohibited the authors from thematizing the capture and destruction of Jerusalem. The victory over Sennacherib rather than the defeat under Nebuchadnezzar is given a central place in their theology of history.'

36 Cf. Hoppe 2000: 71: '[Isaiah of Jerusalem's] insistence on justice of the poor made it possible for those who developed the Isaianic tradition to maintain that the city fell because of its sins (50:1–3) but that God forgave those sins (40:1–2), making possible the city's restoration.'

37 This is at least the traditional view on the message of Isa. 40–55, which recently has been thoroughly criticized; see further in chapter 9. For a study of the way of YHWH in Isaiah, see Lim 2010.

38 Within the present form of Isaiah, Laato sees this exodus predicted in Isa. 11:10–12:6; 14:1–2; 27:12–13; 35:1–10 (Laato 1998: 141).

39 Cf. Laato 1998: 176: 'In Isaiah 40–55 the captivity is understood as a purification whereby the sins of the people have been blotted out.'

40 Blenkinsopp 2002: 310, 327; Berges 2012: 48.

41 For a thorough analysis of Zion as a woman in Isa. 40–55(66), see Wischnowsky 2001: 164–248.

42 Blenkinsopp 2003: 140–1. Nevertheless, Hoppe 2000: 128 states that 'despite [Isaiah 56–66's] devaluation of the Temple's importance, Jerusalem still held a significant place in his prophecy. His anti-temple rhetoric serves to underscore the belief that the status of Jerusalem as God's chosen city was actually independent of the Temple's fate.'

43 Berges 2012: 72 convincingly demonstrates that Isa. 56–66 has a concentric structure: 'In the centre is the announcement of salvation for Zion/Jerusalem (60–62). Three successive frames are concerned (a) with the admittance of proselytes and eunuchs and the mission to the nations (56.1–8; 66.18–24), (b) with words of complaint that lead to a distinction between the wicked and the righteous (56.9–58.14; 65.1–66.17), and (c) communal complaints that deal with the non-arrival of salvation (59; 63.1–64.11).'

44 However, Laato 1998: 200 is right that the Exodus motif is downplayed or altered in Isa. 56–66: '*First*, not all of those who have returned to Judah are willing to follow the commandments of Yhwh even though the texts in Isaiah 40–55 presuppose such fidelity. The disobedience of the audience in Isaiah

ISAIAH

56–66 is the reason why the promised salvation of Isaiah 40–55 has not yet been realized. *Second*, the promise is given in Isaiah 60–62 that other exiles too will in the future return to Jerusalem. Thus Isaiah 56–66 indicates that the final exodus has not yet taken place but even in the future new exiles will be allowed to return to Jerusalem and take part in the new marvelous period which will fall upon the city'; cf. Hoppe 2000: 131: 'The massive return from Babylon to Jerusalem never took place.' Moreover, Hjelm has convincingly stressed that the glorious visions of Zion remain an eschatological hope within the prophetic literature; instead, one needs to look for fulfilment of the visions in the extra-biblical material, especially, in 1 Maccabeans; see Hjelm 2004: 258–93.

45 Cf. McConville 1992: 36: 'By the end of Isaiah, Zion is understood as God's glorified people in a new creation which is at the end of time and on a cosmic scale.'

46 For instance, the first four chapters of the book form two cycles containing oracles of judgement (1:2–31; 2:6–4:1) and of salvation (2:1–5; 4:2–6); see Beuken 2003: 60. See also Dow 2011: 85: 'Interwoven with the message of condemnation and woe in Isa. 1–12 is another picture of a glorious future Zion.'

2

JEREMIAH

Whereas Isaiah only alludes to the great destruction of the city of YHWH, this theme plays a dominant role in the Book of Jeremiah. YHWH will destroy daughter Zion; to be sure, the city and land will be left desolate and without inhabitants. In a fascinating way, however, Jeremiah switches between harsh messages of judgement and comforting messages of hope. Although Jeremiah hardly describes Zion as an invulnerable place, there is constantly a subtle play on motifs associated with the classical tradition of Zion's inviolability.

The term 'Zion'

The term 'Zion' (ציון) occurs seventeen times in Jeremiah: twelve times independently;[1] and five times as part of a construct relation: three times as 'daughter Zion' (בת ציון),[2] one time as 'the height of Zion' (מרום ציון)[3] in 31:12 and one time as 'the inhabitants of Zion' (ישבת ציון) in 51:35. Zion stands next to Judah (14:19), to Jerusalem (51:35) and to Jerusalem and the temple mount (26:18[4]). As in Isaiah, Zion is often depicted with feminine attributes as YHWH's partner.

Although the kingdom of YHWH is closely linked with Zion (8:19), YHWH will reject her (14:19) and destroy her (6:2[5]). Enemies will attack Zion (4:6; 6:23) and make her anguish (4:31), and she will wail over her ruins (9:18). Throughout the book, Zion is both the place of judgement and hope. On the one hand, Zion will be called the outcast that no one cares for (30:17). On the other hand, Zion is the place to which YHWH will bring the faithless (3:14). YHWH will repay all the evil that has been brought upon Zion (51:24, 35); the vengeance for his ruined temple is declared on Zion (50:28); and on that place the people will tell about the work of YHWH (51:10). Finally, Zion is the place to which one goes to encounter God (31:6, 12; 50:5).

Motifs, events and characteristics associated with Zion

Gerhard von Rad begins his examination of Jeremiah by stating: 'The Zion tradition which was determinative for the whole of Isaiah's prophecy has no place whatsoever in Jeremiah.'[6] If von Rad is right, we should end our investigation here. We must, however, keep two things in mind. First, the occurrences of the term Zion – seventeen times – indicate that some sort of Zion motif is present. Second, we should recall that von Rad defined the Zion tradition so narrowly that it could only encompass the classical Zion motif, that is, the image of Zion as the last bastion, which YHWH at the very last moment defends against attacking nations. As observed in the preceding chapter, this definition concerns mainly the passages that scholars have regarded as authentic Isaianic material. However, my examination of Isaiah revealed an entirely different and dynamic picture of Zion as the destination of a return from exile. As we shall see below, Jeremiah contains this dynamic Zion motif to a very high degree.

The agenda of the present form of Jeremiah may be interpreted as a movement from judgement to redemption.[7] As Louis Stulman proposes, we can divide the book into two major parts: Jeremiah 1–25 on the dismantling of Judah's idolatrous world, and Jeremiah 26–52 on the rebuilding out of the ruins.[8] Although Jeremiah is mostly associated with the proclamation of judgement, hope is indeed a central theme within the final form of the book; in particular, in the Book of Consolation (Jer. 30–33).[9]

Unlike Isaiah, Jeremiah has extensive depictions of the destruction of Jerusalem. As a leitmotif throughout the book, Jerusalem must be punished for her iniquities against YHWH. As Jack Lundbom rightly states: 'Behind all of Jeremiah's talk about sin and judgment lies a broken covenant.'[10] The people's transgressions are expressed in terms of violation against this covenant (11:1–17), violation of the Sabbath (17:19–27) and idolatry in the temple (7:1–8:3).[11] In general, the people's adulterous worship of other gods, especially of the Baals, seems to be the main reason behind YHWH's burning wrath (2:1–3:13; 19:3–9; 44:3).[12] Because of this violation, YHWH summons hostile nations from the north to wage war against Zion in order to crush the city (6:22–6). In the classical Zion motif, YHWH would have protected his city against this attack. In Jeremiah, however, we hear that he has forsaken his house and abandoned his heritage (8:19; 12:7; 14:19) and that he has hidden his face from the city because of all its wickedness (33:5). Frequently, it is stated that the city and the whole land will be turned into desolation without inhabitants.[13] Jeremiah 12:10–11 uses the familiar image of the vineyard representing YHWH's beautiful land.[14] Yet the vineyard is being destroyed, the portion has been trampled down and turned into mourning desolation, and the entire land will be made desolate. The land will be completely empty and even those who escape captivity and remain in the land will be killed by YHWH (21:9; 38:2). Crucially, it appears to be of great importance to Jeremiah that the land is made entirely desolate. Only so can the people hope for a new creation. Although Jeremiah regards exile as the punishment of the people's sin, exile and captivity also involve a rebirth of the people which enables the return of a new people to an entirely new city.

The enemy from the north, which marches against Zion, is depicted almost with mythological characteristics. Initially, the passage in 1:13–15 announces that a disaster will come, for YHWH calls all the tribes of the kingdoms from the north. Besides this minor passage, Jeremiah 4–10 contains the most prominent descriptions. The army is portrayed as a hunting lion (4:7), as a storm in which the chariots are like whirlwinds (4:13) and as an earthquake (10:22). The army consists of an enduring and ancient nation; all of them are mighty warriors (5:15–16). The invaders are cruel and show no mercy (6:23). The depiction of the army is even more remarkable than that of Isaiah (cf. Isa. 5:25–30) and with greater success; it wins! The inhabitants of Jerusalem flee, and Zion is destroyed.

There is something ironical about Jeremiah's portrayal of the army.[15] First, he portrays the enemies with similar – and even stronger – images as those of Isaiah, but lets them succeed. Second, he lets the army come from the *north*, from where also the exiled people will return to Zion (cf. 3:18; 16:15; 23:8; 31:8). Third, it is even more absurd that the enemies come from the *north* when one considers the Canaanite inspired mythology of Mount Zion. According to this mythology, Mount Zion lies in the far north (cf. Ps 48). Furthermore, it is identified with the mountain of Baal, the name of which – Zaphon – simply means 'north'. Is the enemy from the north a polemical response against the core of Zion theology: YHWH's unconditional protection?[16]

Who is this army from the north? Some scholars propose that it refers to the Scythians, a nation from southern Russia, which dominated parts of Syria in the latter half of the seventh century BCE.[17] Other scholars propose that it refers to the Babylonians,[18] who we know conquered the area, as the Book of Jeremiah itself frequently informs us.[19] In addition, 'all the tribes of the north' stands next to 'King Nebuchadnezzar of Babylon' in Jeremiah 25:9. However, it remains unsatisfactory, because the army that attacks and destroys Babylon in Jer. 50–1 is also referred to as a hostile nation from the north (50:3, 9, 41; 51:48). Is it the same army or a new one? Should we understand the 'enemy from the north' as a mythological attribute which can be transferred to any new superior force?[20] Or is it again an ironic subtlety of Jeremiah that Babylon, the great power of the first forty-nine chapters of his book, becomes a victim of the enemy from the north in Jeremiah 50–1?[21]

This problem likewise reflects that Jeremiah's perception of the fall of Jerusalem is not consistent throughout the book. In Jeremiah 1–45, YHWH – by means of Nebuchadrezzar and his army – destroys his city as punishment for its idolatry and violation of the covenant. In Jeremiah 50–1, the Babylonians are accused of having arrogantly invaded Judah; therefore YHWH declares war against Babylon to avenge his people.[22]

This lack of consistency also explains the different portraits of the end of exile. In Jeremiah 50–1, YHWH's retribution on Babylon clears the way out of captivity. Just as Babylon raged and consumed Zion, YHWH will repay Babylon for all its evil (51:24, 34–5). This retribution is even illustrated as a divine battle between YHWH and the Babylonian god, Bel (e.g. Marduk); a duel that YHWH wins (51:44). Vengeance will be declared on Zion, that is, the vengeance for the destruction of the temple (50:28; 51:11). In sheer contrast to this dramatic scenario, Jeremiah 1–45 contains a much more moderate promise of return. In this part of the book it is often just simply stated that YHWH will gather and bring his people back.[23] It is also proclaimed that after seventy years, YHWH will punish the Babylonian king and bring his people home (25:11–13; 29:10).

Jeremiah's imagery of the restoration of Zion is not as wonderful and pompous as that of Isaiah. In Jeremiah, there are plain anticipations of restoration of the political balance of power and of a continuation of the simple life with farming and cattle breeding (31:23–4).[24] The land and its towns will be rebuilt and repopulated (30:18; 31:38–40; 33:9–11) and YHWH promises that his people will dwell there in peace and security (30:10–11; 46:27–8). Of particular significance is the hope for reconciliation between the two kingdoms, Israel and Judah (3:18). In the hill country of Ephraim, one will call to go up to Zion, and the people of Israel and the people of Judah will together seek YHWH, their God (31:2–6; 50:4–5). There will be an abundance of food and joy on Zion and mourning will be turned into joy (31:10–14, 25). YHWH will set over the reunited people a new king from the house of David, who will reign with justice and wisdom (23:1–8; 33:15–17). Against this background, we should consider whether Jeremiah merely anticipates a recreation of the time before exile or if he expects something entirely new. Concerning the covenant, for example, some scholars think that the new covenant in Jeremiah is merely a renewal of the Sinai covenant and nothing more.[25] Others, including von Rad, think that the making of what they consider to be an entirely new covenant marks a decisive break between old and new.[26] YHWH will give his people a new heart to know that he is their God (24:7), and the new covenant with Israel and Judah will ensure that everyone – from the least to the greatest – will know YHWH (31:31–4).[27] In sum, the reunification of Israel and Judah plays an important role in Jeremiah.

As demonstrated by the text references, Zion is solely a place that is being destroyed in order to be recreated. Strikingly, Jeremiah again and again emphasizes the complete desolation of Zion. Only out of this desolate region – this empty land – can YHWH create a new Zion for his people returning from exile. Yet what came first? Is Jerusalem going to be restored *because* it was destroyed? Or, maybe better, is Jerusalem going to be destroyed *so that* it will be rebuilt?

Concerning the image of Zion as the last bastion, it seems that the features that commonly characterize the inviolable Zion are transferred to the prophetic figure of Jeremiah.[28] In 1:18–19 and 15:19–21, YHWH makes the prophet into a fortified city, an iron pillar and a bronze wall. No one will prevail against him, for YHWH is with him. Is this yet another ironical statement of Jeremiah that the prophet, not the city, receives special protection?[29] Furthermore, throughout the entire book, there are polemical attacks against faith in the inviolability of the city. The statement that when YHWH is not on Zion, it has no king (8:19) is probably levelled against the dogma that everything is fine as long as YHWH is on Zion.[30] As an illustration of this dogma, the city's prophets tell the people that they will not fear their enemies, because YHWH will provide peace and protection (14:13; 23:17; 27:9). Because of this (false) teaching, the kings and the people wrongly reject the idea that evil will reach them (5:12; 21:13).[31] Additionally, Jeremiah's temple sermon (7:1–8:3) contains a criticism of those who trust in the deceptive words: 'the temple of YHWH, the temple of YHWH, the temple of YHWH!' (7:4). Jeremiah 7:8–11 in particular and its claim to be 'saved' seem to reflect Zion theology.[32]

Some concluding observations: concerning the dwelling of YHWH, we hear that he forsakes and abandons it (12:7), and, moreover, that he roars from on high, from his holy habitation (25:30–1; cf. Am 1:2 and Joel 4:16 [ET 3:16]). YHWH has a throne, which is either called Jerusalem (3:17) or closely related to the temple in Jerusalem (14:21; 17:12). In general, Jeremiah does not appear to be an opponent of the temple institution as such.[33] The prophet gives his famous sermon here (7:1–8:3), and its criticism concerns the people entering the temple rather than the temple itself. As we have noticed, the Babylonian destruction of the temple results in YHWH's vengeance (Jer. 50–1). Finally, the term 'the remnant of Israel' is used twice: first, negatively about the enemies gleaning the remnant as a vine as an indicator of final destruction (6:9);[34] second, positively about YHWH saving his people, the remnant of Israel (31:7).

Summing up: Jeremiah

Zion plays an important role in the Book of Jeremiah. The dynamic Zion motif appears more sharply than in Isaiah, because the destruction of both the city and its surrounding land is constantly stressed. Of special significance is 6:2, where YHWH proclaims that he will destroy daughter Zion. According to Jeremianic theology, it seems to be very important that the city and the land are completely left behind as a desolate and empty place. Only in this way – out of absolute nothingness – can YHWH create a new Zion for a new and reborn people returning from captivity. The New Zion

JEREMIAH

includes the vision of reconciliation and reunification of the two kingdoms, Israel and Judah. This complex offers a kind of theodicy. Facing the fall of Jerusalem, one would initially say that Jerusalem fell because of YHWH's impotence and incapability of protecting his city. Yet by constantly claiming that YHWH is the master of history, working according to a divine plan, Jeremiah 'protects' the sovereignty of YHWH (cf. the battle between gods in Jer. 50–1, which YHWH wins).

Zion as the last bastion exists only as a parody. The prophet Jeremiah, who lives in the middle of the disaster as a witness to the Babylonian invasion, is the inviolable one, not the city. The concept of YHWH's special protection of the city appears only indirectly – and ironically – in the teaching of the false prophets and of the erroneous perception among the people.

Notes

1 Jer. 3:14; 4:6; 8:19; 9:18; 14:19; 26:18; 30:17; 31:6; 50:5; 50:28; 51:10; 51:24.
2 Jer. 4:31; 6:2; 6:23.
3 There are, however, text-critical problems concerning this verse. LXX (with Targum and Vulgate) reads 'the mountain of Zion', and the editors of BHS propose to read [ב]הרים – 'the mountains' – deleting 'Zion'. Nevertheless, I see no reason for these emendations.
4 This verse is, however, explicitly a quotation of Mic. 3:12.
5 Against NRSV's reading, 'I have likened daughter Zion to the loveliest pasture.' The alternative reading, which I choose, is mentioned in the footnote to the particular verse; cf. also Allen 2008: 82: 'That beautiful, refined woman I will destroy – Lady Zion.' Lundbom 1999: 18 has the weaker 'silencing' instead of destroying or annihilating (דמה); see further in my exegesis of this passage in chapter 8.
6 von Rad 1965: 192.
7 Childs 1979: 351.
8 Stulman 2005: 14–15. For other views on the structure of the book, see Allen 2008: 12–14. This at least goes for the Hebrew version of the book, whereas the Greek version may reveal a different structure.
9 Cf. McConville 1992: 39: 'Paradoxically . . . the prophet who was undoubtedly, for the greater part of his ministry, the most hard-bitten opponent of the Zion-tradition, leaves us a book which, taken as a whole, holds out a far more specific hope for restoration of the city than the Book of Isaiah had done.'
10 Lundbom 1999: 145.
11 Cf. Hoppe 2000: 83.
12 Cf. Stulman 2005: 62: 'The central metaphor of the broken marriage, and particularly the portrait of God as scorned lover, has far-reaching implications for theological construction in Jeremiah . . . God's judgement is not to annihilate but ultimately to restore a broken relationship.'
13 See, for instance, Jer. 4:27–9; 6:8; 7:34; 9:10; 10:22; 19:8; 22:6; 25:9, 18, 38; 34:22; 44:6, 22.
14 Cf. Allen 2008: 153.
15 For a general introduction to Jeremiah's use of irony, see the section on 'Humor and Irony' in Lundbom 1999: 133–8.

16 Cf. Douglas Jones' precise observations of the allusions to the Zion tradition in Jer. 1 (see below): 'For his hearers, the young Jeremiah created the greater impact because what he was declaring in this exaggerated, symbolic language was exactly the reverse of what their faith and their Temple worship led them to expect. The reversal of the thought of Ps. 48 is striking. The north is sinister as the source of Judgement, not benign as the home of YHWH. The nations successfully establish their sovereignty in Jerusalem: they are not panicked into retreat' (Jones 1992: 77). See also Hill 1999: 50: 'The designation of צָפוֹן as the source of the threat . . . indicates that the threat is of divine origin.'

17 Cf. in particular the seminal essay by H. H. Rowley (1962); see also Cazelles 1984.

18 See, for instance, Goldingay 2007: 60.

19 See Jer. 20:4–5; 25:8–11; 32:3–5, 24, 29–32; 34:1–2, 7; 37:8; 38:3; 39:1–10.

20 Cf. Childs 1959. Childs, however, argues that 'from the north' only functions as a mythological feature in post-exilic writings such as Ezek. 38–9, Isa. 13 and Joel. To him, the army in Isa. 5:26–30 and Jer. 4–10 does not possess superhuman characteristics. See also Wanke 1966: 87–8: '[Der Feind] bleibt in einem geheimnisvollen Dunkel, wird aber doch von Jeremia als eine menschliche Größe, im geschichtlichen und geographischen Raum existent, verstanden.' Nevertheless, I am not convinced that 'the enemy of the north' refers to concrete elements of the topography of Jerusalem as is suggested by Hoppe 2000: 83, n. 5: 'Iron Age Jerusalem was built on the Ophel hill, which was surrounded on three sides by deep valleys that made approach from any direction other than the north foolhardy. Jerusalem was particular vulnerable to attack from the north, since the northern approaches to the city were actually higher in elevation than the city itself.'

21 For a careful comparison of YHWH's dealings with Judah and Babylon as well as the close linguistic parallels between Jer. 4–6 and Jer. 50–1, see Amesz 2004. For a critical analysis of the different representations of Babylon in the Book of Jeremiah, see Hill 1999; Kessler 2003: 180–3.

22 Carroll 1986: 824.

23 See, for instance, Jer. 12:15; 16:15; 27:22; 29:14; 30:10–11; 31:8, 16–17; 32:37; 46:27–8.

24 Cf. Leslie Allen's comment on Jer. 30:18–22: 'The winsome focus is on the restoration on the status quo ante; there would be a return to the thriving normality that marked life in the land before tragedy struck' (Allen 2008: 339).

25 See the résumé of the scholarly discussion in Lundbom 2004: 466.

26 von Rad 1965: 212–13.

27 For a critical treatment of these themes, see Hjelm 2004: 248–53. I will return to these in part II.

28 Cf. Dow 2011: 91: 'What is very interesting in Jeremiah, however, is that inviolability language is used to describe not Zion but the prophet himself. Protection is attached to faithful people, not a geographic location.'

29 As is indicated in Carroll 1986: 109: 'The imagery of v. 18 presents an obdurate figure who stands like a fortified city against the community (an ironic reflection of the fortified Jerusalem of 588–7?).' For a thorough study of the imagery of the prophetic figure in Jer. 1:18–19 and 15:20, see Riede 2009.

30 Carroll 1986: 236.

31 Cf. Wessel 2006: 741: 'The royal-Zion theology made the leadership and people of Judah self-assured and content. Because of this, they developed an indifferent attitude towards Yahweh with regards to their moral and religious obligations to him.' See also Levenson 1985: 168: 'The fact is that [Jeremiah's]

audience does not adhere to that mythopoetic complex, but to a fragment of it which they have extracted from context. For them, the delicate, highly poetic image of the cosmic mountain has become a matter of doctrine, and the doctrine can be stated in one prosaic sentence: In the Temple one is safe.'

32 Allen 2008: 96.
33 Carroll 1986: 831.
34 Stulman 2005: 77; Allen 2008: 86 list some scholars (W. Rudolph, J. M. Berridge) who regard this metaphor as positive.

3

EZEKIEL

In contrast to Isaiah and Jeremiah, Ezekiel is particularly shaped by priestly concerns.[1] Whereas it is often hard to distinguish Isaiah from Jeremiah and vice versa, Ezekiel largely employs a different language and a different set of metaphors. Nevertheless, our examination will reveal that Ezekiel is closer to Jeremiah, in so far as they both contain the basic features of the dynamic Zion motif.[2] Just as Jeremiah does, Ezekiel proclaims a massive destruction of the sinful city of YHWH. However, after surviving in exile, the people will return to a new and glorified temple.

The term 'Zion'

Ezekiel constitutes a special problem, because the term 'Zion' does not occur throughout the book. Despite this lack of the term, scholars still regard motifs related to the alleged Zion tradition to be present. In the introduction to his seminal commentary on Ezekiel, Walther Zimmerli states: 'The Zion tradition also appears strongly in Ezekiel – admittedly with the striking peculiarity that the name Zion is avoided throughout.'[3] Furthermore, Zimmerli observes that Jerusalem and the land appear as the centre of the world (5:5; 38:12) and that there is a reference to 'the mountain height of Israel' (17:23; 20:40). Ezekiel proclaims YHWH's dwelling-place among his people (37:26–8), and the great vision of the new temple (40–8) seems to employ motifs usually associated with Zion.[4] Unfortunately, however, Zimmerli barely considers why the term – as well as the term 'YHWH Sebaoth', often connected with Zion – has been omitted.[5] In fact, scholars frequently link the temple of YHWH's dwelling-place with Zion, without mentioning that the specific term does not occur.

In his 1999 article 'The Use of the Zion Tradition in the Book of Ezekiel', Thomas Renz reflects this commonly held view:

> Although the term 'Zion' is never used in the book of Ezekiel, motifs usually associated with the Zion tradition are frequently

used in the book, and the temple in Jerusalem is obviously regarded as YHWH's sanctuary with all the consequences this would entail for the significance of this place.[6]

In particular, Renz notices that the term – or any other geographical name – does not occur in the vision of the new temple (40–8); because of this, the temple can be located everywhere.[7] What is important for the new sanctuary is not its concrete location, but rather the presence of YHWH and the consequences of this presence. YHWH will not return to Zion, because Zion *as such* is a holy place. Rather, Zion can again obtain its holiness, if YHWH returns.[8] The best way to make this clear is simply to omit any geographical terms such as Jerusalem or Zion. According to Renz, the mobility and freedom of YHWH – a crucial characteristic of YHWH in Ezekiel – cannot contain a special relation to Zion.[9]

In a slightly different manner, John T. Strong has mounted the case that Ezekiel actually sought to maintain Zion theology through the use of certain tenets surrounding YHWH's glory: tenets that are usually associated with Zion.[10] Because of the chaos of exile and YHWH's abandonment of his temple, Strong argues that Jerusalem and its temple could not be called Zion during this period of crisis. However, rather than breaking with the traditions of Jerusalem's temple cult, Ezekiel translated them into his own time.[11] In contrast, Leslie Hoppe states that

> Ezekiel uses the Zion tradition that honors Jerusalem as 'the city of God' only to turn that tradition against itself. He describes how God abandons Jerusalem and leaves the city and its temple to their total destruction. Ezekiel agrees with his prophetic predecessors, who proclaimed divine judgement against the city.[12]

Finally, Daniel Block explains the deliberate avoidance of the term 'Zion' by stressing the misuse of it that Ezekiel experienced in official temple theology and the shame priests and kings had brought to the place.[13] This view is also reflected by Steven Tuell, as he states: 'The conscious avoidance of the term "Zion" and Ezekiel's negative view on the Jerusalem priesthood could reflect his disillusionment with the religious and political elite of Jerusalem.'[14]

It is, of course, possible that the author(s) of Ezekiel did not know the term at all. This, however, seems rather implausible. The omission of the term is better explained as a subtlety of Ezekiel. As this small review has made clear, the term has most likely been omitted deliberately. Therefore it is not illegitimate to search for a kind of Zion motif within this book as well – that is, the motif that other prophets clearly connect with Zion.

Motifs, events and characteristics associated with Zion

Like Jeremiah, Ezekiel concentrates on the fall of Jerusalem and its future restoration, judgement and salvation.[15] He also interprets the destruction of the city and the succeeding exile as YHWH's righteous punishment of his sinful people. Yet Ezekiel's perspective differs in at least two ways from that of Jeremiah. First, he works in Babylon and addresses primarily the Jewish congregation and their concerns there.[16] Second, Ezekiel is a priest (1:3) and much of the book's imagery concerns YHWH's glory, the temple and regulations for proper worship. Because of this, the idolatry of the people and their profanation of the temple are the main reasons behind the fall of the city in the theology of Ezekiel. Because the inhabitants of Jerusalem have defiled the holy sanctuary, YHWH will punish them without mercy (5:7). YHWH will withdraw his support of the city, and its inhabitants will starve (4:17). To be brief, the city and the land will be turned into desolation.[17]

Most fascinatingly, Ezekiel 8–11 portrays YHWH's abandonment of his temple residence.[18] This text, which contains many important elements, must, however, first be placed carefully within the book's own narrative chronology. According to the superscription in Ezekiel 8:1, the vision of Ezekiel 8–11 appears in the sixth year after the deportation of the prophet Ezekiel and the upper class of Jerusalem. In so far as the historical-critical reconstruction on the basis of Ezekiel's narrative is reliable, the initial deportation is commonly dated to 597 BCE. If this is so, the vision takes place in 592 BCE – that is, five years before the destruction of Jerusalem in 587 BCE.[19] Significantly, the city has not yet fallen when the Spirit brings Ezekiel to Jerusalem. Here, the prophet experiences the inhabitants' idolatry in the temple: they worship an image (8:3–5), idols (8:10) and the sun (8:16). The inhabitants justify their idolatrous worship by stating: 'YHWH does not see us, YHWH has forsaken the land' (8:12). This statement may reflect the fact that the inhabitants in Jerusalem – after the deportation in 597 – did not consider YHWH to be present any more; therefore idolatry accelerated. In any case, *now* he wishes to abandon his city. Ezekiel 10–11 magnificently recounts how the glory of YHWH – on a vehicle with four wheels and with the wings of cherubim – rises up above the temple and leaves it through the eastern gate. From that moment, the city lies unprotected, since YHWH no longer dwells in its temple.

Ezekiel 8–11 not only indirectly explains the fall of Jerusalem in 587 BCE, but also challenges the main claim of the Zion tradition that YHWH protects his chosen city at any cost. Although Ezekiel may regard Jerusalem as YHWH's proper dwelling-place, YHWH is by no means limited to this place.[20] On the contrary, he may leave it when he wishes to and, for example, visit his people in Babylon as it happens in the commission of Ezekiel (Ezek. 1–3). Of significance, however, is that YHWH's abandonment of the temple in Ezekiel 8–11 corresponds closely to his return in the great temple vision in Ezekiel 40–8. In this vision, YHWH returns to his temple through the gate facing east (43:1–12). Again, he places his throne in the temple and will dwell among the people of Israel forever (43:7).

The destruction of Jerusalem does not constitute God's last word. YHWH will spare some survivors who in captivity will remember him (6:8–9) and testify that the destruction of the city was righteous (12:16; 14:22). Frequently, it is stressed that the evil that was brought upon Jerusalem did not appear without cause; rather, it appeared so that the inhabitants will know that YHWH is God (6:10; 14:23). Even the foreign nations will understand that Israel went into captivity because of its sins (39:23). In Ezekiel, the exile involves self-loathing, a process of purification by which the spared people will recognize YHWH as their true God. Salvation occurs in that YHWH – by means of pure grace – brings his people back to their land (11:17; 28:25–6; 34:13; 36:24; 37:12).[21] YHWH will gather his flock, bring them to their land and feed them with good pasture (34:11–16), and he will set over them one shepherd: David (34:23–4). Moreover, YHWH will make a covenant of peace with his people and bless them and the region around his hill. Here, his saved people will dwell in secure places (34:25–31). In 36:8–12, YHWH himself invokes the mountains of Israel to shoot out branches and yield fruit, because Israel will return soon. YHWH will repopulate the cities, restore their ruins and make his people numerous and fertile. The desolate land will become like the Garden of Eden (36:33–8).[22] When the Israelites come home, YHWH will turn the two kingdoms (Israel and Judah) into one and set over them one king. As was indicated, David will be prince forever, and YHWH's sanctuary will be in the midst of his people forever (37:21–8).

The main scenario in Ezekiel of destruction and exile, homecoming, then restoration clearly seems to fit the cluster of motifs, which in the preceding chapters are described as the dynamic Zion motif. Even though the imagery of the empty land and of the recreation of Zion is less exposed and coherent, as in Jeremiah, I still find the same structure present in Ezekiel. This impression is confirmed by Ezekiel's use of motifs to envisage the return from exile and the restoration of the land – that is, essential motifs, which Isaiah and Jeremiah connect explicitly to Zion.

A motif frequently linked with Zion is the notion of 'the high mountain of Israel' (הר מרום ישראל) in 17:23 and 20:40.[23] According to 17:22–4, YHWH will plant a cedar on this high mountain, which will become a gathering point for all kinds of birds.[24] Against the background of 17:1–21, the cedar represents the new kingdom; in addition, we know the shouting 'branch' as a metaphor for the king from other prophetic texts such as Isaiah 11:1 and Jeremiah 23:5–6 and 33:15. Yet it is the tree, not the mountain itself, which will constitute the point of assembly. According to 20:39–44, however, it is the mountain – referred to as 'my holy mountain'

– which will become the centre of the people's worship. On that mountain, YHWH will accept cultic offerings, and he will reveal his holiness to the nations. Interestingly, the mountain here appears to function as the religious centre just as the new temple does according to the vision in Ezekiel 40–8.

Frequently, the phrase 'the mountains of Israel' stands not only for the holy mountain, but for the land in general.[25] In this topography, Jerusalem is located at a cosmic midpoint: YHWH himself set her in the centre of the nations (5:5),[26] known also as the 'navel' or 'centre' (טבור) of the earth (38:12).[27] In the concluding part of Ezekiel, in which the land is divided among the twelve tribes, the city lies in the midst of the middle region, and, additionally, the sanctuary lies in the midst of the city (48:8, 10, 15).

To grasp the overall perspective of Ezekiel, we shall briefly look at the main structure of the book.[28] The book consists of six parts: Ezekiel 1–3, 4–24, 25–32; 33–7, 38–9 and 40–8. The first part accounts for YHWH's commissioning of Ezekiel (Ezek. 1–3), which is succeeded by a larger second part on YHWH's judgement of Judah and Jerusalem (Ezek. 4–24). This part ends with the portrayal of the nations, which – as was the case in Jeremiah – attack Jerusalem from the north (23:22–4) and, under the rule of the Babylonian king, conquer the city (24:2). In the third part, the Babylonian army functions as the instrument of YHWH's wrath and destroys the neighbouring states of Judah as revenge for their glee and arrogance during the fall of Jerusalem (Ezek. 25–32). The main idea seems to be that the entire world must be punished, before salvation can be proclaimed for Judah and Jerusalem, as happens in the fourth part (Ezek. 33–7). Not until the surrounding nations have been crushed into ruins and peace has been restored can the people of Israel return.[29] Salvation is expressed as return, restoration and repopulation of the land, and as a unified people under the rule of one king.

Up until this point, we have seen that the dynamic Zion motif undergirds the main structure of the first thirty-seven chapters of Ezekiel: the city is being destroyed (Ezek. 4–24), but a new one will rise from its ruins (Ezek. 33–7). However, in Ezekiel 38–9 – the fifth part of the book – something remarkable takes place. After the restoration of the land, the gathering of the people from the nations and the establishment of peace (38:8), YHWH will – under the rule of the chief prince Gog – again bring a huge and terrifying army from the far north against the city and its land (38:1–7, 15–16). The army is heavily armed (38:4–5); it is portrayed as a storm (38:9); and it comes to plunder the goods of the people (38:12). Obviously, there are close parallels to the armies in Isaiah 5:25–30 and Jeremiah 4–10. Nevertheless, YHWH will judge Gog and pour down torrential rains upon him and his troops (38:17–23; 39:3–5). By this mighty act of salvation, YHWH reveals his greatness and holiness to his people. Subsequently, the people burn the weapons, bury the dead bodies and cleanse the land.

EZEKIEL

Finally, YHWH will prepare a great sacrificial feast (39:9–20). Ezekiel 38–9 concludes – inappropriately, one could say – with the promise that YHWH will deliver his people from exile and gather it in the land (39:23–9).[30] Nevertheless, the main narrative of 38:1–39:20 fits the classical Zion motif very well, because YHWH at the very last moment protects his people and his land against hostile invaders.

This bombastic victory over the ultimate enemy sets the stage for the concluding part of the book: the new temple (Ezek. 40–8). Already in the introductory verses 40:1–4, it is hard to tell if Ezekiel envisions a human-built city or a 'heavenly' Jerusalem.[31] For the present study, it is significant that YHWH's glory returns to the temple to dwell there (43:1–12)[32] and that a river will flow out from the sanctuary to provide the surrounding land with fertility and prosperity (47:1–12). This imagery of God's presence is commonly connected with Zion; also the new name of the city – 'YHWH is There' (48:35) – seems to express a basic feature of the Zion tradition (cf. the examination of Jeremiah). Steven Tuell, for example, regards it as highly unlikely that Ezekiel should have expected the new temple to be situated in any place other than Zion.[33] In addition, it is interesting that 44:4–9 seems to render a negative view on foreigners' access to the temple (in sharp contrast to Isa. 56–66).[34]

Summing up: Ezekiel

Even though the term 'Zion' does not occur throughout the book, I find that the main features of what we have called the dynamic Zion motif are present in the Book of Ezekiel. As in Jeremiah, survivors will, despite the massive destruction of Jerusalem, live on shattered and in captivity; eventually, they will return as a new and unified people. The motifs of the return from exile and of the restoration of the city are often employed. However, this is not that surprising when we consider that the message of Ezekiel – at least within the narrative setting of the book – is addressed to the community of exiles living in Babylon.

The examination has also revealed that the classical Zion motif, in which YHWH saves the city (or the land) from the aggressive enemies, is present in Ezekiel 38–9. These two chapters function as a bridge between the image of the restored Zion in Ezekiel 34–7 and the vision of the ideal sanctuary and territory in Ezekiel 40–8.

Notes

1 Clements 1982: 128–33.
2 Lawrence Boadt has recently stressed that Jeremiah and Ezekiel, despite their different social locations, personalities and theological concepts, share essential viewpoints on exile, return and restoration; see Boadt 2007.
3 Zimmerli 1979: 41; see also McConville 1992: 40–1.

ZION IN THE OLD TESTAMENT

4 See, for instance, the section 'The Mountain of Ezekiel's Vision as Mount Zion' in Levenson 1976: 7–19.

5 Apart from this short statement in Zimmerli 1979: 53–4: 'What earlier narratives tell of the God of Sinai (Horeb), that [YHWH] came to help his people who had settle in Canaan, Ezekiel experiences in a surprising way the God who, meanwhile, had, according to Israel's faith so far as it lived in Judah, made his abode on Zion. Should we regard as an archaism or as a revolutionary innovation the fact that Ezekiel in his entire message both avoids the name Zion for Jerusalem and also any mention of the God who dwells on Zion by his name?'

6 Renz 1999: 86.

7 Cf. Tuell 2009: 334: 'Ezekiel's connection of Zion with Eden, his disassociation of the mountain and its temple from Jerusalem, indeed his refusal to use the name "Zion", effectively cut Zion free from its geographical, historical, and political referents. The mountain, temple, and river of Ezekiel's last great vision [Ezek. 40–48] have become timeless symbols of divine presence. Though the earthly Zion, with its city and temple, had been a bitter disappointment, the heavenly Zion, the home of the Lord, remained a worthy ground for hope.'

8 Renz 1999: 97; see also Block 1997: 59: 'where God is, there is Zion'.

9 Renz 1999: 101.

10 Strong 2000.

11 Strong 2000: 89, 95: 'Ezekiel's visions of the $k\bar{a}b\hat{o}d$ [were not] new; they were merely an application of beliefs and doctrines that were at home in the Zion traditions.'

12 Hoppe 2000: 94.

13 Block 1997: 551–2, n. 150.

14 Tuell 2009: 137.

15 For an accessible table of the relationship between Ezekiel's judgement and salvation oracles, see Block 1997: 16.

16 Recently stressed by Joyce 2009: 5–6.

17 See Ezek. 5:14; 12:19–20; 15:8; 25:3; 33:27–9; 35:12–15.

18 See in particular Block 2000: 34–41.

19 Joyce 2009: 96.

20 Cf. Tryggve Mettinger's observation: 'in Ezekiel it is important to emphasize that he who sits enthroned above the cherubim in the Temple is fully prepared to abandon his city to hostile powers (chaps. 8–11; cf. 7:22). Thus he subjects the doctrine of Presence to a qualified but decisive modification which explains why it was possible for an enemy to subdue Jerusalem: God abandons his dwelling because of the people's sin' (Mettinger 1982: 109); see further in Rudnig 2007: 281–2.

21 Cf. Joyce 2009: 26: 'in Ezekiel the new future is never earned by righteousness; repentance is never the ground for a new beginning. When a new future is promised it is for God's own reasons; right behaviour follows only afterwards, as a consequence.'

22 Cf. Ezek. 28:14, 16, where the holy mountain of God is identified with Eden; see further in Tuell 2009: 188.

23 Block 1997: 551, 655.

24 Scholars commonly regard this passage as referring to Jerusalem. However, this is never spelled out and it may therefore also allude to the Samaritan Gerizim.

25 Cf. McConville 1992: 41.

26 Steven Tuell, however, suggests that this centrality is far from positive: 'for Ezekiel, that centrality only serves to emphasize all the more Jerusalem's wickedness. Far from living up to its role as an example to the nations, Jerusalem has exceeded them in wickedness' (Tuell 2009: 30).

EZEKIEL

27 Notice the explicit identification of this place in Jub. 8:19: 'Mount Zion [was] in the midst of the navel of the earth'; see further in Hjelm 2004: 260.

28 Here, I roughly follow the structure presented by Joyce 2009: 42, 61–2, although he regards Ezek. 33 as a discrete section (referred to as 'The Turning point').

29 There is, however, no account of the fall of Babylon, which in Isa. 46–7 and Jer. 50–1 prepares the way out of exile.

30 According to Zimmerli 1982: 319, this passage should be interpreted as a look back on the *entire* proclamation of Ezekiel.

31 Tuell 2009: 277. If the vision, however, concerns a heavily reality, we may distinguish between the desolated Jerusalem on earth and the heavenly Zion; cf. Tuell 2009: 329: 'Despite the collapse of Jerusalem and the destruction of the temple, the true Zion yet stands and is accessible to God's people wherever they find themselves.'

32 This entrance to the temple indeed seems to reflect motifs usually related to Zion; for instance, in Ps 24. Furthermore, the relation between God's glory and Zion is explicitly in Isa. 4:5; 24:23; 60:1–2; 66:18–19; Zech. 2:9; Pss 26:8; 85:10; 102:17; see Mettinger 1982: 109–10.

33 Tuell 2009: 284.

34 Cf. Daniel Block's general observation that 'Ezekiel's cartographic vision is extremely narrow. It appears sometimes that he deliberately reins in universalistic tendencies of the so-called Zion-tradition (cf. Isa. 2:1–4; Mic. 4:1–4). Not only does the river that flows from Jerusalem affect only the land of Israel (Ezek. 47:1–12); Ezekiel gives no hint anywhere of expanding his horizons. He is concerned exclusively with the salvation of his people ... Ezekiel's city is open to the twelve tribes of Israel; he is silent on admission to anyone else' (Block 1998: 741).

4

THE BOOK OF THE TWELVE

Far from all of the twelve Minor Prophets are relevant to our present study. Nevertheless, we shall examine all of them book by book to see how they describe Zion and employ motifs associated with it. As David L. Petersen informs us in his illuminating introduction, the concept of the 'Day of YHWH' constitutes a significant motif of the entire collection.[1] This concept is used explicitly throughout all books, apart from those of Jonah and Nahum; the latter, however, contains an allusion to that day (Nah 1:7). Although it was adumbrated in especially Isaiah 5:25–30 and 37:3, the Minor Prophets appear to have linked this concept of the Day of YHWH to Zion.

The Book of Hosea

There is not much talk about Zion in the Book of Hosea. The term 'Zion' does not occur and, in general, Hosea is concerned with a different set of themes, which only marginally overlap with the themes on Zion revealed in Isaiah, Jeremiah and Ezekiel.[2] Some texts, however, may be useful in illuminating motifs which we have already dealt with. These include: Hosea 2:2 [ET 1:11], which accounts for the reunification of the two kingdoms, Judah and Israel, under the rule of one 'head' (cf. Jer. 50:4–5);[3] Hosea 2:20 [ET 2:18], which refers to the covenant that YHWH establishes between his people and the wild animals (cf. Isa. 11:6–9); and Hosea 3:5,[4] which depicts the Israelites seeking YHWH and David, their king (cf. Jer. 30:9).[5]

The Book of Joel

For the present study, the Book of Joel is of great importance. The term 'Zion' occurs seven times: five times independently,[6] once as 'sons of Zion' (בני ציון) in 2:23 and once as 'Mount Zion' (הר ציון) in 3:5 [ET 2:32]. In two of these instances, it is juxtaposed with the holy mountain (2:1 and 4:17 [ET 3:17]), and in three, it appears parallel to or in connection with Jerusalem (3:5; 4:16; 4:17 [ET 2:32; 3:16; 3:17]). In 2:1 and 2:15, one blows the trumpet on Zion as a sign of danger or fast, and by YHWH's

THE BOOK OF THE TWELVE

saving intervention, the sons of Zion rejoice (2:23). Zion is the place of salvation (3:5 [ET 2:32]); YHWH roars from Zion (4:16 [ET 3:16]); and twice it is stated that YHWH dwells in Zion (4:17, 21 [ET 3:17, 21]).[7]

Joel offers an excellent illustration of the classical Zion motif. First, YHWH terrorizes the land and its inhabitants with a locust plague (Joel 1), and then he leads a hostile army of enemies against Zion (2:1–11). It is a great and powerful army (2:2); its consuming fire destroys everything on its way (2:3); and it attacks the city (2:9). Because of this imminent threat, the trumpet of warning sounds at Zion (2:1). The whole scenario is referred to as the 'Day of YHWH' (יום יהוה) and the day of judgement is thereby closely linked to these terrifying events on Zion. Against the background of the danger of invasion, YHWH calls the inhabitants to repent (2:12–14); a fast is proclaimed (2:15); the gathered people are sanctified and the priests pray for mercy (2:16–17). As Leslie Allen has noted, 'the sons of Zion' (referred to in 2:23) represents this national community congregated in the temple.[8] YHWH changes his decision of judgement and removes the attacking enemies by drowning them in the sea (2:18–20).

This text unit certainly has important parallels within the prophetic corpus; for instance, the description of the enemies recalls that of Isaiah 5:25–30; Jeremiah 4–10; and Ezekiel 38–9. More crucially, the motif of the people's repentance to YHWH reminds us of the Isaianic 'theology of decision'. Joel, however, does not demand faith; rather, he calls for repentance in terms of a cultic ritual (cf. Jonah; see below). Here, Joel appears to be influenced by priestly concerns.[9] Throughout the book, the priests play a significant role (1:9, 13; 2:17); the fast and cultic offerings entail great importance (1:9, 13, 14; 2:15, 17); and there are references to the house of God (cf. 1:14, 16; 4:18 [ET 3:18]).

Joel 3:4–5 [ET 2:31–2] repeats the Day of YHWH-motif, including the statement that those who call on the name of YHWH will be saved on Mount Zion. In Joel 4 [ET 3], the judgement concerns the nations of the world, not Judah and Jerusalem. The act of judgement takes place in the valley of Jehoshaphat (4:1–15 [ET 3:1–15]). Furthermore, 4:16–17 [ET 3:16–17] clearly informs readers that YHWH reigns from Zion and that his people will be saved here. The accusations against the foreign nations include their scattering of Israel – YHWH's people and heritage – among the nations; the robbing of the temple treasuries; and the selling of the Judeans as slaves (4:1–8 [ET 3:1–8]).[10] Because of these evil acts, YHWH will crush them (4:9–11 [ET 3:9–11]). Of particular interest is the use of Isaiah's peace vision (cf. Isa. 2:4) in Joel 4:10 turning it upside down:[11] now the ploughshares and pruning-hooks must be beaten into swords and spears! Fortunately, a marvellous portrayal of the future for God's people follows this horrifying scene of judgement: the land will prosper and be fertile; a temple source flows from the house of YHWH; and Judah and Jerusalem will be inhabited forever.[12] Programmatically, the book ends with

53

the statement 'YHWH dwells in Zion', which summarizes the general anticipation that YHWH will protect his people and their city.

The Book of Amos

The term 'Zion' occurs twice in Amos: in 1:2, in parallel to Jerusalem, and in 6:1, in parallel to 'Mount Samaria' (הר שמרון). In 1:2, YHWH roars from Zion (cf. Joel 4:16 [ET 3:16]), and 6:1 includes a cry against those who are at ease in Zion and feel secure on Mount Samaria. Despite these two occurrences, Amos does not contain much of relevance to our inquiry. Two additional passages should be taken into consideration. First, 2:4–5 announces an exclamation against Judah that its people has rejected the law of YHWH and worshipped idols. Second, the entire book concludes with the promise that YHWH will raise the fallen booth of David (9:11–15). However, apart from these four instances centring on Zion or Jerusalem, Amos, like Hosea, appears to focus on a different set of themes.

To explain these peculiar instances within the present form of the book, tradition-historical scholars have argued that Amos – originally stemming from the southern kingdom (cf. Amos 1:1) – certainly knows the David and Zion traditions of this region well. Yet generally addressing the northern kingdom, he employs largely the traditions of this region (e.g. the Exodus traditions) in his preaching.[13] In contrast, redaction critics such as Hans Walter Wolff have distinguished at least six different layers of redaction.[14] According to Wolff, none of the four text passages under consideration – Amos 1:2, 2:4–5, 6:1 or 9:11–15 – belongs to the three oldest layers. Wolff contends that 1:2 was added in the Period of Josiah by the redactor, who brought the 'book' to Jerusalem; 2:4–5 and 6:1[15] were added by the Deuteronomists; and, finally, 9:11–15 clearly reflects the post-exilic period.[16] Wolff's analysis has gained much support, although it has been criticized by some scholars[17] and altered in light of recent canonical concerns.[18] Because of these redaction-historical observations, we must accept that none of the four passages 'fits' the main picture of Amos' theology very well.[19] The Zion motif is almost absent throughout the book and we shall only return to Amos 9:11–15. This passage, however, constitutes a perfect parallel to other passages portraying the rebuilding of Zion and the restoration of the land and its fertility.

The Book of Obadiah

As was the case in Amos, the term 'Zion' occurs twice in the shortest book among the Twelve; both times as 'Mount Zion' (הר ציון) in v. 17 and v. 21. Like Joel 3:5 [ET 2:32], Obadiah 17 portrays Zion as a place of salvation; it is holy and related to the house of Jacob.[20] Obadiah 21 recounts

THE BOOK OF THE TWELVE

how those who have been saved will go up to Mount Zion to judge or rule over the 'neighbour' mountain, Mount Esau.

In general, the Book of Obadiah informs readers about the bitter conflict between Edom and Israel by taking up the Patriarchal narrative of Isaac's two sons: Edom is called Esau and Judah/Jerusalem is called Jacob. Edom deserves revenge because of his pride (v. 3), his passivity when Jerusalem was destroyed (vv. 10–11) and his subsequent *Schadenfreude* (vv. 12–14).[21] Obadiah 15–21, then, offers satisfaction for Judah, which is of special relevance to the present study. On the Day of YHWH, the nations will be punished, but there will be salvation on Zion (vv. 15–17). Then, the reunited people[22] of the northern kingdom (house of Joseph) and southern kingdom (house of Jacob) will not only punish Edom (Esau), but also take possession over other nations as well (vv. 18–20). Finally, they will judge Esau from Mount Zion (v. 21).

As in the Book of Joel, Zion is the secure bastion in the chaos of judgement. It is the place in which those who are saved gather, and from which the judgement against the nations emerges. In addition, Obadiah indicates a reunification of north and south and emphasizes the royal power of YHWH. Finally, the basic structure of the book – judgement against Edom (vv. 1–14) and salvation in Zion (vv. 15–21)[23] – recalls the structure of other prophetic sections as well. In Isaiah 34–5, the revenge against Edom precedes the return from exile; in Ezekiel 35–7, Edom is condemned before the mountains of Judah can be repopulated and Ephraim and Judah can be reunited; finally, in Joel 4:18–21 [ET 3:18–21] and Amos 9:11–15, Edom is destroyed, while the fallen booth of David has been raised and the surrounding land prospers.[24] Obadiah ends with the strong statement that the kingdom will be YHWH's.[25]

The Book of Jonah

The Book of Jonah is not at all useful for our investigation. The term does not occur and the lack of motifs, which are elsewhere related to Zion, is apparent. Of course, we may consider whether the holy temple in Jonah 2 refers to the temple in Jerusalem and if the lament psalm thereby expresses the experience of being far away from Zion. In addition, we may wonder if Nineveh's turning to YHWH – the whole city repents in fear of judgement – reveals the same idea as that in Joel 2, in which the inhabitants of Zion are sanctified because of fear of the approaching army.[26] Nevertheless, I think these parallels are strained and Jonah will not be brought into our discussion again.

The Book of Micah

The term 'Zion' is abundantly present in the Book of Micah, with nine occurrences: four times independently (3:10; 3:12; 4:2; 4:11); four times as 'daughter Zion' (בת ציון) in 1:13, 4:8, 4:10 and 4:13; and one time as 'Mount Zion' (הר ציון) in 4:7. Two times Zion stands parallel to Jerusalem (3:10; 4:2), one time to Jerusalem and the temple mount (3:12; cf. Jer. 26:18) and one time to Migdal-Eder, Ofel[27] and Jerusalem (4:8). It is proclaimed that YHWH will reign over his people on Mount Zion (4:7), that his *torah* will go forth from here (4:2) and that Jerusalem's former sovereignty will be restored (4:8). The references to Zion are both negative and positive. On the one hand, Zion will be ploughed as a field (3:12), because she has sinned (1:13) and has been built with blood (3:10); and the nations will rejoice over her profanation (4:11). On the other hand, Zion will have her revenge and crush many peoples (4:13).

Traditionally, scholars have regarded Micah as one of the eighth-century prophets along with Hosea, Amos and Isaiah, as the superscription in Micah 1:1 indicates.[28] Nevertheless, as in the case of other prophets, this superscription is no proof that the eighth century BCE is the proper – or only – context within which we should understand the book's purpose and content. The Danish scholar Knud Jeppesen has convincingly demonstrated how the message in the present form of the book is addressed to the people in exile.[29] If this is so, Micah's theological concern is closer to that of Second Isaiah, Jeremiah and Ezekiel. As Rick R. Marrs has observed, 'Zion is the object of considerable theological sensitivity and rhetorical interplay.'[30]

In Micah, YHWH comes out of his dwelling to judge Samaria and Jerusalem, and to punish them because of their sin (1:2–5). Daughter Zion has sinned by putting her trust in war material instead of in her God (1:13),[31] and the leaders of the people have built Zion with blood and ruled with injustice (3:10–11). Because of these evil transgressions, the disaster will reach Jerusalem (1:9, 12), the city will be destroyed (6:16) and its inhabitants will go into exile (1:16). Crucially, 3:12 states that Zion will be ploughed as a field; Jerusalem will become a heap of ruins; and the temple mount will become a wooded height. In the preceding verse, the prophet polemicizes against those who incontestably believe that YHWH will protect Zion unconditionally (3:11). Yet in Babylon, YHWH will redeem his people (4:10). He will gather them and bring them to Mount Zion, from where he will reign as king and restore the former dominion of the city (2:12–13; 4:6–8; 7:11–12). Zion will become a midpoint for all nations (4:1–3; cf. Isa. 2:2–4), and peoples will peacefully sit under their vines and walk in the name of YHWH (4:4–5); see further in chapter 10.

The themes explored in this short sketch of Micah remind us of many of the themes that we have encountered in the other prophets as well. Furthermore, the structure of Micah seems to fit the main movement within the dynamic Zion motif: the unfaithful deeds of Judah and Jerusalem demand that YHWH destroys his city and forces his people into exile (Mic. 1–3);[32] yet the exile entails a process of purification, a rebirth that sets a

THE BOOK OF THE TWELVE

new beginning (Mic. 4).[33] Micah 3:9–4:5 is remarkable, because this passage encompasses both extremes: first, the harsh depiction of Zion's destruction; then, the glorious vision of Zion as centre of the *torah* of YHWH and worldwide peace.[34]

The Books of Nahum and Habakkuk

The term 'Zion' does not occur within these two prophetic books, and they do not seem useful for the purposes of our investigation. Nahum focuses on the Assyrian defeat at the end of the seventh century BCE,[35] adumbrating the conquest of Nineveh in Nahum 2–3. The army, which attacks the Assyrian capital (2:4–6; 3:2–3), shares some features with the army elsewhere attacking Zion, including being under the command of YHWH (cf. Jer. 50–1). In Nahum 1:7–8, YHWH is portrayed as 'a stronghold on a day of trouble';[36] he protects those who seek refuge in him (cf. Joel 3:5 [ET 2:32]). Furthermore, in Nahum 1:9–2:1, YHWH will take revenge over the enemies because of their destruction of Judah. However, no clear Zion motif seems to emerge.[37]

Habakkuk, too, has little to offer. An enemy army appears in Habakkuk 1:5–11, which is portrayed as having superhuman characteristics (cf. Isa. 5:26–30); it is not, however, made explicit whom the army will attack. Due to the context, it seems to be the people of God – that is, Judah[38] – because YHWH is accused of not intervening (Hab. 1:12–13). In sum, the passage portraying the attacking enemies may be of relevance to illuminate the motif of the enemies of Zion (see chapter 6).

The Book of Zephaniah

The term 'Zion' occurs twice here: independently in 3:16, and as 'daughter Zion' (בת ציון) in 3:14. In 3:14, it stands parallel to Israel and daughter Jerusalem, and in 3:16, to Jerusalem. Daughter Zion will shout with joy (3:14) and not fear, because YHWH's salvific presence is in her midst (3:16).

As Rex Mason has observed, the Book of Zephaniah is not that original; rather, it mostly reflects and encompasses motifs and features that we find in other prophetic books as well, concerning Zion in particular, the tension between judgement and salvation, and the Isaianic concept of a surviving remnant.[39] Apart from the notions of the remnant of the people of God taking possession of the land of Moab and Ammon (2:9), and of peoples coming from far away to worship YHWH (2:10–11), Zephaniah 3 has most to offer: YHWH has given his obstinate city, generally understood as Jerusalem,[40] numerous opportunities to repent; however, nothing has happened (3:1–6). Because of this, YHWH will assemble foreign nations and pour his anger upon them (the inhabitants or nations?); consequently, the whole world will be consumed by fire (3:7–8). The remnant of survivors

57

will be cleansed, and the scattered people will be gathered (3:9–13). Zion
will rejoice over YHWH's salvific acts (3:14–18), for he will gather his
people and restore their fortunes (3:19–20).

It is not clear if Zephaniah reveals the contours of the classical Zion
motif. On the one hand, the protection of the city is not that significant
and it remains ambiguous against whom the judgement in 3:8 is proclaimed;
the inhabitants of Zion or the foreign nations?[41] On the other hand, the
notion of a remnant on the holy mountain in 3:11–13 indicates that YHWH
has left some survivors on Zion. We shall return to these problems in
chapter 7.

The Book of Haggai

The superscription of the Book of Haggai places its events in the second
year of the Persian King Darius' reign – that is, around 520 BCE in the
biblical chronology.[42] After the end of the exile, a new temple for YHWH
will be built, for his present house lies in ruins (1:9). As we have observed,
other prophetic texts link the building of the new temple with Zion (e.g.
Jer. 50:28), so Haggai is indeed of importance for our study.[43] On the other
hand, the term 'Zion' does not occur and Haggai is more concerned with
priestly matters concerning being clean and unclean (2:10–14), as Zechariah
following him is.[44] However, I think that issues concerning the temple,
including practical details and regulations for offerings and services, are
too far away from what can be contained within a Zion motif. Nevertheless, a text that we certainly will return to is 2:6–9, in which the new
temple is filled with glory (cf. Ezek. 43:5; 1 Kgs 8:11), the nations come
here with treasures and the temple will become a centre of divine peace.

The Book of Zechariah

The term 'Zion' occurs eight times in Zechariah: six times independently;[45]
and two times as 'daughter Zion' (בת ציון) in 2:14 [ET 2:10] and 9:9. The
term stands next to Jerusalem (1:14, 17; 8:3); daughter Zion stands next
to daughter Jerusalem (9:9); and Zion stands next to Judah and Ephraim
(9:13). YHWH is very jealous for Zion (1:14; 8:2), and again he will
comfort her (1:17). The people will escape from Babylon to Zion (2:10
[ET 2:7]) and rejoice (2:14 [ET 2:10]; 9:9), for YHWH will return to the
midst of Zion (8:3). Finally, he will turn Zion into a weapon to defeat
enemies (9:13).

Commonly, the Book of Zechariah is divided into three major parts:
Zechariah 1–8, 9–11 and 12–14. Historical-critical scholars regard the
latter two as larger, secondary additions, referred to as Deutero-Zechariah.[46]
Although we shall not pursue these redaction-historical questions further, we
should still follow this overall division. In *Zechariah 1–8*, the introductory

THE BOOK OF THE TWELVE

superscription, as in Haggai, places the events of this first part in the time of King Darius. To be sure, the proper context of the message is *after* the exile.[47] In addition, the period of exile is registered as seventy years (1:12; 7:5), and is located in the land of the north and in Babylon (2:10–11 [ET 2:6–7]; 6:10) as well as in the east and west countries (8:7–8). The message of Zechariah may thereby be seen as the fulfilment of Jeremiah's prophecy.[48] YHWH will return to Jerusalem, restore his temple here and let prosperity flow from Zion (1:14–17). He will crush the foreign nations (2:1–4 [ET 1:18–21]) and urge his people to flee from Babylon to Zion (2:10–13 [ET 2:6–9]), and Zion will certainly rejoice when YHWH dwells in her midst and many peoples join (2:14–17 [ET 2:10–13]). Jerusalem will lie open without walls because of the multitude of people and animals, and YHWH will be a wall of fire surrounding her and revealing his glory in the midst of her (2:8–9 [ET 2:4–5]).[49] The people will sit under the vine (3:10; cf. Mic. 4:4), and treasures for the new temple will arrive from Babylon (6:10–15).

Already the beginning of Zechariah 1–8 indicates a strong 'before-after' theme, illustrated by references to the ancestors before and in exile: what the ancestors before the destruction did not do – namely return to YHWH (1:2–5) – they did in exile (1:6). Likewise in 8:14–15, YHWH brought a disaster upon the ancestors (the destruction of the city); he will now do good to Jerusalem and to the house of Judah (the restoration of the city).[50] The structure of Zechariah 7–8 summarizes the main idea: initially, there is a reference to the seventy years of exile (7:5). Before this time, Jerusalem was inhabited and it prospered (7:7); yet because of its rebellious and arrogant inhabitants, the lovely land was turned into a desert (7:14). This land is now going to be restored, because YHWH is returning to Zion; peace and joy will fill the streets; and he will gather and bring his people home from the surrounding countries (8:1–8). Nations will come to the city and join YHWH (8:20–3). In sum, the imagery of Zechariah 1–8 fits the main structure of the dynamic Zion motif, in which the primary focus is on the restoration of Zion and the land, because exile has ended.

Zechariah 9–11 continues the motif of the preceding chapters. YHWH destroys the surrounding cities and nations to protect his house (9:1–8), peace for Zion is proclaimed and weapons are destroyed (9:9–10; cf. Isa. 2:4; Ps 76).[51] In 9:11–17, YHWH brings his people home. The return concerns in particular the northern kingdom, referred to as the house of Ephraim and Joseph.[52] Interestingly, 9:13 may indicate a reunification of the two kingdoms. YHWH strengthens first Judah (10:3–5), then Joseph (10:6–7); finally, he assembles the nations from far away (10:8–12). Zechariah 11 is quite difficult to grasp, although the main point seems to be that the peace established with the foreign nations (11:10) and among the two kingdoms (11:14) will be broken. If so, this political chaos provides a bridge to the third part of the book.

Zechariah 12–14 is mainly concerned with the inviolability of Jerusalem as the centre of the world. Zechariah 12 is a fine example of the classical Zion motif: enemies surround Jerusalem (12:2–3); yet when the inhabitants recognize that they receive their strength from YHWH (12:4–5), he protects the city and wipes out the hostile nations (12:6–10).[53] Zechariah 13–14, however, takes a peculiar turn. First, a fountain will cleanse the inhabitants from their sin and idolatry (13:1–2a), and subsequently all prophetic activity is prohibited (13:2b–6). Zechariah 13:7–9 presents an entirely new motif: two thirds of the inhabitants will perish, and YHWH will purge the remaining third. This imagery may, however, be similar to that of the surviving remnant.[54] Yet 14:1–2 surprises once again. Here, the nations conquer Jerusalem; half of the people are forced into exile, the other half remains in the city without being annihilated. Then, abruptly, YHWH enters to protect the (desolate?) city and to judge the nations on the Mount of Olives (14:3–5a). Suddenly, YHWH comes with all the holy ones (the inhabitants, cf. Isa. 4:3?); there is peace; and Jerusalem dwells in security (14:5b–11). In 14:12–15, YHWH strikes the enemies with rottenness and Judah fights against Jerusalem. The entire book, however, ends with a great and glorious vision: the whole city is holy and the remaining nations will come and worship YHWH as king (14:16–21). As has become apparent, Zechariah 1–14 involves many crucial and complex problems, to which we shall return in later chapters.

In sum, the Book of Zechariah contains both Zion motifs: Zechariah 1–11 embodies the dynamic Zion motif by concentrating on the post-exilic restoration of the desolate Zion, whereas Zechariah 12 (along with Zech. 13–14?) illustrates the classical Zion motif of YHWH's protection of the city.

The Book of Malachi

Malachi has a single reference that may be taken up as a parallel: Malachi 3:1. This verse announces the preparation of the way that enables YHWH to enter his temple (cf. Isa. 40:3). That is all.

Summing up: the Book of the Twelve

Among the twelve prophets, *Hosea, Jonah, Nahum, Habakkuk, Haggai* and *Malachi* contain no explicit references to Zion or motifs that other prophets associate with Zion. Some texts, however, may be useful to shed light upon related themes. Although employing the term 'Zion' twice, *Amos* does not refer to the motif at all; because of this, we shall only return to the passage on the restoration of the fallen booth in Amos 9:11–15.

Joel, Obadiah and *Zechariah 12* are fine illustrations of the classical Zion motif, where YHWH protects his city against the aggressive enemies.

THE BOOK OF THE TWELVE

In those texts, the attacking army is closely linked with the concept of the Day of YHWH. To what extent the classical Zion motif is revealed in *Zephaniah* remains uncertain, because of the ambiguous judgement against either the inhabitants of Zion or the hostile nations. We shall scrutinize this problem in chapter 7.

In *Micah*, the destruction of the city is significant, as Zion will be ploughed as a field and its people brought into exile; yet YHWH returns to redeem them and bring them home. In *Zechariah*, the exile has ended, and Zechariah *1–11* mainly portrays the restoration of a new Zion and the re-establishment of the temple cult. There are many indications that the imagery and structure of both Micah and Zechariah reveal the dynamic Zion motif, in which Zion is destroyed by enemies, but eventually rebuilt when the surviving, yet scattered, people of YHWH return from exile.

Notes

1 Petersen: 2002: 170.
2 Cf. the conclusion in Ollenburger 1987: 107: 'there is no mention of Zion or use of those motifs and themes that often occur in association with Zion'.
3 This verse may, however, allude to the Wilderness Narrative, in particular, to Num. 14 (the notion of 'head' in Num. 14:4). In addition, avoiding the word 'king' foreshadows the intense criticism, later in the book, of Israel's sinful kings; see Andersen & Freedman 1980: 208.
4 On this verse's pro-Judean tone, see Emmerson 1984: 101–5. See also the excursus on this verse in Dearman 2010: 142–5.
5 In terms of redaction criticism, it is interesting that Jörg Jeremias considers all of these cases to be exilic or post-exilic additions; see Jeremias 1983: 34–5, 49–51, 57–8.
6 See Joel 2:1; 2:15; 4:16; 4:17; 4:21 [ET 3:16; 3:17; 3:21].
7 Joel 4:16a [ET 3:16a] quotes Am 1:2a, which in Joel is used to move the focus away from the valley of Jehoshaphat to Zion. In addition, Joel 3:5 [ET 2:32] shares some near-verbatim features with Ob 17. In general, Joel contains a lot of quotations from other parts of the Old Testament; for a complete list, see Crenshaw 1995: 26–9; Barton 2001: 22–7; Strazicich 2007.
8 Allen 1976: 92. Cf. the parallelism in Ps 149:2 between 'Israel' and the 'sons of Zion'.
9 Barton 2001: 22.
10 Although this scattering alludes to being in captivity or exile, it is not clear if the author had some specific incident in mind; see Barton 2001: 99–100.
11 For an intriguing study of the play between Isaiah and Joel with regard to this motif, see Fischer 2008.
12 Cf. Allen 1976: 122: 'There is an intimate link between the temple and the land: Yahweh's presence in Zion was the key to the blessing of the whole land.'
13 See especially von Rad 1965: 132, 138.
14 For a general overview of the passages under discussion and the different compositional theories, see Anderson & Freedman 1989: 141–5; Barton 2012: 3–32.
15 To Am 6:1: numerous text-critical attempts have been made to alter or explain the presence of the term 'Zion' in this verse. Already in 1922, Sellin proposed to read 'the city' (העיר) instead of Zion as a reference to the main capital of

the kingdom of Israel, parallel to (and identical with) Mount Samaria in the latter part of the verse; Sellin, however, later abandoned his proposal. Ehrlich along with Maag and Budde have – inspired by Am 6:8 – proposed to read those who are at ease 'sind in ihrem hochfahrenden Wesen' (בגאונם) as is suggested in the footnote in BHS. Yet both attempts involve serious alteration of the consonant text, therefore it seems simpler to regard 'Zion' as a gloss; cf. the conclusion in Wolff 1977: 269–70.

16 Wolff 1977: 121, 163–4, 270, 353.
17 For instance, Shalom M. Paul, who regards all four units as authentic or at least plausible authentic words of the historical Amos; see Paul 1991: 20–4, 36–7, 199–200, 288–90.
18 A fascinating work is Richard James Coggin's commentary on Joel and Amos, in which he – with a reference to S. Bergler's *Joel als Schriftinterpret* (Frankfurt am Main, 1988) – demonstrates how Am 1:2 may be a citation of Joel 4:16 added in the canonical process of binding these two books together as part of the larger framework in the Book of the Twelve. In addition, the notion of David's booth taking possession over Edom (Am 9:12) points forward to Obadiah's judgement of Edom and thereby connects these two books; see Coggins 2000: 60–1, 155.
19 For a different view, see, for instance, Andersen & Freedmann 1989: 559.
20 Cf. Barton 2001: 129: 'Obadiah's message makes sense only against the background of a Zion theology, in which YHWH's chosen mountain, the site of the Temple, is particularly close to his heart.'
21 Cf. Jenson 2008: 18: 'The crime is so serious because the identities of the two nations are bound up with their ancestors.'
22 Cf. Raabe 1996: 253; Jenson 2008: 24.
23 For different views on the overall structure, see Raabe 1996: 18–22; Barton 2001: 118–19.
24 Not surprisingly, Wolff explains these parallels by claiming that all text passages reflect the exilic/post-exilic era in which Edom appears as Israel's primary enemy among the nations; see Wolff 1986: 63.
25 Cf. Johan Renkema's fine résumé: 'The actual basis for judgement and restoration lies in the fact of YHWH's renewed presence in Zion. It is in Zion that YHWH extends the cup of judgement to the nations. In Obadiah's prophecy, the same Zion becomes a place of refuge once again. In the tumult which follows YHWH's judgement of the nations Zion offers a place of sanctuary. Mount Zion alone, however, is unable to offer such protection. Only the renewed presence of YHWH as her guardian makes this possible' (Renkema 2003: 41).
26 Cf. some linguistic parallels between Jon. 3:9 and Joel 2:14; see Wolff 1986: 153–4; Sasson 1990: 260–1.
27 NRSV renders 'Migdal-Eder' as 'tower of the flock' and 'Ofel' as 'hill (of daughter Zion)'.
28 Allen 1976: 241–57.
29 Cf. his Danish dissertation (Jeppesen 1987).
30 Marrs 2004: 82.
31 Jeppesen 1987: 167.
32 Jenson 2008: 100–1.
33 Jeppesen 1987: 260.
34 Marrs 2004: 83: 'Significantly, these two dramatically divergent pictures of Zion are portrayed in starkest contrast in immediately adjacent oracles in 3:9–12 and 4:1–4.'
35 Concerning the historical setting of the book, see Christensen 2009: 52–64.

THE BOOK OF THE TWELVE

36 Cf. Ps 46:2–3[1–2]; see further in Christensen 2009: 222.
37 Although Roberts may be right that 'just as the waters of chaos fled before Yahweh's rebuke . . . so Nineveh's defenders flee' (Roberts 1991: 61–2, 66).
38 Andersen 2001: 168.
39 Mason 1994: 16–17: 'Some easing of the logical tension between the threats of total judgement and these hopes of a glorious future is found here, as in some other prophets – notably Isaiah – in a doctrine of an Israelite "remnant", that band of people whom God will preserve through the crisis and purify so that they may fulfil his ideals for his people as a humble, trusting and righteous community.' See also Roberts 1991: 164.
40 Cf. Berlin 1994: 10.
41 For a short overview of the scholarly positions, see Sweeney 2003.
42 Meyers & Meyers 2010: 4. In addition, notice the unique feature within the Old Testament that the reign of a non-Judean king forms the chronological framework for Haggai's oracles; cf. Hoppe 2000: 112.
43 Cf. Hoppe 2000: 114: 'the prophet's words concern the rebuilding of the Temple, and so they deal with Jerusalem at least indirectly'. Furthermore, Meyers & Meyers 2010: 19 more explicitly claim that the use of the term 'YHWH Sebaoth' indicates that Haggai anticipates YHWH's return to *Zion* and the re-establishment of his mighty power.
44 Cf. Meyers & Meyers 2010: 413: '[The term "Zion"'s] absence from Haggai probably underscores the more developed view of Zion after the temple refoundation ceremony.'
45 Zech. 1:14; 1:17; 2:11 [ET 2:7]; 8:2; 8:3; 9:13.
46 For a short review, see Petersen 1995: 23–9.
47 Cf. Dow 2011: 101: 'although the people are living in Jerusalem, God does not seem to be there, because the Temple is not built and things are not going well.'
48 Hoppe 2000: 115.
49 See Meyers & Meyers 1992: 132: 'The radical blow to that conception [of inviolability] of Jerusalem and the temple represented by the Babylonian conquest may have interrupted the confidence in Zion's sanctity. Yet the early post-exilic community, in agreeing to restore the temple, reactivated the mythic power of the Zion tradition, albeit in a form now distinct in its historical manifestation from the royal Davidic promise . . . The prophecies of First Zech. exhibit in striking measure the mythic consciousness that enabled Zion to be reaffirmed by the devastated post-exilic community.'
50 Meyers & Meyers 2010: 424–5.
51 This juxtaposition of the destruction of the nations (9:1–8) and the proclamation of salvation for Zion (9:9–17) recalls Ezekiel's judgement of the entire world (Ezek. 25–32) and the book's proclamation of salvation for Judah and Jerusalem (Ezek. 33–7); see chapter 3.
52 See further in Conrad 1999: 164.
53 See further in Petersen 1995: 113.
54 Cf. Meyers & Meyers 2009: 405. See also Dow 2011: 102: 'Zechariah does foresee a future attack by the nations on Jerusalem and Judah. Since it is God who will gather the nations, and half of the city will go into exile (Zech. 14.1–2), it appears that this will happen because Jerusalem will again need chastening. The remnant of the city, however, will be saved by God's miraculous intervention (Zech. 12.1–9; 14.3, 12–15).'

5

THE REMAINING BOOKS

This chapter completes the descriptive survey of the Zion motif by briefly examining the remaining books of the Old Testament. However, since my research focuses on the prophetic literature, the following presentation offers nothing more than a cursory overview. Nevertheless, I think it important to examine whether my impression of a dual Zion motif found in the prophets is present in the remaining books of the Old Testament. We shall start by looking at the historical books: Genesis through to 2 Kings as well as Daniel, Ezra, Nehemiah and Chronicles. Then, we shall look at the Psalms, before turning our attention to the Song of Songs and Lamentations. Since I deem Esther, Job, Proverbs and Ecclesiastes to be of no relevance to our present focus, we shall not look at them in the following sections.[1]

The historical books

The term 'Zion' (ציון) occurs six times in the historical books: two times independently (1 Kgs 8:1 [= 2 Chron. 5:2]); and four times as part of a construct relation: two times as 'the stronghold of Zion' (מצדת ציון) in 2 Samuel 5:7 (= 1 Chron. 11:5), one time as 'daughter Zion' (בת ציון) in 2 Kings 19:21 and one time as 'Mount Zion' (בת ציון) in 2 Kings 19:31. Zion stands next to the city of David (עיר דוד) in 2 Samuel 5:7 (= 1 Chron. 11:5) and in 1 Kings 8:1 (= 2 Chron. 5:2); daughter Zion stands next to daughter Jerusalem in 2 Kings 19:21; and Mount Zion stands next to Jerusalem in 2 Kings 19:31.

Zion plays a surprisingly inferior role in the historical books. Although the term occurs six times, it is crucial to notice that it only occurs within a few contexts. In the first context in 2 Samuel 5:7 (= 1 Chron. 11:5), the phrase 'the strongholds of Zion' explains the common name of the city – that is, the city of David (the term preferred throughout the Deuteronomistic Histories).[2] In the second context, 1 Kings 8:1 (= 2 Chron. 5:2) points backward to and repeats 2 Samuel 5:7 when depicting the move of the ark from Zion to the temple. In the third context, the two remaining occurrences (2 Kings 19:21, 31) reflect the Isaianic material of the Hezekiah story taken over by the author(s) of the Deuteronomistic Histories.[3] More significantly, neither the Deuteronomistic nor the Chronistic Histories show any explicit traces of an ideology concerning Zion as YHWH's chosen dwelling (except from 2 Sam. 5:7, perhaps).[4] As Ingrid Hjelm rightly has pointed out, 'to speak about a Zion ideology in the Deuteronomistic history, or for that matter in the Chronistic history, is a kind of *eisegesis* which takes its content from the prophets and Psalms'.[5] Nevertheless, the Chronicler does have an explicit reference to 'Mount Moriah' as the site of Solomon's temple (2 Chron. 3:1) and to 'the mountain of the house of YHWH'; yet, according to Hjelm, these are the exceptions that prove the rule.[6] In addition, as Leslie Hoppe observes, it is crucial that the Deuteronomistic Histories never call Jerusalem 'the city of God'; it is always referred to as 'the city of David' and thereby subject to divine judgement.[7]

Nevertheless, despite this lack of explicit traces of a Zion theology, allusions and hints to God's mountain in Zion/Jerusalem do occur throughout these books. Significantly, however, there is no single narrative depicting the founding of Jerusalem as the main capital of Israel; furthermore, none of the biblical traditions used in the historical books explicitly claims divine foundation.[8] Instead, the 'pagan' Jerusalem appears to be validated by a series of major Old Testament heroes, including Abram, Joshua, David, Ezra and Nehemiah.[9]

In her illustrative examination, Lois Dow lists six allusions to Zion or Jerusalem throughout the Pentateuch. Of particular significance are four of them. First, in Genesis 14:17–24, Abram's meeting with the Jebusite high-priest Melchizedek near a place called 'Salem' validates its legitimacy for later generations (Salem is linked to Zion in Ps 76:3[2]; see below).[10] Second, in Genesis 22:1–19, Abraham's attempt to sacrifice Isaac takes place in the land of Moriah, 'on the mountain of YHWH' (Gen. 22:14; cf. Isa. 2:3). As we have seen, 2 Chronicles 3:1 identifies this Mount Moriah with the place of Solomon's temple. Third, in Exodus 15:1–18, Moses' song after the deliverance at the Red Sea informs readers that YHWH will bring the Israelites and plant them on the mountain of YHWH's possession, the place of his abode and sanctuary (Exod. 15:17). Finding that these terms are often associated with Zion,[11] Dow sees a strong possibility that the song of Moses refers to Zion as the ultimate goal of the exodus.[12] Fourth, and in line with this, Deuteronomy has several allusions to a certain place in the land that YHWH will choose and put his name to dwell.[13] This place is never named, yet later in the historical books, Jerusalem is called the place that God has chosen and where he has put his name.[14] Most scholars therefore assume that Deuteronomy refers to Jerusalem.[15] However, the ambiguity or 'openness' of both Exodus 15 and Deuteronomy concerning the exact location of YHWH's chosen place could also point to Gerizim as maintained in the Samaritan traditions' readings of Deuteronomy 11:29–12:28 and 27:4.[16]

According to Joshua and Judges, the Israelites conquered Jerusalem (cf. Josh. 10; Judg. 1). But they apparently failed to keep it, since the biblical tradition recounts that the Jebusites continued to live there until the conquest by David. Despite its brevity, the account of David's siege of Jerusalem contains serious interpretive problems. In 2 Samuel 5:6–8, David and his men arrive at the city.[17] Yet the Jebusite defenders arrogantly state: ' "You will not come in here, even the blind and the lame will turn you back" – thinking, "David cannot come in here." '[18] As my review of recent studies has revealed, scholars have, by means of this Jebusite claim, argued for a pre-Israelite application of the concept of inviolability to the ridge of Jerusalem.[19] However, it remains uncertain who these blind and the lame refer to. McCarter offers three proposals: (a) because of the city's strength, even its physically disabled citizens can withstand David's attack; (b) the blind and the lame are an instrument of a magic ritual in the defence of the city; and (c) the blind and the lame are David's own troops in comparison with the city's impregnable fortress.[20] The first proposal seems most likely, although the text does not offer much help.[21]

Nevertheless, David conquers the strongholds of Zion through the 'zinnor'. This word may refer to the throat of a man,[22] although the identification of zinnor with the Jebusite water shaft sounds most plausible (either the shaft discovered by Charles Warren in the nineteenth century or the Hezekiah tunnel, if not a literary device).[23] The attack is in particular launched against 'the blind and the lame'. David's hatred of this group is peculiar, if it does not refer to those defenders who have been disabled during the attack on the city. David prohibits them from accessing the temple, as recorded in the purity laws of the Pentateuch.[24] Crucially, following the conquest and the move of the ark to Jerusalem, YHWH promises his support to the Davidic monarchy, not the city as such (cf. 2 Sam. 7).[25] The land for Jerusalem's temple is taken over from a Jebusite inhabitant of the city (Araunah or Ornan; cf. 2 Sam. 24; 1 Chron. 21). However, as the main theological reason in the Deuteronomistic Histories, Jerusalem eventually falls because of the aggressive sins of its kings and people.[26]

The Daniel narrative is set in Babylon. Like in Isaiah 40, the opening of the book presumes that the reader knows that Jerusalem has been left desolate.[27] Daniel 9 refers to the ruined Jerusalem and the period of seventy years of exile (cf. Jeremiah and Zechariah). Following Daniel's lengthy act of prayer and repentance, YHWH's messenger Gabriel delivers a divine promise of a glorious future of restoration and prosperity. Yet, like Ezekiel 38–9 and Zechariah 14 (?), Daniel anticipates another destruction of the rebuilt city before the kingdom of God will rule in eternity.

Ezra and Nehemiah are portrayed as colonists re-colonizing the city.[28] Even though the opening of Ezra–Nehemiah presents the fulfilment of God's promise that the exiles will return after seventy years (cf. Jer. 25:11–12; 29:10–14), the city is not fully restored and the full potential of the divine promises has not been realized.[29] Jerusalem remains a hope for future realization. In Chronicles, Jerusalem is an important place. Again, 2 Chronicles 3:1 combines a set of references, including Solomon's temple, Jerusalem, Mount Moriah, the place where YHWH appeared to David and the threshing-floor of Ornan.[30] This makes it clear that YHWH chose Jerusalem as the site of his temple.[31] Interestingly, in the Hezekiah story, YHWH's statement of 'for my own sake and for the sake of my servant David' has been omitted. Nevertheless, the Hezekiah figure is compared to David and is – in the view of the Chronicler – in the same league as glorious figures such as David and Solomon.[32] The narrative ends with many peoples bringing gifts to Jerusalem. This may indicate the need of the readers of Chronicles 'to be faithful and come to Jerusalem with resources to rebuild it'.[33]

The Book of Psalms

The term 'Zion' (ציון) occurs thirty-eight times in the Psalms: twenty-six times independently;[34] and twelve times as part of a construct relation: five times as 'Mount Zion' (הר ציון);[35] and one time as 'the gates of daughter Zion' (שערי בת ציון) in 9:15[14], 'the gates of Zion' (שערי ציון) in 87:2, 'the fortunes of Zion' (שיבת ציון)[36] in 126:1, 'all who hate Zion' (כל שנאי ציון) in 129:5, 'the mountains of Zion' (הררי ציון) in 133:3, 'the songs of Zion' (משיר ציון) in 137:3 and 'the sons of Zion' (בני ציון) in 149:2. Zion stands next to 'my holy hill' (2:6), 'the sanctuary' (20:3[2]), 'the cities of Judah' (69:36[35]), 'Salem' (76:3[2]), 'the daughters of Judah' (97:8), 'Jerusalem' (102:22[21]; 135:21; 147:12) and 'his habitation' (132:13). In addition, Mount Zion stands next to 'his holy mountain' (48:3[2]), 'the daughters of Zion'[37] (48:12[11]), 'your congregation' (74:2) and 'the tribe of Judah' (78:68).

Zion in particular designates Jerusalem's sanctuary.[38] Traditionally, scholars have regarded Psalms 2, 46, 48, 76, 87, 95–9, 125 and 132 as offering the most proper material for describing Zion in the Psalms.[39] The glorification of Zion and of God's kingship in these psalms is striking. YHWH has chosen Zion and desires it for his habitation (Ps 132:13). He has founded his city on the holy mountains (87:1), and it is the centre of the world (87:4, 7). Psalms 95–9 highlight that God is king (e.g. Pss 95:3; 97:1; 99:1), that he is great in Zion (Ps 99:2) and that he is to be wor-shipped at his holy mountain (99:9).[40] Those who trust in YHWH are compared to Mount Zion: they are unshakable and will stand forever (125:1). God has not only chosen the city, but also anointed and installed his king in Zion (2:6); to be sure, there is a link between the chosen human king and the chosen city (Pss 2; 110; 132).

As we noticed in the introduction, scholars have in particular highlighted Psalms 46, 48 and 76 as sources to a Zion theology.[41] Focusing on Zion (although the term does not occur!),[42] Psalm 46 stresses that God is present in the midst of his city and will protect it against the powers of chaos. God is refuge and strength, when the mountains shake and the water roar (vv. 2–4[1–3]), for he is present and will deliver his city when the morning dawns; the hostile peoples will tremble when he raises his voice (vv. 5–8[4–7]).[43] Having succeeded in the great battle against the nations, YHWH will restore ultimate peace by destroying the weapons and by reigning over the foreign nations (vv. 9–12[8–11]). In sum, the psalm emphasizes that the city is invulnerable to attack from political and cosmic powers, because God has his dwelling in the midst of it. In addition, v. 4[3] depicts a life-giving river which – in contrast to the chaotic waters – makes the city glad.

Psalm 48 commences with a confession to YHWH on Zion: he is great; his holy mountain (and city) located in the far north[44] is a joy for the whole earth; and God is present here (vv. 2–4[1–3]). The psalm continues with the *Völkerkampf*-motif: the kings gather together to battle the city, but are put to flight (vv. 5–8[4–7]), for God will sustain his city in all eternity, and his mercy and righteousness rest in his temple on Mount Zion (vv. 9–12[8–11]). In the last part, peoples are urged to go around Zion, count its towers and consider its citadels. They will thereby understand that the city of God is inviolable,[45] because it will receive special divine protection (vv. 13–15[12–14]).[46]

In Psalm 76, it is not Zion but YHWH who is praised. First, it is highlighted that God has his dwelling-place in Zion, from where he will restore peace by destroying the weapons of war (vv. 2–4[1–3]; cf. 46:9–12[8–11]). However, as Leslie Hoppe notices, 'This assertion is hardly a pacifist manifesto; rather, it follows from the total defeat God has inflicted on Zion's enemies.'[47] Then, God is described as glorious and awe-inspiring; no warrior can hurt him and no one can withstand his wrath (vv. 5–8[4–7]). He will judge the earth and save the humble; those who survive will praise him (vv. 9–11[8–10]). God reigns over all the kings of the earth; to him, vows must be made and gifts brought (vv. 12–13[11–12]). In sum, Psalm 76 stresses the sovereignty of God and his power over heaven and earth as both judge and creator of peace.

Corinna Körting demonstrated that there are different and even contrasting images of Zion in the Psalms.[48] Her study is important because it includes all psalms that mention 'Zion'. Körting operates with three basic categories: (a) Zion/Jerusalem as a centre of peace (Pss 87; 122) and of sincere prayer (Pss 51; 69; 102; 125; 128; 137); (b) God in his sanctuary on Zion (Pss 14; 53; 65; 68; 132; 133; [120–34]); and (c) Zion in mythical time and as a vehicle of religious-political utopia (Pss 2; 46; 48; 99; 110). This survey provides a fresh challenge of traditional ways of regarding Zion as God's unconquerable place.[49] For instance, in Psalm 102, Zion is to be rebuilt and become the place where the name of YHWH is praised.[50] In Psalm 137, the exiles moan in Babylon while remembering Zion.[51] Furthermore, following the alternative translation of Psalm 126:1 – 'When YHWH brought back those who returned to Zion, we were like those who dream' – would strongly indicate a return from exile.[52] These psalms

THE REMAINING BOOKS

at least assume that Zion has been destroyed, and Körting notices that 'Was in den Psalmen von Zion nur in Verbindung mit Jerusalem ausgesagt werden kann, prägt in der Prophetie und den Klageliedern eine ganze Reihe von Texten – Zion, die zerstörte und beweinte Stadt'.[53]

Song of Songs and Lamentations

The term 'Zion' (ציון) occurs once in Song of Songs: in 3:11 as 'the daughters of Zion' (בנות ציון)[54] where it stands next to 'daughters of Jerusalem'. Here, the girls of Zion are called out to view 'Solomon'. It remains unclear why the daughters of Zion are mentioned here. Most plausibly, they are only present to balance the daughters of Jerusalem in poetic parallelism.[55]

A much more profound use of the term is found in Lamentations, where it occurs fifteen times: four times independently (1:17; 2:6; 4:11; 5:11); and eleven times as part of a construct relation: three times as 'daughter Zion' (בת ציון) in 1:6, 2:1 and 4:22; two times as 'the wall of daughter Zion' (חומת בת ציון) in 2:8 and 18; and once as 'the roads to Zion' (דרכי ציון) in 1:4, 'the tent of daughter Zion' (אהל בת ציון) in 2:4, 'the elders of daughter Zion' (זקני בת ציון) in 2:10, 'virgin daughter Zion' (בתולת בת ציון) in 2:13, 'sons of Zion' (בני ציון) in 4:2, and 'Mount Zion' (הר ציון) in 5:18. Zion stands next to Jacob and Jerusalem in 1:17 and the cities of Judah in 5:11; and daughter Zion stands next to daughter Jerusalem in 2:13 and daughter Edom in 4:22.

Lamentations consists of a kaleidoscope of images all focusing on the miserable fate of Zion. The city suffers shame, destruction and abandonment. Zion is portrayed as a female in all kinds of roles: a widow, a princess, a whore, a rape victim, a betrayed lover and an abandoned wife.[56] The condition of exile illustrates the hopeless situation (cf. Lam. 1:3: 'she lives now among the nations').[57] In general, the five chapters present a public mourning or reflection on the national catastrophe of destruction. In a word, Lamentations is 'a call to God to be Zion's comforter'.[58] Yet, despite this sincere call, God remains silent throughout the book. Undergirding the entire composition, he is really angry with Zion.

Lamentations appears to draw upon a set of Deuteronomistic features. The destruction of Jerusalem and exile are interpreted as YHWH's righteous punishment of his people who have transgressed against him.[59] As Adele Berlin states,

> the book does not construct a theology of its own, nor does it present in any systematic way the standard theology of its time. It assumes the 'theology of destruction' in which destruction and exile are the punishment for sin ... The sin that warranted such severe punishment is idolatry, the code word for the rejection of God and his commandments.[60]

In the description of the inhabitants' transgressions, Lamentations refers both to impurity (priestly concerns) and to rebellion (political concerns); both, however, highlight that exile is God's final judgement of his people's cruel deeds.[61] YHWH stands behind the disaster, employing the Babylonians in fulfilling his judgement. As many of these theological motifs are also present in Jeremiah, this partly explains why tradition has assigned him the authorship of these laments (cf. the canonical order in Christian Bibles).

Of particular interest is the image of the desolate Zion. This image illustrates the first stage of what we have referred to as the dynamic Zion motif. Obviously, Zion is no invulnerable place in Lamentations.[62] Zion has lost her sovereignty and has been abandoned by her comforter. She is left alone and dethroned. Interestingly, Lamentations appears to reverse several motifs that we have encountered in the previous chapters. Instead of joy and gladness for exiles returning to Zion (cf. Isa. 35:10), the roads to Zion mourn, because no one comes to her festivals (Lam. 1:4).[63] Instead of Zion being left like a booth in the vineyard (cf. Isa. 1:8), YHWH has destroyed his booth like a garden (Lam. 2:6).[64] Instead of enemies being consumed by divine fire in Zion (cf. Isa. 30:33; 31:9), YHWH has kindled a fire in Zion that consumes its foundations (Lam. 4:11). Mount Zion is by no means inviolable, but left destroyed with jackals prowling over it (cf. Jer. 9:10). Eventually, daughter Zion's exile will come to an end (4:22).

Summing up: the remaining books

The examination of the remaining books of the Old Testament supports my impression of a dual Zion motif. In the historical books, Jerusalem is an object of divine wrath and destruction and it might also be the idealized goal of the Egyptian Exodus. Both themes – destruction and return – match the cluster of motifs that we have defined as the dynamic Zion motif. The imagery of Lamentations also belongs to this cluster. The Psalms illustrate both Zion motifs. On the one hand, a series of psalms reveals the classical Zion motif by depicting Zion as the mythological and inviolable heritage of YHWH. On the other hand, as Körting has demonstrated, another series of psalms reveals the dynamic Zion motif, in which Zion occurs as a place of destruction and restoration.

Conclusion: Zion in the Old Testament

An initial reading of Isaiah made it clear that the book exhibits different perceptions of Zion. On the one hand, there is an image of Zion as the last bastion where YHWH at the very last moment defends a faithful remnant against attacking enemies. On the other hand, there is an image of Zion as a wilderness that will be restored and repopulated by the people of YHWH returning from exile. The examination of Jeremiah, Ezekiel and the Book of the Twelve has revealed that Zion suffers different fates throughout the discrete books. In Jeremiah, Ezekiel and Micah, for instance, the destruction of the city by enemy attack is inevitable and a surviving remnant is forced into exile. Hereafter, however, there are hopeful anticipations that YHWH will bring his people home to a restored Zion. The brief survey of the remaining Old Testament books supports the impression of Zion's dual fates.

These preliminary observations suggest that it is appropriate to distinguish between two Zion motifs, which express the two different fates of the city and its people between divine judgement and divine salvation. According to the first motif, the city is saved and a remnant of its inhabitants is left on Zion. According to the second motif, the city has been destroyed and its survivors are brought into exile. Apparently, these fates stand in serious tension. Within the Bible's own narrative structure, these fates are expressed in two key accounts: Sennacherib's unsuccessful siege in 701 BCE and Nebuchadrezzar's successful siege in 587 BCE. As Chris Seitz asserts, 'the correlation between 701 and 587 events would appear to be antithetical: Zion was delivered in 701 – it was destroyed in 587.'[65]

I will refer to the first motif as the classical Zion motif because the idea of the inviolability of Zion and YHWH's defeat of the enemies has determined tradition-historical concepts of a *Zion tradition*. As demonstrated in the introduction, this is the motif that scholars most commonly associate with Zion.

The second motif is my own attempt to create order out of a wide range of texts and ideas that relate to Zion, but do not 'fit' the classical motif. These include Zion as a wilderness, as a ploughed field and as abandoned by YHWH, Zion as the goal of a return from exile and of the nations' peaceful pilgrimage, and Zion as a destroyed city that is to be rebuilt. I will refer to this motif as the dynamic Zion motif, because Zion undergoes a development and a transformation: it is destroyed and abandoned, but eventually rebuilt and repopulated.[66]

The following constructive proposal, laid out in the succeeding five chapters, displays these two contrasting views on Zion: common for both motifs is that the people have offended YHWH either by means of violation against common justice and the covenant, or by means of idolatry and profanation of God's temple. Because of this, divine judgement is imminent. The enemies arrive as an instrument of YHWH's judgement and attack Zion. In this great battle with the nations, there are only two possibilities: either YHWH personally intervenes and saves his city and its faithful remnant survives the enemy attack, or YHWH does not intervene and lets the enemies destroy the city and bring the surviving remnant into foreign captivity. Eventually, YHWH will redeem his people in exile and bring them home to Zion, which is to be rebuilt.

Crucially, then, both motifs begin with the *Völkerkampf*-motif: enemies attacking Zion.[67] Instead of just focusing on the victory of the inviolable Zion as scholars have tended to do, our examination will also bring attention to the defeat of Zion. As we have seen in Jeremiah and Ezekiel, motifs associated with the alleged tradition of Zion's inviolability are deliberately turned against Zion itself when depicting its defeat. Jeremiah's portrait of the defeat of Zion especially stands in opposition to the classical Zion motif, which dominates Isaiah.

Notes

1 Dow 2011: 43, n. 1.
2 For a classical study of the name Zion in relation to the city of David, see Simons 1952: 60–4.
3 Cf. Hjelm 2004: 100–15 who – by means of a comparative analysis of shared themes – very convincingly argues in favour of an Isaianic authorship of the Hezekiah narrative.
4 Hjelm 2004: 6–7.
5 Hjelm 2004: 41.
6 Hjelm 2004: 254.
7 Hoppe 2000: 104.
8 Bolin 2003: 179.
9 Bolin 2003: 196: 'As did Abram, Joshua, David, Ezra, and Nehemiah, so every good Jew should acknowledge the primacy of Jerusalem, make offerings to Yahweh there and nowhere else, and maintain strict fidelity to the Torah despite, or because of the presence foreign influence.'
10 Bolin 2003: 183–4: 'At work in Genesis 14 is a founder tradition that portrays the great hero [that is, Abram] visiting a city . . . his presence as a hero in the city and the honor he extends to the place validates it.' Dow 2011: 45: 'Salem is identified with Jerusalem and the story probably functions to tell how Jerusalem became God's holy city and shrine, and to underline Abraham's connection with Jerusalem.' See also Schreiner 1963: 69; Weinfeld 1983: 103.
11 For instance, 'mountain' in Ps 48:1–2; Isa. 2:3; 'dwelling-place' in 2 Sam. 15:25; 1 Kings 8:13; and 'sanctuary' in Pss 20:2; 78:68–9; cf. Dow 2011: 47.
12 Dow 2011: 48.
13 See Deut. 12:5, 12, 14; 14:23; 16:5–7, 11, 16; 26:2, etc.
14 See 1 Kgs 9:3; 2 Kgs 21:4, 5; 2 Chron. 6:6; Ezra 6:12; Neh. 1:9.
15 See the review in Bolin 2003: 179; cf. Hoppe 2000: 44–5: 'Deuteronomy does affirm that Jerusalem is God's city . . . [However,] the book purposely avoids mentioning any proper names that might sound anachronistic'; and Dow 2011: 50: 'Even if Deuteronomy is not referring directly to Jerusalem, it sets up the expectation of a central shrine in which Israel will do the kinds of things that Abraham did at Salem and Moriah (i.e. pay tithes, receive priestly blessing and make sacrifices).' In addition, we should remember that the central aim of Deuteronomy is to centralize all sacrificial activity in one site, which Josh.–2 Kgs interpret as Jerusalem; cf. Hjelm 2004: 296: 'The intentionality of Deuteronomy's ambiguity both reflects and is a precondition for exactly such implicit narrative discourse, which establishes Yahweh's choice through prophetic interpretation.'
16 Hjelm, *forthcoming*.

THE REMAINING BOOKS

17 Within the larger context of 2 Samuel, Willis has noticed two important elements in the narrative. First, David captures Jerusalem with his own men (in Chronicles, it is David and all Israel), which indicates that it is his possession ('the city of David'). Second, Zion or Jerusalem is located geographically between Israel and Judah, but belongs to neither; see Willis 2004: 137–8.

18 Cf. NRSV. Alternative translations read 'You would first have to drive away the blind and lame who say' (see Hertzberg 1964: 266, n. a) or '"You shall not come in here!" (For the blind and the lame incited them, saying, "David shall not come in here!"'; see McCarter 1984: 135).

19 See, for instance, Hayes 1963: 424; Levenson 1985: 94.

20 McCarter 1984: 138. See also the review in Campbell 2005: 56–7.

21 This interpretation is supported, for instance, by Bolin 2004: 186; Campbell 2005: 56–7; Thompson 2005: 84.

22 If so, see McCarter's paraphrase of David's statement: 'Whoever strikes down a Jebusite must deal a fatal blow, for otherwise the city will be filled with mutilated men whom we have wounded but not slain, and I find such men intolerable' (McCarter 1984: 140).

23 Bolin 2003: 187–8 rightly points out that 'the possibility that the *tzinnor* of 2 Samuel 5 refers to [Hezekiah's] water channel has not been seriously explored by scholars, since most agree that Hezekiah's Tunnel was built roughly three centuries after the putative time of David, and the assumption of 2 Samuel's historicity makes it imperative either to identify the *tzinnor* with a known pre-ninth century archaeological feature in Jerusalem or to translate the term so that its meaning has nothing to do with the topography of Jerusalem. It seems more likely that the author of 2 Samuel is referring to Hezekiah's Tunnel anachronistically because he is recounting a legend about a heroic king set many centuries in the past.'

24 See Lev. 21:16–23; Deut. 32:2[1]; cf. Thompson 2005: 84: 'The key to the riddle is its anachronistic use as an etiology or origin story for the purity law in Leviticus, preventing the lame and the blind from offering sacrifice in the temple.'

25 Cf. Bolin 2003: 180–1: 'It is not David who will build a house (i.e. temple) for Yahweh, but Yahweh who will build a house (i.e. dynasty) for David. Similarly in 1 Kgs 8:16 Yahweh declares that he did not choose a *city* (i.e. Jerusalem) but a *man* (i.e. David).'

26 However, as 'Deuteronomy Revisited', the apocryphal Book of Tobit proclaims the future of a restored Jerusalem where God's holy name will be praised forever; see further in Hoppe 2000: 54–5.

27 Cf. Dow 2011: 96.

28 Cf. Bolin 2003: 189: 'The picture in Ezra-Nehemiah is thus one in which the city is built from the ground up, complete with a temple, walls, population and necessary social structures.'

29 Dow 2011: 74–5.

30 The name 'Moriah' plays on the word 'to see' and designates the place where Abraham and David have visionary experiences; see Levenson 1985: 94–5; Hjelm 2004: 243–4; Dow 2011: 69.

31 Hoppe 2000: 119.

32 Dow 2011: 70.

33 Cf. Dow 2011: 70. For a recent and thorough study on the utopia in Chron., see Schweitzer 2007.

34 See Pss 2:6; 9:12[11]; 14:7; 20:3[2]; 48:13[12]; 50:2; 51:20[18]; 53:7[6]; 65:2[1]; 69:36[35]; 76:3[2]; 84:8[7]; 87:5; 97:8; 99:2; 102:14[13]; 102:17[16]; 102:22[21]; 110:2; 128:5; 132:13; 134:3; 135:21; 137:1; 146:10; 147:12.

ZION IN THE OLD TESTAMENT

35 See Pss 48:3[2]; 48:12[11]; 74:2; 78:68; 125:1.
36 Following LXX, an alternative reading suggests 'צִיּוֹן שְׁבוּת': 'When YHWH brought back those who returned to Zion, we were like those who dream' (cf. footnote in NRSV).
37 NRSV reads 'the towns of Judah'.
38 Cf. Kraus 1986: 73.
39 Since Hermann Gunkel, several of these psalms have been known as 'songs of Zion', building upon the idea that 'the songs of Zion' in Ps 137:3 refers to a clearly defined group of pre-exilic hymns; see Gunkel & Begrich 1933: 42; cf. Kraus 1988: 58; Miller 2010: 667. Cf. also Dow 2011: 76: 'The Psalms are the main source for ideas that are usually known as "Zion Theology" or the "Zion Tradition".'
40 Cf. Ben Ollenburger's main thesis that 'Zion symbolized security because the divine king who resided there exercised his royalty in his dual activity as creator and defender' (Ollenburger 1987: 74).
41 In terms of content, Joseph Schreiner sees three major themes: (1) YHWH's kingship, (2) the expressions of the old traditions and motifs connected with the divine mountain and (3) the glorification of YHWH (Schreiner 1963: 219–35). On form-critical grounds, Jörg Jeremias has demonstrated that Pss 46, 48 and 76 (and 87) share the same syntactical constructions in their chief statements. However, not only in terms of form but also in terms of content theses psalms share themes and conceptions (Jeremias 1971: 189–96; cf. Kraus 1988: 459–60). Nevertheless, Ben Ollenburger is very critical towards the juxtaposition of those three psalms (and the concept of Zion songs in general). To him, they do not share the same *Gattung* and should not be regarded as rendering some general dogma of Zion's inviolability (Ollenburger 1987: 16).
42 See Wanke 1966: 35: 'Die Korachitenpsalmen setzen es als selbstverständlich voraus, daß alles das, was über den heiligen Berg Zion gesagt ist, in gleicher Weise auch für die Gottestadt Jerusalem gilt'; cf. Körting 2006: 179.
43 Kraus 1986: 82: 'the decisive reason for the invincibility of the city of God is the fact that Yahweh is "in the midst of her" . . . This is no area of taboo protected by magic.' Cf. Ollenburger 1987: 71: 'Zion has this symbolic power not because of some mythological power inherent in the mountain itself, but because it is the site of Yahweh's royal dwelling and hence the site of his defeat of the hostile kings.'
44 Mitchell Dahood translates this verse as 'Mount Zion is the heart of Zaphon, the city of the Great King' to stress the play on the Canaanite mythological motif of the mountain of Baal (Dahood 1963: 288). See also Levenson 1985: 146: 'No psalmist was so inept as to imagine that Jerusalem was in the north; rather, Zion as the sacred mountain of YHWH had attracted the name of the sacred mountain of his Canaanite arch-rival Baal.' Nevertheless, NRSV like other modern translations has 'Mount Zion, in the far north, the city of the great King'; see further in Hoppe 2000: 25–6.
45 Hjelm 2004: 146–7: 'It does not seem to be their qualities as fortifications that the author wants to present, but their inviolability.'
46 Kraus 1988: 474–5: 'it is not the city of God as such, with its this-worldly might, that possesses the radiance of transcendent inaccessibility. Yahweh is the one that here proves to be the protection. He is the one who gives to the city of God its invincibility.' See also Maier 2010: 662–3.
47 Hoppe 2000: 31.
48 Körting 2006: 221: 'Zion ist in den Psalmen mit einer Vielzahl von Bildern, Stimmungen und Intentionen verbunden. Doch ist auch Zion selbst Ausdruck

THE REMAINING BOOKS

für diverse Motive und Vorstellungen. Zion ist nicht zu reduzieren auf den Berg als Osthügel bzw. Nordberg oder auf die Stadt, sei es unbezwingbar oder zerstörte und wiederaufbauende Stadt. Zion evoziert verschiedene Assoziationen, trägt einen Bedeutungsüberschuß in sich und verwiest dennoch im Kontext des einzelnen Psalms nur auf einen Teils seines potentiellen Bedeutungsspektrums.' Cf. Dow 2011: 80: 'there is a tension in the psalmists' view of Zion'.

49 Cf. Dow 2011: 76, who notices that Pss 74, 79, 102 and 137 picture Zion as a vulnerable earthly city.

50 Körting 2006: 41: 'Zion, in den vv 14 und 17 derjenige, dem Gott sich zuwendet und der wieder erbaut werden soll, wird nach den vv22f. zu dem Ort, an dem der Name Jhwhs verkündet wird und wo die Völker sich versammeln.'

51 Cf. Hoppe 2000: 23: 'The psalms also give voice to those Judahites who lamented the fall of Jerusalem and the destruction of the temple. They also express the hope for the city's restoration.'

52 Körting 2006: 143: 'Wenn Ps 126,1 als Schicksalswende mit Bezug auf die Vergangenheit verstanden wird, dann kann nur, wie auch die prophetischen Texte es andeuten, die Wende des Exils, die Rückkehr und die Wiederherstellung der Gottesdienstgemeinde gemeint sein.' Cf. Kraus 1988: 450; Dow 2011: 82: 'The returned exiles sing in Psalm 126 of their hope of future joy.'

53 Körting 2006: 228.

54 Notice that it is omitted in the LXX.

55 See the short review in Snaith 1993: 56–7; Pope 1977: 447: 'Although the expression "daughters of Zion" is not elsewhere attested, there is no reason to expunge it since it forms a perfect poetic parallel to "daughters of Jerusalem".'

56 Berlin 2002: 47. See also Porteous 1961: 237–9.

57 Berges 2000: 16.

58 Berlin 2002: 48.

59 Hoppe 2000: 89.

60 Berlin 2002: 18.

61 For a short and accessible overview of the theology of Lamentation, see Berlin 2002: 17–22.

62 According to Bertil Albrektson's classic suggestion, '"The key to the theology of Lamentations" is in fact found in the tension between specific religious conceptions and historical realities: between the confident belief of the Zion traditions in the inviolability of the temple and city, and the actual brute facts' (Albrektson 1963: 230); cf. Berges 2000: 5; and Dow 2011: 93. See also Dobbs-Allsopp 2004: 21: 'The Zion tradition and its central dogmas could not be maintained in the face of the catastrophic events surrounding the Babylonian destruction of Jerusalem. The poem's opening movement (vv. 1–8) depicts Yahweh's assault on Jerusalem. The city, its temple, and supporting mythologies are razed. What survives this verbal carnage is the uneasy figuration of Yahweh as enemy and the literary image of personified Zion ... the poem seeks to counterfeit the Zion tradition.' Hoppe 2000: 92, however, does not find this to be the case: 'The book of Lamentations did not arise to deal with the problem of suffering or to resolve the tensions between the Zion tradition and the experience of 587.'

63 Indeed, both in terms of themes and style, Lamentations is close to the language of Isa. 40–55; cf. Berges 2000: 18–19; Mandolfo 2007: 103–19; Tiemeyer 2011: 347–61.

64 Notice also the allusion to Isa. 51:3: 'YHWH will comfort Zion ... and will make her wilderness like Eden, her desert like the garden of YHWH.'

65 Seitz 1991: 123.

66 Other scholars have stressed this double fate of Zion too. In his work on Zech. 12:1–8 and 14:1–5, Hanns-Martin Lutz observes that Jerusalem plays a different role within these two passages (see Lutz 1968: 209–10; cf. Hoppe 2000: 133: 'Zechariah 12–14 contains two accounts of Jerusalem's future. Both use the motif of "the nations against Jerusalem."'). In Zech. 12–13, Jerusalem remains untouched by the enemy attack; yet an outpouring of the spirit leads to repentance and purging of the sins of its inhabitants. In Zech. 14, however, Jerusalem is conquered and destroyed and half of its people exiled: 'Erst nach dieser tiefsten Demütigung ersteht das neue Jerusalem' (Lutz 1968: 210). Eventually, YHWH enters the city and is proclaimed as king of the world. As we have seen, Lois Dow has called for more emphasis on the dual role of Jerusalem/Zion as a place of inviolability and a sinful capital vulnerable to divine judgement; cf. Dow 2011: 83: 'Side by side with the prophets' denunciation of the sin of Israel and their predictions of the ruin this would bring to Jerusalem and the nation is the theme of a gloriously renewed Zion.'

67 As portrayed by Edzard Rohland; see the introduction.

Part II

THE ZION MOTIFS: BETWEEN JUDGEMENT AND SALVATION

6

THE ENEMY ATTACK ON ZION

YHWH's battle against the nations was, according to Edzard Rohland, one of the four main features of the classical Zion tradition (cf. the introduction). The arrival of hostile nations and their attack on Zion function as the initiatory element of the dramatic scenario. Who are these enemies? From where do they come? And why do they attack the place of YHWH's people?

In order to answer these questions, this chapter will begin in a detailed analysis of Joel 2:1–11. This pericope explicitly mentions Zion in 2:1 and its eleven verses form a literary continuum centred on the attack of the enemies. In short, the text encompasses many important aspects of the attack motif. After analysing the unit, we shall look for similar motifs in other texts describing the enemy attack on the city.[1]

The enemy attack in Joel 2:1–11

The notion of the 'Day of YHWH' (יום יהוה) in v. 1 and v. 11 frame the entire unit of Joel 2:1–11; this day is indeed the subject matter of the text. Initially, v. 1 indicates that Zion is the target of this outrageous day, which involves a major attack by enemies. Significantly, it is YHWH who sounds the alarm (cf. the reference to *my* holy mountain in 2:1), although the prophet appears to be the proclaimer of the content of the Day of YHWH in the rest of the pericope.[2] It remains unclear to whom YHWH and the prophet speak. Yet because the trumpet sounds on Mount Zion, it is likely that it is the people living there who are warned. The text unit consists of three parts: vv. 1–2a announce the Day of YHWH; vv. 2b–10 depict the approach and behaviour of the hostile nations; and v. 11 demonstrates YHWH's sovereignty over the attacking army.

Before scrutinizing these three parts, we must establish its context within the Book of Joel. Chapter 2:1–11 follows immediately the locust plague in Joel 1, where a swarm of locusts attacks the land and consumes its crops. Yet the question remains whether this locust army continues its attack in 2:1–11[3] or whether a new army enters the stage. Scholars have defended

79

THE ZION MOTIFS: BETWEEN JUDGEMENT AND SALVATION

both views. Hans Walter Wolff especially has strongly argued for the latter view: it is a military invasion pictured by means of apocalyptic features.[4] Nevertheless, the text remains vague and does support both interpretations. In our analysis, however, we shall focus more intensively on the 'military' character of the swarm.

Verses 1–2a: YHWH's announcement of the Day of YHWH. At first the danger does not concern the enemy attack as such, but more broadly the phenomenon of 'the Day of YHWH'. This is underlined by the use of 'for' (כִּי) in v. 1: 'Let all the inhabitants of the land tremble, *for* the Day of YHWH is coming, it is near!' The particle forms of 'to come' (בּוֹא) and 'to be near' (קרב) emphasize that judgement day is imminent.[5] In general, Joel's 'Day of YHWH' includes an event of war expressing God's judgement on either Israel itself or the foreign nations.[6] Here, the judgement clearly concerns the chosen people. However, the city's inhabitants are described in universal categories; they are the inhabitants of the *land* (or earth), although the people who are involved hardly exceed the borders of Judah.[7] Nevertheless, the employment of this broader perspective gives the scenario a more wide-ranging significance. Four nouns in v. 2a picture the day itself: it is a day of darkness and gloom, and a day of clouds and thick darkness.

Verses 2b–10: the enemy army. Of initial importance is that the army in v. 2b is referred to as a great and powerful people (עַם רַב וְעָצוּם).[8] This reference to a *people* may indicate that it is an army of humans; unfortunately, similar terms are used in Joel 1 to depict the swarming locust (e.g. in 1:6, although by another term [גּוֹי]). The army in Joel 2 is indeed unique: none of its like has ever been, and no one will ever arise (cf. v. 2c). Still, we do not hear from where it comes. However, if we look a bit further in 2:20 and presuppose that this verse refers to the same enemy, then, the army comes from the north (cf. 'the northern [army]'; הַצְּפוֹנִי). Verses 3–5 and 7–9 depict the activities of the army. Its approach is likened to a fire, which burns the fruitful fields and leaves them as desolate deserts (v. 3). Its appearance and movement are like that of warhorses (v. 4), which indicate the army's superior force. The sound – or infernal noise – of the army is like the rumbling of chariots on the tops of the mountains, like the crackling fire and like a mighty army ready for battle (v. 5). War is ahead. Verses 7–9 depict the attack of the city: the invaders run like warriors and soldiers, each man keeping to his own course (v. 7). It is an army of tremendous coordination and discipline; no one pushes the man running next to him. Even when the army is being shot at,[9] it is not halted, but continues determinedly (v. 8). Verse 9 intensifies the invasion of the city: first the soldiers leap upon the city, then they are on its walls, they climb in the houses, and finally, they come through the windows like thieves.

The reaction to this intense and dramatic encounter with the enemies is fear. The people living in Zion are terrified and their faces grow pale (v. 6). Also v. 10 expresses the reaction to the enemy attack: 'the earth quakes before them, the heavens tremble. The sun and the moon are darkened, and the stars withdraw their shining.' This cosmic reaction points backward to the first part of the text unit. As the inhabitants *tremble* at the announcement of the Day of YHWH in v. 1, so does the earth *tremble* (רגז); and the darkness of that day in v. 2 is caused by the darkening of the celestial bodies. This judgement portrayal has clear parallels in, for instance, Isaiah 13; Amos 5:18–20; and Zephaniah 1:14–16, where the darkness, the clouds and the earthquake are common elements.[10] The image also shares some important features with the depiction of YHWH's theophany: in Exodus 19, there are clouds, smoke, an earthquake and sound of trumpets, when YHWH reveals himself on Mount Sinai; such elements are also alluded to in Joel. One may see the suffix in לפניו in vv. 3, 6 and 10 as referring to God, not the army (or 'them'; cf. NRSV). If this is so, the consuming fire – a common expression of YHWH's divine nature – devours in front of *him* (v. 3), and people, the heavens and the earth tremble before *him* (vv. 6 and 10). The ambiguity may be deliberate, namely that YHWH and the army approach simultaneously. In other words, they are two sides of the same coin. In all cases, Joel obviously associates the army with the work of YHWH.[11]

Verse 11: YHWH's sovereignty over the army. In this crucial verse, it becomes abundantly clear that the army depicted in the preceding verses belongs to and takes orders from YHWH. To be sure, YHWH utters his voice to the chief of *his* army (חילו), and *his* camp (מחנהו) is vast. Zion's enemies are not self-appointed and autonomous; they are instruments of YHWH and obey his command. The concluding verse reiterates the central motif of the Day of YHWH in v. 1: 'Truly the Day of YHWH is great; terrible indeed'; and the prophet rhetorically asks: 'Who can endure it?'

In sum, the analysis of Joel 2:1–11 has revealed three essential features of the enemy attack:

(1) YHWH summons and leads the hostile army against Zion.
(2) The event of war is referred to as 'the Day of YHWH', a day of darkness and clouds.
(3) The army is portrayed as invincible.

We shall now examine how other texts dealing with the attack on Zion/Jerusalem make use of similar features. Additionally, in Joel 2:1–11, the lack of reasons for YHWH's attack on the city is peculiar; therefore we shall consider this important issue as well.

YHWH summons and leads the army

It is apparently a recurrent feature in biblical texts that YHWH summons and leads aggressive armies against the city of his people. In Isaiah 5:26, YHWH – in his anger – raises a signal (נס) for a nation far away and

THE ZION MOTIFS: BETWEEN JUDGEMENT AND SALVATION

whistles (שרק) at them that they will come to Zion (cf. also Isa. 7:18).[12] In Isaiah 8:7, YHWH lets the mighty flood waters – that is, the Assyrian king – sweep (Hiphil of עלה) into Zion. Furthermore, in Isaiah 36–7, it is interesting that the Assyrian Rabshaqeh, the king's messenger, regards his task to be commanded by God: 'YHWH said to me, Go up against the land, and destroy it' (cf. Isa. 36:10). In Jeremiah, YHWH's crucial role is repeated more than once: 'For now I am calling [הנני קרא] all the tribes of the kingdoms of the north' (Jer. 1:15) and 'I am bringing [אנכי מביא] evil from the north' (Jer. 4:6); the scorching hot wind in Jer. 4:11 comes *from* YHWH; and YHWH states: 'I am going to bring [הנני מביא] upon you a nation from far away' (Jer. 5:15).[13]

Ezekiel confirms this picture when YHWH states: 'I will arouse [הנני מעיר] against you your lovers'; and further: 'I will bring them [הבאתים] against you from every side' (Ezek. 23:22). Also in the narrative about the attack of Gog of the land of Magog, YHWH says to Gog: 'I will bring you [הבואתיך] against my land' (Ezek. 38:16). Finally, some of the Minor Prophets have similar formulas expressing YHWH's deep engagement: 'For I am rousing [הנני מקים] the Chaldeans' (Hab. 1:6); 'For my decision is to gather [אסף] nations, to assemble [קבץ] kingdoms' (Zeph. 3:8); and, finally, very clearly: 'For I will gather [אספתי][14] all the nations against Jerusalem to battle' (Zech. 14:2). In sum, it is indisputable that Joel is far from being the only prophet to assert that YHWH stands behind the enemy attack on Zion.

As we have seen in Joel, YHWH plays a dual role: he brings the enemies to Zion and he warns his people of imminent disaster. This peculiar dualism is revealed by other prophets as well. In Jeremiah 6:1, YHWH summons the people of Bethlehem to let them flee from Jerusalem, and the warning trumpet will sound in Tekoa (cf. Joel 2:1). Likewise in Jeremiah 4:5–6, the trumpet sounds and a signal or standard (נס) is raised towards Zion. In general, we can observe that YHWH often proclaims the threat of imminent events. In particular, in Jeremiah, where the discrete units frequently are introduced by YHWH's address: 'Declare in Judah' (4:5); 'it will be said to this people and to Jerusalem' (4:11); 'Tell the nations' (4:16); and 'thus says YHWH' (5:14; 6:22; cf. Ezek. 23:22).

The attack as the Day of YHWH

The association of the enemy attack with the Day of YHWH, however, is not as significant in the remaining textual material as in Joel. The term 'Day of YHWH' (יום יהוה) occurs only in Zechariah 14:1, where it introduces the imminent invasion. Besides that, however, there are a few similar, yet crucial, expressions of the Day-motif. In Isaiah 5:25–30, the passage about the approaching army ends with the statement that the enemies will roar 'on that day' (ביום ההוא);[15] in addition, darkness and distress cover the land, and the light grows dark with clouds (cf. Joel 2:2). Furthermore, in Isaiah 36–7, King Hezekiah describes the day of the Assyrian attack as 'a day of distress, of rebuke, and of disgrace' (cf. 37:3).[16] Also Ezekiel 38:1–6 contains a reference to 'that day', on which evil thoughts will come into Gog's mind and he will initiate the attack on God's people (cf. 38:10). In the verse immediately preceding, we hear how Gog will come like a storm and cover the land like a cloud. Finally, in Zechariah 12:3, the attack on Jerusalem takes place 'on that day'. In sum, the attack of the enemies is regarded as a central feature of the Day of YHWH.

Despite the numerous proposals explaining from which traditions the concept of the Day of YHWH has emerged, scholars generally agree that its primary content is YHWH's judgement of either his people or the foreign nations.[17] In what way does the enemy attack represent YHWH's judgement against his people? In Jeremiah 1:16, YHWH will – by means of hostile kings – utter his judgement (משפט);[18] furthermore, in Jeremiah 4:12, concerning the hot wind, YHWH speaks his judgements (משפטים) against his people. Of special importance is Ezekiel 23:24, in which YHWH has aroused Jerusalem's former lovers against her, saying to her: 'I will commit the judgement to them, and they shall judge you according to their ordinances' (ונתתי לפניהם משפט ושפטוך במשפטיהם). Significantly, the enemies are not only in the service of YHWH, but also the executors of his judgement. Their *ordinances* most plausibly refer to the destruction of the city that the army carries out in the succeeding verses (cf. Ezek. 23:25–7).[19]

In all these texts, it is also significant that YHWH gives a reason for calling the enemies to execute his judgement. In Jeremiah 1:16, the charges against the people of YHWH include that they have forsaken God, they have made offerings to other gods and they have worshipped the work of their own hands. Furthermore, in Jeremiah 4:17–18, the obstinacy, misdeeds and cruelty of the people have brought in the enemy from the north. In Ezekiel 23:22–5, YHWH punishes Jerusalem for her infidelity and adultery against him as her God. The portrayal of the approaching army in Isaiah 5:25–30 continues a larger unit in 5:8–24, which lists several social and ethical iniquities. Finally, in Isaiah 8:5–8, YHWH brings the Assyrian king to Zion, because the people have sought political support from Rezin and the son of Remaliah instead of YHWH.

Besides these instances, the prophetic books contain numerous accusations against God's people and their city because of their sins. I have, however, limited my examination to the accusations that are closely connected with passages describing the attack of a hostile army. Concerning these passages, we can conclude that all texts (except Habakkuk) link the attack with either the 'Day of YHWH' and 'on that day', or settings in which the enemies execute YHWH's judgement. In sum, the approaching army represents an instrument of YHWH's judgement. This is especially clear when YHWH personally leads the army.

The invincible army

As in Joel 2:1–11, the army is generally referred to as a *people* or *nation* in either singular[20] or plural.[21] It is, furthermore, presented in two ways: as anonymous[22] or as one of the great powers of the Ancient Near East – in Isaiah, as Assyrians (8:7; 36–8); in Jeremiah, as Babylonians and Chaldeans (34:1); in Ezekiel, as Babylonians and Assyrians (23:23), but also Persians, Nubians and Parthians under the rule of Gog (38:2); and in Habakkuk, as Chaldeans (1:6). In Jeremiah 34:1, King Nebuchadrezzar is in charge of not only his own army of Babylonians, but also all the kingdoms of the earth and all peoples. Also in Zechariah 12:3, it is all nations who attack Jerusalem. In sum, the identity of the enemies is either anonymous, a great power of the region or simply all nations of the world gathered to fight against Zion.

The places from which the enemies come confirm this impression. In Jeremiah, they come from the north (1:13–15; 4:6; 6:22; cf. also Isa. 14:31) and likewise in Ezekiel (38:6, 15). Of importance also are the several geographically undefined locations: 'from far away' (מרחוק in Isa. 5:26; Jer. 5:15; Hab. 1:8); 'from a distant land' (מארץ הרחוק in Jer. 4:16); 'from the ends of the earth' (מקצה הארץ in Isa. 5:26); 'from the farthest parts of the earth' (מירכתי־ארץ in Jer. 6:22); and 'from the breadth of the earth' (מרחבי־ארץ in Hab. 1:6). Crucially, it is a 'new' enemy arriving from far away, not – one is tempted to say – the usual and local enemies such as Ammon, Moab and Edom.[23]

The numerous and mighty enemies are described with extraordinary elegance: they are men of beauty, governors and commanders (Ezek. 23:23), all clothed in full armour (Ezek. 38:4). It is an enduring and ancient nation and alien because one cannot understand what they say (Jer. 5:15). They are a swift and speedy people (Isa. 5:26; Hab. 1:6), and none of them is tired, stumbles or needs to rest (Isa. 5:27). Furthermore, the people are dread and fearsome (Hab. 1:7); the warriors are cruel and show no mercy (Jer. 6:23). The approaching army is like mighty floods (Isa. 8:7),[24] like a hot desert wind (Jer. 4:11–12) and like a great earthquake (Jer. 10:22). It comes up over the city like clouds (Jer. 4:13; Ezek. 38:9, 16) and its noise is like the roaring of the sea (Isa. 5:30; Jer. 6:23) or like that of a lion (Isa. 5:29). Habakkuk asserts that the army acts on its own accord and arrogantly despises every king, ruler and fortress (1:7, 10). The horses of the army are swifter than leopards and eagles, more frightening than wolves and fly like an eagle to devour (Jer. 4:13; Hab. 1:8). The hoofs of the horses are like flint and the chariots like the whirlwind (Isa. 5:28; Jer. 4:13). In addition, the army is formidably equipped with swords, helmets, shields, bows and arrows. It is indeed an invincible army!

Other texts and motifs

I will briefly bring some texts into the discussion that may add other features to the picture gained through the preceding examination. In Isaiah 8:9–10 and 17:12, and Zechariah 12:2–3, we hear nothing about YHWH's calling of the hostile nations. On the other hand, it is not stated that they come of their own accord. These passages more clearly relate to – or maybe are reflective of – the classical motif of the *Völkerkampf* as we know it from the Psalms (see chapter 5). In Psalm 2, the kings attack autonomously and independently of YHWH and his anointed on Zion; in addition, Psalms 46, 48 and 76 contain no references to the idea that YHWH should summon the enemies. Yet a deeper examination of this topic lies outside the scope of the present study.[25] According to Hanns-Martin Lutz, Isaiah 29:1–8 (especially vv. 1–4a) illustrates how YHWH himself besieges the city without making use of an army as instrument.[26] Nevertheless, these minor exceptions do not sufficiently threaten the main point that the enemy army in the prophetic literature primarily is in the service of YHWH.

Summing up: the enemy attack on Zion

The investigation has confirmed the three features of the enemy attack proposed after the analysis of Joel 2:1–11. First, YHWH raises the army, summons the nations and leads the enemies to Zion. The army belongs to YHWH and obeys him. Surprisingly, however, YHWH also warns his people of imminent attack. Second, the attack is frequently associated with 'the Day of YHWH' or 'on that day', a day which brings the darkness of judgement to the land. In addition, the attack is often understood as an execution of YHWH's judgement (משפט) against his people. Third, the army is pictured as extraordinarily powerful, determined and invincible. Its strength is compared with cosmic phenomena such as a storm, a flood and an earthquake, and its horses are swift. The army is ancient, embodies great powers and comes from far away.

Why is the army portrayed as that powerful? Why is YHWH behind it? To make the threat of imminent danger as ultimate as possible! Several passages express this scenario: 'no one can rescue' (Isa. 5:29); 'nothing escapes it' (Joel 2:3); and one can only cry, as in Jeremiah: 'Woe to us, for we are ruined!' (Jer. 4:13). Joel 2:1–11 ends in the same vein: 'Who can endure it?' Such a dramatic scenario has only two possible endings: either YHWH intervenes and protects his city, or YHWH abandons his people to total annihilation. The next two chapters concern an examination of these two possibilities.

Notes

1 These passages include: Isa. 5:25–30; 8:5–8; 36–8; Jer. 1:13–16; 4:5–7, 11–13, 16–18; 5:14–17; 6:1–5, 22–6; Ezek. 23:22–5; 38:1–16; Hab. 1:5–11; Zeph. 3:8; Zech. 12:1–3; 14:1–2. Texts such as Isa. 13 and Jer. 50–1 are not included in the analysis because they deal with Babylon rather than Zion.

2 Fleer 1983: 152.

3 Cf. David Fleer, for instance, who sees the locust invasion in Joel 1–2 as a literal event, stating that 'in Joel, as well as nonbiblical sources, locusts are compared with human soldiers but should not be misconstrued to be symbols' (Fleer 1983: 149–50). See also Crenshaw 1995: 128; Barton 2001: 44, 69–70.

4 Wolff 1977: 41–2, who lists three major arguments in favour of his position; for a challenge of these arguments, see Barton 2001: 69. See also Garrett 1985, 289–90.

5 Wolff 1977: 43.

6 Fleer 1983: 153–5.

7 Crenshaw 1995: 118.

8 As Ingrid Hjelm has demonstrated, the term 'mighty' or 'plentiful' (עצום) is applied to both Israel and the nations and frequently implies a warlike situation; see, for instance, Isa. 8:7 and 31:1, where the enemies are described as 'mighty nations' (cf. below); Hjelm 2004: 135–6.

9 Like Wolff 1977: 38; Barton 2001: 68, I understand השלח as referring to 'missiles' or 'weapons' (cf. LXX). Crenshaw 1995: 116 renders the half verse as 'they descend into a tunnel'.

10 For a thorough analysis of the use of or allusions to other biblical texts in Joel 2:1–11, see Strazicich 2007: 113–41.

11 Lutz 1968: 123–4; Fleer 1983: 160.

12 For a recent study of the images of enemies in the book of Isaiah, see Eidevall 2009.

13 See further in the section on 'The Superpower's Subordination to Yhwh' in John Goldingay's illuminating article on the superpower in Jeremiah (Goldingay 2007: 60–8).

14 Cf. NRSV; Meyers & Meyers 2009: 412, although the verb is in perfect.

15 Hanns-Martin Lutz argues that 'on that day' may be identical with the 'Day of YHWH'. He, however, observes that Isa. 2:12–17, which portrays the events 'on that day', does not contain the notion of an enemy attack (Lutz 1968: 132–3). For a review of the Day of YHWH in Isaiah, see Laato 1998: 85–96.

16 The common interpretation is that this dark day refers to YHWH's judgement against his people by means of the Assyrian army (cf. Kaiser 1974: 387; Blenkinsopp 2000: 474; Wildberger 2002: 401). However, scholars such as J. D. W. Watts and W. A. M. Beuken have argued that this dark day refers to the actions YHWH will take against Assyria; cf. the review in Hjelm 2004: 142–3. Nevertheless, terms such as 'on that day' also designate the day of YHWH's salvific intervention (e.g. Isa. 30:26; see chapter 7).

17 Fleer 1983: 153–5; Crenshaw 1995: 48.

18 However, due to the ambiguous 'them' in v. 16 (אותם), it is not clear against whom the judgement is proclaimed – the foreign kings or Jerusalem? Yet because the accusations mentioned in this verse – forsaken YHWH, offered to other gods, worshipped the work of their hands – are commonly directed at Jerusalem and Judah throughout the book of Jeremiah, v. 16 presumably concerns the judgement against God's own people, not the assembled nations; cf. Carroll 1986: 107; Fischer 2005a: 140.

THE ENEMY ATTACK ON ZION

19 Zimmerli 1979: 488 refers to these judgements or ordinances as 'barbaric methods of war' indicating a military terminology. In addition, in his depiction of the approaching army, Habakkuk states that 'their justice (מִשְׁפָּט) and dignity proceed from themselves' (cf. Hab. 1:7). Importantly, however, מִשְׁפָּט has a broad semantic range of meanings, including also legal right, custom and manner.

20 עַם in Jer. 6:22; גּוֹי in Jer. 5:15; 6:22; Hab. 1:6.

21 עַמִּים in Ezek. 23:24; 38:6, 9, 15; Zech. 12:2–3; גּוֹיִם in Isa. 5:26; Zeph. 3:8; Zech. 12:3; 14:2.

22 Isa. 5:26; Jer. 4:16; 5:15; 6:22; Zeph. 3:8; Zech. 12:2–3; 14:2.

23 Cf. Carl F. Keil's observation: 'The farther the land is from which the enemy comes, the more strange and terrible he appears to the imagination'; cf. Allen 2008: 91.

24 Scholars commonly take these waters as referring to the chaotic waters of the flood; however, for an intriguing reading of the water metaphor in light of Assyrian royal ideology, see Hjelm 2004: 130–5.

25 See further in Lutz 1968: 40–51; Kraus 1986: 78–84, 126–9.

26 Lutz 1968: 100.

7

THE DELIVERANCE OF ZION

This chapter investigates how the motif of Zion as the last bastion is used within the prophetic literature. As we have seen, the theme of the city being attacked by hostile nations but eventually saved by YHWH constitutes one of the basic features of the classical Zion tradition. It is usually held implicit when scholars refer to the Zion motif. The motif as such is quite simple: YHWH defeats the attacking enemies and leaves Zion as an invulnerable place. In the following examination, I will first present this basic motif as well as its nuances and differences within the Book of Isaiah. This will be continued with an examination of Ezekiel 38:1–39:22; Joel 2:1–4:21 [ET 2:1–3:21]; Obadiah 15–21; Micah 4:11–13; Zephaniah 3:1–20; and Zechariah 12:1–13:1. Common to these texts is their portrayal of the deliverance of Zion.

The main pattern in Isaiah 1:4–9

The opening verses of the Book of Isaiah – *Isaiah 1:4–9* – sketch the fundamental structure of the motif in a condensed manner: because the people have rebelled against YHWH (vv. 4–6), enemies ravage the land (v. 7), but Zion is left impregnable with a few survivors (vv. 8–9). In other words, these six verses reveal a movement from the people's transgressions to harsh judgement to graceful salvation.[1] According to vv. 4–6, the charge is laid against the sinful nation (גוי חטא) and the people laden with iniquity (עם כבד עון) – in short, the people who have forsaken YHWH (עזבו את־יהוה). Provoked by the people's unfaithfulness to YHWH, aliens (זרים) have attacked the land and left its cities desolate and burned with fire all the way towards Zion (cf. Joel 2:3). Nevertheless, in the middle of this chaos, daughter Zion has been left isolated like 'a booth in a vineyard' (cf. v. 8).[2] There are two important things to notice in this verse: first, the image of Zion as the last bastion, as 'a besieged city' (עיר נצורה); second, the fact that Zion receives its fate *passively* due to the Niphal form of the verb יתר. However, it does not seem clear who has left the city in this way: the aliens or YHWH? Yet the verb יתר occurs once again in v. 9, although in the

THE DELIVERANCE OF ZION

Hiphil, with YHWH as subject. It is, therefore, plausible that YHWH stands behind the presence of the enemies as well as the subsequent deliverance of Zion. Verse 9, however, clearly states that YHWH is responsible for the few survivors. The verse opens with a condition: '*If* YHWH Sebaoth had not left [הותיר] us a few survivors, we would have been like Sodom, and become like Gomorrah.' In other words, without the saving mercy of YHWH, the city and its inhabitants would have been totally extinct like Sodom and Gomorrah.[3] In addition, v. 9 briefly sketches the concept of a remnant – that is, some survivors of Zion – a concept that will turn out to be an essential feature of the motif (see below). Lacking in this short passage is an account of the defeat of the enemies. Still, up until this point, the main pattern appears as follows:

(a) Enemies, who are called by YHWH and have devastated the land, attack Zion.
(b) YHWH delivers Zion which thereby appears as the sole inviolable place.
(c) The concept of a surviving remnant constitutes a component of the deliverance of Zion.

YHWH's sudden intervention

A fairly obvious text in this context is *Isaiah 29:1–8*, which even has been called a 'key passage' for understanding the theological message of Isaiah.[4] The passage consists of two sub-units: vv. 1–4 and vv. 5–8, with vv. 5–6 as the turning point of YHWH's sudden intervention.[5] The first sub-unit commences with a 'woe', addressed to Ariel,[6] which, due to the context of the whole unit, is Zion (cf. 29:8). As a consequence of the city's arrogance (cf. v. 1b), YHWH will attack and besiege her; there will be moaning and lamentation (vv. 2–3). In so far as the city will suffer the greatest distress, the humble and whispering speech may be interpreted as a silent prayer for help.[7] The saving help is introduced in v. 5, where the multitude of strangers[8] and tyrants will be spread like chaff in the wind, for in an instant – suddenly – YHWH will *visit* his people with thunder, earthquake and whirlwind (v. 6). The enemy attack will be like a dream from which one awakens (v. 7). The section concludes in v. 8 with the moral lesson: so it will be for those who fight against Mount Zion.[9]

There are, however, some exegetical difficulties in connection with this passage, especially in the latter sub-unit. First, in v. 5, it does not seem clear who will be scattered like dust. Even though BHS reads 'your strangers' (זריך), 1QIsaᵃ, LXX and Peshitta read 'those who scorn you' (זדיך). The latter could indicate an 'internal' confrontation with the haughty political leaders of the city (parallel to 'your tyrants'), rather than with foreign nations.[10] Nevertheless, in my view, we should maintain 'your strangers' in reference to those enemies whom YHWH has called to besiege his city (cf. 'the aliens' (זרים) in Isa. 1:7). In the same breath, we must consider whether the 'afflict' or 'visit' (פקד)[11] of YHWH in the succeeding verse is negative or positive.[12] This depends on the interpretation of 'your strangers' and 'your tyrants' in v. 5 and the subsequent theophany of YHWH. If YHWH's visit is negative, it entails a judgement of the scornful and violent leaders of Zion by means of the enemies and the natural disasters associated with the judging act of YHWH. If the visit is positive, it is an expression of salvation and mercy that YHWH, with all his might, intervenes against the enemies to deliver his city. Kaiser, Wildberger and Childs advocate for the latter proposal, but Wildberger rightly asserts that the term פקד has deliberately been chosen because it corresponds to the ambivalence of YHWH's way of acting.[13] The ambivalence is also indicated in the segment as a whole, in so far as YHWH first attacks his city (vv. 1–4) and, then, delivers it by destroying the enemies (vv. 5–8).[14] Apparently, YHWH stands behind both.

Verse 5 contains another remarkable feature, namely that the intervention occurs suddenly and surprisingly, as is expressed by the use of לפתע and פתאם. In the middle of distress and humiliation, YHWH unexpectedly enters and annihilates the very enemies he had brought to Zion. We do not hear much about their defeat, in so far as the whole scenario is presented as a dream, or rather a nightmare, from which the inhabitants of Zion awaken. Verse 8 applies the dream metaphor to the hostile nations: they suffer from hunger and thirst, although they in dreams imagine the opposite, and they are weak (הנה עיף).[15] In short, the invincible enemies are slain by YHWH's intervention.

Before summing up, we shall briefly compare Isaiah 29:1–8 with *Isaiah 17:12–14*. Even though these three verses do not contain a direct reference to Zion (or a city as such!), the composition of the text is similar to 29:1–8, with which it shares an abundance of linguistic parallels. As in 29:1, Isaiah 17:12–14 opens with a 'woe' (הוי), but it is addressed to the foreign nations. The enemies are described as a 'multitude of many peoples' (המון עמים רבים) like the 'multitude of all the nations' (המון כל־הגוים) in 29:7–8. According to vv. 12–13, the nations roar like the sea (cf. Jer. 6:23), yet YHWH intervenes and frightens them so that they flee far away (מרחק) to where they came from (cf. Isa. 5:26). Like the work of YHWH in 29:5–6, the enemies are chased like chaff (מץ) before the storm (סופה). Verse 14, similar to 29:7–8, plays on the rhythm of day and night: in evening time, there is fear and dread among God's people – that is, the 'us' to whom the oracle is addressed;[16] but, before morning, the enemies are gone. Accordingly, Wildberger emphasizes the simplicity and precision of this short statement in the description of the sudden and surprising intervention of YHWH ('a most surprising turn of event') which, as in 29:7–8, is compared to being awakened from a dream.[17] Finally, 17:12–14, too, ends with a moral: this is what happens to those who try to plunder from the people of YHWH (cf. 29:8).

THE DELIVERANCE OF ZION

To sum up, Isaiah 29:1–8 and Isaiah 17:12–14 share similar points of departure, namely that enemies have surrounded Zion and infused its inhabitants with fear and humiliation (cf. 29:4; 17:14). Isaiah 29:1–4 contends that it is YHWH who attacks the city. Due to the divine control of the army, the sudden change appears the stronger in 29:5–6 when the scenario of judgement becomes turned into salvation because of YHWH's presence. The element of surprise is not quite as dominant in 17:12–14, even though the change is presented by an abrupt shift between evening and morning as well as between dream and reality (cf. 29:7). In the following, it will be of relevance to pursue whether YHWH's sudden, unexpected and ambiguous way of acting is present in other passages.

YHWH's plan

In contrast to YHWH's sudden intervention, several passages in Isaiah speak about a divine plan. *Isaiah 10:24–34* is part of the larger unit of Isaiah 10, which accounts for both the imminent threat by the approaching Assyrian army and the possible deliverance. Initially, we may divide the text into two sub-units: vv. 24–7 and vv. 28–34. The first sub-unit is introduced in v. 24 by a common formula within the prophetic literature: 'therefore thus says YHWH Sebaoth'. This formula implies that the following verses are to be perceived as a direct speech of YHWH. The oracle addresses 'my people who live in Zion' (עמי ישב ציון) and announces that they will not be afraid of the Assyrian army, even if the army beats them with a rod. The rod and the staff are used as poetic metaphors for military power and they represent the Assyrian Empire as the tool of YHWH's judgement (cf. Isa. 10:5–6).[18] The summon 'do not be afraid' is closely related to the succeeding verse, which states that, 'in a very little while' (עוד מעט מזער), the indignation of YHWH will come to an end; instead, his anger will be directed to the destruction of the Assyrians.

We notice a crucial difference between 29:1–8; 17:12–14 and this passage. The intervention of YHWH does not occur suddenly, but, on the contrary, is announced beforehand and is part of a message of consolation and salvation *after* YHWH's judging wrath. Still, as in the former texts, a similar ambiguity is at stake. First, Assyria appears as the servant of YHWH *against* his people (v. 24); then, YHWH will wield a whip against the Assyrians and beat them on behalf of his people (v. 26).[19] That YHWH uses a whip instead of a regular weapon underlines his supremacy and punishment of the Assyrians.[20] This whole event takes place 'on that day' (ביום ההוא), when the Assyrian burden and yoke will be removed from the inhabitants of Zion.

In continuation of vv. 24–7, vv. 28–34 reveal the same undergirding structure of judgement and salvation. This sub-unit dramatically reports how an anonymous army makes its way from the north towards Zion. The

91

THE ZION MOTIFS: BETWEEN JUDGEMENT AND SALVATION

advance of the army causes cries of terror in the cities (v. 30); Ramah trembles in fear (v. 29); and the inhabitants of the cities flee (v. 31). As a primary illustration, vv. 28–31 display how the invaders from the north terrorize the land all the way to the final battle at Zion (cf. Isa. 1:7). According to v. 32, the enemy army now halts at Nob, just next to the mount of daughter Zion,[21] shaking its fist at her. The succeeding vv. 33–4 are ambiguous, in so far as it is unclear *whom* YHWH is acting against. 'The tallest trees' that he will cut down may, on the one hand, refer to the leaders of Zion, who are guilty of political arrogance (cf. the possible interpretation of Isa. 29:5); on the other hand, 'the tallest trees' may point backward to the destruction of the Assyrian army in 10:18–19.[22] The former proposal makes sense within the larger context of Isaiah 1–12, since Isaiah 11:1 speaks about the branch growing out of the root (of a cut down tree). The latter proposal, however, concerning the judgement of the enemies, fits the context of Isaiah 10 unfolding YHWH's rejection and destruction of the Assyrian army.[23] In addition, it remains unclear if the city is actually invaded. Verses 33–4 are another case of the troubling, yet fascinating ambiguity of Isaiah's proclamation.

If we assume that the judgement in vv. 33–4 concerns the enemies, then vv. 24–7 and vv. 28–34 apparently display the same theological structure:

(a) YHWH's judgement – 24: the Assyrians ravage / 28–32: an anonymous army ravages
(b) YHWH's salvation – 25–7: YHWH intervenes / 33–4: YHWH intervenes

This structure is helpful to shed light upon the ambiguous way in which YHWH acts. In 29:5–6, it was not certain if his 'visit' (פקד) signified judgement or deliverance. As we may recall, the ambiguity basically consists of the paradox that YHWH calls and leads the enemies, who attack Zion, while *at the same time* YHWH delivers Zion from the imminent danger of invasion. In continuation of this paradox, Wildberger asserts that, according to Isaiah, Assyria appears as both *instrument* of divine wrath and *object* of divine judgement.[24] Isaiah 10:12 grasps this tension: when YHWH has finished all his work (מעשה) on Mount Zion and on Jerusalem (i.e. to judge and to punish his people), he will visit (פקד!) the king of Assyria to punish him because of his arrogance.[25] Here, God's visit is definitely positive, since the destruction of Assyria results in the deliverance of Zion. Nevertheless, we should notice that the destruction of the Assyrians in this verse as well as the entire text is grounded in the arrogance and disloyalty of the Assyrian king, who has appointed himself as the lord of the world (cf. Isa. 10:7–14).[26]

Isaiah 10:12 provides a fine link to the next text passage that I will bring into the discussion. *Isaiah 14:24–7* constitutes the most crucial contrast to the concept of YHWH's sudden intervention. Here, YHWH's plan (עצה) is

THE DELIVERANCE OF ZION

the central matter. The passage summarizes and confirms YHWH's decision to destroy Assyria.[27] Like in 10:24, the unit opens with the formula of speech: 'YHWH Sebaoth has sworn' – as he has designed and planned, so will it be. In that manner, the divine plan has – from the very beginning – contained the defeat of the Assyrian king and the removal of the yoke oppressing God's people. In v. 26, the perspective is extended, in so far as the judgement concerns the whole earth, not only the Assyrians; in a word, YHWH's hand is stretched out over all the nations (כל־הגוים). Whereas the hand once was stretched out against the people of YHWH (cf. 5:25; 10:4), it is now turned against the Assyrian army and the nations of the world. The whole event will take place 'in my land' and 'on my mountains',[28] which, as 29:1–8 and 10:28–34 do, refer to the place of the chosen people. The concluding v. 27 underlines the validity of the plan: 'for YHWH Sebaoth has planned, and who will annul it?'[29] In short, the whole scenario of enemies attacking Zion and YHWH's intervention is by no means a sudden whim of his, but part of a careful, predetermined plan.

Following 14:24–7, two minor half verses – *v. 30a* and *v. 32b* – express the special protection that, by virtue of the plan, is being offered on Zion. First, in v. 30a, we hear about the poor and needy lying in safety (בטח);[30] furthermore, in. v. 32b, we hear that the needy among the people will find refuge here because YHWH has founded Zion (כי יהוה יסד ציון). This might suggest that the place is believed to be safe *in itself* and not depending on the decision of YHWH.[31] In other words, is the place safe because the intervention of YHWH is thought to occur automatically? We shall return to this problem in the next section. What we, however, find in these verses is the immediate faith in permanent safety on Zion.

As a final and dramatic illustration of YHWH's slaughtering of the enemy army, we shall turn to *Isaiah 30:27–33*. This passage contains a set of fascinating features. First, it is of great importance that the approach of YHWH is depicted similarly to that of the enemies. Like the enemy army, YHWH arrives from far away (מרחק) and is not already on Zion.[32] He comes from far off to protect his people against the enemies who are referred to as גוים and עמים (cf. 29:7; 17:12; 14:26) and אשור (cf. 10:24; 14:25). Precisely like the advancing enemies, YHWH appears as burning fire accompanied by vicious noise and cloudburst. According to 30:28, the parallel to the enemies is made indisputably clear since the breath of YHWH is 'like an overflowing stream that reaches up to the neck'; the exact same image was employed to describe the Assyrian attack on Zion (cf. Isa. 8:7–8). Accordingly, this implies that the invincible strength of the enemies is turned against themselves. The rod, once in the hand of the Assyrians, is now the weapon with which they are beaten.

Second, the moaning, the lamentation and the whispering speech (cf. 29:2–4) as well as the fear (cf. 10:29–31) are turned into song and gladness in the hearts of the inhabitants as if they celebrated a holy festival. YHWH's defence of his people calls for a festival, and he, thus, fights to the sound of timbrels and lyres (cf. 30:32).

Third, in the concluding verse, the strange word 'Topheth' (תפה) occurs, probably referring to some kind of cultic altar.[33] The 'Topheth' is made ready for the king, who, in this context, seems to be the Assyrian king (cf. Isa. 10:12). The pyre of the altar has been made deep and wide with enough fire and wood so that the breath of YHWH can consume all the enemies. The wider significance of this fire or offering institution will be taken up below.

Finally, if we read 30:26 as a prologue to the following passage, we may discover another striking parallel. Verse 26 accounts for the day on which YHWH will bind up the injuries of his people and heal their wounds; the light of the moon will be like the light of the sun, and the light of the sun will be seven times brighter. In contrast to this bright day of salvation, the day of judgement was a day of clouds and thick darkness, that is, the day of the enemy attack (Isa. 5:30; Joel 2:2, 10).[34] On the day on which YHWH delivers his people, there will be plenty of light.

In sum, Isaiah 30:26–33 represents the odd phenomenon that the approach of the enemy army and the coming of YHWH to defend his people share the same linguistic features and motifs. In the end, the attackers have been attacked, lamentation turned into gladness, and the day of darkness replaced by a day of light.[35] The text sums up one of the main points so far: the deliverance of Zion is the sole work of YHWH, a work over which the inhabitants of Zion have no influence. Or do they?

Conditions for the deliverance of Zion

In his 1963 article, John H. Hayes claims that Isaiah radically altered the tradition of the inviolability of Zion by introducing 'a condition of salvation and protection'.[36] Before we look closer at this issue, we shall begin with an analysis of *Isaiah 31:4–9*. This passage consists of three parts: vv. 4–5 express YHWH's judgement and deliverance of the city by the means of two animal metaphors; vv. 6–7 constitute a call to repentance and abolition of idolatry; and, finally, vv. 8–9 describe YHWH's intervention against the Assyrians. Once again, v. 4 illustrates the profound ambiguity that dominates these texts. Apparently, YHWH will descend to fight *against* Mount Zion. The Hebrew text states: כן ירד יהוה צבאות לצבא על־הר־ציון. A similar linguistic formulation was employed in Isaiah 29:7, where the nations fight *against* Ariel (הצבאים על־אריאל). Indeed, 'to fight against' is a perfectly possible interpretation and translation and not that odd when we consider that YHWH, according to previously examined passages, calls for and stands behind the enemy army.[37] Verses 4–5 thereby capture the tensions within God's single work, encapsulating his judgement and salvation.[38]

Nevertheless, that YHWH should fight *against* Mount Zion seems too extreme for most interpreters. Instead, they assert that the preposition (על)

94

THE DELIVERANCE OF ZION

relates to the descent of YHWH – that is, YHWH comes down to fight *upon* or *for* Mount Zion.[39] If this were so, it affects our understanding of the lion metaphor in v. 4: as a lion, YHWH *protects* his prey against the shepherds (i.e. the Assyrians, or the leaders of Zion?) by descending upon Mount Zion.[40] At least v. 5 becomes clearer, since YHWH's protection of Jerusalem is emphasized five times with five different words.[41] In vv. 6–7, the motif of repentance is introduced directly: 'turn back' (שׁוּבוּ) to him, that is, to God whom the sons of Israel have betrayed. Interestingly, the deliverance of Zion and the return to YHWH are juxtaposed (for the relation between v. 6 and vv. 4–5, see below). The betrayal or unfaithfulness (סרה; cf. Isa. 1:5 as prelude to 1:7–9) from which the people are urged to turn back probably explains the presence of enemies as an instrument of YHWH's wrath. The acknowledgement of YHWH as the one true God, as part of the act of repentance, therefore implies that idolatry is abolished. Furthermore, vv. 8–9 underline that the defeat of the Assyrian enemies is the work of YHWH alone; cf. the 'sword, which is not of humans' (חרב לא־אישׁ/לא־אדם). On the other hand, it is not obvious if the 'sword' refers to YHWH's personal intervention (cf. 29:5–6; 10:33–4; 30:27–33), or to an agent (cf. 37:36; see below). The Assyrians flee and their young men are forced into slavery. Finally, 31:4–9 concludes with a reference to the fire on Zion (cf. 30:33).

Yet the question remains: how should we understand the call for repentance? On the one hand, Lutz contends that the call in v. 6 constitutes the turning point of the entire passage: YHWH *can* save Zion (vv. 4–5); however, only if Israel repents (v. 6) will he save his city from the Assyrian threat (vv. 8–9).[42] In a similar manner, Hayes states that 'the return is joined with the promise of Yahweh's victory'.[43] On the other hand, Wildberger argues that 'the sons of Israel are not to repent *so that* Jerusalem can be saved, but *because* this deliverance has been promised, because of the experience of the unheard-of faithfulness of God'.[44] According to Wildberger, this must be the case here, because the call to return occurs *after* the proclamation of salvation in vv. 4–5. Roughly speaking, there seem to be two options: the return is either a condition for salvation or a result of deliverance.

To shed light upon this theme, we shall briefly include two famous texts, namely Isaiah 7:1–9 and 28:14–18. In those passages, it appears that *faith* (אמן), rather than conversion, is the central matter. *Isaiah 28:14–18* contains a criticism of the leaders of Jerusalem who, in order to protect the city against the enemies, have entered into political alliances with foreign powers and solely have faith in them (cf. Isa. 31:1–3). In v. 16, YHWH proclaims that he has laid (יסד) a tested stone in Zion.[45] However, it is not the stone (or Zion, cf. 14:32) *itself* that guarantees the inviolability of the place, but the faith that YHWH will save it.[46] This concern is expressed in the statement: 'one who trusts will not panic' (המאמין לא יחישׁ). Likewise, *Isaiah 7:1–9* informs that YHWH's protection of the Davidic monarchy is not

95

unconditional; rather, it depends on the people's faith in him.[47] That it is so is negatively expressed in the concluding v. 9: 'if you do not stand firm in faith, you shall not stand at all' (אם לא תאמינו כי לא תאמנו).[48] In sum, the crucial message of both passages is that failing to trust in YHWH results in a political defeat.

Another relevant illustration is *Isaiah 30:15–17*. Apparently, v. 15 is in line with the interpretation proposed by Hayes and Lutz: 'in returning [שובה] and rest you shall be saved; in quietness and in trust shall be your strength'. Wildberger, however, insists that this verse, within its immediate context, concerns the particular way of acting in facing the imminent threat.[49] Rather than an inner transformation, this passage concerns the observance of and adherence to concrete prophetic instructions, that is, the trust in YHWH's help (cf. Isa. 7:4). Wildberger thereby makes his interpretation of the verse fit into what he considers to be the political programme of the prophet Isaiah: to stay out of coalitions with foreign nations and to call for a serenity that only faith can provide ('remaining still' means not to look around for outsiders).[50] The overall matter in 30:15–17, however, is that the people and their leader *do not* keep calm, which implies that only a few of them are left alive.

Summing up, Hayes, Lutz and Wildberger agree that faith (although it is only mentioned twice) constitutes an essential condition for YHWH's salvation. Furthermore, Hayes and Lutz regard conversion as a precondition as well. By contrast, Wildberger regards the conversion as the people's *reaction* over against the experience of salvation (cf. 31:6) or downplays its spiritual nature (cf. 30:15). We shall return to these questions in the examination of Joel. Until now, we have seen that YHWH's intervention occurs either suddenly or in accordance with a plan, and that it might depend on the faith and conversion of the inhabitants. In addition, a single text supported the concept that the place itself guarantees safety.

Hezekiah: the faithful king

Whereas most of the textual material examined so far has been minor, discrete oracles, *Isaiah 36–7* forms a coherent narrative. As Antti Laato has argued, Isaiah 36–7 is the culmination of Isaiah 1–35, in so far as all the passages recently examined relate to or point forward to the events described in Isaiah 36–7.[51] These chapters account for the siege of Jerusalem by the Assyrian king, Sennacherib, and for the miraculous deliverance of the city and the fate of the king Hezekiah.[52] My focus will be *37:14–38*, but important observations must be noticed concerning 36:1–37:13.

It is worth noting that Sennacherib does not send his army against Jerusalem until all the fortified cities of Judah have been captured (cf. 36:1). While all the other cities have been conquered and destroyed, Jerusalem remains intact (cf. Isa. 1:7–9). Furthermore, it is remarkable that Hezekiah's

THE DELIVERANCE OF ZION

sincere faith in YHWH, which constitutes a leitmotif throughout the narrative, initially is mediated only indirectly through the Assyrian Rabshaqeh, that is, the chief messenger of Sennacherib. Through him, we receive a list of significant statements about the faith of the inhabitants of Jerusalem: 'we rely [בטח] on YHWH our God' (36:7). Consequently, the inhabitants are warned by the Rabshaqeh not to be deceived by Hezekiah when their king asserts: 'YHWH will surely deliver [נצל] us; this city will not be given into the hand of the king of Assyria' (36:14–15). Again in 36:18, the following words are assigned to Hezekiah: 'YHWH will save [נצל] us.' According to 36:20, the Rabshaqeh is bluntly arrogant, when he answers: 'Who among all the gods of these countries have saved their countries out of my hand, that YHWH should save Jerusalem out of my hand?' It is not before 37:1 that the piety of Hezekiah is presented straightforwardly, in so far as he, as a reaction to the briefing on the immediate threat, tears his clothes, covers himself with sackcloth and enters the temple as an expression of deepest penance.[53] Yet again in 37:10–11, in a letter, the Assyrians warn Hezekiah not to be deceived by his God, by maintaining that Jerusalem will not be given into the hand of the king of Assyria. Apparently, Assyria has displayed tremendous military force, so how on earth should Jerusalem be saved? With these observations in mind, we shall now turn to my focal text.

Isaiah 37:14–38 may be divided into five parts:

(1) Hezekiah's prayer in the temple (vv. 14–20);
(2) YHWH's words against the Assyrian king (vv. 21–9);
(3) the promise of a surviving remnant on Zion (vv. 30–2);
(4) the promise of protection and deliverance of the city (vv. 33–5); and
(5) the defeat of the Assyrians and the death of Sennacherib (vv. 36–8).[54]

In vv. 14–15, Hezekiah, carrying the letter conveying the Assyrian threat, enters the temple to pray. His prayer opens with a confession to YHWH. He is God of Israel and of all the kingdoms of the earth (implicitly including the Assyrian empire in his realm!), and creator of heaven and earth. The pious and humble confession thereby forms a sharp contrast to the arrogance of the Rabshaqeh (36:20; 37:11).[55] In vv. 17–19, Hezekiah introduces YHWH to the central matter: Sennacherib has mocked him, the living God. The Assyrian king's invasion of all the countries was only possible, because the gods of all those countries were no gods at all; YHWH alone is the one, true God. The prayer culminates in v. 20, which contains two elements. First, Hezekiah prays: 'so now, YHWH our God, save [ישע] us from his hand'. We have not yet met such a direct address to YHWH asking for his help. Second, in the latter part of the verse, a new motif is introduced: the deliverance must take place so that all kingdoms of the earth may *know* (ידע) that YHWH alone is God.[56] This recognition of the

97

sovereignty of YHWH among the foreign nations, in fact the world at large, constitutes a new feature and we shall return to it in the analysis of Ezekiel 38–9. In short, the content of the prayer is a call for help.

The prophet Isaiah presents YHWH's reply in 37:21. First he scorns Sennacherib because of his arrogance (vv. 22–5); then he assures him that he will turn him back (vv. 26–9). In vv. 30–2, YHWH gives Hezekiah a sign: in the years to come, agriculture will be restored, and the survivors going out from Jerusalem will regenerate and prosper. The concept of a remnant was introduced in Isaiah 1:9, and we shall deal with that topic in the next section of the present chapter. Finally, YHWH arrives at the decisive matter: the deliverance of Zion. In vv. 33–4, YHWH's assessment of the siege of Sennacherib forms a structural frame: 'he shall not come into this city!' Neither an arrow nor a siege ramp will reach the city; by the way that he came, he will return. In v. 35, YHWH makes his support abundantly clear: 'I will defend this city to save it' (וגנותי על־העיר הזאת להושיעה). In this verse, the same word for salvation (ישע) is employed as in the prayer of Hezekiah (cf. 37:20) and, in addition, גנן occurs (cf. the promise of YHWH's intervention in 31:5). Now, YHWH will save his city for his own sake and for the sake of his servant David.[57] His honour is at stake! To whom this 'David' refers is not clear; yet within its larger context, it seems to refer to Hezekiah as a representative of the Davidic monarchy.

Finally, vv. 36–8 report on the promised defeat of the Assyrians. During the night, an angel of YHWH sets out and kills 185,000 in the Assyrian camp; when the inhabitants of Zion wake up, the Assyrians are dead bodies. It is often stressed that this verse shows how the intervention of YHWH occurs by means of miraculous circumstances (cf. the 'sword not of humans' in 31:8). Likewise, the idea that the victory or deliverance is realized at sunrise (cf. 17:14) is apparent: YHWH saves at daylight. Sennacherib, however, returns to Nineveh, but is killed there as predicted in 37:7.

To sum up, Isaiah 36–7 represents the classical Zion motif in a narrative form: the Assyrian army, having captured and desolated the cities of Judah, stands at the walls of Jerusalem; yet by means of the inhabitants' faith and Hezekiah's prayer, YHWH intervenes and protects his city in terms of a miraculous deliverance. As part of the deliverance, there is a promise of a surviving remnant sprouting from Mount Zion.

The surviving remnant on Mount Zion

In Isaiah 37:30–2, the promise of a remnant of survivors sprouting from Mount Zion functions as an illustration of the time following the decisive victory over the enemies. As has been indicated, the concept of a remnant is central in Isaiah.[58] In Isaiah 1:9, we have already noticed the idea that *if* YHWH Sebaoth had not left a few survivors, Zion would have been totally extinguished like Sodom and Gomorrah. The temple vision likewise

THE DELIVERANCE OF ZION

foreshadows that only a remnant will remain: a tenth part will be the holy seed of a new people (cf. Isa. 6:11–13). In the King Ahaz narrative in 7:1–9, the concept of a remnant returning to YHWH and his saving power plays a significant role. Meeting Ahaz, the prophet Isaiah is accompanied by his son, who carries the symbolic name 'Shearjashub', which means 'a remnant will return'.[59] Despite the Assyrian threat, the people will not be annihilated, because a remnant will be saved. The return (שוב) may, however, also refer to the repentance in 31:6 as a possible condition for salvation. If this is so, everyone has been given the offer, but only a few have in fact returned to YHWH. This scenario was displayed in 30:15–17, where the people were urged to return and to remain calm; however, they ran away in fear. The people fled until their abandoned place was like a flagstaff on the top of a mountain (Zion?) and like a signal on a hill. Such a scenario recalls the main figure of 1:7–9 (נתר occurs in both passages): only daughter Zion will be left like a booth in a vineyard.

Three passages elaborate in more detail the concept of the remnant on Zion: Isaiah 4:2–6, 10:20–3 and 37:30–2. In *10:20–3*, it is announced that 'on that day' (ביום ההוא) the remnant of Israel (שאר ישראל) and the survivors of the house of Jacob (פליטת בית־יעקב) will lean on YHWH in faith (אמת). The remnant (שאר) – the remnant of Jacob (שאר יעקב) – will *return* (שוב) to their mighty God. Here, it seems that a remnant at last repents and fulfils the condition introduced in 7:9, 28:16, 30:15 and 31:6.[60] According to vv. 22–3, the return is vital, because YHWH's destruction of all the earth *has* been decreed. The phrase 'destruction is decreed' (כליון חרוץ) underscores the validity of YHWH's decision (cf. the plan in 14:24–7). And although the people of Israel are like the sand of the sea, only a remnant of them will return (שאר ישוב!); everyone else is lost without hope. Rather than only presenting a vision of a future time of salvation, 10:20–3 marks the ultimate line of demarcation: only a remnant of the people will return to YHWH and be saved.[61]

Isaiah 37:30–2 is more concerned with the future for the survivors. As a result of the ravage by the Assyrian army, agriculture will not be restored until three years later; people will then plant vineyards and eat their fruit. In v. 31, we hear that the surviving remnant of the house of Judah (הנשארה פליטת בית־יהודה,) will take root downwards and bear fruit upwards. The specific reference to the 'root' indicates that the language is figurative; the remnant which has survived the great judgement of YHWH is the root from which a new people will emerge.[62] Verse 32 points in the same direction, because the remnant (שארית) and the survivors (פליטה) will *sprout* (יצא) from Jerusalem and from Mount Zion. Finally, it is the zeal of YHWH (קנאת יהוה) that carries all this out. YHWH himself will see to it that his people once again will bloom.

As in 10:20–3, the events in *4:2–6* take place on ביום ההוא, the day when misery is turned into prosperity. After the judgement, there will be

99

THE ZION MOTIFS: BETWEEN JUDGEMENT AND SALVATION

a new beginning.[63] Verse 2 looks similar to 37:30 with regard to its use of plant metaphors; the branch of YHWH (צמח יהוה) and the fruit of the land will be beautiful, glorious and the pride of the survivors of Israel (פליטת ישראל).[64] The verse also recalls 28:5–6 concerning YHWH as a garland of glory and a diadem of beauty to the remnant of his people (שאר עמו). In vv. 3–4, those who are left (הנשאר) in Zion and those remaining (הנותר) in Jerusalem will be called holy, because YHWH will wash away their filth and their bloodstains by the spirit of judgement and burning (רוח בער, רוח משפט). The notion of a spirit of judgement[65] also occurs in 28:5–6, where the spirit supports the one who sits in judgement. As an expression of salvation, there is a purge of the surviving remnant. In vv. 5–6, YHWH creates (ברא) over the whole site of Mount Zion and over its places of assembly a cloud by day, and smoke and the shining of fire by night. The cloud and the fire, which during the wilderness wandering symbolize the presence of YHWH, are here linked with YHWH's protection of Zion.[66] Here, the cloud and the fire also function as a canopy. There will be a booth (cf. Isa. 1:8) as shade and shelter from the heat, the storm and the rain – phenomena that in other texts describe the approach and attack of the enemy army.[67]

To sum up, the concept of a surviving remnant provides an important conclusion to the enemy attack and YHWH's deliverance of Zion. The remnant that has returned in time and has been saved from the devastating attackers (cf. 10:20–3) becomes the root from which the people once again will increase (cf. 37:30–2); this happens after the sins of the survivors have been washed away and a new, sheltered Zion has been created (cf. 4:2–6). In short, the purpose of the remnant is to secure a new beginning, a new people and a new creation after the time of judgement.

The purging of Zion and the presence of YHWH

The purging of Zion occurs in other texts as well, for instance, in *1:21–8*, which is part of the large introductory chapter to Isaiah as a whole, presenting a set of themes that occurs throughout the book. Verse 21 commences with the astonishing observation that the faithful city (קריה נאמנה), formerly full of justice (משפט) and righteousness (צדק), has become a whore. It is filled with murders. Verses 22–3 show the present state of the city: its silver has become dross, and its wine is mixed with water. The leaders of the city revolt, take bribes and do not care about orphans and widows. As a result of the violation of justice, YHWH intervenes in vv. 24–6. He will avenge the foes, remove the dross and install new judges in the city. The intervention of YHWH is thereby aimed at the leading circles which, according to v. 23, did not live up to their obligations and must be replaced.[68] When this is done, Zion will again be called the city of righteousness (עיר הצדק) and the faithful city (קריה נאמנה). The epilogue in vv. 27–8 is of special importance: 'Zion

100

THE DELIVERANCE OF ZION

shall be redeemed by justice [מִשְׁפָּט], and those in her who repent,[69] by righteousness [צְדָקָה].' Now, it becomes clear that it is the remnant of penitence who has been delivered from its corrupt leaders and the enemies of YHWH. Subsequently, v. 28 accounts for the destiny of those who did not return: the rebels (פֹּשְׁעִים), the sinners (חַטָּאִים) and those who forsake YHWH (עֹזְבֵי יהוה; cf. Isa. 1:4) will be consumed. In short, 1:21–8 is concerned with the removal of the leaders who distort life in the city. Thus, it is an 'internal' confrontation between the faithful flock who has returned to YHWH and those who did not and will perish (cf. 10:22–3).

The same theme is generously presented in *33:14–24*. According to v. 14, the sinners (חַטָּאִים) in Zion and the godless (חֲנֵפִים) are afraid, for who can live with the devouring fire (אֵשׁ אוֹכֵלָה) and with the everlasting flames (מוֹקְדֵי עוֹלָם)?[70] In other words, the devouring fire constitutes the means by which sinners will be removed from Zion. As we have seen, this fire often characterizes YHWH's judging appearance (cf. 30:27, 30) and, in 30:33, it is turned against the enemies (or the arrogant leaders!). YHWH has his fire in Zion (31:9) and the name 'Topheth' (תֹּפֶת) designates some sort of sacrificial fire for the enemies (cf. 30:33). In that manner, the devouring fire of YHWH is a purging fire that removes the enemies, frightens sinners away and establishes Zion as a stronghold of righteousness.

Verses 15–16 present the moral ideal for the righteous inhabitant: he who fulfils these commandments will live on the heights, his refuge will be the fortresses of rocks, and he will have an abundance of food and water. Protection and providence are offered to the faithful on Zion. The righteous will see the king in his beauty and observe a land that stretches far away (אֶרֶץ מֶרְחַקִּים); the land once ravaged by enemies is now under the rule of the king. Verses 18–19 assure the inhabitants that the enemies have left; no one counts the towers,[71] and the alien people (עַם נוֹעָז) whose language was obscure (cf. Jer. 5:15!) have disappeared. In vv. 20–2, Zion is a city of festivals (cf. Isa. 4:5). It is now a quiet habitation which will not be moved; the city is safe and solid.[72] The water is not chaotic as in Isaiah 8:7–8, but flows as calm streams; and YHWH himself is the judge, ruler and king of the city. Whereas v. 23 is odd and probably refers to events outside the text,[73] v. 24 summarizes the entire passage: there is no longer illness in the city, and the iniquity of the people who live there has been forgiven (הָעָם הַיֹּשֵׁב בָּהּ נְשֻׂא עָוֹן). In that manner, the concluding verse points backward to the sinners, who disappeared (cf. vv. 14–15). In fact, in the context of the Book of Isaiah as a whole, v. 24 recaptures the introductory verses in Isaiah 1 concerning the sinful people who had forsaken YHWH and deserved punishment.[74] In sum, 33:14–24 constitutes a final stage within the classical Zion motif: YHWH is present on Zion with his devouring fire; sinners and enemies are gone; there is an abundance of food and water; the kingdom extends; there are festivals instead of illness and iniquity; and YHWH is the king of the city.

101

Summing up: the classical Zion motif in Isaiah

The saving intervention of YHWH occurs as a response to the enemy's attack against the city, either suddenly (לפתע פתאם; cf. 29:1–8; 17:12–14), or announced as part of a preconceived plan (עוד מעט מזער; cf. 10:24–34; 14:24–7). A single passage seems to assert that Zion is a safe place in itself (cf. 14:30a, 32b). YHWH's intervention is, however, characterized by ambivalence; first, it is not clear whether his 'visit' means judgement or salvation of his people (cf. 29:5–6; 10:33–4; 31:4); second, YHWH seems to judge and save *at the same time*. On the one hand, he calls the enemies as an instrument of his wrath; on the other hand, he delivers his people from the imminent danger of invasion. Neither faith nor conversion as conditions for deliverance are certain, and this issue will be investigated more closely in the following sections of the present chapter. In any case, by the mercy of YHWH, a remnant of survivors is saved and, after their iniquities have been washed away, they will become the root of a new and righteous nation. The deliverance of Zion thereby implies that the sin – which originally provoked YHWH's calling of enemies as a tool of his divine judgement (cf. 1:4–6) – has been forgiven (cf. 4:2–6; 1:21–8; 33:14–24).

Ezekiel 38:1–39:22: They shall know that I am YHWH!

Although the narrative in Ezekiel 38:1–39:22 appears to have been reworked several times, which has resulted in a number of literary tensions within the present text, we shall attempt to read the two chapters according to their final form.[75] Ezekiel 38–9 contains no reference to Zion, a city or even a mountain. Nevertheless, the narrative refers to 'the mountains of Israel' (38:8; 39:2, 4, 17), 'my land' (i.e. the land of YHWH; 38:16) and 'the centre of the earth' (טבור הארץ; 38:12). Furthermore, YHWH addresses his people as 'my people Israel' (38:14, 16; 39:7) and the region as 'my mountains' (הרי; 38:21; cf. Isa. 14:25). Just as YHWH's plan in Isaiah encompassed that the Assyrians should suffer defeat on 'my mountains', so will Gog and his entire army fall on 'the mountains of Israel' (Ezek. 39:1–5). Both texts therefore share the feature that the deliverance from the enemy attack will occur in the place (city, mountain(s) or land) in which the people of YHWH dwell.[76]

In the context of the Book of Ezekiel as a whole, Ezekiel 38–9 is placed after the deliverance and return from the Babylonian exile (Ezek. 1–37).[77] Crucially, 38:8 states that the inhabitants of the land have been gathered from many nations and live in safety (בטח) on the mountains of Israel, which had lain a wasteland for a long time. In 38:1–9, YHWH calls for Gog and his troops in the north and asks them to be ready, for after some time, he will send them to fight the land of his people. The text, however, does not express the idea that these enemies will function as an instrument

THE DELIVERANCE OF ZION

of YHWH's wrath; neither are there any charges against the people of YHWH.[78] Whereas Gog in 38:1–9 bluntly follows the divine instructions, 38:10–13 accounts for his own, personal decision: he will rob from the unprotected land. We may see this aim as a parallel to the arrogance displayed by the Assyrian king (cf. Isa. 10; 36–7), which eventually led to YHWH's punishing anger. Whereas Gog will invade the land, YHWH's plan is different. Gog and his many peoples will approach the land, *so that the nations may know YHWH* (38:14–16). In my view, this worldwide recognition of the holiness and sovereignty of YHWH constitutes the key motif of the entire narrative, and we shall make a closer examination of it below. Verse 17 places Gog and his army within the larger context by stressing that he is the ultimate enemy with whom YHWH formerly has threatened his people. Yet according to 38:18–23, the picture is turned upside down. On that day (ביום ההוא) when Gog enters the land of Israel, the wrath of YHWH will be aroused. The defeat of the hostile army even involves cosmic phenomena: a great earthquake will shake the entire world. YHWH will judge (שׁפט) Gog with all means including fire and sulphur (cf. Isa. 29:6; 30:27–33). All this happens so that nations may know who YHWH is (38:23).

Ezekiel 39:1–5 reiterates the motif in a more condensed form. YHWH catches and leads Gog from the north against the mountains of Israel (39:1–2). Here, he will fight him – man against man – and strike the bow and the arrows from his hands (39:3). In 39:4–5, YHWH twice announces that Gog and his troops will fall in the mountains of Israel. Their bodies will be left on open ground as food for birds of prey and wild animals. In 39:6–8, it is once again emphasized that all these events happen so that the foreign nations will know that YHWH is Lord. In 39:9–20, the inhabitants of the land will burn the weapons, which number so many that it will take seven years.[79] The bodies will then be buried in order to purge (טהר) the land. Finally, YHWH will host a huge sacrificial feast where the wild animals, as in 39:4, will consume the horses, the chariots and the warriors.

The perspective revealed here is indeed rather different than that of the Book of Isaiah. Nowhere is it stated that Gog and his troops must fulfil YHWH's judgement against his people.[80] Moreover, there are no charges against the people at all. Only Gog and his troops are judged (38:22).[81] Until after the slaughtering of the foreign enemies, the people of YHWH only play a minor role. The judgement of the sinful nation, which constituted a key motif in Isaiah, is completely absent from these chapters of the Book of Ezekiel.[82] On the contrary, YHWH's motivation is to demonstrate his ultimate power and sovereignty. This motivation is frequently expressed in the 'Recognition Formula', which forms a central feature in the composition of the book as a whole. In 38:16, YHWH explains the planned attack: 'so that the nations [הגוים] may know [דעת] me, when *through you*, O Gog, I display my holiness [בהקדשי] before their eyes'. In other words, the holiness

103

THE ZION MOTIFS: BETWEEN JUDGEMENT AND SALVATION

of YHWH will be revealed by the work he performs through Gog. As in other passages, holiness is closely linked with the faithful care that YHWH shows for his people.[83] In 38:23, YHWH states: 'I will display my greatness and my holiness [התקדשתי] and make myself known [נודעתי] in the eyes of many nations [גוים רבים]. Then they shall know that I am YHWH [כי אני יהוה].' And again in 39:6-7: 'they shall know that I am YHWH . . . the nations [הגוים] shall know that I am YHWH, the Holy One in Israel'. As an obvious parallel, we noticed in the prayer of Hezekiah that YHWH's deliverance of Zion would involve all kingdoms of the earth knowing (ידע) that YHWH alone is God (cf. Isa. 37:20). In sum, a purpose of both Isaiah and Ezekiel with regard to the presence of enemies and the following deliverance is to show and make the nations understand the divine nature of YHWH.

Ezekiel 39:21-2 sums up the preceding material.[84] The content of the two verses is uttered by YHWH: 'I will display my glory among the nations; and all the nations [כל־הגוים] shall see my judgement [משפטי] that I have executed, and my hand that I have laid on them.' In short, the judgement of Gog and his army by which YHWH reveals his glory has a worldwide audience and will imply a worldwide recognition of his divine supremacy. Furthermore, according to v. 22: 'The house of Israel shall know [ידעו] that I am YHWH their God [כי אני יהוה אלהיהם], from that day forward.' This sentence is remarkable, because it is the only passage in the entire Book of Ezekiel in which 'the house of Israel' is subject of 'knowing' YHWH forever. Thus, the defeat of Gog is the final act of YHWH in order to gain faith and support from his people. The deliverance of his people will, once and for all, reveal the sovereignty of YHWH as God and master of the universe.

Joel 2:12–4:21 [ET 2:12–3:21]:
repentance and judgement of the nations

The four chapters of the Book of Joel present a coherent argument. Joel 1 accounts for the swarming locusts destroying the land, while Joel 2:1–11 depicts the enemy army governed by YHWH. The enemy attack motivates the call for repentance that sounds in 2:12–14. YHWH in 2:1 announced the approach of the enemies, and in 2:12 he calls for repentance: 'Return to me!' (שבו עדי). Verse 13 repeats the central term שוב – 'Return to YHWH, our God' – and in v. 14, YHWH is the one who might 'return' – that is, regret and change his decision to punish his people.[85] While Wildberger strongly rejected interpreting repentance in terms of an 'inner transformation' in Isaiah 30:15 and 31:6, this is precisely what appears to be the case in Joel.[86] The repentance will involve 'all your heart' with fasting, weeping and mourning (cf. 2:12) and the people must rend their heart instead of their clothes (cf. 2:13). Verse 13 apparently reflects the anxiety that repentance

104

THE DELIVERANCE OF ZION

will occur mechanically as part of an empty ritual rather than being authentic and sincere.[87] Furthermore, v. 13 points forward to vv. 15–17, where repentance takes place in midst of the assembly led by the priests.[88] In the end, however, the avoidance of the threat through repentance and submission is only possible because of the mercy of YHWH (cf. 2:14).

Joel 2:15–17 recalls the call in 2:1 to blow the trumpet on Zion. Whereas the trumpet in the first case should warn the people, the trumpet in v. 15 calls for the people to repent. The people of all ages will be gathered, and the assembly will be sanctified. In v. 17, the priests will stand, cry and pray: 'Spare your people, o YHWH!' Being the heritage (נחלה) of YHWH, the people should not become a mockery among the nations. In short, the people are the heritage that YHWH will deliver from attacking enemies. In sum, 2:12–17 concerns the condition for deliverance, which entails that the people repent, gather in the temple and pray for mercy.[89]

Crucially, 2:18 illustrates the ultimate expression of grace: 'Then YHWH became jealous for his land, and had pity on his people.' According to Wolff, this statement marks the 'decisive turn' within the book as a whole.[90] Everything from here on must be read in light of this statement. Whereas Joel 1:1–2:17 describes the judgement of the people of YHWH, 2:19–4:21 describes the salvation of Zion and the judgement on the foreign nations. Verses 19–20 present YHWH's response to the repentance in 2:12–17. YHWH will restore the land that the swarming locusts destroyed. He will not make his people a mockery among the nations. And, finally, he will remove the enemies – referred to as 'the northern' (הצפוני) – and drive them into the desolate land, where he will drown them. The removal of the enemies leads to joy and fertility for the land, the animals and the sons of Zion (cf. 2:21–5).

The chapter closes in 2:26–7 with two significant elements: praise and acknowledgement. In v. 26, the name of YHWH is praised for the restored fertility and all the gracious things that he has done for his people; never again will his people be put to shame. Similarly to Isaiah 37:20 and Ezekiel 38–9, v. 27 introduces a formula of recognition: 'You shall know' (ידעתם). The deliverance of Zion occurs with a specific purpose in mind: the people's acknowledgement of YHWH as their only God. This acknowledgement consists of three steps. First, they will know that YHWH is in the midst of Israel; second, they will know that YHWH is their God; and third, they will know that there is no other God than YHWH. Finally, YHWH repeatedly assures them that the people will never again be put to shame. Wolff, however, does not perceive 2:27 as a conclusion. Rather, he sees the verse as a forerunner of the succeeding two chapters and especially of the acknowledgement in 4:17.[91] YHWH's promise that his people will not be put to shame is abundantly fulfilled in these last chapters of Joel.

Up until this point, YHWH has led the army to judge his people (cf. 2:1–11) and, in the light of repentance (cf. 2:12–17), showed mercy to his people

105

THE ZION MOTIFS: BETWEEN JUDGEMENT AND SALVATION

and restored their fortunes (cf. 2:18–27). The introductory words in 3:1 (אחרי־כן) point forward to the next phase: the final slaughtering of the hostile nations. This ultimate battle will happen 'in those days' (בימים ההמה; cf. 3:2; 4:1). Surely, a new set of events takes place in these two final chapters. Joel 3:1–5 constitutes a discrete textual unit, which consists of three sub-units: vv. 1–2 on the outpouring of the spirit, vv. 3–4 on the Day of YHWH and v. 5 on the salvation on Zion.

In vv. 1–2, YHWH will pour out (שפך) his spirit upon all humans (presumably his people and their slaves), and they will prophesy and see visions. What does the spirit (רוח) of YHWH represent? Wolff suggests 'vital power',[92] and Crenshaw renders it 'vital force'.[93] Yet the question remains of whether the spirit also leads to a purging of the people's sins (as in Isa. 4:3–4). This matter will be discussed later, in the examination of Zechariah 12:1–13:1.[94] Wolff, furthermore, argues that this spirit creates a new and prophetic relationship to God, in which everybody relates directly to YHWH.[95] This new individual relationship is allegedly expressed in the salvation on Zion in v. 5, and may imply a reduction of the significant role of the priests (cf. 2:17). The outpouring of the spirit clearly happens *after* the repentance and the acknowledgement of YHWH as God.

Verses 3–4 once again announce the Day of YHWH. YHWH will show wonders in the heavens and on the earth: the sun will be turned into darkness and the moon to blood. As in 2:1–11, the day is called 'great and terrible' (הגדול והנורא). Yet the context is different. Everyone who calls on the name of YHWH will be saved. Since the name of YHWH was an object of praise in 2:26, we may presume that the salvation encompasses the people, who have already returned to YHWH and praised his name.[96] Against this background, we ought to understand the confident faith of the people in their future salvation on Mount Zion and in Jerusalem. In other words, the preceding repentance, acknowledgement and outpouring of the spirit determine the salvation on Zion.

Verse 5 spells out the implications of YHWH's dwelling in the midst of Israel (cf. 2:27). On Mount Zion, there will be escape (פליטה) from the army from which there formerly was *no* escape (cf. 2:3). This turn thereby indicates that the Day of YHWH in 3:3–4 – in light of the overall 'turn' in 2:18 – concerns the enemies rather than the people, as displayed in the following judgement of the nations in Joel 4. However, the Day of YHWH will bring salvation to Zion (cf. Isa. 4:2; 10:20), when he will call on the survivors (שרידים; cf. Isa. 1:9).

In Joel 4, the judgement of YHWH is clearly directed against the foreign nations. In 4:1–3, YHWH will restore (שוב) the fortunes of Jerusalem and revenge his people, that is, his heritage (נחלה; cf. 2:17). YHWH will gather the enemies in the valley of Jehoshaphat – the valley of judgement[97] – and judge (שפט) all the nations who ruined the land and its inhabitants. Joel 4:9–15 functions as a counter-motif to 2:1–11. As in 2:7, the army consists

106

THE DELIVERANCE OF ZION

of warriors and soldiers, and they are urged to gather and prepare for battle. Joel 4:14 reiterates the statement that the Day of YHWH is near (cf. 2:1), and 4:15 quotes 2:10b word for word. As observed in Isaiah, so also Joel 4:9–15 turns things around: the peoples, formerly appointed as an instrument of YHWH, now become the object of monstrous judgement. They will gather so that YHWH can utterly destroy their warriors (4:11). This whole scenario is set in the valley of Jehoshaphat; yet in 4:16–17, the focus shifts to Zion. Now, YHWH roars from Zion and is a refuge for his people.[98] The judgement of the nations will, as in 2:27, involve a specific acknowledgement of the people: 'So you shall know [וידעתם] that I, YHWH your God, dwell in Zion, my holy mountain.' Thereafter the city will be holy (cf. the holy remnant in Isa. 4:3?) and strangers will not pass through it. As Isaiah announced a cleansing and renewal of Zion (see Isa. 1:21–8; 4:2–6; 33:14–24), Joel 4:18–21 envisions a future restoration. The land is full of prosperity (cf. v. 18) and political independency (cf. vv. 19–20). Just as Isaiah 33:14–24 proclaimed the ongoing presence of YHWH, the Book of Joel ends on a similar note: 'YHWH dwells in Zion' (יהוה שכן בציון).

In sum, the Book of Joel's sincere repentance (2:12–17) causes not only deliverance from enemies (2:20), but also an acknowledgement of YHWH as God (2:27) and the outpouring of the spirit (3:1–2). This evokes a faithful belief that there is escape on Zion (3:5). Joel 4, like Isaiah, turns the motif of judgement upside down: the attacking enemies become the attacked. In the end, this turn rests on the mercy of YHWH, which in 2:18 constitutes the key statement in the composition of the book as a whole. Before this point, the judgement of YHWH is directed against his people, while after this point, the judgement is directed against the nations. Joel's concept of the Day of YHWH (יום יהוה) thereby expresses the same kind of ambivalence about YHWH's judgement as does the Book of Isaiah. In Joel 1:15, 2:1 and 2:11, the concept designates the judgement against the people of YHWH, while in 3:4–5 and 4:14–16, it designates the judgement against the nations and concordant salvation of Zion.

Obadiah 15–21: the deliverance of Zion and the control over the territories

The small Book of Obadiah also employs the motif of escape in Zion, especially in Obadiah 15–21, which consists of three sub-units: the Day of YHWH (vv. 15–16), the escape in Zion (vv. 17–18) and the people of YHWH taking control over the surrounding territories (v. 19–21). As in Joel 2:1 and 4:14, the Day of YHWH is near and applies to all nations. Yet the following statement spoken by YHWH is problematic: 'For as you have drunk on my holy mountain, all the nations around you shall drink.'[99] Who does this 'you' refer to? It may refer to Edom, who

THE ZION MOTIFS: BETWEEN JUDGEMENT AND SALVATION

in vv. 1–14 is under accusation.[100] If this is so, the judgement is extended to encompass not only Edom, but also all the nations.[101] On the other hand, 'you' may refer to the political leaders of Zion, who have been drinking on the mountain of Zion (cf. the ambiguity in Isa. 29:5–8).[102] If so, the judgement has formerly been directed against Zion and is now transferred to the nations. Both interpretations are indeed plausible, although the latter seems preferable because of the parallels in Isaiah. In sum, however, vv. 15–16 clearly state that the evil deeds of Edom and the nations will be turned against them; they will drink and become as though they had never been.

Verses 17–18, subsequently, depict the sincere trust that there, in the middle of this chaos, will be escape (פליטה) in Zion. That this place will be holy recalls both the scene in Joel 4:17, where Jerusalem will become holy, and the notion of the holy remnant on Zion in Isaiah 4:3. There will be escape for those of the house of Jacob. Here Jacob is explicitly linked with Zion (cf. Isa. 10:20), and his house will take possession of the surrounding nations, who dispossessed it. The key term is 'to take into possession' (ירש), which points forward to vv. 19–21. At the same time, v. 18 presents a new and remarkable feature: the houses of Jacob and Joseph will be a flaming fire, which will consume the enemies of the house of Esau. This statement is significant for two reasons. First, the two houses are endowed with the punishing and consuming fire, which is usually an attribute of YHWH. Second, the houses of Jacob and Joseph, not YHWH, defeat the enemies of Esau. In this manner, the people of YHWH appear as the tool of YHWH's judgement, which is a task that in other prophetic texts has been given to foreign nations. The destruction of the house of Esau is total. There will be no survivors (שׂריד).

As a consequence of the judgement against the nations, the escape to Zion and the destruction of the 'local' enemies, the people of YHWH – referred to as the house of Jacob – will take control of the surrounding territories (cf. v. 19).[103] In the succeeding v. 20, the perspective becomes expanded. Not only the house of Jacob on Zion, but also the exiles of the Israelite army and the exiles of Jerusalem will participate in the invasion of the neighbour states. Yet the notion of these exiles indeed contrasts with the assumption that the only survivors of the enemy attack escaped in Zion. For this reason, Wolff regards the expanded perspective to be a later addition.[104] Nevertheless, it is significant that Zion now becomes the centre of a considerably larger state. Verse 21 underlines this by stating that those who have been saved (מושעים; cf. v. 17), will go up to Mount Zion to judge or rule (שׁפט) their neighbour and enemy, Mount Esau. Finally, the last statement emphasizes that the power over Esau and the surrounding territories does not come from the people itself, but rather from YHWH: 'The kingdom shall be YHWH's!'

108

THE DELIVERANCE OF ZION

Micah 4:11–13: daughter Zion defeats the nations

Micah 4:11–13 constitutes a minor unit that, like Obadiah, to some extent diverges from the views presented so far. The scenario is simple: many nations gather to fight against Zion (v. 11), but they do not understand that they are gathered to be destroyed (v. 12), and daughter Zion herself will crush the nations (v. 13). Although v. 11 does not clearly state whether the enemies have arrived of their own will (cf. Isa. 17:12),[105] v. 12 surely emphasizes that YHWH has gathered them.[106] Nevertheless, the nations do not understand the implied cause, as they do not know YHWH's plan. The notion of the divine plan (עצה) also occurred in Isaiah 14:24–7, where the plan encompasses the destruction of the Assyrians. In Micah, however, the content of the plan is further explained: 'YHWH has gathered them as sheaves to the threshing-floor.' The nations will be threshed and crushed. The parallel to Joel 4 is obvious. YHWH gathers the nations with one intention, and his judgement is depicted by means of threshing-metaphors (cf. Joel 4:13).

The special feature in Micah is the statement in 4:13. Whereas Isaiah, Ezekiel and Joel present YHWH as the destroyer of the enemies, Micah depicts how daughter Zion as the people of YHWH fulfils this task.[107] Although YHWH has prepared the judgement (v. 12), the inhabitants of Zion execute it (v. 13).[108] The people of YHWH, *not* the foreign nations, appear as the tool of divine judgement. Nevertheless, it is still YHWH who gives the inhabitants horn of iron and hoofs of bronze, so that they can crush the many nations.

Zephaniah 3:1–20: the ambiguous judgement and the poor remnant on Zion

The third chapter of Zephaniah presents one line of thought. The chapter consists of three minor units: the judgement against the political leaders of Zion and the nations (vv. 1–8); the purging of Zion and the surviving remnant (vv. 9–13); and the praise for salvation (vv. 14–20). The first part consists of two minor sub-units, where vv. 1–5 function as a prelude to vv. 6–8. The themes and structure of vv. 1–5 recall those of Isaiah 1:21–8. Following a cry of woe over the unjust and corrupt city (v. 1), vv. 2–4 introduce a long list of accusations for not trusting (בטח) YHWH. The accusations are mainly directed against the leading circles of the city: its officials, judges, prophets and priests. They have all failed to recognize their responsibility. In sharp contrast to this deceit, v. 5 illustrates that YHWH is righteous within his city; here, he daily renders his judgement.

Verse 6 recounts how YHWH has defeated the (hostile) nations, laid waste to their streets and made desolate their cities. Nevertheless, this divine power and activity does not seem to make any impression on the people

109

of YHWH or their leaders. They simply continue their evil deeds (v. 7). In addition, the urge to fear YHWH and accept correction may indicate a condition for preventing that YHWH gathers foreign nations to judge the city.[109] The people of YHWH apparently do not follow the invitation, because, in v. 8, YHWH announces judgement against them. Or does he? Verse 8 is highly problematic because of its ambiguity, a feature that also undergirds some of the most important passages in Isaiah. A close analysis reveals that the verse consists of four parts:

לכן הכו־לי נאם־יהוה ליום קומי לעד

Therefore wait for me, says YHWH, for the day when I arise as a witness. (Zephaniah 3:8a)

כי משפטי לאסף גוים לקבצי ממלכות

For my decision is to gather nations, to assemble kingdoms, (Zephaniah 3:8b)

לשפך עליהם זעמי כל חרון אפי

to pour out upon them my indignation, all the heat of my anger; (Zephaniah 3:8c)

כי באש קנאתי תאכל כל־הארץ

for in the fire of my passion all the earth shall be consumed. (Zephaniah 3:8d)

Line (a) begins with 'wait for me', a common phrase within the psalmodic literature, where it usually expresses the anticipation of YHWH's salvation.[110] The following 'the day when I arise as a witness' stands for the 'Day of YHWH'.[111] On that day, YHWH will stand as a witness against (or in support of?) his people, for his decision or judgement (משפט) is to gather nations and kingdoms (cf. Jer. 1:15). Line (c) presents the ambiguous statement: 'to pour out upon *them* my indignation'. Upon whom? It is either the people of YHWH and their arrogant leaders, or the nations and the kingdoms.[112] The interpretation of the plural suffix in עליהם may refer to the sinful people who were accused in 3:1–7. If this is so, the nations and kingdoms are gathered as an instrument of YHWH to judge them.[113] Alternatively, the suffix may refer to the nations and the kingdoms, which means that YHWH will judge them in front of his people as an act of salvation.[114]

In his commentary, Hubert Irsigler has a keen eye for this ambiguity. He suggests that the verse has originally expressed the judgement against the cruel leaders of Zion.[115] This judgement naturally follows the serious accusations in 3:1–7 and points forward to 3:11–13 about the surviving

110

THE DELIVERANCE OF ZION

remnant after the eliminations of the leaders. Eventually, however, some redactors have wished to establish a link to the judgements against the nations (Joel 4; Obad. 15–16; Mic. 4:11–13), as a result of which they have added line (d) to express the greater and cosmic judgement of all the earth. By means of this addition, the scene is set for 3:9–10, in which the peoples are turned into pious servants of YHWH.

In short, v. 8 witnesses a clash between two different scenarios: judgement against the sinful people of YHWH instrumented by the foreign nations, and judgement against the nations leading to the salvation of the people. It is difficult to say which one is the proper one, in particular because the context of the verse seems to support both interpretations. Indeed, this ambiguity seems similar to that of Isaiah 29:5–6. Zephaniah 3:1–13 is perhaps an even better illustration of two plausible but conflicting interpretations of the same message.

Even if 3:8 is understood as a judgement against the arrogant leaders of Zion, the enemy attack does not result in a total destruction of the city. As in Isaiah, Zephaniah 3:11–13 employs the concept of a surviving remnant. Whereas the remnant in Isaiah was the few who repented in time, the remnant in Zephaniah is negatively defined. The remnant is those who were not proudly exultant and haughty, as their leaders were.[116] As vv. 11–12 inform us, YHWH will remove the arrogant ones who believed in the autonomy of the city, and mercifully leave a remnant (השאיר) in the midst of his city. This remnant will be 'a people humble and lowly' (עם עני ודל) and be called 'the remnant of Israel' (שארית ישראל). In contrast to the deceitful leaders, the remnant will seek refuge in the name of YHWH. As in Isaiah 33:15, Zephaniah 3:13 describes the surviving people as righteous. They do not act wrongly and utter lies. On the contrary, they show the deepest trust in YHWH by resting and pasturing in peace (cf. Isa. 14:30a).[117] The people will live silently in the presence of YHWH. However, there is not, as in Isaiah 37:30–2, any anticipation that this remnant will become the root of a new, great and powerful people.

The last seven verses praise the time of salvation, which succeeds the divine judgement. Daughter Zion will rejoice (v. 14). The enemies are gone, and, instead of corrupt leaders, YHWH rules as the king of Israel in the midst of the city (v. 15). There is nothing to fear (v. 16). YHWH is in the midst of his people and rejoices over his renewed city (v. 17–18). The passage ends with a euphoric depiction of YHWH punishing the oppressors, gathering the weak and making them a blessing for the whole world (v. 19–20).

In Zephaniah 3:1–20, Zion is delivered, but only after massive charges against its leaders, who, along with the foreign kings, must be removed. On Zion, then, YHWH spares a small remnant. Because of its weakness, YHWH will take care of it. In sum, Zephaniah outlines a 'theology of the poor', in which YHWH brings salvation to the poor and afflicted, who remain on Zion.

Zechariah 12:1–13:1: Jerusalem and Judah

The last passage that will be examined occurs in the final chapters of the Book of Zechariah. It concerns two issues: the inviolability of Jerusalem (12:1–9) and the subsequent lament and purging of its inhabitants (12:10–13:1). According to 12:3, the enemy attack is ultimate: 'all the nations of the earth shall come together against it'. YHWH turns the city into a 'cup of reeling' for the surrounding peoples, who in their eagerness to storm Jerusalem include the surrounding region Judah in chaos (cf. Isa. 1:7; 36:1). Nevertheless, the cup signifies judgement for the attackers. YHWH will turn Jerusalem into a heavy stone; all who struggle to lift this stone will wound themselves incurably. In other words, the metaphors of the cup and the stone refer to the same matter: through Jerusalem, YHWH will fulfil his judgement against the foreign peoples.[118] Yet it remains uncertain whether YHWH has actually called for the nations to come. In any case, the attractiveness of the city tempts its enemies.

In v. 4, YHWH miraculously intervenes and strikes the enemies' horses and riders with panic and madness. This action entails recognition. But by whom? As noticed in other cases, those who recognize are the kingdoms (Isa. 37:20), the nations (Ezek. 38–9), Israel (Ezek. 38:22) or the people on Zion (Joel 2:27; 4:17). In Zechariah, however, it is the clans of Judah who say to themselves: 'The inhabitants of Jerusalem have strength through YHWH Sebaoth, their God.'[119] This recognition underlines the fact that Judah, as distinct from the rest of the attacking enemies, supports Jerusalem.[120] Verse 6 even illustrates how YHWH will turn Judah into a protective rampart of fire ('a flaming torch among sheaves'; cf. Obad. 18). Judah will consume all the surrounding peoples (*contra* Joel 2:3, where the enemies consume everything with fire!) and Jerusalem will remain in safety. In short, Judah becomes the instrument of YHWH's destruction of the enemies, while Jerusalem remains untouched (cf. Isa. 1:8).

Verse 7, too, confirms the special status of Judah. First, YHWH will save (הושיע) the tents of Judah, so that the glory of the house of David and the inhabitants of Jerusalem will not 'be exalted over that of Judah'. The exact meaning of this phrase remains unclear; it may be a commentary that Jerusalem, despite its inviolability, will not reveal the same arrogance as the Assyrian king in Isaiah 10:12.[121] In any case, in these verses of Zechariah, Judah plays a far more dominant role within the motif than in the texts examined so far. In these, focus has been the city (Isaiah, Joel, Obadiah, Micah and Zephaniah) or the land as a whole (Ezekiel). In Zechariah, YHWH's deliverance encompasses not only the city, but also Judah. Verse 8 expresses the special protection of the inhabitants of Jerusalem (cf. the term גנן, which is also employed in Isaiah 31:5; 37:35). Verse 9 concludes the preceding eight verses with this strong statement of YHWH: 'I will seek to destroy all nations that come against Jerusalem.' This promise definitely undergirds the inviolability of the city.

THE DELIVERANCE OF ZION

Within a Christian context, v. 10 is one of the most famous statements in the Old Testament. The notion of a human (or YHWH?), who is pierced and for whom the inhabitants will mourn, has been interpreted as a prophecy of Christ. The verse is tremendously difficult to understand within its present literary context – and it is beyond the scope of the present study to handle this complex issue.[122] Nevertheless, v. 10 begins with an outpouring of the spirit. YHWH declares: 'I will pour out [שפך] a spirit of compassion and supplication [רוח חן ותחנונים] on the house of David and the inhabitants of Jerusalem.'[123] Now, what does this spirit represent? As we have observed, in Joel 3:1–2, the spirit indicates a new and unmediated relationship to YHWH. In Zechariah, however, it seems to be a precondition for mourning the pierced one. Or does the spirit of compassion refer back to the deliverance of the inhabitants stated so strongly in v. 9? In Ezekiel, the outpouring of the spirit means that YHWH will never again hide his face (cf. Ezek. 39:29). Furthermore, in Isaiah 4:3–4, the spirit of judgement and burning (רוח משפט, רוח בער) should purge the survivors *after* their deliverance. Is the same at stake here that the inhabitants after deliverance from their enemies receive a spirit for repenting their sins? Unfortunately, the text is too vague to present any clear answer. Zechariah 13:1, however, does speak about a fountain (מקור) opened for the house of David and the inhabitants of Jerusalem to cleanse them from sin (חטאת) and impurity (נדה). Since a purging does take place, the spirit plausibly has the same function.[124] In any case, it is notable that in Isaiah, Joel, Ezekiel and Zechariah an outpouring of the spirit occurs after the deliverance.

Summing up: the deliverance of Zion

Our investigation has made clear that the prophets employ the motif of the deliverance of Zion and the defeat of the enemies in different ways and with different purposes. *Isaiah, Joel* and *Zephaniah* interpret the enemy attack as YHWH's judgement against his people and its leaders because of their sins. As a necessary precondition for deliverance, Isaiah calls for faith and conversion, whereas Joel depicts an act of repentance in the temple. In Isaiah, only a small and righteous remnant returns in time; in Joel, the people as a whole led by its priests repent; and in Zephaniah, YHWH removes the haughty leaders and leaves a remnant of the humble. All these texts deeply express the theological ambivalence that YHWH judges his people by summoning the enemies and delivers his people (or parts of it) from these enemies.

YHWH's judgement against his people is almost absent in *Ezekiel 38–9, Obadiah, Micah 4:11–13* and *Zechariah 12:1–13:1*. In these texts, the foreign nations gather not to judge, but to be judged. In Ezekiel, YHWH defeats Gog so that the nations will see his mighty power. In Obadiah, the destruction of Edom results in Jacob's and Joseph's dominance over the

113

surrounding regions. In Micah, the enemies gather in order for daughter Zion to crush them as sheaves on the threshing-floor. And in Zechariah, the judgement of the nations implies that Judah recognizes that Jerusalem – the inviolable city – takes her strength from YHWH. Finally, the scenario in Joel 4 illustrates an act of revenge. The defeat of the enemies is either the work of YHWH (Isaiah, Ezekiel, Joel and Zephaniah) or the work of the people/Judah as a consuming fire or as a threshing-sledge (Obadiah, Micah and Zechariah).

Since YHWH's judgement of his sinful people plays such a significant role in Isaiah, Joel and Zephaniah, some sort of cleansing occurs after the deliverance. In Isaiah and Zephaniah, the arrogant leaders are removed from the community of the righteous. Nevertheless, Isaiah also depicts how a spirit of judgement and burning purges the surviving remnant on Zion. The linking of sin-purging and spirit-outpouring also occurs in Joel and Zephaniah. In Joel, the spirit creates a new and direct relationship with YHWH, whereas in Zechariah, the outpouring of the spirit appears in connection with a fountain, which cleanses Jerusalem from her sin. In short, after the deliverance, the divine spirit transforms the surviving people by purging out their sins and offering knowledge of God.

Both Isaiah and Zephaniah use the concept of a surviving remnant on Zion. Whereas the remnant in Isaiah is the few righteous who were faithful and returned to YHWH, the remnant in Zephaniah is the weak ones who are left when the arrogant leaders have been removed. In addition, the remnant in Zephaniah indicates a theology of the poor where YHWH takes care of the afflicted, while the remnant in Isaiah becomes the root of a new, great and powerful people of YHWH.

In sum, after the defeat of the enemies, Zion will be filled with righteousness, knowledge, political independence and prosperity, and it will enjoy the presence of YHWH as king and God.

Notes

1 Cf. Childs 2001: 18–19 who notices the abrupt shifts in the imagery between vv. 4–6, 7 and 8–9.

2 This 'booth' (סֻכָּה) may allude to God's shelter or abode in Pss 27:5, 31:21 and 76:3; Isa. 4:5–6; see Wildberger 1991: 31; Williamson 2006: 71.

3 Cf. Hans Wildberger's conclusion: 'Yahweh, who is the Holy One of Israel, is the God who surrounded Israel with all good things before he demanded any responses in the form of obedience, and he was protecting them faithfully; it would have naturally followed that it is God alone who is responsible for keeping the activities of the people from resulting in a complete destruction, which would have otherwise followed, that the remnant which remained still had a chance to make it, but also, that the sins were not rooted in the trespasses of individual commandments, but rather in the total abandonment of fellowship with God' (Wildberger 1991: 32).

THE DELIVERANCE OF ZION

4 Cf. Wildberger 2002: 70. Against Eidevall 2009: 185 who regards its ambiguous motif as marginal within the Book of Isaiah.

5 For an analysis of Isa. 29:1–8 within the context of Isa. 28:1–29:8 and with a specific concern for the Zion motif, see Hoppe 2000: 58–63.

6 According to Laato 1998: 106, the use of the name 'Ariel' (that is, the altar hearth) is highly ironic. First, Jerusalem has now become like the sinful Canaanite city that David once conquered. Second, the feast mentioned in v. 1 points forward to YHWH's feast of sacrifice where the sacrificial altar will be Jerusalem itself.

7 Kaiser 1974: 267.

8 Cf. BHS; against NRSV; see below.

9 Hoppe 2000: 62: 'The prophet does not explicitly say that Jerusalem will be delivered but that the nations who make war against Zion will have their day of judgement. This does not mean that Jerusalem will escape unscathed but merely that the nations arrayed against it will also experience God's anger.'

10 Kaiser 1974: 263 renders it as 'the strangers', while Lutz 1968: 100 and Wildberger 2002: 63 have 'your presumptuous ones'. Blenkinsopp 2000: 39 changes it into 'your enemies' (צֶרָיִךְ); cf. Childs 2001: 211.

11 The term פקד has a quite wide semantic range, see further in Williams 1997: 657–63.

12 Childs 2001: 217.

13 Kaiser 1974: 268; Childs 2001: 217–18; Wildberger 2002: 69, 76–7.

14 Cf. Childs 2001: 218: 'The seeming incomprehensibility of God's first attacking and then delivering Jerusalem does not derive from a tendentious redactional process that tries to replace a "pessimistic" message with an "optimistic" one. Rather, the complexity of the oracle derives from its basic theological content. God both kills and brings to life. The description of God's plan provides explanatory reasons; it is not dependent on Israel's response, but is derived solely from the mystery of God's hidden counsel.' See also Seitz 1991: 124–5.

15 The weakness of the enemies has its counterpoint in the depiction of the army in Isa. 5:25–30, where none of the enemies is weary (אֵין עָיֵף) and none slumbers and sleeps.

16 Childs 2001: 138.

17 Wildberger 1997: 201.

18 See further in Childs 2001: 90–3.

19 Cf. Eidevall 2009: 53: 'A clear distinction is made between the rod beating those who dwell in Zion (v. 24b) and the whip wielded by YHWH (v. 26a), between the staff lifted by Assyria (v. 24b) and the one lifted by YHWH (v. 26b). Assyria and YHWH are pictured as opponents, equipped with similar weapons, bur far from equal. When YHWH strikes, Assyria is apparently unable to strike back.'

20 Kaiser 1983: 245.

21 BHS actually has 'the temple mount of Zion' (הר בית ציון); NRSV as many other translations follows the Masoretic qere by reading בת (cf. 1QIsaᵃ, LXX, Vulgate and Peshitta); cf. chapter 1.

22 For support of the former view, see Kaiser 1983: 251; Wildberger 1991: 456–7; for support of the latter view, see Clements 1980: 43; Blenkinsopp 2000: 261–3; Childs 2001: 97. See also Laato 1998: 105.

23 Wildberger 1991: 458 admits that 'the redactor, who placed this section at this point, doubtlessly interpreted vv. 33–4, along with the majority of modern interpreters, in reference to the failure of Assyria to take Jerusalem'. Eidevall even suggests the Babylonians and notices that the possibilities are legion. However,

THE ZION MOTIFS: BETWEEN JUDGEMENT AND SALVATION

'it is preferable to regard the passage – in its present context – as programmatical, and to presuppose a more general reference: As part of the preparations for a new era (11:1–9), YHWH will humble and "bow down" all enemies' (Eidevall 2009: 74).

24 Wildberger 2002: 70.

25 This verse indeed supports Childs' thesis that the 'shift in Isaiah's description of the role of Assyria does not derive from a change in the prophet's own attitude . . . but was a part of Yahweh's plan from the beginning (14:24–27)'.

26 This criticism concerns Babylon in Isa. 14 as well; cf. Berges 2012: 37: 'Because neither of them [Assyria and Babylon] understood themselves to be tools in the hand of Yhwh, considering themselves instead to be like God (cf. Isa. 10.5ff.; 14.12ff.; 37.23–24), they are both equally condemned.'

27 Cf. Childs 2001: 127.

28 In BHS, the notion עַל־הָרַי is vocalized in plural: 'on my mountains'. It only requires a small alteration of the vocalization to change the expression into singular 'on my mountain' to make the association with Zion clear. However, the editors of BHS do not indicate that there is textual evidence for this emendation. In addition, 'on my mountains' provides a crucial link to another important passage on the deliverance of God's people (cf. Ezek. 38–9 below).

29 The content of 14:24–7 runs parallel to that of 8:9–10, where those who plan Israel's destruction are an object of ridicule; cf. 'speak a word, but it will not stand'.

30 This imagery indeed alludes to the well-known motif of the good shepherd protecting his flock (cf. Ps 23; Isa. 40:11; Ezek. 34 [cf. below]); see Kaiser 1974: 55.

31 Wildberger 1997: 100 suggests that Isaiah employs 'dogmatic' sentences from the Zion theology, which took shape within Jerusalem's cultic liturgical celebrations.

32 See further in Barth 1977: 101 for a list of parallel elements.

33 Cf. Kaiser 1974: 309; Blenkinsopp 2000: 424; Wildberger 2002: 203. NRSV renders the term as 'burning-place'.

34 Cf. Laato 1998: 80–1: 'Isa 30:26 is antithetic to 1:5–6. It emphasizes that in the day of salvation Yhwh will dress (חֲבֹשׁ; cf., 1:6) the wounds of the people and heal the scars of the blows (מַכָּתוֹ; cf., 1:6).'

35 Laato 1998: 108, however, points out that Isa. 30:27–33 may contain prophecies of both doom and salvation: 'Yhwh comes from afar up to Jerusalem (28aα) with Assyria to destroy the transgressors among the people of Judah (cf., 10:5–6) but at the same time brings Assyria to the place where it will meet its destruction (30–31 and 33; cf., 10:16–19).'

36 Hayes 1963: 425.

37 Childs 2001: 233.

38 Childs 2001: 234: 'Israel's judgement and Israel's redemption cohere in God's purpose even when it often appears mysterious and incomprehensible to human logic.' Laato 1998: 109: 'Isa 34:4–5 explains, on the one hand, how the Assyrian threat is regarded as a cleansing whereby the sinners are annihilated from Zion and, on the other hand, how Assyria cannot conquer the city.'

39 See Hayes 1963: 425; von Rad 1965: 159; Lutz 1968: 154; Kaiser 1974: 316; Blenkinsopp 2000: 425; Wildberger 2002: 216; cf. NRSV. In contrast, Clements 1980: 32 and Childs 2001: 229 have: 'to do battle against Mount Zion'. For a critical review, see Childs 2001: 232–3.

40 The lion imagery is highly problematic, because the enemy army in Isa. 5:29 and Jer. 4:7 is also portrayed as a lion. However, it may be a subtle feature that YHWH is the lion *against* the Assyrians (cf. the reversal of motifs in 30:26–33). This is confirmed by 31:5, where YHWH rescues (הִצִּיל) his people from the

THE DELIVERANCE OF ZION

army from which there was no rescue (מציל; cf. 5:29); see Eidevall 1993; Laato 1998: 109.

41 Hoppe 2000: 68, however, argues that the bird imagery of v. 5 is most as ambiguous as the lion imagery: 'Bird circling a city under siege does not conjure up an image of protection – quite the opposite. It presents an image of scavengers looking for carrion . . . While the text does imply that God will not abandon Jerusalem, it also says that Jerusalem's salvation will be more like a timely escape than a glorious deliverance.'

42 Lutz 1968: 154.

43 Hayes 1963: 425.

44 Wildberger 2002: 224. Cf. Childs 2001: 234: 'Always after God's plan has been described and his will for Israel and the nations has been announced, then Israel is challenged to respond to the One who has embraced it.'

45 It is, however, uncertain what this stone represents. Kaiser 1974: 253 offers a review of the classical proposals, including the law of YHWH, the temple as the refuge of those faithful in YHWH, the Davidic monarchy, the city of Jerusalem, the saving work of YHWH, YHWH's relationship to his people and so on. Childs 2001: 209–10 argues that the stone 'serves as a metaphor unifying central themes that have been nuanced in different ways throughout the book . . . The symbolism of the stone encompasses the reality of the new community, a faithful remnant, which is a foretaste of the coming righteous reign of God and which is ushered in by the promised messianic rule of Zion.' For a recent and thorough study of this single verse, see Dekker 2007.

46 Lutz 1968: 153.

47 Cf. Childs 2001: 64: 'unless Judah, the people of God, understands itself as a theological reality – a creation of God and not merely a political entity – the state will have no future existence'.

48 See further in Hjelm 2004: 120–6.

49 Wildberger 2002: 160–1.

50 Cf. Ollenburger 1987: 116: 'The fundamental position of Isaiah's salvation message is then that Yahweh associates himself with Zion as the place of security and peace for those who do not attempt to secure their own or Jerusalem's defense through "practical", military means, leaving the matter of security absolutely in the hands of Yahweh.'

51 Laato 1998: 124–5; see also Webb 1990: 69.

52 For exhaustive studies of historical, literary, canonical and ideological aspects of these chapters, see, for instance, Childs 1967; Clements 1980; Seitz 1991; Laato 1998; Hjelm 2004. For a synopsis of the versions in Isa. 36:1–39:8 and 2 Kgs 18:13–20:11, see Wildberger 2002: 481–93. For a critical survey of the biblical Hezekiah narrative in light of Assyrian sources, see Hjelm 2004: 33–7. For a critical review of recent literature, see Clements 2011: 101–27.

53 Kaiser 1974: 389. In addition, Laato 1998: 80 argues that Hezekiah thereby presents the ideal behaviour towards God, which constitutes a focal point in Isaiah as a whole: 'Isaiah 1 together with Isaiah 39 . . . suggest to potential readers that they regard Isaiah 36–9 not only as the great salvation of Jerusalem but as offering the people of Judah two alternatives: to obey and prosper or to rebel and be destroyed.'

54 Cf. the outline in Childs 2001: 272–3.

55 See further in Blenkinsopp 2000: 476.

56 By adding אלהים; cf. 1QIsaᵃ and 2 Kgs 19:19 as well as LXX and Peshitta.

57 As Christopher Seitz has noticed, this goes against the concept of Zion's inviolability: 'The Hezekiah-Isaiah narratives maintain a focus on the figure of the king,

117

THE ZION MOTIFS: BETWEEN JUDGEMENT AND SALVATION

and it is clear that Zion's deliverance is the consequence of royal obedience as well as divine grace ... It is not Zion's inviolability that is at issue in the Hezekiah-Isaiah narrative traditions, but rather the singular example of divine grace and royal obedience that confirms Isaiah's earlier Zion proclamation and leads to Zion's wondrous deliverance' (Seitz 1991: 147).

58 For general studies of the concept of a remnant in Isaiah, see Hasel 1974: 216–372; Hausmann 1987: 139–70; Webb 1990: 72–81; Laato 1998: 74–85; Clements 2011: 206–11.

59 Wildberger 1991: 296–7 lists several proposals to understand and translate the phrase שאר ישוב: 'a remnant returns', 'the remnant, which returns', 'a remnant (at least) returns', or more threatening '(only) a remnant returns'. Concerning שוב, he further asks: 'Is it an internal or an external return to Yahweh ... ? Is the return in the sense of a conversion or an inward soul-searching? Or is it return in a secular sense [that is, returning from a battle] ... ? Finally, שוב also means to turn oneself away, to the side, so that the translation "a remnant turns itself away" would be theoretically possible.' According to Wildberger, we should understand the phrase as '[o]nly a remnant will turn back through all the catastrophes which will press in upon Israel, that is, only a remnant will return to Yahweh in faith'.

60 Kaiser 1983: 242.

61 Cf. Childs 2001: 95: '[Shearjashub] is both a sign of judgement "only a remnant will return" and also a concrete pledge of a promise ("surely there will be a [faithful] remnant") [cf. Wildberger above] ... The remnant will experience all the terrors of judgement, but the promise of new life through the destruction is affirmed.'

62 Kaiser 1974: 396–7.

63 Childs 2001: 34–5 rightly reads this passage of salvation as a response to that of judgement in Isa. 2–3; cf. Beuken 2003: 60; Williamson 2006: 305.

64 Blenkinsopp 2000: 203 argues that although the history of interpretation testifies to several serious attempts to read the צמח יהוה as a reference to the king, his reign or the coming Messiah, it is more likely – due to the parallelism with the fruit of the land – that the term refers to the prosperity after the desolation (cf. 37:30–2). Childs 2001: 36 states that although 'the literal rendering of the passage as a promise of renewed fertility and beauty to the land is not wrong ... the exalted style of the entire passage warns against a too flat and prosaic interpretation'. See also the review in Williamson 2006: 306–9.

65 NRSV has 'spirit of justice'.

66 See a list of references and allusions in Wildberger 1991: 171–2.

67 The booth (סכה) appears in Ps 31:21 as a place in which YHWH hides those who take refuge in him. Likewise, in Ps 27:5, the psalmist hides in his shelter (סך) in the day of trouble! Interestingly, YHWH's abode (סך) in Salem is parallel to his dwelling-place in Zion in Ps 76:3. Intriguingly, Berges 2012: 29 finds an allusion to the *Sukkot* festival (cf. Zech. 14:16–20): 'Zion/Jerusalem, the temporary "booth" in the cucumber field (Isa. 1.8), will become a lasting Sukkah as a salvific sign for Israel and the nations!' Likewise, Hoppe 2002: 67 states that 'the use of *sukhah* ("shelter") in 4:6 is deliberate. The prophet wants to contrast his vision of the future of Zion with the inflated rhetoric of the Zion tradition. What God will provide Judah for its protection is a humble hut rather than a monumental structure like the temple.'

68 Kaiser 1983: 43.

69 However, the rendering of ושביה is not straightforward. Wildberger 1991: 60–1 lists at least three proposals: first, as 'her captivity' (cf. LXX), which along with

THE DELIVERANCE OF ZION

Isa. 35:10 indicates that it is those who return from captivity (cf. Kaiser 1983: 40: 'those who return to her'); second, as שׁביה (cf. the footnote in BHS), that is, the inhabitants of Zion (cf. Isa. 10:24); third, as the remnant that returned to YHWH (cf. Isa. 10:21) in opposition to the sinners in v. 28 (cf. Wildberger; Blenkinsopp 2000: 179; Childs 2001: 15: 'her repentant ones'; Williamson 2006: 147: 'those in her who repent').

70 Isa. 33:14–16 appears to draw upon the sort of 'liturgy of the gate' that, for instance, occurs in Pss 15 and 24.

71 I regard 'Where is the one who counted the towers?' (איה ספר את־המגדלים) as a play on Ps 48:13[12], where the enemies are told to go around Zion and 'count its towers' (ספרו מגדליה). Since no one counts, the enemies have left; see chapter 5.

72 Here, Wildberger 2002: 304 finds an image play on older traditions: 'The ancient concepts concerning the mount of God that would not be shaken, even when stormed by enemy, reappear now, recast in an eschatological form.'

73 Childs 2001: 248.

74 Interestingly, Marvin Sweeney among others divides Isaiah into two main parts, Isa. 1–33 and 34–66, in which Isa. 33:14–24 closes the first part; Sweeney 2012: 270–1.

75 Zimmerli 1983: 298 regards Ezek. 38:1–9, 39:1–5 and 39:17–20 as the oldest elements which eventually have been altered, expanded and relocated within the present form. For a review of redaction-critical issues, see Block 1998: 424–32.

76 Zimmerli 1983: 300. Cf. Block 1998: 443: '[The mountains of Israel are] the homeland of Ezekiel and his fellow exiles, the land that Nebuchadrezzar's forces had devastated, and which will have lain desolate for a long time.'

77 Joyce 2009: 214–15. Interestingly, Daniel and Zech. 14 (?) also anticipate a final battle after the restoration of the land.

78 Nielsen & Strange 1988: 216 propose that the safety (בטח) in which the people dwell could be understood as an accusation. After returning from exile, the people have become *too* secure and need to be reminded of the sovereignty of their God. However, this proposal seems strained. As we noticed in Isa. 14:30a, the ideal is to lie down in safety (בטח) on Zion.

79 The image of the destruction of the weapons occurs in other texts as well. In Isa. 9:4[5], the boots and garments are burned, and in Pss 46 and 48 (the important Zion psalms), the bow, the spear and the sword are being broken, while the shields are burned. See also my analysis of Isa. 2:2–4 in chapter 10. The seven years indicate the massive quantity of weapons and thereby highlight the magnitude of YHWH's victory; see Joyce 2009: 216.

80 Joyce 2009: 215: 'Gog is not commissioned to serve as an agent of punishment – Babylon has already fulfilled that role for Ezekiel's age. Rather, Gog is raised up only to manifest YHWH's holiness.'

81 Block 1998: 463 identifies the latter group as 'the Mediterranean shores and island regions represented by Tarshish in 38:13, referring to the maritime forces allied with the land armies headed by the Anatolian hordes'.

82 Zimmerli 1983: 308.

83 Zimmerli 1983: 312.

84 Zimmerli 1983: 319 argues that Ezek. 39:21–2 looks back on the Gog pericope, while 39:23–9 reflects on the entire proclamation of the prophet (Ezek. 1–39).

85 Barton 2001: 35: 'YHWH's unpredictability, which can be perceived as threatening, also contains the seeds of hope, for he may turn out, when he acts, to do so in love and mercy just as much as in hostility and anger.'

86 Hoppe 2000: 137: 'The Day of the Lord can bring either judgement or salvation to Jerusalem. The people of Jerusalem will decide which by the quality of their repentance.'

87 See Crenshaw 1995: 135. In addition, John T. Strong has convincingly argued that Joel does not reject the ritual acts of piety as such. Since the rending of garments refers to the act of a funeral lamentation, the prophet is therefore 'poetically stating alternative fates: one can either repent, or realize the darkness of death intrinsic in the day of the Lord' (Strong 1996: 152).

88 For an illuminating comparison between Joel 2:12–17 and Moses' prayer in the golden-calf-episode, see Schmitt 2004.

89 It is noteworthy that Joel does not give any reasons for the enemy attack and the judgement of the people. Crenshaw 1995: 146 lists numerous proposals from modern scholarship to explain the transgressions of the people, including insincere cult, religious syncretism, excessive ritual and cultic self-sufficiency, breach of covenant, failed leadership, presumption arising from election, reluctance to be identified with a loser in battle and an impotent deity. In the end, however, Joel is as silent as the grave.

90 Wolff 1977: 57.

91 Wolff 1977: 65.

92 Wolff 1977: 66: 'the pouring out of God's spirit upon flesh means the establishment of new, vigorous life through God's unreserved giving of himself to those who, in themselves, are rootless and feeble, especially in the approaching time of judgement.'

93 Crenshaw 1995: 163–4. See also Barton 2001: 94–5.

94 An outpouring of the spirit also occurs in Ezekiel after the defeat of Gog. In Ezek. 39:29 – concluding the retrospective view on Ezek. 1–39 – YHWH promises that he will never again hide his face from his people, since he pours out his spirit upon the house of Israel. Interestingly, like in Joel, this outpouring of the spirit happens immediately after the people's acknowledgement of YHWH as their God (cf. Ezek. 39:28).

95 Wolff 1977: 66–7.

96 Barton 2001: 97.

97 Wolff 1977: 76: 'The name, being symbolic, is completely determined by the significance of the place where Yahweh's act of "judgement" (שׁפט vv 2b, 12b) will come to pass ... It is possible that the memory of the battle of king Jehoshaphat, as it may have been known to Joel from the account in 2 Chron. 20, could have had a part in determining the expression, but this cannot be demonstrated.'

98 The term 'refuge' (מחסה) is also used in connection with the booth in Isa. 4:6, concerning the fake refuge in Isa. 28:15 and 17, and in Ps 46:2[1]: 'God is our refuge and strength!'

99 Since Julius Wellhausen, scholars have commonly reversed vv. 15a and 15b so that v. 15b concludes the section on Edom and v. 15a begins the section on the nations; see further in Barton 2001: 118.

100 See the arguments, including a thirty-seven-page excursus on 'Drinking the Cup of Yahweh's Wrath' in Raabe 1995: 202–42.

101 Or in Philip Peter Jenson's review: 'A more contextual interpretation (cf. v. 15) is that the "you" in the first line refers to the Edomites (as in Amos 4:21; Jer. 49:12). Drinking then represents their feasting and celebration in the abandoned and conquered Jerusalem ... Their literal drinking will result in the opposite kind of metaphorical drinking ("the cup of punishment" Targ.)' (Jenson 2008: 23); see also Hjelm 2004: 144, 279.

THE DELIVERANCE OF ZION

102 See Wolff 1986: 65. Cf. Barton 2001: 152: 'This second interpretation is supported by the fact that "your" drinking has occurred "on my holy mountain", that is, in Jerusalem, which is hard to explain if Edom is being addressed.'

103 Wolff 1986: 60–1, 67. This interpretation, however, requires that we regard בית יעקב in v. 17b as the subject to יושו in v. 19.

104 Wolff 1986: 67. Likewise indicated in Renkema 2003: 211. Interestingly, the Edom-motif of Obadiah and Isa. 34; 63 is elaborated in 1 Macc. 5, in which Judas and his brothers will return to Zion; see Hjelm 2004: 279.

105 Wolff 1990: 140.

106 Allen 1976: 336: 'The magnet that drew [the nations] to Jerusalem was not merely their war lust but God's providential will.'

107 Jenson 2008: 154: 'In the metaphor Yhwh is the owner of the harvest, the sheaves are the nations, the threshing-floor is the field of battle and the thresher is the army of Jerusalem (daughter Zion).'

108 See further in Lutz 1968: 94.

109 Vlaardingerbroek 1999: 183.

110 Lutz 1968: 98.

111 Sweeney 2003: 180.

112 BHS proposes to read 'upon you' (עליכם) in order to make clear that the judgement concerns the people of YHWH. However, this proposal is not supported by textual evidence. See also Sweeney 2003: 181–2: '[Wilhelm] Rudolph goes so far as to argue that the original עליכם was deliberately changed to עליהם in the Second Temple period in order to divert judgement from Israel to the nations who were to serve as God's instrument of punishment. This is sheer invention on Rudolph's part. There is no textual support for such an emendation.'

113 For this interpretation, see Roberts 1991: 210, 215–16; Berlin 1994: 133.

114 For this interpretation, see Sweeney 2003: 179.

115 Irsigler 2002: 342, 356–7, 361.

116 Cf. Berlin 1994: 'Jerusalem's sins will no longer be held against her, for those causing the sins, the haughty elite, will have been removed, and only the humble God-fearing folk will remain.'

117 The parallels to Isa. 14:30a and 32b are obvious. In Isaiah, the people are also portrayed as poor and needy (דלים, עניים); the same terms for to pasture and to lie down are used (רעה, רבץ); and the weak find refuge (חסה) here; see further in Irsigler 2002: 398–9.

118 Lutz 1968: 18.

119 Cf. the note in BHS in which לי ישבי is emended into לישבי; cf. Lutz 1968: 11; Conrad 1999: 181; NRSV. Meyers & Meyers 2009: 307 have 'There is strength for the leaders of Jerusalem in Yahweh of Hosts their God'. Petersen 1995: 155, however, renders the statement without emendations: 'My strength resides in the inhabitants of Jerusalem.' He argues that Judah will find support in Jerusalem, because YHWH already supports her.

120 Conrad 1999: 181–2.

121 Petersen 1995: 116.

122 Petersen 1995: 120–1; Conrad 1999: 183; Meyers & Meyers 2009: 337–40 do not present any clear solution. Petersen, tentatively, suggests reading the verse within the context of the attack on Jerusalem. If so, the verse could indicate a kind of ritual act, that is, child sacrifice; cf. 2 Kgs 3:27.

123 Petersen 1995: 106 translates the phrase into 'a favorable spirit, in answer to (their) supplications'. Meyers & Meyers 2009: 307 have 'a spirit of favor and supplication'.

124 Lutz 1968: 210.

8

THE DEFEAT OF ZION AND THE EXILE

In this chapter, we shall investigate the cases in which YHWH does not save his chosen city against the attacking enemies, but rather leaves it unprotected and open to invasion and destruction. The chapter seeks to establish a counter-motif to the ideas and images that we examined in the previous chapter. We shall begin with an analysis of Jeremiah 6:1–9, which – perhaps even deliberately – confronts and reverses the main features of the classical Zion motif. This analysis will provide the foundation for a closer look at Jeremiah as well as Ezekiel, Micah and Zechariah.

As noted, Isaiah has surprisingly little to say about the destruction of Zion. There are some general allusions in Isaiah 39 and spread throughout 40–66, which indicate that a destruction will take or has taken place. Nevertheless, only two small passages – *Isaiah 6:11–13* and *64:9–10* – describe the terrible catastrophe more closely. Isaiah 6:11–13 foreshows the desolation of the land, the waste cities and the emptiness in the midst of the land. No people will live there; those who remain will be burned. Instead, YHWH will send some people far away. Isaiah 64:9–10 is part of a prayer to YHWH that he will support his people in the present distress: 'Your holy cities have become a wilderness, Zion has become a wilderness, Jerusalem a desolation. Our holy and beautiful house, where our ancestors praised you, has been burned by fire, and all our pleasant places have become ruins.'[1] It is this ultimate destruction to which we now turn in the non-Isaianic prophetic books.

Jeremiah 6:1–9: the destruction of daughter Zion

Jeremiah 6:1–9 constitutes a minor unit within the larger context of 4:5–6:30, which intensely accounts for the danger of invasion. Peoples are urged to flee (v. 1). YHWH himself will destroy daughter Zion (v. 2) and enemies have surrounded the city (vv. 3–4). However, the presence of enemies is not without cause, for the city is accused of fostering violence and oppression (vv. 6–7). Accordingly, YHWH threatens to turn the city into an uninhabited land (v. 8) and to glean the remnant of Israel as a vine (v. 9).

THE DEFEAT OF ZION AND THE EXILE

Surprisingly, it is the sons of Benjamin who are urged to flee. However, the flight will take place from the midst of Jerusalem. Apparently, the 'fleeing' motif undergoes a transformation throughout Jeremiah 4:5–6:30. In 4:5–6, the trumpet sounds, peoples are urged to gather in the fortified cities and a warning sign is raised: towards Zion![2] In 4:29, however, the entire city (כל־העיר)[3] flees to hide in the thickets and in the mountains, while the city is left without inhabitants. Likewise in 6:1, the people flee to Tekoa, south of Jerusalem. The main capital in particular is the target of the enemy attack. The urge to escape occurs in 4:6, 4:29 and 6:1 against the background of a very specific, terrifying observation: evil (רעה) comes from the north and will result in a great destruction (שבר גדול).[4]

Verse 2 contains one of the strongest expressions of YHWH's wrath against his people in the Old Testament: 'I will destroy daughter Zion!'[5] This verse, which may serve as the headline for Jeremiah 1–25 as a whole, forms a sharp contrast to the main thought of the classical Zion motif:

נותרה בת־ציון

Daughter Zion is left. (Isaiah 1:8)

דמיתי בת־ציון

I will destroy daughter Zion. (Jeremiah 6:2)

Verses 3–5 portray the invasion. The shepherds and their flocks will surround Zion (cf. 4:17), and rise against her to attack and destroy her palaces.[6]

Verse 6 contains two striking features. First, YHWH commands that the enemies will cut down trees and cast up a siege ramp against Jerusalem (שפכו על־ירושלם סללה). In Isaiah 37:33–5 – one of the most important passages concerning the protection of Zion – YHWH ensured that the king of Assyria would *not* cast up a siege ramp against the city (לא־ישפך עליה סללה). This is indeed another illustration of the difference between the classical Zion motif and the main motif of Jeremiah. Second, Jerusalem is a city that must be 'punished' (הפקד).[7] As we may recall, this term forms the turning point of Isaiah 29:1–8. Here, however, it is clearly addressed to daughter Zion in terms of judgement.

Verse 7 spells out the reason behind the judgement: the midst of the city is full of wickedness, violence and destruction, and sickness and wickedness are everywhere. As Douglas Jones rightly asserts, 'it is not a question simply of particular sins but of her total condition'.[8] Verse 8 offers a last chance for salvation – 'take warning' – so that YHWH will not turn from his people in disgust and make the land into a desolation without inhabitants (cf. 4:7). This opportunity to prevent the disaster from happening recurs many times throughout Jeremiah, and we shall return to it later. Verse 9 contains a final and significant contrast to the classical Zion motif as revealed in

123

Isaiah: the remnant of Israel (שארית ישראל) will not be saved, but gleaned as grapes on a vine. The gleaning represents divine judgement. It is not clear who the grape-gatherer is; however, the plural form of 'glean' (יעוללו) indicates that it is the enemies (cf. v. 6).[9] No one will survive, for the hand of grape-gatherers will return to the vine to ensure that its branches are empty of fruit. Nothing is to be left.

In sum, Jeremiah 6:1–9 presents three major themes that we shall pursue in the following three sections:

(a) YHWH's or the enemies' destruction of Jerusalem;
(b) the people's opportunity to prevent the evil disaster; and
(c) Jeremiah's rather peculiar concept of a surviving remnant (the good and bad figs).

As we shall see, these themes differ significantly from the main elements of the classical Zion motif.

The fall of Jerusalem

In a condensed form, *Jeremiah 9:10–15[11–16]* reveals the main characteristics of Jeremiah's portrait of the great destruction. In v. 10, YHWH thunders: 'I will make Jerusalem a heap of ruins [גלים], a lair of jackals [מעון תנים]; and I will make the towns of Judah a desolation [שממה], without inhabitant.' In other words, the disaster encompasses not only a destruction of the capital and its surrounding cities, but also the annihilation of its inhabitants; instead of peoples, jackals will live in the ruins (cf. Jer. 10:22). Verse 11 considers what reasons could lie behind this ruination: 'Why is the land ruined and laid waste like a wilderness?' In his response, YHWH offers no fewer than five reasons (vv. 12–13) followed by five different kinds of judgement (vv. 14–15).[10] Desolation has come upon the people of YHWH because they have forsaken (עזב) his *torah*, they did not obey his voice and they did not walk in accordance with his will; they have stubbornly followed their own hearts and, even worse, worshipped idols, namely the Baals. Because of these serious abominations, YHWH will give them poisonous food and water, he will scatter (פוץ) them among peoples that they do not know and he will send the sword after them until he has consumed them. In short, idolatry and disobedience against YHWH's *torah* are the main reasons behind the desolation and scattering of the people.[11]

A series of laments follows this bleak prospect. In v. 18, a sound of wailing is heard from Zion: the inhabitants have left their land. Again, we encounter the motif that it is the whole land that is abandoned; furthermore, the idea of an exile is even more significant than in v. 15. In addition, the use of the term עזב points backward to v. 12. As the people have abandoned YHWH's *torah*, they will abandon their land and houses. As an important

THE DEFEAT OF ZION AND THE EXILE

feature in Jeremiah, this 'logic of retribution' appears in 5:19 too.[12] The people will ask why all this is happening and YHWH declares: 'As you have forsaken [עזבתם] me and served foreign gods in your land, so you shall serve strangers in a land that is not yours.' The same motif and structure recur in Jeremiah 16:10–13.

In *19:3–9*, the people's idolatry is closely linked to the destruction of the city. These verses contain an interpretation of a symbolic act that the prophet Jeremiah makes to illustrate the fate of the people and their city. In v. 3, addressing Judah and the inhabitants of Jerusalem, Jeremiah proclaims that YHWH will bring a disaster (רעה) upon this place. 'This place' (המקום הזה) refers to the city of Jerusalem and occurs five times throughout this small passage. Verses 4–5 present the charges against the inhabitants, which include that they have forsaken (עזב) YHWH. They have profaned his holy city by making offerings to other gods and by building high places for child offerings to the Baals. None of this has YHWH asked for, and consequently judgement is near (vv. 6–9). In these days, this place will no longer be called Topheth or the valley of the son of Hinnom.[13] Rather, the place will be called the Valley of Slaughter, where YHWH will judge his people. Verse 7 focuses on the punishment of the inhabitants: their plan (עצה) will be made void (cf. the Assyrians' fate in Isa. 8:10); they will fall by their enemies' sword; and their dead bodies will become food for wild animals (cf. Gog's fate in Ezek. 39:4). According to v. 8, YHWH will make his city a horror; it will be hissed at (in contrast to Joel 2:27); and everyone who passes it will be horrified.

Finally, v. 9 pictures a terrifying scenario: YHWH will make his people eat their own children and each other. This form of cannibalism is indeed a strong expression of how people may react during a siege (cf. 2 Kgs 6:24–7:20; Lam. 4:10) and furthermore forms an ironic requital for the sacrifice of children (cf. vv. 4–5).[14] However, viewed within a canonical context, Jeremiah seems to employ a prophecy-fulfilment-motif.[15] Penalties for disobedience against YHWH's covenant are preserved in a series of covenant curses in the Pentateuch, including Leviticus 26:27–9: 'But if . . . you disobey me, and continue to be hostile to me, . . . you shall eat the flesh of your sons, and you shall eat the flesh of your daughters.'[16] In the end, YHWH's judgement against his people derives from their covenantal infidelity.

Within Jeremiah as a whole, several of the themes in 19:3–9 have already been presented in *7:30–8:3*. Here, the accusations also include idolatry and a profaned cult (vv. 30–1). In v. 32, Topheth will become a burial ground – a mass grave that will be full of the dead bodies of the inhabitants. In v. 33, the image of the bodies becoming food for the birds of the air and animals of the earth reappears.[17] This imagery may recall that of Ezekiel 39:4 and 39:17–20, where Gog and his army are consumed by vultures and wild animals. However, whereas Ezekiel assigns this fate to the enemies, Jeremiah assigns it to the people of YHWH. Likewise, Jeremiah 8:1–2

125

informs readers that the bones will be brought out of the tombs and spread like dung on the surface of the ground. Interestingly, this fate is reversed in Ezekiel 39:11–16, in so far as the bones are gathered and buried in the valley of Hamon-gog. Still, the passages share the motif that the destruction is so great that the dead bodies will cover the entire land. Furthermore, 8:3 touches upon the concept of a surviving remnant. Yet the situation is so terrible that the remnant (השארית) that remains in all the places to which they have been driven will prefer death to life; a parody of Deuteronomy 30:19.[18] That the survivors now live in other places indicates that YHWH's judgement against his city and its sinful cult implies a total removal of the surviving remnant to a wholly new place.

That YHWH has turned his back on his people emphasizes the desolation of the city, its land and its inhabitants. As an illustration, *Jeremiah 12:7–12* begins with YHWH's statement: 'I have forsaken [עזבי] my house, I have abandoned my heritage.' The heritage (נחלה) can refer to his temple, his city, his land or even to his people (cf. Joel 2:17), whose fate he has set in the hands of their enemies.[19] Crucially, YHWH himself has left his people's fate in the hands of their enemies. Verses 8–9 take up different metaphors concerning the same matter: the people of YHWH have become a rebellious lion and a hyena. YHWH thus calls for the wild animals: 'Come, assemble, eat!' The parallel to Ezekiel 39:17 is apparent. Both passages refer to the animals as כל חית השדה and both use the terms 'to assemble' (אסף) and 'to eat' (אכל). Like Jeremiah 6:3–5, vv. 10–11 use the image of the foreign shepherds that trample down YHWH's vineyard and turn it into a desolate wilderness (מדבר שממה).[20] The term שממה is used three times within these two verses to highlight the ultimate desolation.[21] In v. 12, the sword of YHWH will – like the grape picker in 6:9 – devour from one end of the land to the other. No one will be saved.

Jeremiah 1–25 as a whole concerns the destruction of Jerusalem, Judah and the land. Throughout these chapters, this very theme is taken up again and again. Initially, 1:15 opens with the foreign kings from the north, who have surrounded the city; 4:5–6:30 speaks of imminent disaster; and towards the end of the twenty-five chapters, the threat becomes extremely concrete. The enemies are no longer portrayed as anonymous kings or by means of metaphors (animals, shepherds). In Jeremiah 20, there are references to Babylon, and in Jeremiah 21, the enemies are consequently referred to as the Babylonians or the Chaldeans under the rule of King Nebuchadrezzar. In the following, we shall take a closer look at 21:4–10 and 25:8–14, which envision the culmination of the destruction.

Jeremiah 21:4–10 offers a response to how the city will behave when threatened by the imminent danger of invasion. As we observed in the preceding chapter, according to Isaiah 30:15, the inhabitants should stay calm and wait for YHWH's salvific intervention. In Jeremiah, on the contrary, the inhabitants are told to surrender. The situation here is highly

THE DEFEAT OF ZION AND THE EXILE

critical. YHWH will defuse the weapons of his people (v. 4) and – through the enemies – he will fight against his people with an outstretched hand and a mighty arm (v. 5).[22] As the enemies were made into dust by YHWH's burning wrath in Isaiah 30:27–33, this judging wrath is turned against the people; in Jeremiah, the decision will not be changed. Verse 7 makes clear that such a sudden intervention that saved the city in Isaiah will not occur. Instead, YHWH will give Jerusalem's king and his people into the hands of Nebuchadrezzar and his army and they will show no mercy. Furthermore, vv. 8–10 clearly present two possible scenarios (cf. Deut. 30:15): either you stay in the city and get killed, or you leave it and survive. Verse 9 emphasizes the central motif in Jeremiah that there will be left no survivors in the besieged city.[23] Finally, v. 10 summarizes the fate of the city: this city (עיר הזאת) is doomed to disaster (רעה), for it will be given into the hands of the Babylonian king, who will burn it with fire.

The defeat reaches its climax in *25:8–14*. Verse 8 briefly introduces YHWH's main charge against Jerusalem: 'because you have not obeyed my words'. The succeeding portrayal of punishment in vv. 9–11 compiles several of the motifs and images that have been used throughout Jeremiah 1–25. This indicates that the judgement reaches its final end in this passage.[24] Verse 9 reiterates that it is YHWH who calls and brings the tribes from the north; King Nebuchadrezzar of Babylon is even referred to as 'the servant of YHWH'.[25] The enemies will invade both Judah and the nations around her, and leave them as an everlasting disgrace. Verse 9 thereby recalls the image of the total destruction of the land. As in 7:34, YHWH silences the sound of mirth (cf. v. 10). However, v. 11 constitutes the most interesting element of the passage. The first clause emphasizes the destruction: 'this whole land shall become a ruin and a waste'. Yet the second clause outlines the implications of the defeat: 'these nations shall serve the king of Babylon seventy years'. Jeremiah 5:19 and 17:4 have already foretold that the people will serve a foreign power, but 25:11 gives this foreign power a name and provides a limited period of time. Verse 12 briefly announces the end of this period: after seventy years, YHWH will 'visit' (פקד) Babylon, punish its inhabitants and make their land an everlasting waste. We shall return to the symbolism of the seventy years below. For now, it is important to notice that YHWH's judgement against his people involves not only a destruction of the cities and the land, but also a removal of the surviving inhabitants into captivity under a foreign power.

The possible prevention of the destruction

In Jeremiah, it is often stated that the sins of the inhabitants of Jerusalem have caused the destruction. They had been given a chance to repent and prevent its realization. *Jeremiah 25:4–7* illuminates this scenario. Verses 4–6 inform us that YHWH has persistently sent his prophets to make his

127

THE ZION MOTIFS: BETWEEN JUDGEMENT AND SALVATION

people repent. Verse 5 clearly sketches the basic causality at stake: 'turn [שׁובו] now, every one of you, from your evil way and wicked doings, and you will remain [שׁבו] in the land that YHWH has given to you and your ancestors from of old and forever'. In other words, turning away from evil deeds will secure the future of the land; this 'turn' also implies an abolition of idolatry and false worship (cf. v. 6). If the people do this, YHWH will not hurt them. However, v. 7 strongly questions the realization of this future vision by the refrain 'yet you did not listen to me' (לא־שׁמעתם אלי).[26] As Leslie Allen has pointed out, the failure to pay attention to the prophetic message is the ultimate sin in Jeremiah (cf. 6:17; 7:13, 25–6).[27] Moreover, as a bridge to the Babylonian invasion in 25:8–14, 25:7 contends that the people's provocation of YHWH will lead to their own harm (רע).

In 26:1–6, the prophet Jeremiah stands in the court of the temple and proclaims what YHWH commands him to say. In v. 3, YHWH speaks and he apparently still hopes for a change of attitude among his people: 'It may be that they will listen, all of them, and will turn [ישׁמעו ושׁבו] from their evil way.' In that case, YHWH will change (נחם) his mind about the disaster that he intends to bring upon them. Verses 4–6 conversely reveal the consequence if his people do not listen and do not obey his *torah*. They will suffer the same fate as the temple in Shiloh (i.e. abandonment, cf. Jer. 7:14–15; Ps 78:60); in short, this city (העיר הזאת) – that is, Jerusalem – will become a curse among the nations.[28]

A similar structure undergirds a part of the potter's parable in *Jeremiah 18:7–12*. In vv. 7–10, YHWH addresses an anonymous nation or kingdom, which he will pluck up, break down and destroy. However, if this nation turns (שׁב) from its evil deeds, YHWH will change (נחם) his mind about the disaster. The return to YHWH will even result in prosperity in the land, but only if the people do good deeds. In vv. 11–12, this pattern is transferred directly to Judah and the inhabitants of Jerusalem. Since YHWH plans to do evil (רעה) against them, the call for repentance is sounded: 'turn [שׁובו נא] now, all of you from your evil way, and amend your ways and your doings'. The use of אישׁ emphasizes that *everyone* is responsible for the imminent danger of invasion and must seize this opportunity for salvation.[29] As in 25:7, however, this return fails, because everyone will instead follow their own plans and act according to their stubborn hearts.

The passage on the holiness of the Sabbath, *17:19–27*, illustratively grasps this relation between evil deeds and disaster vis-à-vis good deeds and peace.[30] At the gates of Jerusalem, the prophet Jeremiah will admonish the people to hallow the Sabbath (vv. 19–22); yet as so often before the result is poor: 'they did not listen' (לא שׁמעו). Verses 24–7 present two possible outcomes in two conditional clauses. According to vv. 24–6, 'if you listen to me' (אם־שׁמע תשׁמעון אלי), then the city will become an international centre and will be inhabited forever (ישׁבה העיר־הזאת לעולם). Verse 27 pictures the opposite motif: 'if you do not listen to me' (אלי אם־לא תשׁמעו), YHWH

THE DEFEAT OF ZION AND THE EXILE

will kindle a fire in the city's gates and the palaces of Jerusalem will be burned down.

The great desolation could have been prevented, but the people failed to repent. In Jeremiah, as we have seen, there is a clear connection between the disobedience of the people and the destruction of the city and the land. This connection is plainly and straightforwardly presented in 4:18 about the people's behaviour: 'your ways and your doings have brought this upon you' (דרכך ומעלליך עשו אלה לך). Nevertheless, although the call for repentance resounds throughout Jeremiah 1–25, I do not think there is much reality in it after all: the people will not listen. In contrast to this (unrealistic) call to repent, 4:28 offers a different view on these matters.[31] According to this verse, what YHWH has planned to do (i.e. to make the land a desolation), will not be changed; he will not change his mind and turn back.[32] Here the great desolation actually appears to be unpreventable. In addition, this verse shows a different image of God than that which we encountered in Joel. What formed the root of hope in Joel – that YHWH may change his mind and turn back – is not an option in Jeremiah 4:

כי־דברתי זמתי ולא נחמתי ולא־אשוב ממנה

For I have spoken, I have purposed; I have not relented nor will I turn back. (Jeremiah 4:28b)

מי יודע ישוב ונחם

Who knows? He might turn and relent. (Joel 2:14a)

Apparently, YHWH judges and saves his people in two different ways. In Joel and the classical Zion motif, YHWH changes his mind and leaves a remnant of faithful 'returners' while all others perish. In Jeremiah and the dynamic Zion motif, YHWH will destroy everything and eventually allow a group, which has survived in foreign captivity, to return to a new Zion. In sum, the option that YHWH will change his mind by means of his people's repentance was fundamental to the salvation announcement in Joel. In Jeremiah, the plan of disaster will not be changed.

The good and the bad figs

In Jeremiah 8:3, we heard that the survivors, exiled to foreign places, would prefer death to life. Yet a surprisingly different image is found in *24:1–10*'s parable about the good and the bad figs. The passage offers an allegory that sharply illustrates the contrast between two groups: those who are brought into exile and those who remain in the land or flee to Egypt.[33] It consists of three minor units: vv. 1–3 form an introduction and display the riddle; vv. 4–7 concern the good figs; and vv. 8–10 concern the bad figs.

129

In vv. 1–3, YHWH shows the prophet Jeremiah two baskets of figs in front of the temple. According to v. 1, this happens after the deportation of King Jeconiah and Jerusalem's upper class, which is usually dated to 597 BCE by historical-critical scholars. One basket contains very good figs (תאנים טבות מאד) and the other contains very bad figs (תאנים רעות מאד) – so bad that they are inedible.

YHWH likens the Judean exiles (גלות יהודה), whom he has sent from this place to the land of the Chaldeans, to the good figs. The phrase 'I have sent' (שלחתי) underlines the fact that the removal and deportation of a part of Judah is the work of YHWH.[34] Good things await the exiled for YHWH will make them return (השבתים) to their land and he will care for them. In other words, the exile is a limited period of time (cf. 25:11–12). After the return from exile and the restoration of the land, the people will receive a new heart to know YHWH. They will understand that 'I am YHWH' (cf. e.g. Ezek. 38–9), they will be his people and YHWH will be their God, and they will return (ישבו) to him with all their heart.[35] Interestingly, this 'return' appears not to take place as a condition for salvation; rather, it appears as a *consequence* of salvation. It thereby illustrates Wildberger's point in his commentary to Isaiah 31:6 that the return follows the proclamation of salvation (see above in chapter 7).

Just as good things will happen to the good figs, evil things will happen to the bad figs. That is 'the remnant of Jerusalem [שארית ירושלם] who remain [הנשארים] in this land, and those who live in the land of Egypt', those who are not in Babylonian captivity.[36] The fate of those who remain will become a horror for all the foreign nations, for they will be the victims of punishment – sword, famine and pestilence – and they will perish. Verse 10 thereby recalls the central motif of Jeremiah that the land will be completely empty of inhabitants. As in Jeremiah 21:8–10, the people of YHWH will only survive in exile, while those who remain in the city, in the land or in Egypt will be killed. Here we can notice a significant difference to the classical Zion motif as explored in Isaiah. Isaiah 36–7 and Jeremiah 1–25 obviously depict different events within their distinctive narrative settings (Isaiah that of 701 BCE; Jeremiah that of 597/87 BCE), and they reveal important differences regarding their concepts of a remnant. In Isaiah 37:30–2, a new people will emerge from the surviving remnant on Mount Zion, while in Jeremiah 24:4–7, the creation of a new people will happen *after* their return from foreign places. Accordingly, the classical Zion motif of Isaiah posits a positive image of the remnant on Mount Zion – a future hope – whereas in Jeremiah, the remnant of Jerusalem will be extinguished and replaced by the 'good figs' who have survived in exile.

Furthermore, *Jeremiah 29:10–20* modifies the theme of the two kinds of figs, yet without explicitly mentioning the good. First, YHWH addresses the good (figs) living in exile, pictured as a state of welfare in which YHWH cares for his people. Yet according to v. 10, YHWH will visit (פקד)

them after seventy years and fulfil his promise of bringing them back (הֹשִׁיב) to 'this place', that is, Jerusalem. That the exile lasts seventy years was foreshadowed in 25:11–12. As indicated above, I perceive the number of years as a symbol: seventy designates a whole (like the forty years in the wilderness) and, in addition, such a long period of time implies that it is *a whole new population* that returns to Zion.[37] The old and sinful people who had been deported to Babylon is now gone; instead, a new and purified people return to the city and their land. The reason for the return is not clear, because there seem to be two distinctive views at stake.[38] On the one hand, vv. 10–11 highlight YHWH's plans (הַמַּחֲשָׁבֹת) of peace, future and hope. On the other hand, vv. 12–13 inform readers that when the people cry to YHWH and seek him, he will hear and let them find him. In short, the former verses depict salvation in terms of grace – YHWH's decision – whereas the latter verses depict salvation in terms of repentance and compensation. However, the outcome remains the same, when v. 14 proclaims that YHWH will restore (שַׁבְתִּי) the fortunes of his people (cf. Joel 4:1; Zeph. 3:19–20), gather them and bring them back to (exactly) the place from which their ancestors seventy years earlier had been sent into exile.

Like 24:1–10, 29:16–19 sharply contrasts with those who remain in Jerusalem, that is, King Zedekiah and his people, with those who have been deported (however, hardly King Jehoiachin; cf. the curse against him in Jer. 22:28–30). As 24:8–10, vv. 17–18 assign them the fate of sword, famine and pestilence. Like many other passages, v. 19 offers one particular reason: 'they would not listen' (לֹא שָׁמְעוּ). By contrast, according to v. 20, the exiled, whom YHWH has sent away from Jerusalem to Babylon, will listen and obey.

Summing up: the destruction and exile in Jeremiah

Most significant in Jeremiah is his proclamation of total destruction. YHWH himself stands behind it: the city will be turned into ruins; the land will be turned into desolation; and the entire land will be empty of inhabitants. It is persistently stressed that no one will survive, the remnant of Jerusalem will be crushed and only a small group of 'good figs' will survive in Babylon. This imagery certainly provides the foundation for the myth of the empty land.[39] The chosen land is left uninhabitable and only the return of the righteous ones from exile will make the desert bloom.

In general, I think that this perspective of Jeremiah differs in three ways from that of the classical Zion motif of Isaiah (see chapter 7). First, according to the classical motif, Zion is left as an invulnerable place, whereas Jeremiah anticipates a total destruction of the city and the land. Second, the classical Zion motif contains the element of a faithful remnant that repents to YHWH and in time, whereas no one returns in Jeremiah and – despite YHWH's innumerable efforts – the people continue their evil

THE ZION MOTIFS: BETWEEN JUDGEMENT AND SALVATION

deeds. Third, the classical Zion motif regards the cleansed remnant on Mount Zion as the root of a new people, whereas the new people in Jeremiah will emerge out of exile as a new generation.

The destruction and exile in Ezekiel

The destruction of Jerusalem also constitutes a pivotal point in the Book of Ezekiel. Following the marvellous account of the call of Ezekiel, Ezekiel 4–5 offers a detailed depiction of that destruction. Initially, we shall examine *Ezekiel 5:5–17*. This passage can be divided into three minor parts: vv. 5–7 about the sinful Jerusalem; vv. 8–9 about YHWH's intervention; and vv. 10–17 about the content and nature of the punishment. Verse 5 depicts the present condition of the city. YHWH states: 'This is Jerusalem; I have set her [שמתיה] in the centre of the nations, with countries all around her.' Two things are important here. First, the city has been founded by YHWH; second, the imminent event – YHWH's judgement – will take place not in some remote place, but in the centre of the world.[40] Since v. 5 attaches this great importance to the city, the greater is its fall in vv. 6–7. According to these verses, the inhabitants have been rebellious, rejected YHWH's ordinances (משפט) and not followed his statutes. Their covenantal infidelity is emphasized, as the people of YHWH are judged to be even more wicked than all the nations around them.[41] Against this background, YHWH enters the stage (cf. vv. 8–9): 'I am also coming against you [עליך גם־אני]; I will execute judgements among you in the sight of the nations.' YHWH will treat Jerusalem as he has never done before and never will do again. In sum, the imminent disaster is unique, and its like has never been seen before.

Verses 10–17, then, carefully depict the judging act of YHWH through a long series of discrete sentences. Like Jeremiah 19:9, v. 10 indicates cannibalism, and similar to Jeremiah, it is likely to be seen as a prophetic fulfilment of YHWH's covenantal curses (cf. Lev. 26:29; Deut. 28:53–7), in particular, the terrifying image of YHWH pursuing the inhabitants of Jerusalem with a sword.[42] Furthermore, the few survivors (שאריתך) will be scattered to every wind. Verse 11 presents the indictment that the sanctuary has been defiled (a typical expression of the priestly theology in Ezekiel);[43] because of this, YHWH will massacre without mercy and pity. Verse 12 informs readers that the inhabitants will die of pestilence, famine and sword, and v. 13 highlights the anger, fury and jealousy of YHWH. Verses 14–15 recall central motifs of Jeremiah: YHWH will turn the city into a ruin (cf. Jer. 7:34; 25:9) and the land will be a taunt and a warning to the nations passing by (cf. Jer. 19:8). Verse 16 highlights the famine, and v. 17 contains a breathless list of all kinds of horrors, including famine, wild animals, kidnapping, pestilence, bloodshed and sword. The catastrophe is final.

THE DEFEAT OF ZION AND THE EXILE

Dispersed throughout the following chapters, there are different references to the great destruction. In 6:14 and other places, YHWH will stretch out his hand against his people and make their land desolate and waste (שממה ומשמה). In 12:19–20, the land of Israel and the inhabited cities (הערים הנושבות) will be laid waste without people. In 15:8, all this takes place 'because they have acted faithlessly' (יען מעלו מעל).

It is a special feature of the Book of Ezekiel that everything is viewed from an exilic perspective. Already before the final destruction of Jerusalem, Ezekiel has accompanied a part of the Judean population brought to Babylon, and it is from here that the prophet perceives and portrays current events. Because of this, the final account of the fall of Jerusalem occurs only indirectly in *33:21–9*. In the initial v. 21, a survivor (הפליט) from Jerusalem comes to the prophet Ezekiel and announces that the city has fallen (הכתה העיר).[44] Yet the following vv. 24–9 are difficult to grasp. Verses 24–6 relate that those who are left in Jerusalem's ruins after the destruction will claim the land as their property. Just as Abraham got possession of the land, so will the many who are left take possession of the land. What is the problem? Zimmerli rightly asserts that whereas the land was given to Abraham as an act of divine mercy, the survivors of Jerusalem will *claim* possession of the land.[45] This may explain the sarcastic comments in vv. 25–6: do you really think that you will possess the land, when you eat and shed blood, worship idols, trust your sword and commit abominations (accusations that are typical of the Holiness Code; see Lev. 17–26)?[46] In other words, the claim of the survivors is arrogant and deserves punishment. Thus, divine judgement is pronounced in vv. 27–9. The arrogant survivors will fall by the sword, be given to wild animals and die of pestilence. Again, we sense a strong tension between the exiled and those remaining in the homeland (cf. Ezek. 11:14–21; see also Jer. 24:1–10; 29:10–20). Verse 28 relates that YHWH will turn the land into a desolation and a wasteland (שממה ומשמה); also the mountains of Israel will become so waste that no one will pass through them (אין עובר). In sum, 33:21–9 recalls the central motif of Jeremiah: that even if some survive the great destruction, they will definitely be killed afterwards (cf. Jer. 24:8–10; 29:16–19), and the land emptied of its inhabitants.

Fortunately, however, some will survive. In *6:8–10*, YHWH will spare (הותרתי) some survivors from the sword (פליטי חרב), although they will be scattered among the nations. First, the use of הותרתי emphasizes that it is by YHWH's will that there will be survivors after the judgement.[47] Second, and crucially, due to the use of linguistic terms, the content of v. 8 is close to the concept of the remnant in Isaiah. Indeed, v. 8 employs יתר about those who are left (cf. Isa. 1:8–9) and פליט about those who survive or are being saved (cf. Isa. 4:2; 10:20; 37:31). A significant difference, however, is that the remnant in Isaiah is left on Mount Zion, whereas the remnant in Ezekiel (and Jeremiah) is scattered among foreign peoples and countries (בארצות, בגוים).

133

THE ZION MOTIFS: BETWEEN JUDGEMENT AND SALVATION

Nevertheless, we should not forget that Isaiah and Ezekiel refer to different events within their distinctive narratives, that is, Isaiah refers to the remnant surviving the Assyrian assault in 701 BCE, whereas Ezekiel (and Jeremiah) refers to the survivors after the Babylonian invasion of Jerusalem in 597/87 BCE. Ezekiel 12:16 contains a motif similar to that of 6:8. According to this verse, YHWH leaves (הותרתי) a few escapees from the sword, famine and pestilence, who among the peoples (בגוים) will tell of their abominations. The escapees function thereby as witnesses of the people's sin and the inevitable judgement of YHWH, while they at the same time *as survivors* function as witnesses of his gracious mercy.[48] Living in captivity also entails a process of self-loathing and cleansing. As Ezekiel 6:9–10 clearly illustrates, the survivors will undergo a 'spiritual renaissance' at three decisive levels: they will remember (זכר), be loathsome (קוט) and recognize (ידע).[49] Spelled out, they will remember YHWH and the destruction he has caused; they will loathe themselves for the evils that they have committed; and they will recognize that YHWH did not bring the disaster upon them in vain (לא אל־חנם). As Steven Tuell states, 'true self-knowledge comes not through introspection, but through an encounter with the Lord.'[50] Fortunately, this encounter will lead to a sincere reflection and break with the abominations and idolatry of the past.

The recognition-motif recurs in *14:21–3*. Initially, v. 21 presents YHWH's four deadly acts of judgement (ארבעת שפטי הרעים): sword, famine, wild animals and pestilence. Both the figure four and the nature of the acts symbolically illustrate the totality of the destruction. Also here, it is YHWH who sends (שלחתי) his punishments directed against Jerusalem to kill humans and animals. However, v. 22 informs readers that some survivors (פלטה) will be left (נותרה) and brought to Ezekiel and those in exile. When Ezekiel's community sees their ways and deeds, they will be consoled for the evil that was brought upon Jerusalem. Still, it remains difficult to understand why. Yet the best explanation available suggests that the escape of a group from Jerusalem – after all – testifies to the mercy of YHWH: he will take care of them.[51] Along with the consolation follows an act of self-loathing and recognition (cf. 6:9–10), and the survivors will finally realize that the desolation of the city did not happen without cause (לא חנם).[52] In sum, that a remnant survives the great catastrophe is solely an expression of YHWH's saving grace.

In terms of imagery and themes, *Ezekiel 7:21–7* indeed looks similar to Jeremiah 12:7–12. As YHWH has abandoned his house in Jeremiah, Ezekiel 7:22 informs his audience that YHWH turns his face away from his people. Ezekiel 7:21–7 consists of two parts: vv. 21–4 concerning the profanation of the temple and vv. 25–7 concerning the people's fear of imminent attack. Verses 21–4 emphasize that YHWH summons the enemies. Accordingly, he gives his city and its people as booty to strangers and the wicked, and he mobilizes the evil nations. Notably, YHWH will allow foreigners to

THE DEFEAT OF ZION AND THE EXILE

desecrate the temple.[53] The image of the profanation of the temple is of particular significance. In vv. 21–2, the term חלל occurs three times designating the effects of the presence of enemies. Furthermore, in v. 24, the nations take possession of the holy places. Verse 23 accuses the city and the land of being full of crimes and violence. Verses 25–7 then describe how the people of YHWH fear the judgement and seek the peace of which there will be none (cf. Jer. 12:12). Verse 27 illustrates the retribution-motif: YHWH now does to the city, as the city has done to him.

The profanation of the temple in 7:21–7 forms an excellent introduction to Ezekiel 8–11. We have already dealt with these important chapters (see chapter 3); accordingly here, we shall focus on a single element: YHWH's abandonment of his temple and city. As we were told in Jeremiah 12:7 and Ezekiel 7:22, YHWH will go far off (רחק) from his sanctuary and his glory will ascend from the middle of the city (cf. Ezek. 8:6; 11:23). Character-istically for both Jeremiah and Ezekiel, YHWH leaves the city before it is conquered by the enemies. Or even more importantly: because YHWH leaves the city, it can be conquered. When YHWH is no longer in the city or in the land, Zion is left as a desolation, emptied of people, animals and God. Zion has become a godforsaken place.

The ploughed field in Micah

It is primarily the first three chapters of the Book of Micah that portray the destruction of Jerusalem/Zion. The suspense is built rather cleverly throughout these chapters. In 1:2–4, YHWH enters to judge. This judgement-motif recurs and is reiterated within these three chapters, culminating in 3:9–12, where Zion is ploughed as a field. In the following, we shall focus on 1:8–16, 2:2–4, 2:8–10 and 3:9–12.

In *1:8–16*, the destruction of Judah and Jerusalem follows immediately after the desolation of Samaria in 1:6–7. There is a close connection between these two cities, because the disaster reaches Jerusalem from the north. According to Knud Jeppesen, 1:8–16 constitutes one of the most difficult passages within the Old Testament and it is hard to translate because of numerous text-critical problems. Still, the content or central matter of these verses – that is, the destruction of Jerusalem – ties them together.[54] In v. 8, the whole scenario provokes a sincere lament and sorrow of the prophet Micah, which is further explained in the crucial v. 9. For her wound or stroke (מכותיה)[55] is incurable. Yet who is 'she'? According to the context, it can be either Samaria or Jerusalem. Jeppesen, however, argues in favour of Samaria, so that the verse establishes a close link between the two disasters.[56] And he reaches or touches (נגע) the gate of my people. Yet who is 'he'? It is hardly the wound, because that is feminine, as a result of which Jeppesen proposes to read YHWH. It is YHWH who reaches the gate of the people as part of his judgement.[57] Indeed, this interpretation is plausible,

135

THE ZION MOTIFS: BETWEEN JUDGEMENT AND SALVATION

as we have often observed that YHWH plays an active role in the destruction. Thus the destructive nature of YHWH, which first laid Samaria waste, now reaches Jerusalem.[58]

Verses 12–13 confirm this picture. While the inhabitants of Maroth wait for good (טוב),[59] disaster (רע) will come down *from* YHWH to the gate of Jerusalem. The term שׁער occurs both in v. 9 and v. 12, which supports an impression that the imminent disaster comes from YHWH. In continuation, v. 13 clearly states that the destruction will take place because of the people's sin. Interestingly, the verse refers to daughter Zion's *main sin* (חטאת ראשׁית).[60] This sin includes the fact that the chariots are made ready in Lachish and that the inhabitants thereby trust in their own military force rather than in the support of YHWH. As we have seen, this was a main charge as well in Isaiah (e.g. Isa. 31:1–3). Here the sinful act will cause the great disaster in so far as the transgressions of Israel (פשׁעי ישׂראל) are in Zion. Annihilation is inevitable and will, according to v. 16, lead to a deportation: 'for they will go from you into exile' (ממך כי גלו; cf. Jer. 24:5 and Ezek. 33:21). In short, exile and captivity succeed the great disaster.

Micah 2:3–4 highlights the paradigmatic retribution-motif in, for instance, Ezekiel 7:27. Because of this evil family (המשׁפחה הזאת רעה), YHWH will bring disasters upon it, and it will become an evil time (עת רעה).[61] In addition, v. 3 clarifies that the evil comes from YHWH (cf. 1:9, 12). Verse 4 is introduced by the well-known ביום ההוא and consists of a lament over YHWH's judgement: 'we are utterly ruined' (שׁדוד נשׁדנו). The cries end with the lament that the fields are given to foreigners, referred to as 'rebellious'.[62] *Micah 2:8–10* continues in the same mode. The people rise against YHWH as an enemy;[63] women and their children are driven out (cf. 1:16); and v. 10 again indicates that exile will follow the destruction. The latter part of v. 10 takes up a priestly motif in Micah, similar to what we have already encountered in Ezekiel. In Micah 2:10, it is explicitly announced that the place will be destroyed because of its uncleanness (טמאה)[64] and that it will be a grievous destruction.

The culmination of judgement is reached in *3:9–12*. Initially, vv. 9–11 present a series of accusations against Zion's political and religious leaders, while v. 12 portrays YHWH's intervention. The criticism against the leaders recalls that of Isaiah 1:21–8 and Zephaniah 3:1–8. In Micah 3:9, it primarily concerns the corruption of justice. Wolff points out that this corruption entails three different kinds of behaviour: the leaders mistreat people (v. 10), they accept bribes (v. 11a) and they are hypocritical in their faith in God (v. 11b).[65] In v. 10, we hear that they (or 'he', i.e. the ruler) build Zion with blood and Jerusalem with wrong. It is uncertain what it exactly means to build a city with blood and wrong, yet Jeppesen is right that doing so will always bring new disasters.[66] As was mentioned, the charge in v. 11a is well-known. The traditional authorities such as rulers, priests and prophets do not do their jobs in love of justice, but in love of money and bribes.

THE DEFEAT OF ZION AND THE EXILE

The final charge in v. 11b is remarkable. The leaders allegedly rely on YHWH when they state: 'Is YHWH not in our midst [הלוא יהוה בקרבנו]? No harm [רעה] shall come upon us.' The statement – as in Isaiah – indirectly reveals a criticism of the idea that YHWH will protect his city unconditionally.[67] However, Micah does not mention any particular conditions for salvation and the destruction appears to be unpreventable. Yet v. 11 illustrates the hypocrisy among the leaders that they, despite their corrupt deeds, still arrogantly anticipate YHWH's protection.

Nevertheless, destruction is inevitable. The close connection between the imminent disaster and the sinful leaders is emphasized in v. 12 by stating 'because of you'. Because of them, Zion will be ploughed into a field,[68] Jerusalem will become a heap of ruins and the temple mount will become a wooded height. The main point in Micah is thereby similar to that of Jeremiah and Ezekiel: the whole area will be left desolate and without inhabitants.

A different image in Zechariah 14:1–5

The last passage that we shall bring into discussion in this chapter is *Zechariah 14:1–5*. We can divide the passage into three sub-units: v. 1 announces the Day of YHWH; v. 2 depicts the conquest of Jerusalem; and vv. 3–5 portray YHWH's counter-attack. The short v. 1 announces that the Day of YHWH is coming (יום־בא ליהוה), which unmistakably reminds us of the other designations of this event (ביום ההוא, יום יהוה). Verse 2 is highly interesting, because it contains imagery that is both familiar and unfamiliar to us. On the one hand, YHWH gathers the nations to do battle against Jerusalem: the city is conquered (נלכדה העיר), houses are robbed, women raped and half of the population goes into exile (גולה). All this is well-known, in so far as these images have dominated our examination until now. Yet the following motif is different: 'the rest of the people [יתר העם] shall not be cut off from the city'. Ostensibly, there is a mixture of the two versions we have explored: either the remnant survives on Zion, or the remnant lives on in captivity. Zechariah 14:2 seems to anticipate both scenarios. Furthermore, the destruction is only treated briefly, for in vv. 3–5, YHWH enters the stage to judge the attacking enemies (a motif similar to that of Joel 4). Jerusalem is saved and restored throughout the rest of the chapter. In sum, Zechariah 14:1–5 presents quite a different scenario than that of Jeremiah, Ezekiel and Micah concerning the destruction of Jerusalem (for Zech. 1–8, see the succeeding chapter).

Summing up: the defeat of Zion and the exile

Jeremiah, Ezekiel and Micah share three motifs. First, there is a clear connection between, on the one side, the idolatry, abominations and unrighteous

THE ZION MOTIFS: BETWEEN JUDGEMENT AND SALVATION

leaders as manifestations of sins against YHWH and, on the other side, the great destruction as the judgement of those sins. In Jeremiah, it is stated several times that this destruction could have been prevented, *if* the inhabitants had returned to YHWH; obviously, they never did. Furthermore, the logic of retribution is explicit. Second, the destruction is final. The main capital Zion/Jerusalem, the cities of Judah and the entire land are turned into a desolation by the enemy attack and left as a ruined wasteland, emptied of both humans and animals; only jackals will live there. Third, the few who did survive have been led into exile far away. In addition, it is remarkable that Jeremiah and Ezekiel set the destruction within a fulfilment of the covenantal curses of the Pentateuch (see Lev. 26; Deut. 28).

It is worth noting that YHWH plays a significant role in all these events. He summons and instructs the enemies, he destroys the city and he spares a few only to bring them into foreign captivity (cf. Jer. 24:5; Ezek. 6:8). Yet the exile contains a process of cleansing. The period of exile is seventy years, to ensure that it is an entirely new generation which eventually returns to restore the empty land (Jer. 29:10–20). Exile also entails a process of self-loathing and recognition among the survivors by which they recognize their evil deeds (Ezek. 6:9–10). In the preceding chapter about the classical Zion motif, we observed that the survivors remain on Mount Zion where the cleansing of sin took place (cf. Isa. 4:2–6). In Jeremiah and Ezekiel, it is the reverse. The survivors are led far away, into exile, where they will be cleansed from their sins. In the classical Zion motif, the remnant on Zion is the root of the new people of YHWH; in Jeremiah and Ezekiel, the survivors in exile will become that root. In the classical Zion motif, the restoration of the righteous Zion takes place in Zion, whereas in Jeremiah and Ezekiel, the restoration is pushed into a distant future. The destruction of Zion and the subsequent exile therefore only constitute one of three stages in the dynamic Zion motif, that is, (a) destruction and exile; (b) return; and (c) recreation of a new Zion. We shall investigate the two latter stages in the next two chapters.

I will close this chapter by mentioning a passage that may bridge the following chapters. It is a small literary pearl wedged between the many harsh oracles of judgement in Jeremiah 4:5–6:30. I am thinking of *4:23–6*. In four visions, the poet portrays the land after the enemy attack, the fall of the city and the deportation of its people into exile. Chaos rules. According to v. 23, the land (or the earth) has become waste and void – a *tohu wa-bohu* – as before the divine creation in Genesis 1:2; the heavens have no light. As we have seen in Isaiah 5:30, the marching enemies brought darkness to the land and such they have left it dark and desolate. The depiction of this state of chaos continues in v. 25, where the mountains quake and the hills tremble. Verse 25 shows that the land is empty for there are neither humans nor birds. All life has been extinguished. The

138

THE DEFEAT OF ZION AND THE EXILE

fruitful land (הכרמל) has been turned into a desert (מדבר) as a consequence of the aggressive enemies (cf. Joel 2:3), and the cities have been laid in ruins. All this has been caused by YHWH, by his burning wrath. That his chosen land is now waste and void is YHWH's ultimate judgement against his people. Everything is chaos. Only a divine act of recreation will offer a new beginning.

Notes

1 It is important to note that the destruction of Zion does not necessarily refer to an actual historical event; cf. Laato 1998: 55: 'Isa 63:7–64:11 does not presuppose any concrete historical destruction of Jerusalem in the post-exilic period, but can be interpreted as a community lament which speaks of the city's distress in figurative terms by using metaphors of Jerusalem's destruction.'

2 BHS has שְׂאוּ נֵס צִיּוֹנָה, where נֵס refers to a sign or a standard. Probably fitting the context better, LXX reads *pheugete* = נֻס, that is, 'flee to Zion'; see further in Carroll 1986: 160.

3 Against NRSV's 'every town'.

4 Cf. Jones 1992: 131 describes Jer. 6:1–8 as the climax of the scroll.

5 As was indicated in chapter 2, I follow the alternative reading of NRSV supported by Carroll 1986: 190: 'The comely and delicately bred I will destroy, the daughter of Zion'; Lundbom 1999: 413: 'The lovely one, the delicate one I am silencing daughter Zion'; and Allen 2008: 82: 'That beautiful, refined woman I will destroy – Lady Zion.' The text-critical issue at stake concerns the term דמה, which may be derived from roots meaning 'be destroyed' or 'be like'. NRSV follows the latter meaning: 'I have likened daughter Zion to the loveliest pasture.' However, within the context of Jer. 6:1–9, this reading seems rather unlikely. For a critical review of text-critical issues, see Jones 1992: 132; Fischer 2005a: 259; Allen 2008: 83.

6 Cf. Allen 2008: 85: 'The shepherds are kings, as in 2:18, and their flocks are the regional companies under their command. A siege is envisioned.' See also Carroll 1986: 191: 'In vv. 2–3 the images used are those of grassy meadow land and shepherds pasturing their flocks in it, with their tents surrounding the meadow. An idyllic picture! . . . But these terms also are only metaphors, metaphors standing for the invading army about to besiege Jerusalem (cf. 1.15). The beautiful meadow infested with shepherds grazing their sheep is in reality a city under siege from a formidable enemy. Sheep may *not* graze safely here.'

7 According to BHS, הפקד is masculine, which is badly congruous with the feminine עיר; furthermore, the Hophal-vocalization causes problems. Georg Fischer suggests changing the vocalization into Niphal; see Fischer 2005a: 259.

8 Jones 1992: 133 also notes that Jer. likely takes up the metaphor of illness employed in Isa. 1:4–9.

9 Cf. Carroll 1986: 195. See Lundbom 1999: 424 for a larger review of proposals, including Bernhard Duhm's suggestion that the prophet Jeremiah is the gleaner.

10 Fischer 2005a: 357–8.

11 Cf. Stulman 2005: 'The disaster is no accident of history, or sign of divine impotence; rather, the nation has fallen because of its own covenant failures.'

12 Cf. Thompson 2003: 244: 'This principle of retribution – that God will deal with Israel as they themselves deal – set the logic which the story requires to hold. It is a message to the reader: "Punishment fits the crime" or "evil turns

back upon itself"'; cf. Hjelm 2004: 144. See also Thompson 2005: 116–17: 'The logic of retribution reflects the ancient political structures of patronage. If Yahweh is acknowledged as God, his mercy and compassion follow in course. To those who are not his servants, however, all that remains is retribution ... There is belonging and there is rejection; there is no middle way.'

13 Scholars disagree about where this valley of Hinnom is geographically located, what Topheth – the ritual burning place – refers to and whether the notion of sacrificing of children is literal or metaphorical. For extensive reviews of the many proposals, see, for instance, Carroll 1986: 220–4, 385–9; Fischer 2005a: 317–21, 596–9. Within the context of our study, it is interesting that Topheth in Isa. 30:33 was made ready to consume the attacking, yet defeated enemies and thereby serves a 'positive' function. However, in Jeremiah, it clearly forms the basis of a central charge. Crucially, in Jer. 19:12, the entire city is turned into a Topheth, therefore the destruction of the city may be interpreted as a gigantic sacrificial feast.

14 Allen 2008: 227.

15 Hjelm 2004: 88. Cf. Dow 2011: 65: 'This kind of divine retribution for sin and blessing for obedience is often seen as a staple interest of the "Deuteronomistic History" recorded in Deuteronomy to 2 Kings.'

16 Cf. Deut. 28:53–7: 'In the desperate straits to which the enemy siege reduces you, you will eat the fruit of your womb, the flesh of your own sons and daughters whom YHWH your God has given you. Even the most refined and gentle of men among you will begrudge food to his own brother, to the wife whom he embraces, and to the last of his remaining children, giving to none of them any of the flesh of his children whom he is eating, because nothing else remains to him, in the desperate straits to which the enemy siege will reduce you in all your towns. She who is the most refined and gentle among you, so gentle and refined that she does not venture to set the sole of her foot on the ground, will begrudge food to the husband whom she embraces, to her own son, and to her own daughter, begrudging even the afterbirth that comes out from between her thighs, and the children that she bears, because she is eating them in secret for lack of anything else, in the desperate straits to which the enemy siege will reduce you in your towns.' For parallels in the Vassal-Treaties of Esarhaddon, see Lundbom 1999: 840.

17 For parallels in the Vassal-Treaties of Esarhaddon as well as in the Old Testament literature, see Lundbom 1999: 499.

18 Allen 2008: 104.

19 Jones 1992: 192.

20 See Allen 2008: 153: '[The disaster's] executors are kings leading their military detachments on the rampage through the vineyard or field that represents Yahweh's beautiful land (cf. 3:19; 6:3) ... Behind these agents lies a divine cause.'

21 The term שממה is used frequently within the prophetic literature (fifty-four times) and especially by Jeremiah (fifteen times) to designate destruction and desolation. Interestingly, a close parallel is employed in the passage about the fulfilment of Jeremiah's prophecy in 2 Chron. 36:21.

22 Cf. McConville 1992: 38: '[Jeremiah's] inversion of the Zion-tradition is so complete that he can even use the language of "holy war" – typical of that tradition – in reverse: far from his fighting for Jerusalem to defend it (recall Isa. 31:4f.), God is now its resolute enemy, ready to bring destruction on his own heritage because of its treachery (21:4–7).' See also Allen 2008: 240–1 who speaks of 'an ironic use of the motif of disarmament in the Zion tradition (cf. Pss 46:9[10]; 76:3[4])'.

THE DEFEAT OF ZION AND THE EXILE

23 Fischer 2005a: 638.

24 Cf. Carroll 1986: 496.

25 Also used in Jer. 27:6 and 43:10. Designating Nebuchadrezzar as servant is significant, because the Old Testament except here never gives an enemy of the people of YHWH this title. Frequently, the title is applied to Jacob or David; Cyrus, too, is called the servant of YHWH (Isa. 44:28), yet as a servant of YHWH's salvation; see further in Lundbom 2003: 247.

26 The term 'to hear' (שׁמע) is here as often within the Old Testament more likely to be translated into 'obey' – that is, 'yet you did not obey me'.

27 Allen 2008: 285.

28 Allen 2008: 298.

29 Fischer 2005a: 581.

30 See also Jer. 22:4–5: 'For if you will indeed obey this word, then through the gates of this house shall enter kings who sit on the throne of David, riding in chariots and on horses, they, and their servants, and their people. But if you will not heed these words, I swear by myself, says the YHWH, that this house shall become a desolation.'

31 See Carroll 1986: 171: 'This addition [that is, v. 28] to the cycle may need to be balanced by the other reflections which make the invasion the responsibility of the community, but the absoluteness of its theology should not be ignored completely.'

32 Cf. Lundbom 1999: 362.

33 Stulman 2005: 219.

34 Fischer 2005a: 719.

35 This covenant formula forms a central element in Jeremiah, see further in Lundbom 2003: 232.

36 Carroll 1986: 486.

37 The seventy years may, however, literally refer to the historical period either between the fall of Assyria in 605 BCE and the victory of Cyrus in 539/6 or between the fall of Jerusalem in 586 BCE and the completion of the Second Temple in 516 BCE. In addition, we also know the seventy years from the Black Stone of Esarhaddon (dated to 680 BCE), which refers to a period of that length concerning Babylon's desolation. To support my view of the number as a literary artistic form, see Carroll 1986: 495: '[the phrase of seventy years] stresses the fullness of . . . judgement'; Lundbom 2003: 249: 'If [the number seventy] corresponds to anything, it is the conventional description of a full life-span'; and Allen 2008: 287: 'the prediction has an impressionistic quality, an exceptionally long period of Babylonian hegemony and Judean impotence'. See the discussion in Carroll 1986: 493–6; Jones 1992: 326–7; Lundbom 2003: 249–50; Fischer 2005a: 741–2; Allen 2008: 286–7.

38 Cf. Carroll 1986: 559.

39 See further in Barstad 1997.

40 Zimmerli 1979: 174–5.

41 Block 1997: 198.

42 Cf. Dow 2011: 83: 'The Pentateuch predicted that the result of these sins of forsaking God would be foreign invasion, death of most of the people, scattering of the remaining population into other countries, scorn of other nations, and the virtual end of national life (Lev. 26.33–39; Deut. 4.27; 28–36, 64–68; 29.28).'

43 Notice Ezekiel's extensive use of the theologically important term 'abomination' (תועבה), often viewed as a sign of Deuteronomistic influence. Ezek. 8–11, for instance, vividly illustrates the abominations of the people of YHWH; see further in Block 1997: 203–4; Joyce 2009: 89.

THE ZION MOTIFS: BETWEEN JUDGEMENT AND SALVATION

44 Joyce 2009: 190 notices that this news forms a turning point of the book. After this announcement of the fall of Jerusalem, the book shifts to themes of promise and restoration.

45 Zimmerli 1983: 198–9. Cf. Joyce 2009: 193, who speaks of an arrogant and decidedly materialistic claim.

46 Cf. Tuell 2009: 231: 'the survivors of Jerusalem's fall assume that their presence in the land is a sign of divine approval . . . The survivors have no right to claim patriarchal promise; indeed, their actions show that they have less in common with Abraham than with the foreign nations, whom God displaced so that Israel could possess the land.'

47 Zimmerli 1979: 189. Cf. Tuell 2009: 31: 'for Ezekiel there *is* no righteous remnant. Those whom the Lord has spared from destruction have escaped not because of any virtue of their own, but because the Lord chose to deliver them.'

48 Zimmerli 1979: 274.

49 Block 1997: 231–3.

50 Tuell 2009: 34.

51 Zimmerli 1979: 316; Joyce 2009: 128.

52 Block 1997: 452.

53 Cf. Joyce 2009: 95.

54 Jeppesen 1987: 169.

55 'Her wound' (מכותיה) is plural with a feminine suffix referring to the city; yet the verb 'has come' (באה) in v. 9a is feminine singular and the verb 'has reached' in v. 9b (נגע) is masculine singular. To solve this problem, Wolff 1990: 43 proposes to read (וה)מכת יה, that is, 'the wound that YHWH inflicts' (cf. the footnote in BHS); then, the wound is feminine singular and is congruous with 'has come'; and YHWH as masculine singular is subject for 'has reached'. This emendation, however, is not attested in any of the ancient translations. A slighter emendation is to read 'wound' in singular; cf. Jeppesen 1987: 159. See also Allen 1976: 267; Jenson 2008: 111.

56 Jeppesen 1987: 161; Jenson 2008: 111.

57 Jeppesen 1987: 162.

58 Cf. Jenson 2008: 111 who observes that v. 9 forms a kind of bridge within the passage: v. 9a recalls the defeat of Samaria in vv. 6–7; v. 9b anticipates the judgement of Judah and Jerusalem in vv. 10–16.

59 This 'good' probably refers to that Maroth hoped for good from the invaders or that they foolishly expected YHWH to save them; see Jenson 2008: 115.

60 I prefer 'main sin' to 'the beginning of sin'; cf. Allen 1976: 277.

61 Cf. Wolff 1990: 79: 'A synthetic manner of thinking is represented in the word (ה)רע: it means "evil" in the sense of active wickedness, and "disaster" in the sense of suffering brought on by wicked actions – two sides of the same coin.'

62 NRSV has 'our captors'.

63 NRSV has: 'But you rise up against my people as an enemy.' For the interpretation I have chosen, see further in Jenson 2008: 125–6, although he concludes that any interpretation of this verse must remain tentative.

64 See Jenson 2008: 127: 'Although uncleanness is a priestly ritual term, it is also used to describe the result of certain kinds of unethical behaviour ("moral filth", Allen 1976: 293; cf. Lev. 18:24–28; Num. 35:33; Deut. 21:23). This seems to fit the context better than other prophetic texts, where it is a cultic metaphor for sin (Ps 51) or a term for idolatry (Jer. 19:13; Ezek. 22:4).'

65 Wolff 1990: 106.

66 Jeppesen 1987: 222. Surprisingly, Wolff 1990: 106–7 understands the expression quite literally. According to him, it is the blood shed by all the workers,

THE DEFEAT OF ZION AND THE EXILE

for instance, from Micah's home territory, while constructing the Siloam tunnel! See also Allen 1976: 317; Jenson 2008: 138. On the other hand, the expression may articulate a common phraseology designating guilt; cf. 2 Kgs 21:16; 1 Chron. 28:3.

67 Jenson 2008: 139–40: 'To "lean upon Yhwh" is synonymous with trusting him (Isa. 30:12; Prov. 3:5). It is an attitude that is linked to salvation (2 Chron. 16:8), but these people had forgotten that moral integrity is a necessary pre-condition of this trust. When this happens the result will be judgement not salvation (Isa. 30:12; 31:1).'

68 Cf. the observation in Jenson 2008: 141 that 'the image is not of farmers cultivating land, but enemies making a thorough job of destruction. Even the foundations will be ploughed up, leaving uninhabited open country, fit only for animals.'

9

THE RETURN TO ZION

The great desolation and the succeeding exile do not constitute YHWH's final plan. In a varied range of texts, Zion and Jerusalem occur as the goal of an exodus from exile. This topic will be the primary concern of the present chapter. First, we shall examine Isaiah 35:1–10, which depicts the holy way to Zion. Then, we shall interpret a series of parallel texts from Isaiah 40–55, Jeremiah, Ezekiel, Micah and Zechariah, in order to shed further light upon the motif of return.

The holy way

Isaiah 35:1–10 presents a way, which leads to Zion through the wilderness. The text appears as an 'open' text that is difficult to place within one particular context.[1] Within its present canonical form, Isaiah 35 succeeds the account in Isaiah 34 of the vengeance of YHWH and the destruction of Edom. In that context, the way through the wilderness constitutes a way through the desolate neighbouring land of Judah.[2] Interpreters, however, generally assert that Isaiah 35 employs a great bulk of images, themes and motifs especially associated with Isaiah 40–55.[3] Within the present composition, chapter 35, along with chapter 34, forms a bridge roughly between the themes of judgement and salvation in Isaiah.[4] Isaiah 35 points forward to chapters 40–55[66] and these chapters' announcement of a new beginning after destruction and exile (as alluded to in Isa. 39).[5] Although the way in Isaiah 40–55 apparently leads from the Babylonian captivity to a restored Zion (see below), such is by no means clear in Isaiah 35.[6] Indeed, Isaiah 35 only states to which place the redeemed will go, but not whence they came.[7]

Isaiah 35:1–10 consists of four minor textual units: the transformation and blossoming of the desert (vv. 1–2); the call for a renewed hope (vv. 3–4); the healing of the weak and the lame and the growing prosperity in the desert (vv. 5–7); and, finally, the depiction of the holy way leading to Zion (vv. 8–10). In vv. 1–2, three different words are employed to describe the region; they include 'the wilderness' (מדבר), 'the dry land' (ציה) and 'the

144

THE RETURN TO ZION

desert' (ערבה). The region will be glad and rejoice, for it will bloom and become like Lebanon, Carmel and Sharon, known throughout the Old Testament as beautiful and fertile places. Yet to what does this 'desolate' land refer? As mentioned above, the passage is ambiguous. However, we shall attempt to read Isaiah 35 in light of the great desolation, examined in the previous chapter. It means that the wilderness and the dry land may not be random places, but Zion and the surrounding land that have been ravaged by enemies and left desolate and without inhabitants. It is these places that will bloom and rejoice. The fruitful land, which was turned into a desert (cf. Jer. 4:26), will once again become fertile (cf. Isa. 29:17; 32:15).[8] A similar motif occurs in Isaiah 51:3, in which YHWH will comfort Zion and make her wilderness (מדברה) and her desert (ערבתה) like Eden and the garden of YHWH. In addition to this richness of prosperity and plants, 'they' will, according to 35:2, experience the glory of YHWH (כבוד־יהוה). Who are 'they'? Due to the context of the verse, it is most plausibly the landscape. On the other hand, it may, as we shall see in the following sub-units, refer to individuals, that is, the weak ones seeking consolation (35:3–4) or the redeemed people (35:10).[9]

The transformation of the wilderness implies a consolation in vv. 3–4. The weak hands will be strengthened and the feeble knees made firm. Verse 3 thereby forms a contrast to, for instance, Ezekiel 7:17, where the people are discouraged by the attack of the enemies. According to v. 4, the consolation is based upon the vengeance of YHWH: 'Here is your God. He will come with vengeance, with terrible recompense. He will come and save you.' This vengeance (נקם), also mentioned in Isaiah 34:8 (the vengeance upon Edom), is indeed one of the features linking Isaiah 34 and 35 closely together. In Isaiah 35, however, vengeance does not seem to involve a slaughter of hostile nations. Rather, it seems to be an expression of the presence of YHWH; consequently the word 'vengeance' has an unpleasant ring.[10] The important thing about this 'vengeance' or the parallel phrase 'terrible recompense' (literally: 'the work of God' [גמול]) is the emphasis on YHWH's support to his people; in short, he is coming to save them.

Furthermore, vv. 5–7 underline the fact that it is not only the geographical place that will be transformed, but also the individuals here: the blind will see, the deaf will hear, the lame will walk and the dumb will speak.[11] The transformation of individuals in vv. 5–6b is closely linked to that of nature in vv. 6b–7. Both the weaklings and the dry landscape will be 'healed'. Waters and streams break forth in the wilderness, and the burning sand and thirsty ground become life-giving sources.[12] Of particular importance here is the statement in v. 7b: 'the habitation of jackals shall become a swamp'. As was indicated above, jackals are often present when a city is destroyed (see Isa. 34:13 regarding the desolate fortresses of Edom).[13] Moreover, in Jeremiah 9:10, YHWH made Jerusalem a lair of jackals. As the wilderness is transformed into a fruitful garden, the region will be

THE ZION MOTIFS: BETWEEN JUDGEMENT AND SALVATION

cleansed from its remaining inhabitants, the jackals. The people of YHWH will then take possession of the land.

The transformation of the landscape and the people functions as a figurative introduction to the subject matter of the text, namely the redemption of the people of YHWH and their return to Zion.[14] The three last verses of the passage present the way, which the redeemed will follow. The adverb שם occurs three times: *there* is the way! It will be called 'the Holy Way'. No unclean or godless will walk upon it; neither will lions or beasts pass it. The lion as such is of course a dangerous animal, yet as a metaphor, it also refers to the enemies. As we have seen, the enemy is depicted as a lion going up from its thicket (cf. Jer. 4:7); and in Ezekiel, the wild animals represent one of four deadly acts of judgement (cf. Ezek. 14:21). The absence of these animals indicates that the enemies have left and the danger is over. The redeemed (גאולים) can walk in safety. Verse 10 contains three significant features. First, it is stated that the ransomed of YHWH will return or repent (ישבון). As noticed in previous chapters of our investigation, Old Testament usage of this particular term שוב designates both 'repentance' and 'return'.[15] Here, it seems to refer to the act of physical return: they will return to Zion. However, we should consider whether this physical return also involves a spiritual transformation, repentance and conversion.[16] If so, the repentance to YHWH is part of or a precondition for the people's return to Zion. Second, Zion is the explicit goal of the return. Third, the journey is accompanied with joy and gladness. The sorrow and sighing will flee. We find a reversal of its counter-motif associated with the destruction, namely the sound of wailing (e.g. Jer. 9:19), when the sorrow and lamentation become replaced by joy and cries of happiness because of YHWH's redemptive act.

The return to Zion in Isaiah 40–55

Isaiah 40–55 opens with a prologue in *Isaiah 40:1–11* introducing some of the main themes within the sixteen chapters. The eleven verses may be divided into four smaller parts: vv. 1–2 announce that the guilt of the people has been removed; vv. 3–5 prepare a way for YHWH; vv. 6–8 reveal the status of man before God; and, finally, vv. 9–11 present the good tidings concerning the presence and compassion of YHWH. In the following, we shall focus on vv. 1–2, 3–5 and 9–11. Initially, v. 1 presents the momentous proclamation: 'Comfort, O comfort my people, says your God.' The addressees (note the plural form of the imperative) of the divine message are not spelled out;[17] yet, according to v. 2, the call concerns 'Jerusalem' representing the people.[18] The proclamation addresses decisive matters: 'she has served her term' (צבאה) and 'her iniquity [עונה] has been pardoned'. צבא is frequently translated into 'army' or 'war', although Wilhelm Gesenius, in this particular case, proposes a more figurative meaning.[19] In addition,

146

THE RETURN TO ZION

some scholars strive to understand the word in terms of 'indentured service' – that is, parallel to the iniquity, rather than to the military service.[20] The people's iniquities have been forgiven (cf. 44:22).[21] Verse 2 thereby constitutes a pivotal turning point: the exile as penalty for all the transgressions of the people is over, their sins have been cleansed and the way home to Zion has been reopened.

Verses 3–5 begin with the famous call: 'In the wilderness prepare the way of YHWH, make straight in the desert a highway for our God.' Terms similar to those in Isaiah 35:1 are employed to portray the wilderness (מדבר, ערבה) and the way (דרך יהוה, מסלה). In Isaiah 35, the way was a way for the people to follow, whereas in 40:3 it designates YHWH's return to his people.[22] Although the preparation of YHWH's way does not affect the surrounding land as magnificently as in Isaiah 35, it still has an immense impact on the region. According to v. 4, valleys will be lifted and mountains be made low, uneven ground will become levelled and the rough places plains. Furthermore, in v. 5, the glory of YHWH (כבוד יהוה) will be revealed and all people will see it. In 1 Kings and Ezekiel, for instance, the 'glory' is closely connected with the temple (1 Kgs 8:11). However, in Ezekiel, it is significant that YHWH's glory leaves the temple (Ezek. 11:22–3) and reveals itself to the exiled in Babylon (Ezek. 1–3).[23] As was noted above, Isaiah 35's account of the transformation of the region and its individuals contained the phrase 'to see the glory of YHWH' (cf. 35:2).[24] The whole world will witness the return of YHWH to his people.

Verses 9–11 inform readers that the good news will be proclaimed. The messenger in v. 9 is referred to as מבשרת ציון. How should we understand this phrase? It may be read as a construct relation, that is, 'the messenger of/to Zion' (cf. Isa. 41:27; 52:7).[25] Or it may be read as apposition, that is, 'the messenger, Zion' (cf. Isa. 41:14).[26] This would mean that Zion and Jerusalem – the people or a part of the people – will ascend to a high mountain and proclaim to the cities of Judah. In other words, Zion, who has already been consoled (cf. 40:1–2), will render the comforting words to others: 'Here is your God' (הנה אלהיכם; cf. 35:4)! Verses 10–11 unfold this announcement. YHWH comes (יבוא) with might; he will gather (יקבץ) his people and be their shepherd. As in vv. 3–5, vv. 9b–11 concern the way of YHWH to his people, rather than the people's way out of exile. Indeed, a way is prepared for YHWH to save his people, gather them and bring them out of captivity. The redemption and return of the people are YHWH's work, as were the destruction and deportation also.

In *43:14–21*, the theme of the way in vv. 16–21 succeeds the proclamation of redemption in vv. 14–15. The term גאל is a predominant expression for the salvific act of YHWH within Isaiah 40–55 (cf. also Isa. 35:9). According to 43:14–15, YHWH is his people's 'Redeemer' (גאלכם), and his redemption involves an attack on Babylon to break down all its bars.[27] Although the plural form of בריח has often caused interpretive problems,[28] it makes good sense to maintain the understanding of 'bars'.[29] The premise for the people's return to Zion is precisely the deliverance from the Babylonian captivity – that is, when YHWH redeems his people by bursting the gates of Babylon.

Verses 16–21 present the way out of captivity. The text is of special interest because it in a peculiar way combines the deliverance from Babylon with the Egyptian Exodus. Although neither Egypt, Moses nor Pharaoh are mentioned by name, vv. 16–17 clearly imply the Exodus tradition: YHWH makes a way in the sea and the mighty army cannot withstand the power of YHWH, but is quenched like a wick. However, this mighty act constitutes a past that should not be remembered (v. 18), because YHWH will do a new thing (הנני עשה חדשה) by making a way in the wilderness and rivers in the desert (v. 19). This verse, in particular, combines two main motifs in Isaiah 40–55: the preparation of a way through the wilderness and bringing forth water for the people to drink and live (cf. 41:17–20; 42:14–17). Just as YHWH led the Israelites out of Egypt, he will lead his people out of Babylon; and just as he took care of them during the forty-year wilderness experience, he will provide for them on their way to Zion.[30]

Isaiah 48:20–1 provides a similar link between the Egyptian Exodus and the New Exodus. Verse 20 opens with an imperative of יצא – 'Go out from Babylon' – which is one of the central verbs in the Book of Exodus. It stands next to ברח, which marks the exodus as an escape. Yet joy and happiness will spread to the ends of the earth, for YHWH has redeemed his servant Jacob. Verse 21 asserts that the people will be safe in the wilderness.[31] They will not thirst, because water will flow from the rock (as Moses strikes water from the rock in the Exodus narrative; cf. Exod. 17:6).

In *49:9–13*, the announcement of the way is addressed to the prisoners and to those in darkness. This imagery interprets exile in terms of captivity or imprisonment and in terms of darkness from which one must be redeemed. As in the previous examples, the term יצא occurs frequently, and vv. 9b–10 reiterate trust in the care of YHWH; he will lead them and guide them to springs of water. Interestingly, v. 12 states: 'lo, these shall come from far away' (הנה־אלה מרחוק יבאו) – that is, from the north and from the west as well as from the land of Sinim (this might be the same as Syene, located on the border of Egypt; cf. NRSV). In any case, the perspective is expanded, in so far as the returners are not only those exiled to Babylon, but also in the wider Diaspora. Like 44:23, v. 13 utters the cosmic exultation that YHWH has comforted his people.

Unlike 48:20–1, the people are not forced to flee in haste in *52:11–12*. Verse 11, too, employs the term יצא, but the following v. 12 clearly states that they will not go out in haste and flight (חפזון, מנוסה). They will walk in full safety for YHWH will go before them and be their rearguard. That YHWH leads and protects his people was announced in 40:9–11 and is also proclaimed in *52:7–10*. According to v. 7, a herald announces peace and salvation saying to Zion: 'Your God reigns.'[32] According to vv. 8–10,

148

THE RETURN TO ZION

salvation involves the fact that YHWH returns to Zion (בשוב יהוה ציון).
The ruins of Jerusalem will rejoice, for YHWH has comforted his people,
redeemed Jerusalem and reveals his salvation to the whole world. After
this good news, the urge to leave Babylon follows (cf. 52:11–12).[33] In sum,
52:7–12 underlines that YHWH's return to his people appears simultaneously to the deliverance of the people from exile and their return to Zion.[34]

Scholars have often noticed that the imagery of a way leading from
Babylon (and from other places) to Zion functions as a frame for the
overall composition of Isaiah 40–55. The prologue (40:1–11) introduces
the way prepared for YHWH and the concluding textual unit (55:12–13)
contains an urge to depart (an indefinite 'you'). The two concluding verses
of Isaiah 40–55 consist of four different motifs that all have been used
throughout the sixteen chapters. To some extent, they thereby summarize
the main message or tone of this prophetic book. Chapter 55:12a exhorts
a departure in joy and a return in peace. Verse 12b depicts the mountains,
hills and trees of the field bursting into song because of redemption. Verse
13a describes, although in other terms, the transformation of the wilderness
into fertile land; instead of the thorn and the brier, the cypress and the
myrtle will come up. Finally, in v. 13b, this entire act of salvation will be
a memorial (שם) for YHWH, an everlasting sign of his divine mercy, which
will not be cut off.

In sum, Isaiah 40–55's proclamation of the way is twofold: it describes
the way of YHWH's return to his people and it prepares the way for the
people's escape from captivity and return to Zion and their God.[35] From
the very beginning, the forgiveness of the people's sin against YHWH serves
as a condition for the deliverance from exile and captivity (40:2; 44:22).
Among basic features of Isaiah 40–55 are also the image of YHWH as a
shepherd who gathers his flock and the typology between the redemption
from Babylon and the deliverance from Egypt.

The return in Jeremiah

In Jeremiah, the return from exile is a significant motif also, however not
as predominant as in Isaiah 40–55. According to Jeremiah, the exile is
limited to seventy years. When this period is completed, YHWH will bring
his people back to the place from which they were expelled (Jer. 29:10–14).
As in Isaiah 40–55, Jeremiah portrays YHWH as a shepherd who gathers
his people from the lands to which they have been driven (Jer. 23:3). The
theme of the way, which – as we have seen – often stands in close relation
to the restoration of Zion, occurs only sporadically. It is largely concentrated
within chapters *30–1* and *50–1*, which we shall examine below.

The theme of return is presented in Jeremiah 30:3. YHWH will restore
(שבתי) the fortunes (שבות) of his people, Israel and Judah, and bring them
back (השבתים) to the land that he gave to their ancestors and they will take

149

THE ZION MOTIFS: BETWEEN JUDGEMENT AND SALVATION

possession of it.[36] It is worth noting that the term שוב occurs three times with different meanings.[37] In the third case, it seems to refer to a physical 'return' to the land, hardly involving any spiritual transformation. Moreover, the verse underlines the fact that the goal for the people's journey is exactly the place that had been desolated and abandoned seventy years earlier. According to vv. 30:8–9, YHWH will break the yoke from off his people's neck and burst its bonds, and they will serve God and David instead of being enslaved by strangers. As in Isaiah 10:27, the image of a broken yoke appears to be a figurative illustration of the rupture with a foreign supremacy, supported by the image of bonds being burst.[38] The exile is thus seen as a captivity under the rule of a foreign power (cf. Isa. 40:2), which in v. 10 is expressed as 'the land of their captivity' (ארץ שבים).[39] The deliverance from exile is referred to as YHWH's salvific act (הנני מושיעך) and this entails that Jacob will return (שב) and dwell in safety. Accordingly, this also implies the defeat of the foreign nations, as YHWH will make an end of all the nations among which he scattered his people.

In *Jeremiah 31*, it is clearly stated that Zion is the goal of the journey (cf. vv. 6, 12). *Verses 7–9* and *vv. 10–14* are of special interest, because the language and imagery of these sections look very similar to the language of Isaiah 40–55. In v. 7, YHWH's salvation of his people will give rise to joy and gladness (cf. Isa. 35:1; 44:23; 49:13). Besides that, the people are referred to as 'the remnant of Israel' (שארית ישראל); the remnant that in the Book of Jeremiah has survived in exile. In v. 8, the blind and the lame (cf. Isa. 35:6–7), as well as those with child and in labour, will return (ישובו) together, gathered in a great assembly.[40] In v. 9, the wandering people are led to brooks of water (cf. Isa. 43:19–20) and in a straight path (cf. Isa. 35:8). Furthermore, in vv. 10–11, YHWH is depicted as a shepherd gathering and keeping his flock (cf. Isa. 40:10), and he is worshipped as the one ransoming and redeeming (גאל) Jacob (cf. 43:14). In vv. 12–14, they come to Zion in exultation and their mourning is turned into joy (cf. Isa. 35:10). In sum, Isaiah 35 and 40–55 and Jeremiah 30–1 share a number of themes and linguistic terms.[41] Both prophets speak of the exile in terms of captivity; both anticipate that it is YHWH who redeems and gathers his people; finally, both describe how YHWH prepares a way for his people and leads them to streams of water.

Jeremiah 31:8 is crucial to the present study. The structure of this verse reminds us of the portrait of the approaching army in Jeremiah 4:6 and 6:22:[42]

הנני מביא אותם מארץ צפון וקבצתים מירכתי־ארץ

See, I am going to bring them from the land of the north, and gather them from the farthest parts of the earth. (Jeremiah 31:8)

כי רעה אנכי מביא מצפון

For I am bringing evil from the north. (Jeremiah 4:6)

THE RETURN TO ZION

הנה עם בא מארץ צפון וגוי גדול יעור מירכתי־ארץ

See, a people is coming from the land of the north, a great nation is stirring from the farthest parts of the earth. (Jeremiah 6:22)

As we can see, YHWH is behind both the gathering of the enemies in 4:6 and the gathering of his returning people in 31:8. Likewise, the enemies and people of YHWH arrive *from the same place*, referred to as 'the land of the north' and 'the farthest parts of the earth'. As in 30:10, YHWH brings the people to Zion from far away (רחוק), from where the hostile nations came (cf. 5:15). Moreover, 31:16–17 clearly asserts that they will come back from the land of the enemy (מארץ אויב) to their own country (גבולם). The appearance of identical terms serves a structural purpose. Whereas the enemies came from the north to Zion, destroying and ravaging on their way through the region (cf. Joel 2:1–11), the movement is reversed in regard to the return of the people.[43] They come from the north to Zion, which will be rebuilt, and the desolated land becomes recreated during their journey towards Zion (cf. Isa. 35:1–10). As Jeremiah interprets the desolation of the land and the succeeding exile as an expression of YHWH's judging wrath and punishment against his people, he interprets the return to and restoration of Zion as an expression of YHWH's salvific act.

Jeremiah 31:21–2 highlights that the exiles' way from Zion into exile is identical with the returnees' way from exile to Zion. Road markers and signposts will mark the road by which the people went, for one day they will return by the very same. In v. 22, the people are called 'faithless daughter' (הבת השובבה), which might suggest that the double invitation to 'return', as presented in v. 21, promotes both meanings of שוב – that is, in the first case, the sincere repentance to YHWH, and in the second case, the physical return to their home towns.[44] The invitation to return emerges against the background that YHWH has created a new thing on the earth (כי־ברא יהוה חדשה בארץ; cf. Isa. 43:19).

Whereas Jeremiah 30–1 in general offers a moderate call to return from exile, *Jeremiah 50–1* is far more dramatic. Babylon is under attack and conquered by a people from the north, meaning that the people of YHWH must hurry and flee.[45] The call occurs three times throughout the two chapters – in Jeremiah 50:8: 'Flee from Babylon, and go out of the land of the Chaldeans'; Jeremiah 51:6: 'Flee from the midst of Babylon, save your lives, each of you!'; and Jeremiah 51:45: 'Come out of her, my people!' The depiction of the desolation of Babylon in these chapters is almost identical with the depiction of the desolation of Zion in Jeremiah 1–25. Just as similar descriptions portray both the arriving enemies and the people's return to Zion, so the descriptions of the destruction of Zion as part of YHWH's judgement against his people mirrors Babylon's destruction as a precondition for his salvation of the people.[46] Fugitives and refugees from the land of Babylon now declare in Zion the vengeance of YHWH for his

151

people (cf. 50:28; see also 50:11). This vengeance is depicted in detail in 51:24–6, where YHWH repays Babylon and all the inhabitants of Chaldea for all the wrong that they have done to Zion. YHWH himself attacks the city, and Babylon will be left behind as a perpetual wasteland.

A final observation concerns *50:19–20*. According to this unit, YHWH will restore Israel to its pasture. If anyone in those days seeks the iniquity of Israel (עון ישראל) and the sins of Judah (חטאת יהודה), none will be found. YHWH states: 'I will pardon the remnant [אשאיר] that I have spared.' In my view, this indicates that the exile and return are perceived in terms of a purification process (cf. Isa. 44:22).[47] As we noticed in chapter 7, the classical Zion motif contains the purification on Zion after the prevention of the enemy attack (see Isa. 4:2–6). Yet in Isaiah 40–55 and Jeremiah, the purification takes place in exile, far away from the abandoned Zion.

The return in Ezekiel

As Isaiah 40–55, *Ezekiel 20:33–44* alludes to the Exodus narrative in its portrayal of the return as a new exodus from foreign lands.[48] Verses 33–4 recount the authority of YHWH: he will reign as king with an outstretched hand, a motif frequently used in Isaiah 40–55 (e.g. 40:10; 52:7–10).[49] Ezekiel 20:34–5 contains three verbs that occur in connection with the motif of return in other parts of the Book of Ezekiel. YHWH will perform his act in three stages (cf. 20:41–2; 34:13; 36:24). First, he will *bring* the people *out* from the peoples; then, he will *gather* them *out* of the countries where they were scattered; and finally, he will *bring* them *into* 'the wilderness of the peoples' (20:35), 'the land of Israel' (20:42) or 'their/your own land' (34:13; 36:24).[50] In these verses, all three verbs are first person singular with YHWH as the agent of the people's return. YHWH himself brings his people out (Hiphil of יצא), which, as in Isaiah 40–55, alludes to the deliverance from Egypt. The term קבץ designates YHWH's gathering of his people (cf. Isa. 40:11; Jer. 23:3; 31:8, 10). Yet in Ezekiel, the gathering of the people does not relate to one particular geographical place (e.g. Babylon), but to many different places, that is, from 'the peoples' and from 'the countries where they were scattered'. In Ezekiel 6:8, the survivors of the great desolation should be scattered throughout the countries, and it is exactly from these places they are gathered. The use of the Hiphil form of בוא in regard to YHWH's bringing up his people is remarkable, because קבץ and הביא also occurred in the depiction of YHWH's calling the enemies. In other words, just as he gathered and brought enemies to Zion, he now gathers and brings his people home (cf. Jeremiah). We shall investigate this shift more carefully in the examination of Zechariah (see below).

Returning to Ezekiel 20:33–44, vv. 35–8 state that YHWH will bring his people into the wilderness of the peoples to judge them.[51] Eventually, however, all the house of Israel will serve YHWH on his holy mountain, the

THE RETURN TO ZION

mountain height of Israel. Despite Ezekiel's avoidance of the term, Zion is clearly the setting of these events.[52] At this place, YHWH will welcome his returning people (v. 40). Verses 41–2 repeat the fact that YHWH will bring his people out, gather them and, in these verses, bring them back into the land of Israel which he swore to give to their ancestors. According to vv. 43–4, the inhabitants will undergo a process of purification by which they remember and loathe themselves for all the evils that they have committed (cf. Ezek. 6:9–10). This process entails both the recognition of YHWH as their God and a self-awareness of their guilt.

In *34:11–16*, YHWH reappears as the shepherd taking care of his flock (cf. Isa. 40:11). Most interestingly, however, is the statement in v. 12: YHWH will search out his flock and rescue (נצל) them 'from all the places to which they have been scattered on the day of clouds and thick darkness'. The exile is here described as a worldwide scattering, and the day on which the people were scattered is referred to as 'the day of clouds and thick darkness' (יום ענן וערפל). As we may recall, similar expressions were employed in the depiction of the Day of YHWH in Joel 2:2. In Ezekiel, however, YHWH's judgement resulted in the destruction of the temple and the scattering of his people. His salvation involves the gathering of his people. Verse 13 contains the three verbs of 'bringing home' mentioned above and vv. 14–16 conclude the unit with an illustration of the pastoral care of YHWH.[53]

In the Book of Ezekiel, it is not only the people who return, but also YHWH. As was previously noticed, the destruction of the main city was possible because the glory of YHWH ascended and he abandoned the temple (cf. Ezek. 8–11). In *43:1–9*, this image is reversed. The text consists of two sub-units: vv. 1–5 account for the return of YHWH, whereas vv. 6–9 assert that he will dwell among his people forever. Verses 1–5 persistently underline the idea that the glory of YHWH[54] comes *from the east*, since it was into that very direction that the glory once left the temple (cf. Ezek. 11:22–4).[55] The entire chapter is presented as a vision given to the prophet Ezekiel, and v. 3 suggests an amazing link. The vision that Ezekiel now receives is similar to those he received when he (or YHWH)[56] came to destroy the city (cf. Ezek. 8:4; 9:3, 10) and at the river Chebar (cf. Ezek. 1:4–28).[57] The three visions depict stages in the dynamic Zion motif: the destruction of the city and the land; the residence in exile; and the return to the desolate and abandoned city and land. The movement of YHWH and the movement of his people are parallel. Both will leave the city; both will stay in foreign places; both will return after a designated time. In vv. 6–9, YHWH speaks to Ezekiel to assure him that the divine throne will remain in this place forever. The people will not defile the holy name of YHWH again. The fatal accident resulting in the desolation of the city will not recur. In a former time, YHWH was driven far (רחק) from his sanctuary (cf. Ezek. 8:6); now, he will let the people put their idolatry and the corpses of their kings far away (רחק), so that the holiness of the temple can be maintained. In sum, YHWH accentuates that he will live among his people forever.

The return in Micah

Three passages in the Book of Micah allude to a return. These include Micah 2:12–13, 4:6–8 and 4:9–10. Like the three Major Prophets, *2:12–13* employs the image of a shepherd gathering his flock (cf. Isa. 40:11; Jer. 23:3; 31:10; Ezek. 34:13).[58] The appearance of this image indicates that these verses concern the return from exile, although the texts are silent about the place of departure as well as the goal of the journey.[59] The motifs of breaking through the gates and of YHWH leading his people (cf. v. 13) call forth associations to other passages describing the return.[60] These include the broken bar in Isaiah 43:14, the leadership of YHWH in Isaiah 52:12 and the frequent use of יצא. Therefore, it seems likely that Micah too anticipates a return from exile.[61]

According to *4:6–8*, YHWH will assemble the lame and the cast-off, those whom he has afflicted (הרעתי). It is worth noting that, in Micah, the desolation of Zion is described as a disaster (רע) from YHWH (cf. 1:12) and as an evil time (עת רעה; cf. 2:3). Now, the afflicted will be gathered by YHWH, and the survivors, who have been driven far away (cf. Jeremiah), will become a strong nation (גוי עצום). An almost similar expression (עם עצום) was employed in Joel 2:1 and 2:5 about the enemy army. This similarity indicates that the defeated and exiled people will grow as strong and mighty as were the attacking enemies. In this time of prosperity, YHWH will reign as king over his people on Mount Zion (cf. Isa. 43:15; Ezek. 20:33), and daughter Zion will regain her former dominion. According to 4:6–8, this happens on 'this day' (ביום ההוא) as a shining contrast to the dark day of judgement (cf. Isa. 4:2).[62] Just as the great desolation took place 'on that day', the redemption of the exiled people of YHWH will happen 'on that day'. In addition, the notions of YHWH as king, of the people as his flock and of a 'sheep-tower' artfully play on the shepherd-motif.[63]

Finally, *4:9–10* portrays the destruction of the city. Depicted as a woman giving birth, daughter Zion will writhe and groan, for she will go forth from her city. Accordingly, the people will go to Babylon. Yet in a condensed form, v. 10b alludes to the main structure of Isaiah 40–55 and Jeremiah: the people of YHWH are forced into captivity in Babylon (cf. Mic. 1:16); but there, far away from Zion, will they be saved.[64] YHWH will redeem (גאל) them from the hands of those enemies who once destroyed Zion and forced the people into exile. That the surviving remnant will become a strong nation and regain its former dominance (cf. 4:6–8) presupposes that the sin against YHWH has been forgiven during the stay in Babylon where the redemption and deliverance will take place.

THE RETURN TO ZION

The return in Zechariah

In the Book of Zechariah, the people's conversion to YHWH is a fundamental precondition for the salvific intervention of YHWH (cf. Joel; see chapter 6). Therefore, the divine salvation is initiated towards the end of exile and the people's return to Zion. In the opening verses of the book, *Zechariah 1:3–6*, there is a brief yet vigorous call from YHWH: 'Return to me – and I will return to you' (שׁובו אלי – ואשׁוב אליכם). The people must return to YHWH before he will return to them.[65] Accordingly, שׁוב is the key word within this passage, appearing four times. YHWH's appeal to his people is presented in the light of his wrath against their ancestors, who did not follow the earlier prophets' call to repentance and who thus caused the great desolation and the succeeding exile (Zech. 1:4; cf. Jer. 25:3–7). Therefore, a rhetorical question succeeds in v. 5: 'Your ancestors, where are they?' Well, they are either in captivity or dead.[66] Just as Ezekiel several times operates with self-loathing among the exiles after their experience of the great desolation (Ezek. 6:9–10; 20:43–4), Zechariah indicates a similar motif. Eventually, the ancestors repented and recognized that YHWH acted in this manner because of their evil ways and deeds (cf. v. 6).[67] When their children truly repent, YHWH is ready to return to them and save them from exile.

Zechariah 8:14–15, too, plays on the relation between YHWH's judgement against the ancestors and his salvation of their descendants. Verse 14, which accounts for the disaster brought by YHWH, appears to quote or allude to Jeremiah 4:28b:

כי־דברתי זמתי ולא נחמתי ולא־אשׁוב ממנה

For I have spoken, I have purposed; I have not relented nor will I turn back. (Jeremiah 4:28b)

כאשׁר זממתי להרע לכם בהקציף אבתיכם אתי (. . .) ולא נחמתי

Just as I purposed to bring disaster upon you, when your ancestors provoked me to wrath, and I did not relent. (Zechariah 8:14)

The imminent salvation in Zechariah 8:15 is closely linked with the disaster in the previous verse by means of an antithetical compound statement. In the same way as YHWH in his wrath planned and brought evil and did not relent, he will now return (שׁוב) and purpose to do good to Jerusalem and to the house of Judah. In so far as the 'disaster' stands for the great desolation of Zion,[68] the return of YHWH, conditioned by the return of the descendants (cf. Zech. 1:3), involves a blessing and a restoration of the region that was formerly left in ruins by the enemies.

The saving actions of YHWH also encompass his return to Zion. This seems evident in *Zechariah 1:12–17*, which constitutes the latter part of a vision given to the prophet Zechariah. According to vv. 12–13, the angel

155

of YHWH asks how long YHWH will withhold his mercy from Jerusalem and the cities of Judah, with which he has been angry for seventy years (cf. Jer. 25:11; 29:10). The answer lies implicit in the angel's question: since the seventy years of humiliation and decline have passed, YHWH will finally intervene and change the present situation. This positive change is expressed in v. 13 by 'gracious and comforting words' (cf. 8:15) and, furthermore, as a delightful message of the compassion of YHWH that the prophet will proclaim (vv. 14–17).

Verses 14–15 display a crucial 'logic' in the temper of YHWH. On the one hand, he is very jealous for Jerusalem and Zion. This jealousy or passion is often expressed in YHWH's wrath against his people, but here it is positive (cf. Joel 2:18; Ezek. 39:25). On the other hand, YHWH shows great anger with the nations that are at ease. As Meyers and Meyers rightly assert, 'God's wrath against the nations will allow him to restore his "compassion" for Jerusalem.'[69] According to v. 15b, the reason for his anger is that the nations 'helped' to make the disaster (רעה) worse, even though YHWH was only a little angry.[70] What does this mean? The wrath may point backward to the situation in v. 12. The point, then, is that YHWH was only angry for a short while (מעט as a temporal adverb), but the nations extended the period to seventy years. Or – as a more daring proposal – the verse may be read in the context of the desolation of Zion. If so, YHWH was angry with his people; yet he had not planned that the attack of the hostile nations should result in total devastation. We might then maintain that the nations somehow have exceeded the bounds of their commission and called forth the wrath of YHWH (cf. Assyria in Isa. 10; 37).

In continuation of v. 14, v. 16 states that YHWH has returned to Jerusalem with compassion and that his house will be built in it. In other words, YHWH returns with a compassion (רחמים) he did not show for seventy years (cf. 1:12). Nevertheless, the use of שוב is ambiguous. Does YHWH *return* physically to Jerusalem (cf. Ezek. 43:1–9); or does he in compassion *turn* to his city and people (cf. 1:3; 8:15)? The ambiguity may be deliberate allowing for the passage to contain both aspects: YHWH's return to Zion happens as a part of his turning to his people. Verse 17 emphasizes the prosperity of the recreated land by means of the fourfold use of עוד: again the good news will be proclaimed; again the cities of YHWH will overflow with prosperity; again YHWH will comfort Zion; and again he will choose Jerusalem.[71]

In *2:10–17* [ET 2:6–13], the link between the return of YHWH and that of his people is apparent. According to vv. 11–12, Zion, who lives with daughter Babylon, is urged to flee from the land of the north (cf. the 'fleeing' motif in Isa. 48:20; Jer. 50–1). The focus here is alone on Babylon in the north (cf. Isa. 40–55, Jeremiah and Micah). According to v. 14, daughter Zion will sing and rejoice for YHWH will come and dwell in her midst (הנני־בא ושכנתי בתוכך). The coming of YHWH is described in the

THE RETURN TO ZION

same manner as in Isaiah 35:4 and 40:10 by the term בוא (cf. Zech. 9:9: 'Lo, your king comes to you'). It is assumed that YHWH will take up residence in the city (cf. vv. 14–15). Verse 16 repeats the election of Zion (cf. 1:17) and adds that Judah will become YHWH's portion in the holy land.

The theme of YHWH's return recurs in *Zechariah 8:1–8*, which elaborates upon several phrases and motifs from Zechariah 1:12–17. Verse 2 expresses the great jealousy but also the great wrath that YHWH has for his people (cf. 1:14). According to v. 3, this jealousy leads to YHWH's return to Zion (שבתי אל־ציון; cf. 1:16). Here, the use of שוב appears to refer to the physical return because the verse additionally informs us that YHWH will dwell in the midst of Jerusalem (ושכנתי בתוך ירושלם). For that reason, Jerusalem will be called the faithful city (cf. Isa. 1:26) and the mountain of YHWH Sebaoth will be called the holy mountain. In v. 6, the divine act is described as miraculous (פלא), and although the surviving remnant regards it as impossible, YHWH demonstrates that he can do it. Without doubt, this 'miraculous' act refers to the return of YHWH (vv. 2–3), to the peace restored in the city (vv. 4–5) and to the gathering of the people and their return to Jerusalem (vv. 7–8). The verses concluding YHWH's return also imply a return of his people, whom he will save from the east and the west (cf. Isa. 43:5–6; Jer. 30:10–11) and bring home. Just as YHWH will dwell in Jerusalem (v. 3), his people will live there as well (ושכנו בתוך ירושלם). There is indeed a symbiotic relationship between the return of YHWH and the return of his people to Zion and their common settlement in the city. YHWH will be their God and they will be his people in faithfulness and in righteousness.[72] This new relationship with God shares qualities with the new city in v. 3.[73]

Like Zechariah 8:14–15, 10:6 plays on the theme 'before-after'. YHWH will bring the houses of Judah and Joseph back, and they will be as though he had not rejected them. Repudiation and exile become replaced by salvation and return. Finally, *10:8–10* renders a magnificent picture of YHWH's gathering of the scattered people from Egypt and Assyria. Several of the terms are familiar. He gathers (קבץ) the people (10:8, 10), he redeems (פדה) them (10:8; cf. Isa. 35:10) and he brings them home (השיב; 10:10). Yet the perspective is expanded from Babylon to Egypt, Assyria and 'far away countries' (cf. Ezekiel). The people of YHWH will return to the land demarcated by Gilead and Lebanon, and this area will not be spacious enough for them, as they will be so many in number.[74] Verse 8 introduces another familiar term: YHWH as a shepherd who will *whistle* (שרק)[75] for his people. According to Gesenius, the term in this particular sense ('jem. pfeifen, ihn durch Pfeifen herbeirufen') only occurs three times within the Old Testament as a whole.[76] Besides this verse in Zechariah, it occurs two times in Isaiah where YHWH sends for a nation far away (Isa. 5:26) and for Egypt and Assyria (Isa. 7:18). This indicates that YHWH whistles for his people scattered in Egypt and Assyria like he whistled for the enemy

157

THE ZION MOTIFS: BETWEEN JUDGEMENT AND SALVATION

army located in the same places. We have already noticed that the terms קבץ and אסף are used to describe YHWH's gathering of his people from exile.[77] The very same terms were employed in the portrait of YHWH's gathering of the enemies to attack Zion (see e.g. Zeph. 3:8; Zech. 14:2). There exists a structural parallelism between YHWH's calling of the enemies as a tool of his judgement and YHWH's calling of his people to their salvation. Whereas the former is negative, involving the devastation of the land and the desolation of the city, the latter is positive, inasmuch as the redemption makes the desert bloom, the people return and Zion become restored.

Summing up: the return to Zion

In the previous chapter, we observed that the city and its surrounding land were left desolate and without humans. A remnant of survivors was brought into exile. In Isaiah 40–55, Jeremiah and Micah, it is an essential feature that this exile is regarded as a captivity from which the people of YHWH must be redeemed. In addition, the exile is regarded as YHWH's righteous punishment of his people because of their evil sins causing great destruction. Yet in exile, YHWH forgives his people's sins and brings them home. However, it remains unclear from where the return will take place. Isaiah 40–55, Jeremiah, Micah and Zechariah refer to Babylon and the land of the north, whereas Ezekiel – surprisingly unspecifically – refers to 'all the places to which they have been scattered'. Occasionally, Egypt and Assyria are mentioned as well as east and west. The exile, therefore, is not located in one particular place, but many. This indicates a centralistic world view in which Zion or God's mountain is the centre to which the people of YHWH returns from all the corners of the world. Zion is either referred to by its name (Isa. 40–55, Jeremiah, Micah and Zechariah) or referred to as 'the land of Israel' or 'the mountain height of Israel' (Ezekiel).

It is YHWH who as a shepherd gathers his scattered people and brings them through the wilderness. Furthermore, a central characteristic of the homecoming-motif is that YHWH also returns. This is spelled out in Ezekiel's magnificent temple vision; yet Isaiah 40–55 and Zechariah also depict YHWH's physical return to Zion. The ambiguous term שוב poses a special problem, in so far as it contains at least two different meanings. On the one hand, 'return' means *turn to* – that is, a sincere, spiritual transformation or conversion, in which the sinner or sinful people turns to YHWH in their repentance. On the other hand, 'return' means *return to* – that is, a concrete, physical return to a particular geographical location. As we have seen, it is often difficult to decide which meaning is implied in the texts; sometimes, the ambiguity even appears to be deliberate. The spiritual conversion to YHWH and the physical return to Zion may

158

THE RETURN TO ZION

thereby be two sides of the same coin. The forgiveness of sins – through the people's self-loathing in exile – results in a redemption from captivity and return to the desolate city.

Within a broader context, I find that the motif of return has its structural counterpoint in the attack of the enemies, which we examined in chapter 6. In both motifs it is YHWH who gathers and brings them to Zion. Yet, whereas the enemies come as an instrument of YHWH's judgement, the people of YHWH return as an expression of his merciful salvation. In Jeremiah, this is made abundantly clear through a series of literary devices: as the city of YHWH was destroyed by the Babylonians, Babylon is destroyed by YHWH; and as the enemies came from the north, the returning people will come from the north. However, whereas the hostile nations brought destruction, the people of YHWH will bring restoration. YHWH had left the city so that it could be conquered by the enemies; now, he returns and will choose the rebuilt temple and city as his dwelling-place.

The motif of return constitutes the second stage of the dynamic Zion motif. It forms a bridge between desolation and exile and the theme of the New Zion, which we shall explore in the following chapter.

Notes

1 Lim 2010: 151: 'Since ch. 35 is not a historical narrative, but rather a poetic vision, the wilderness mentioned in the poem need not be a reference to Judah's desolate topography in 701.' In addition, for a thorough study of Isa. 34–5 within the canonical context of Isaiah as a whole, see Mathews 1995.

2 See, for instance, Watts 2005: 539–40: 'The effect of YHWH's judgment is felt most immediately by those parts of Judah nearest the borders to the south and east.'

3 See Wildberger 2002: 347–8.

4 Cf. Childs 2001: 253: 'The two major themes of the chapters, namely, the divine judgment of the nations and the return to the redeemed to Zion, point both backward to the earlier Isaianic prophecies as well as forward to the ensuing chapters.'

5 However, Childs notes that since Isa. 35 is placed before the historical episodes of the Assyrian and Babylonian attacks, this passage projects the divine plan beyond a certain historical period and 'focuses on the final eschatological exaltation of Zion and the entrance into the ultimate joy of the kingdom of God' (Childs 2001: 256).

6 Cf. Childs 2001: 258: 'the imagery of the return to Zion has been extended far beyond the concrete historical situation depicted in chapters 40ff.'

7 Due to this ambiguity, the passage may refer to a return from Babylon (cf. Isa. 40–55) and to a return from all the other countries and regions where the people of YHWH have been brought, for instance, Assyria and Egypt (cf. Isa. 11:11–16). Furthermore, the passage can be read as a general depiction of pilgrimage, which constitutes a central part of the life of the pious Israelite (cf. in particular Pss 120–34). We shall return to the pilgrimage motif and the nations going up to Zion in chapter 10.

8 Notice that in Jer. 4:26, the fruitful land/Carmel (הכרמל) was turned into a desert (מדבר), whereas in Isa. 35:1–2, the desert (מדבר) will be transformed into 'the majesty of Carmel' (הדר הכרמל).

THE ZION MOTIFS: BETWEEN JUDGEMENT AND SALVATION

9 Cf. Kaiser 1974: 363: 'The first obvious suggestion, that it is the desert and wilderness as the scene of the manifestation of the glory of Yahweh going before his liberated people to Zion . . . , does not stand up to examination.'

10 See Wildberger 2002: 351.

11 According to Thompson 2005: 107–35, these motifs draw upon a common Ancient Near Eastern genre, that is, 'the song of the poor man', which includes representatives of the poor or outcast, often coupled in pairs: widows and orphans, the blind and the lame, or the weak and oppressed. In Isa. 35, '[Isaiah] brings together the death-like barrenness of a desert's aridity and the life-giving fertility of spring rain to create a transcendent metaphor for the reversals that the kingdom determines. He joins this life-affirming imagery to an eightfold song for a poor man' (Thompson 2005: 121).

12 Ps 84:6–8[5–7] indicates a striking connection. The wandering in itself makes the dry valley of Baca into a place of springs. In other words, because the people of YHWH *go* through the valley of Baca, it becomes full of prosperity.

13 Cf. Kaiser 1974: 365.

14 Wildberger 2002: 353.

15 With over 1,050 occurrences, the term is extraordinarily widely attested in the Old Testament; it indeed ranks twelfth in frequency among words (cf. Fabry 2004: 472). In his highly informative article, Heinz-Josef Fabry distinguishes between a secular semantic category, that is, the physical movement of turning, turning around and returning, and a theological semantic category, that is, the religious repentance; see Fabry 2004: 478–81.

16 Wildberger 2002: 356–7.

17 LXX adds 'o Priests'.

18 Blenkinsopp 2002: 180.

19 Gesenius 1921: 671: 'v. d. Mühsal, v. Elende des Lebens'.

20 See Westermann 1987: 35; Blenkinsopp 2002: 180.

21 Westermann 1987: 35. See also Childs 2001: 298, who notices that much of Isaiah's attack on Israel has focused on a 'people laden with iniquity' (1:4; cf. 5:18). Another pregnant example of YHWH's salvation is *44:21–3*. Verse 21 ensures that YHWH will not forget his people, which are called 'Jacob', 'Israel', and 'servant (of YHWH)'. Verse 22a repeats the opening motif in 40:2 where YHWH sweeps away the transgressions of his people as a precondition for their return. Strikingly, v. 22b states: 'return to me, for I have redeemed you' (שׁובה אלי כי גאלתיך). Here, 'the return' (שׁובה) very likely means repentance to YHWH as a response to his redemptive intervention, rather than a physical return. Verse 23 concludes with a cosmic acclamation that praises YHWH as the redeemer of Jacob.

22 Blenkinsopp 2002: 181.

23 Blenkinsopp 2002: 183.

24 Cf. Childs 2001: 299: 'When 40:3–5 is read in light of chapter 35, then the prologue signals not just a general expectation of a coming redemption, but points explicitly to the end of God's judgment upon Judah, symbolized by its blindness and inability to see: "Then the eyes of the blind will be opened" (35:5).'

25 Cf. footnote in NRSV, LXX, Targum and Vulgate.

26 Cf. NRSV; Westermann 1987: 31; Childs 2001: 294; Blenkinsopp 2002: 184. As Childs states, 'Zion and Jerusalem are now personified as evangelists of good tidings. They are appointed to proclaim the news to the cities of Judah.'

27 An important motif within Isa. 40–55 is YHWH's commission of the Persian King Cyrus. Particularly in Isa. 44:24–45:8, Cyrus defeats Babylon so that the people of YHWH can escape captivity. Cyrus likewise stands behind the restoration of Jerusalem; see further in chapter 10.

THE RETURN TO ZION

28 Although we should prefer this alternative reading, the ambiguity may be deliberate. In the end, however, both images testify to the same subject matter: Babylon is punished for the sake of the people of YHWH; cf. Childs 2001: 336; see further in Poulsen 2012: 101.
29 Cf. NRSV.
30 Blenkinsopp 2002: 227.
31 In opposition to NRSV, I understand v. 21 as referring to the future (cf. the use of prophetic past tense; cf. LXX) rather than to the past; see further in Poulsen 2012: 96.
32 Cf. Berges 2011: 114: 'The proclamation of Yhwh's kingship in Isa. 52:7 sounds as a positive answer to the desperate question in Jer. 8:19: "Is Yhwh not in Zion? Is her king not in her?"'
33 However, Babylon is not explicitly mentioned in this passage, only the vague 'from there' (מִשָּׁם). Hans Barstad understands 'from there' as Jerusalem. To him, it is the inhabitants of Jerusalem, who in continuation of vv. 7–10 will go out with the weapons of YHWH (כְּלֵי יהוה) to fight the enemies of Jerusalem; see Barstad 1989: 102–6. Childs 2001: 406–7 suggests the 'place where God's holiness is not respected' (cf. 52:1–6).
34 Westermann 1987: 251.
35 For studies of the way imagery in Isa. 40–55, see Kiesow 1979; Barstad 1989; Laato 1998: 131–41; Lund 2007; Lim 2010; Tiemeyer 2011: 155–202. Many of these interpreters, especially H. Barstad, Ø. Lund and L.-S. Tiemeyer, however, are highly critical of the alleged centrality of the new exodus in Isa. 40–55. Rather than proclaiming a return from the Babylonian exile, Isa. 40–55 as a whole concerns YHWH's return to Zion, the return from the Diaspora as such and the destruction of the enemies of Zion as part of its restoration and glorification; see further in Poulsen 2012: 93–6.
36 The motif of return and restoration in Jeremiah shares a set of features with God's promises in Deut. 30:1–10. Therefore, just as the destruction of Zion was seen as prophetic fulfilment of YHWH's covenant curses (cf. chapter 8), the return and restoration can be seen as prophetic fulfilment of YHWH's covenant promise; cf. Dow 2011: 84.
37 However, according to Allen 2008: 334–5, the 'repetition of the Hebrew verb *šûb* provides a narrower definition of restoring fortunes envisioned as a return to the promised land'. Cf. Jones 1992: 377, who informs us that older English versions of the verse render the phrase 'restore the fortunes' as 'turn again the captivity'.
38 Carroll 1986: 576: 'Judah-Israel will be freed from foreign domination (cf. v. 3), and the only servitude it will know in the future is to Yahweh and its own king . . . No longer will the nation serve foreign kings but their own Davidic king will be their ruler.' See further in chapter 10.
39 Cf. Gesenius 1921: 802: 'Land der Gefangenschaft'; see also Carroll 1986: 577; NRSV.
40 Notice the use of motifs related to 'the song of the poor man'; see further in Thompson 2005: 115–30.
41 In general, there is a series of verbal parallels between Jer. 30–1 and Isa. 40–55, see Lundbom 2004: 371–2.
42 Lundbom 2004: 423–4.
43 For a useful list of examples of YHWH's reversal of the judgement against Judah/Israel, see Stulman 2005: 260–1.
44 See also Lundbom 2004: 450–1: 'Hebrew *habbat haššôbēbâ* plays on the two occurrences of *šûb* in v 21 and embellishes the idea of virgin Israel as a people who turns here and turns there.'

THE ZION MOTIFS: BETWEEN JUDGEMENT AND SALVATION

45 According to Carroll 1986: 814, 'two themes dominate the poems: the fall of Babylon and the restoration of the exiles to their own land . . . and these are interwoven together without any marked degree of progress of thought'.
46 Cf. Stulman 2005: 387.
47 Allen 2008: 514: 'The former sins that hung over Israel's survivors like a cloud, causing its punishment and preventing their covenantal fellowship with God, would be forgiven.'
48 Zimmerli 1979: 414–15.
49 The expression 'with a mighty hand and an outstretched arm' (בְּיָד חֲזָקָה וּבִזְרוֹעַ נְטוּיָה) is familiar in the Pentateuch (see Deut. 4:34; 5:15; 7:19; 26:8). In the Pentateuch, however, YHWH's hand is manifested against the enemies of his people. As Tuell 2009: 134 indicates, that hand is now manifested against the people of YHWH itself: 'God will deliver Israel against its will!' Cf. Martens 2001.
50 The terms יצא, קבץ and בוא occur in all four instances, except from 36:24 where יצא has been replaced by לקח.
51 It is rather peculiar that Ezekiel – after the deliverance – anticipates another act of judgement in which the people will be brought within the bond of the covenant and the rebels are prohibited access to the land. Whereas the wilderness in Isa. 40–55 is turned into a place of prosperity (cf. Isa. 43:19b–20), the wilderness in Ezekiel constitutes a thematic link to the Exodus narrative and serves as a place of judgement and segregation. See further in Baltzer 1971: 25–6. Cf. Joyce 2009: 153: 'Ezekiel's use of [Exodus language] here transforms the model from one of salvation to one of judgement, or at least one that is about judgement before it is about salvation.'
52 Cf. for instance Joyce 2009: 154.
53 For a list of references to other Old Testament and Ancient Near East 'shepherd' texts, including Ps 23, see Block 1998: 290–1.
54 The image of the glory of YHWH filling the temple (cf. v. 5) echoes Exod. 40:34 and 1 Kgs 8:11; see Joyce 2009: 227.
55 Cf. Block 1998: 578–9: 'the present course signifies a reversal of the tragedy described in chs. 10–11. The last time the prophet had encountered the divine glory the latter hovered over the east gate and then disappeared over the mountain east of the city (11:19, 23), symbolic of Yahweh's abandonment of his people. The present movement affirms that the nation's period of separation from his presence is past; Yahweh has taken up residence in his temple in their midst.'
56 With good reason, some manuscripts alter בבאי into בבאו to clarify that 'he' – that is, YHWH – came to destroy the city; cf. Zimmerli 1983: 407–8.
57 According to Ezek. 1:1, the river Chebar designates the place of the exiles where Ezekiel received his call (אֲנִי בְתוֹךְ־הַגּוֹלָה עַל־נְהַר־כְּבָר).
58 Marrs 2004: 88: 'It is noteworthy that Micah uses common Near Eastern shepherd imagery to depict Yahweh's royal protection of his people. Zion's ultimate destiny cannot be divorced from the vision of Yahweh as royal protector and triumphant leader.'
59 Jeppesen 1987: 197.
60 Jenson 2008: 129.
61 Wolff 1990: 86: 'the main theme of the passage is clear. It is Yahweh who, going before his people, prepares a way for their escape from prison and their exodus into freedom'.
62 Jeppesen 1987: 245.
63 Allen 1976: 331.
64 See further in Allen 1976: 333–4.
65 Meyers & Meyers 2010: 93: 'The issue of the people's return to obeying God's word is coupled with Yahweh's "return" . . . The latter concept implies that

162

Yahweh has temporarily turned away, a condition represented by the destruction and exile.'

66 Cf. Petersen 1984: 133 who, in addition, refers to Lam. 5:7: 'Our ancestors sinned; they are no more, and we bear their iniquities.'

67 Cf. Meyers & Meyers 2010: 99: 'Whereas the earlier age brought about the punishment of destruction and exile because of their "evil ways" and "evil deeds" (v 4), the present age holds forth promise because the people have "returned" (v 6b).'

68 See Meyers & Meyers 2010: 424.

69 Meyers & Meyers 2010: 121.

70 Cf. Meyers & Meyers 2010: 122. I see no reasons to read עזר as having an alternate root meaning 'to be copious' (i.e. 'the nations multiply calamity') or to emend the root to זרע meaning 'to plough'.

71 The divine election of Jerusalem (ובחר עוד בירושלם) is thereby actually a re-election of the city that, according to Ps 132:13, formerly was chosen by YHWH (כי־בחר יהוה בציון).

72 Notice the reminiscence of the election formula in the Pentateuch (see Exod. 19:5; 29:45; Lev. 26:12) as it is employed in Jeremiah's vision of the new covenant (Jer. 31:31–4); see further in Meyers & Meyers 2010: 418–19.

73 Cf. Petersen 1984: 303.

74 Petersen 1995: 77.

75 NRSV has 'signal for' (see note below).

76 Gesenius: 1921: 864. The term שרק occurs in several passages, yet with two different meanings: either *to whisper* as a signal to call somebody or *to whisper* as a taunt. We encountered the latter meaning, for instance, in Jer. 19:8, where the desolated city will be 'a thing to be hissed at'. Meyers & Meyers 2009: 213 count twenty attestations, of which only Zech. 10:8 has positive connotations.

77 See, for instance, Isa. 40:11; Jer. 23:3; 31:8, 10; Ezek. 20:34, 41; Mic. 2:12; 4:6.

10

THE NEW ZION

The imagery of the New Zion is rich. The text material extends from plain anticipations of restoration and repopulation of the desolate city to, more or less, wonderful pictures of Zion as the holy centre for all nations of the world. Apparently, the imagery of the New Zion is stretched out between concrete reality – that is, a rebuilt city and the ideal: a dream, a hope and a vision of a bright and peaceful future without division, destruction and death.

The structure of this chapter illustrates this span of anticipations. First, we shall focus on the national political aspect of the New Zion concerning the rebuilding and repopulation of the city, and the reunification of the two kingdoms, Israel and Judah, under the rule of a Davidic monarch. Second, we shall look at the cultic aspect in relation to the new temple and its life-giving fountain. Third, we shall investigate the international aspect concerning the gathering of the nations of the world. Finally, we shall explore the cosmic aspect, including the future of a harmonious coexistence between God, man and animal, and the abolition of death.

Rebuilding and repopulation

In *Isaiah*, the plans for restoration are initially foreshadowed in *Isaiah 44:26–8*. YHWH pronounces about Jerusalem: 'it shall be inhabited', and of the cities of Judah: 'they shall be rebuilt'. He assures them of the fact, saying: 'I will raise up their ruins.' In v. 28, a promise is given concerning Jerusalem: 'it shall be rebuilt'; and its temple[1] will be founded.[2] The interesting point in this short section is that the rebuilding and repopulation of the city and YHWH's command to the deep to dry up are intertwined (cf. Gen. 1; Ps 74:12–17).[3] The portrayal of YHWH as rebuilder and creator, therefore, suggests that the restoration of Zion is not merely a reconstruction of the desolate Zion; a new and different Zion may emerge by the creative power of YHWH.[4] Moreover, the vision of Isaiah 44:26–8 introduces the succeeding chapter concerning YHWH's commission to the Persian king, Cyrus, as his servant. According to Isaiah 45:13, Cyrus will build the city of YHWH and set the exiles free. We may ask: who is going to rebuild

THE NEW ZION

Zion? Is it YHWH (cf. 44:26), Cyrus or even 'the foreigners' (cf. 60:10)? It is hardly an either/or question, in so far as all three actors make good sense within their distinctive contexts. Obviously, YHWH stands behind it (as he stood behind the great desolation and return of his people). Yet Cyrus, too, plays a prominent role as a main agent within Isaiah 41–8. Nevertheless, a rebuilding initiated by foreigners makes sense within Isaiah 60, which portrays the worldwide pilgrimage to Zion.

In *Isaiah 54:11–17*, the restoration becomes more fanciful. Verses 11–12 describe how the city will be built with malachite and sapphires, and how its walls and gates will be covered with precious stones.[5] YHWH will provide a unique protection, because anyone who dares to attack will fall (cf. vv. 14–17).[6] Verse 13 contains a minor text-critical problem, as it states: 'all your [that is, the city's] children shall be taught by YHWH' (כל־בניך למודי יהוה). This scenario does not appear to be implausible, in so far as parallels do exist in texts such as Isaiah 48:17 and Jeremiah 31:31–4, where the people will be taught by YHWH. Nevertheless, Westermann proposes, by changing the vocalization, to read 'your builders' instead of 'your children'.[7] Such a modification thereby highlights that the sovereignty of the new city is anchored in the divine will, because its builders are taught by YHWH himself (cf. the temple in Exodus and 1 Chronicles).

Isaiah 62:1–12 energetically expresses YHWH's passion for Zion. The text consists of three minor sub-units: YHWH's care for Zion (vv. 1–5), the guards on the walls (vv. 6–9) and the prepared way to Zion (vv. 10–12). Already in the introductory verse, YHWH shows his care: 'For Zion's sake I will not keep silent, and for Jerusalem's sake I will not rest, until her vindication shines out like the dawn, and her salvation like a burning torch.' The nations will, according to v. 2, come to witness the salvation of Zion, and the city is to receive a new name. The names associated with the city, the old and the new ones, all symbolically illustrate the destiny of the city (vv. 4b–5). Formerly, Zion was called 'Forsaken' (עזובה; cf. Jer. 9:18; 12:7) and its surrounding land was called 'Desolate' (שממה). Now the city will be called 'My Delight Is in Her', and the land will be called 'Married'. These symbolic names draw upon the wedding metaphor, which is a common Ancient Near Eastern image of a people's relationship with God, depicted as the relationship between bride and bridegroom (cf. the Merneptah Stele, Hosea and Ezekiel).[8] Nevertheless, a text-critical problem arises concerning the statement 'your children shall marry you' (יבעלוך בניך).[9] As in Isaiah 54:13, it is the vocalization of the word בניך that causes problems; in short, can *children* marry their mother?[10] Blenkinsopp supports this idea by maintaining the expression 'your children'; however, he translates בעל more modestly: 'so will your children *be united* with you'.[11] In addition, a footnote in BHS proposes to change the subject into singular, indicating that YHWH is marrying his city. This emendation, however, is without text-critical warrant. The picture of the children of the city being united with Zion is not that

165

unrealistic when we pay attention to the former name of the city, 'Forsaken'. Moreover, the term 'children' or 'sons' commonly designates the inhabitants of a place. Indeed, the entire passage concludes with a reference to the redeemed of YHWH returning home.

We shall make a cursory reading of the following sub-unit (vv. 6–9), noticing that the guards, watching day and night, will remind YHWH to establish (כון) the city. Initially, vv. 10–12 appear to recall the Exodus motif in Isaiah 40–55.[12] The inhabitants of Zion are urged to go through the gates, to prepare a way for the people (העם) and to raise a signal for the peoples (העמים). Yet for whom is this way prepared? According to Westermann, 'the people' stands for the surviving remnant still waiting in exile to return.[13] Blenkinsopp, too, argues for a return from the Diaspora, although he understands the way in an eschatological perspective concerning the way of pilgrimage to the sanctuary on Zion.[14] We may thus assume that the way is not only restricted to the people of Israel, but to *the peoples* as such. The text likely advocates for the universalism revealed in other texts where the nations gather around Zion (especially Isa. 2:2–4; see below). In any case, the new city will become the centre for some kind of migration, and, therefore, the city is given a new name: 'Sought Out' (דרושה). The people coming to Zion will be called 'The Holy People' (עם־הקדש) and 'The Redeemed of YHWH' (גאולי יהוה). Finally, the city will bear the name 'A City Not Forsaken' (עיר לא נעזבה). In sum, the 'forsaken' city of v. 4 has become assured that she will not be abandoned again.

In the visions of *Jeremiah*, YHWH's restoration of the fortunes of his people (cf. Jer. 30:3) involves a restoration of Zion. Furthermore, in Jeremiah 30:18, YHWH will restore the fortunes of the tents of Jacob and have compassion for his dwellings. The use of שוב and רחם indicates the unmistakable shift taking place, which mirrors the past: 'the city shall be rebuilt upon its mound, and the citadel set on its rightful site'. The citadel or palaces (ארמון), which were destroyed in Jeremiah 6:5, will be re-established.[15] The ruined buildings will be rebuilt on the exact spot on which they formerly stood.[16] Just as the people will return to the land given to their ancestors (cf. Jer. 30:3), the cities will reappear where they once stood. In *Jeremiah 31:23–5*, the people in the land of Judah and in its towns will – because of this new situation – joyfully say: 'YHWH bless you, O abode of righteousness, O holy hill!' The blessing concerns a particular place, reflected in the term 'holy mountain' (הר הקדש, or rather הר קדשי), which occurs parallel to Zion in some texts (cf. Joel 2:1). Here, 'the holy mountain' parallels the apparent identical 'abode of righteousness' (נוה־צדק). Who, then, will live in this abode? Is it the abode of YHWH, the same as the holy hill belonging to him? If so, the verse announces that YHWH will again dwell on Zion. Or does the expression 'abode of righteousness'[17] refer to the abode of the people (i.e. the land and cities of Judah)? If so, Judah will again be blessed by YHWH. The succeeding v. 24 supports the

THE NEW ZION

latter proposal, as it states: 'and Judah and all its towns shall live there [לל] together' – that is, in the land as such or on the mountain (cf. Ezek. 20:40).[18] Nevertheless, the point is that the abandoned and desolate land will be repopulated.

In Jeremiah, it appears to be a subtle composition strategy that several motifs are contrasted and turned upside down. We have previously observed correspondence between the attacking enemies arriving from the north and the people returning from the north. Accordingly, as Zion was ruined, Babylon became ruined. With regard to the restoration and repopulation, many motifs are reversed: the cities will lie in the places where they once stood, and there will again be people in places that had been emptied and deserted. This is also the case in *Jeremiah 31:27–8*. According to v. 27, YHWH will 'sow' with the humans and the animals he once killed (cf. Jer. 21:6)![19] Verse 28 constitutes, according to Georg Fischer, a theological key statement.[20] In this verse, the connection between the desolation and the restoration is made unambiguously clear: YHWH is responsible for both. As he watched over his people when they were plucked up and broken down, he will watch over them as they are built and planted (cf. Jer. 1:10). This coherence elucidates that the destiny of both the people and Zion, from the very beginning, has been anchored in the providence of YHWH.

The restoration of the city is described in detail in *31:38–40*.[21] As Leslie Allen states, 'this passage provides a climax to a topic that has kept on surfacing in this compositional block, the importance of Zion in Yahweh's purposes and in Israel's future'.[22] The city will be rebuilt for YHWH; it is his city (cf. Ps 48). In v. 40, it is of particular significance that the valley, once filled with dead bodies (7:30–8:3), will become sacred. This new sacredness of the city thereby contrasts with the imagery of its sinfulness, for instance in 7:30–8:3.[23] Finally, v. 40 concludes the unit with this powerful statement: 'it shall never again be uprooted or overthrown!' In short, the restoration of Zion implies a divine promise concerning protection and inviolability (cf. Isa. 62:12).

Jeremiah 33:1–11 adds four significant elements. First, YHWH is portrayed as the creator and maker of the earth (cf. v. 2).[24] Thus the proclamation of the New Zion is related to the creative power of YHWH (cf. Isa. 44:26–8). Second, the recalling of the great desolation in vv. 4–5 forms a sharp contrast to the salvific action of YHWH in the succeeding vv. 6–11 (cf. the similar structure in Jer. 31:28). Third, the action of YHWH is portrayed by three expressive images in vv. 6–9. According to v. 6, YHWH, who formerly hid his face in anger, will now heal his people and reveal to them prosperity and security; according to v. 7, he will restore the fortunes of Judah and Israel (cf. 30:18) and rebuild them as they were at first; and, finally, in v. 8, YHWH will cleanse (טהר) his people from all their sins and forgive (סלח) all their guilt and rebellion (cf. 31:34). The cleansing of the sin that caused destruction and exile forms a central element in the creation

167

THE ZION MOTIFS: BETWEEN JUDGEMENT AND SALVATION

of a New Zion. Fourth, the place that was left waste and without humans and animals (cf. 4:23–6) will be filled with sounds of joy and gladness. The sound of mirth, brought to silence in 7:34, will once again be heard in the city. Moreover, it is striking that thank-offerings will be brought to the house of YHWH (בית יהוה). The locus for the happiness of the new city seems to be the temple institution, which, in the canonical composition of the Book of Jeremiah, appears to be almost absent after the exile. We shall return to this issue later in the present chapter.

According to *Ezekiel 36:33–8*, the purging of sin is also closely connected with the restoration and repopulation. As YHWH proclaims in v. 33:

ביום טַהֲרִי אתכם מכל עונותיכם וְהוֹשַׁבְתִּי אֶת־הערים וְנִבְנוּ החרבות

On the day that I cleanse you from all your iniquities, I will cause the towns to be inhabited, and the waste places shall be rebuilt. (Ezekiel 36:33)

Ezekiel employs the same terms (בנה, יָשַׁב) to portray the recreation of the ruined Zion as are used in Isaiah 44:26–8 and Jeremiah 30:18. As in Isaiah 35:1–2, the desolate land will be transformed into exuberance; it will become like the Garden of Eden; and cities and ruined towns are to be inhabited (vv. 34–5; cf. v. 10). Verse 36 depicts YHWH as a gardener rebuilding the ruined places and replanting the desolate, employing the same terms (בנה, נטע) as used in Jeremiah 31:28. In sum, Ezekiel, too, anticipates a new great people, in so far as YHWH will increase the population of his people like a flock, and this flock will fill the ruined towns (cf. vv. 37–8).[25]

Although the Book of Amos does not have much to say about Zion, its concluding passage in *Amos 9:11–15* is of relevance to shed light upon the anticipations we examined above. As YHWH raised up the ruins of his city in Isaiah 44:26, he will, according to Amos, raise up 'the booth of David that has fallen' (סֻכַּת דויד הנפלת). To what does this phrase refer? Apparently, there are two possibilities. It may refer to a restoration of the Davidic monarchy,[26] or it may refer to a restoration of the 'booth' associated with Zion in texts like Isaiah 1:8 and 4:6.[27] The latter proposal is most plausible when the phrase is read along with the second half of the verse – that is, YHWH repairs its breaches, raises up its ruins and rebuilds (בנה!) it as in former times.[28] On the other hand, the allusions in v. 12 to the invasion of Edom and the slaughtering of the nations suggest that the 'booth' refers to the reinstatement of a new Davidic king. Uncertainty remains. Verse 13 portrays the prosperity brought to the land. In the succeeding v. 14 (cf. Jer. 30:18), YHWH will restore the fortunes of his people, and they will rebuild (בנה) the ruined cities and inhabit (יָשַׁב) them. Again, the terms בנה and יָשַׁב are employed to express the change that takes place. Also v. 15 provides an essential parallel to Jeremiah: YHWH will plant (נטע) his people in their land (cf. Jer. 31:28), and they will never again

168

THE NEW ZION

be plucked up (cf. Isa. 62:12; Jer. 31:40). The passage of Jeremiah concerns the new city rather than the people as such. The vision of Amos 9:11–15 recalls much of the imagery revealed in Isaiah, Jeremiah and Ezekiel,[29] and, in addition, ties the Davidic figure to the New Zion.

The depiction in Isaiah 54:11–17 of God's special protection by means of solid walls resonates with the scenario in *Zechariah 2:4b–5 [ET 8b–9]*, although the latter appears to be slightly different. In this passage, there are no walls, because the new city will be inhabited as open fields, where humans and animals will dwell in it. Again, humans and animals are juxtaposed, as they happen to be in texts concerning their extinction by YHWH (cf. Jer. 21:6; Ezek. 14:21) and in texts concerning their restoration (cf. Jer. 31:27; Ezek. 36:11). An astonishing feature of Zechariah 2:4b–5 is the depiction of YHWH forming a wall of fire (חומת אש) around the city and showing his glory within it. As observed in chapter 7, YHWH uses the fire to defeat his enemies (cf. Isa. 30:27–33) and the fire purges Zion from sinners (cf. Isa. 33:14). Here, the fire provides a bulwark against hostile nations and is, at the same time, closely related to the glory and permanent presence of YHWH. As Meyers and Meyers conclude, 'with God himself as guarantor of Jerusalem's integrity, the existence of actual fortifications becomes meaningless'.[30]

The reunification of the two kingdoms under a Davidic monarch

A remarkable characteristic of the New Zion is the reunification of the two Israelite kingdoms: the northern kingdom of Israel and the southern kingdom of Judah. This reunification is rather peculiar, because the disruption of the Davidic-Solomonic Empire constitutes an inferior theme within the prophetic literature as such. Only a few verses allude to this event (e.g. Isa. 7:17); therefore a more elaborate account of the conflict and the disruption of the empire must be looked for in other parts of the Old Testament. Nevertheless, some of the prophets presuppose a great separation in earlier times.

In *Isaiah*, the reunification is referred to only in Isaiah 11:13, where the jealousy and hostility of the two kingdoms will disappear.[31] Especially in *Jeremiah* is the reunification of the kingdoms related to Zion. In *Jeremiah 50:4–5*, we are told that the people of Israel and the people of Judah come together weeping as they seek YHWH their God and ask about the way to Zion. This suggests that the reunification happens as part of the return to Zion. Two separate peoples will become one, seeking YHWH on Zion. Furthermore, the reunification of Israel and Judah involves a covenant with YHWH (cf. Jer. 31:31–4): an everlasting covenant not to be forgotten. In *Jeremiah 3:18*, too, the reunification takes place in relation to the return. The house of Judah will go to the house of Israel, and together they will

169

THE ZION MOTIFS: BETWEEN JUDGEMENT AND SALVATION

come from the land of the north (i.e. the exile) to the land that YHWH gave their ancestors for a heritage (cf. Jer. 30:3). There are two important elements to note in this verse. First, the reunification happens in the movement towards Zion, 'together they shall come' (ויבאו יחדו), as in the case of Jeremiah 50:4–5. Second, the two houses are juxtaposed (i.e. בית ישראל and בית יהודה). According to Georg Fischer, this juxtaposition occurs only ten times within BHS and eight times in Jeremiah, but also once in 1 Kings 12:21.[32] This is crucial, because 1 Kings 12:21 accounts for the assembling of the house of Judah and the tribe of Benjamin to fight against the house of Israel. Consequently, the schism, initiated and enlarged in 1 Kings, is brought to an end in the visions of Jeremiah. Finally, according to Jeremiah 31:1, YHWH will be the God of *all* the families of Israel (כל משפחות ישראל), and they will be his people (cf. the covenant in Jer. 31:31–4 encompassing both Israel and Judah). Moreover, Jeremiah 31 is intensely concerned with the northern kingdom, in so far as the name 'Ephraim' – a common designation for this kingdom – occurs four times (Jer. 31:6, 9, 18, 20).[33] According to Jeremiah 31:6, the watchers in the hill country of Ephraim will call to go up to Zion, to YHWH their God (cf. Jer. 50:4).[34]

Jeremiah 23:1–8 employs the metaphor of the shepherd in the depiction of the people as a flock of sheep and their leaders as shepherds. YHWH's raising up shepherds over his people (הקמתי עליהם רעים) in v. 4 forms a close linguistic parallel to Ezekiel 34:23 (see below), although the passage in Jeremiah presupposes more shepherds than one.[35] The *single* leader, however, appears in Jeremiah 23:5–6. YHWH promises that the Davidic monarchy will not suffer extinction (cf. Ezek. 34:23; 37:22–5).[36] The imagery of the righteous branch surely seems similar to the growing branch in Isaiah 11:1.[37] In general, the Davidic figure is portrayed as the ideal king, wisely executing justice in the land and ensuring salvation and safety for Israel and Judah. This passage alludes to prominent texts such as Isaiah 8:23–9:6, 11:1–5 and Micah 5:1–5. Like the city in Isaiah 62:1–12, the new king is given a new symbolic name: 'YHWH is our righteousness' (יהוה צדקנו; cf. Jer. 23:6).

The promise of an everlasting Davidic monarchy continues in *Jeremiah 33:14–26*. Here, YHWH will fulfil his promise to the house of Israel and the house of Judah. Despite some differences, vv. 14–16 repeat or rework the language of Jeremiah 23:5–6. YHWH will cause a righteous branch to spring up, and it will bring salvation and peace for Judah and Jerusalem. The unique element in 33:14–16 is the juxtaposition of the promise of a new David and the promise of new Levitical priests. According to vv. 17–18, YHWH's affirmation that Israel will never lack a man to sit on the throne also embraces the Levites serving in the temple. In the following vv. 20–22, YHWH's covenant with the king as political leader and the Levites as temple ministers is compared to the covenant that he made at the time of creation; only God is able to break it.[38] Verse 24 contains an essential element: the disheartened people claim that 'the two families that

170

THE NEW ZION

YHWH chose have been rejected by him'. Who are those families? Due to the context of the passage, it may be the families of David and the Levites, who have been dismissed from their posts in the great desolation.[39] Nevertheless, the reference to 'two families' relates to those two nations and kingdoms in Ezekiel 37:22 (see below), Israel and Judah, which are also referred to in the introductory verse of Jeremiah 33:14–26.[40] Thus, the reunification of the two nations might presuppose the reunited offspring of Abraham, Isaac and Jacob mentioned in Jeremiah 33:26. The central matter, however, is YHWH's promise that never again will he reject his people, and that leaders from the seed of David will rule over them.

The gathering under a single ruler is also a predominant theme in Ezekiel. *Ezekiel 37:21–8* offers an exposition of the preceding symbolic action (cf. 37:15–20). The reunification happens after the return when YHWH unites the returning peoples (גוי אחד) and appoints one king (מלך אחד) to rule over them all, assuring them that never again will they be two nations (שתי גוים), and never again will they be divided into two kingdoms (שתי ממלכות).[41] Undoubtedly, the two kingdoms stand for Ephraim and Judah, inasmuch as they occur in the symbolic action of the preceding verses.[42] The idolatry that once caused the division of the two (cf. 1 Kgs 11) will not recur, and YHWH will purge them for their misdeeds (cf. Jer. 33:8). As part of the reunification, there is an announcement of one king portrayed in detail in vv. 24–5: his name is David, the servant of YHWH, and he will be king so that there will be but one shepherd (רועה אחד) over them all. And David will be prince forever.[43]

Within the composition of the Book of Ezekiel as a whole, the new king has already been portrayed in *Ezekiel 34:23–4*, where YHWH will set over his people one shepherd (הקמתי עליהם רעה אחד). According to 34:24, the people's relationship to God and to their king is closely connected. YHWH will be their God, and David, his shepherd, will be prince (נשיא) among them.[44] In 37:24–5, the accession and position of the new king will make the people follow the ordinances of YHWH, and in generation after generation they will live in the land of their ancestors. In vv. 26–8, YHWH will make an everlasting covenant with them (cf. Jer. 50:5) – that is, a new relationship with God, which, as we have observed, means that the new sanctuary and the dwelling of YHWH will be among his people (cf. Ezek. 20:40; 40–48).

The metaphor of the king sprouting like a plant is thoroughly envisioned in *Ezekiel 17:22–4*. In the chapter as a whole, the three verses constitute a positive response to – or even early midrash on[45] – the humiliation and defeat of the Judean king in the preceding vv. 1–21. According to v. 22, YHWH himself will take a sprig from a cedar and plant it on a high and lofty mountain. Verses 23–4 are interesting for two reasons. First, the new king will be planted on the mountain height of Israel. As we may recall, this is, according to Ezekiel 20:40, the location of the sanctuary to which

171

the house of Israel will come to worship YHWH with offerings. This suggests that there is a conjunction between the place of the king's throne and the place of the temple (cf. the offices in Jer. 33:14–26).[46] Second, the new plant will become a focal point for all the birds – that is, the people of YHWH. They will come and seek protection. Just like the new temple will be the religious focus, the king will be the new political focus.[47]

As Isaiah does, *Hosea* alludes to reconciliation in a single statement: 'the people of Judah and the people of Israel shall be gathered together, and they shall appoint for themselves one head [ראש אחד]; and they shall rise up from[48] the land' (Hos. 2:2 [ET 1:11]). If we understand the vague 'they shall rise up from the land' (עלו מן־הארץ) as the departure from exile in the Diaspora,[49] the reunification in Hosea is also related to the return. Besides that, the reconciliation implies a gathering under the rule of *one leader*. As in Ezekiel 17:22–4, the combined centre of political and religious authority appears in *Hosea 3:4–5*, even though the significance of Zion is minimal within the book of this prophet. Being without king and temple for a long time, the sons of Israel will repent or return (ישבו), seeking YHWH, their God and David, their king.[50] Notice here that the people, as in Jeremiah 50:4, will 'seek' (בקש) YHWH. Furthermore, it is stated that they will come in awe to him and to his goodness 'in the latter days' (באחרית הימים). As we shall see, exactly the same formula introduces the famous vision of Isaiah 2:2–4, which portrays the pilgrimage of foreign nations to Zion in order to be taught the instructions of YHWH. In light of this vision, Hosea 3:5 offers a concentrated expression of the characteristics of the New Zion; through pilgrimage, peoples will seek YHWH (worship) and David (political protection). We shall now turn to the religious and international aspects of the New Zion concerning the new temple and the worldwide pilgrimage.

The new temple on Zion

As was mentioned above, the foundation and restoration of a new temple was foreshadowed in Isaiah 44:28 and constitutes a leitmotif throughout *Isaiah 56–66*. Isaiah 56:1–8 begins with the house of prayer situated on the holy mountain and Isaiah 66:18–24 concludes with the many nations bringing offerings to Zion. Similarly to Isaiah 56–66, *Zechariah* expects the new temple to be founded on Zion, and this book, likewise, ends with the nations' pilgrimage to Jerusalem. This indicates that the new sanctuary constitutes a central theme of the New Zion in both Isaiah and Zechariah.

The picture is less clear in *Jeremiah*. I have already stressed that, although the prophet is extremely critical about the practice in the temple – for instance, in his sermon in Jeremiah 7:1–8:3 – he does not reject the temple institution as such (see chapter 2). Furthermore, the thank-offerings for the rebuilding of Jerusalem will be brought to the house of YHWH (בית יהוה;

THE NEW ZION

cf. Jer. 33:11), and the Levitical priests will be reinstalled in their former positions (cf. Jer. 33:14–26). Jeremiah's account of a new temple is, however, restrained (if not almost absent) throughout the book. Because of this apparent lack of concern for the temple, interpreters have understood Jeremiah's resentment against the Ark of the Covenant in *Jeremiah 3:16–17* as a direct criticism of priestly temple theology and of the written *torah* presented in the Pentateuch; indeed, the latter is to be replaced by the law written on hearts (Jer. 31:31–4).[51] In v. 17, it is Jerusalem and not the Ark of the Covenant that will be called the throne of YHWH (כסא יהוה). All the nations of the world will gather to this throne.[52] The city of Jerusalem thereby functions as the vital meeting point, not the temple institution as contended by Isaiah and Zechariah (see below). It remains, however, uncertain whether Jeremiah expects a temple or not.

The importance of the sanctuary is striking in *Ezekiel*, inasmuch as the concluding nine chapters are concerned with this topic. As we have previously observed, the house of Israel will serve YHWH on his holy mountain, the mountain height of Israel (Ezek. 20:40), and this location of the sanctuary among the people is part of the vision of the reunited kingdom under the rule of a Davidic monarch (Ezek. 37:21–8). In Ezekiel 40:2, the prophet, having been transported by YHWH to a very high mountain (הר גבה מאד), observes a structure like a city to the south. The phrase 'a very high mountain' appears in Ezekiel 17:22 in connection with the new monarch as the political centre. Therefore, it does not seem unreasonable that the location in Ezekiel 40:2 is the same as that of Ezekiel 17:22–3 and Ezekiel 20:40.[53] The new temple will be founded in the heart of the political and religious sphere. As was mentioned in chapter 3, the term 'Zion' is omitted in Ezekiel, yet interpreters generally consider the location here to be identical with the place named Mount Zion by other prophets.[54]

The temple source

As was shown in the introduction, the imagery of the river of paradise flowing from the mountain or the sanctuary constitutes one of four basic motifs of the classical Zion tradition (cf. E. Rohland). Many interpreters have intensely grappled with the nature of this river. Some posit that the river refers to a geographical reality (e.g. the Gihon river); others propose that the river refers to the divine river in common Ancient Near Eastern mythology.[55] As an illustration of this mythological perspective, Psalm 46:5[4] portrays the river whose streams please the city of God (cf. Ps 65:10[9]). The river also springs from the Garden of Eden in Genesis 2:10–14 to water the garden and its outside surroundings. Besides these occurrences, three relevant passages are located within the prophetic literature, namely Ezekiel 47:1–12, Joel 4:18 [ET 3:18] and Zechariah 14:8, although the imagery varies within the three.[56]

173

In *Ezekiel 47:1–12*, water wells up from below the threshold of the temple (מפתן הבית) and flows towards the east through the Wadi Arabah valley into the Dead Sea.[57] The stream becomes gradually deeper, until it is impossible to cross by foot. The fertile and life-giving source serves a twofold purpose: first, it will soften the desolate region so that trees with edible fruit will emerge; second, it will neutralize (literally 'cure') the saline and stagnant water in the Dead Sea for fish to fill it and people to begin to fish. In other words, the river functions as 'water of life', healing the land and restoring fertility *after* the great desolation (cf. Ezek. 37:1–14). In the concluding verses, it is explicated that these streams flow from the sanctuary (המקדש) and give nourishment to fruit trees. Because of the unfailing fruit and the evergreen leaves, the trees will constantly provide food and healing plants.

In *Joel 3:18*, all the valleys of Judah (כל־אפיקי יהודה) will flow with water and a source (מעין) will emerge from the house of YHWH (בית יהוה) irrigating Wadi Shittim. In so far as this Wadi Shittim is to be located in the area between Jerusalem and the Dead Sea, the depiction of Joel seems similar to that of Ezekiel:[58] a source flows from the temple towards the east and waters the valley.[59] Likewise, Joel portrays a rich and life-giving fertility filling the land.

In *Zechariah 14:8*, it is not a river but 'living waters' (מים־חיים)[60] flowing from Jerusalem (and not explicitly from the sanctuary). Other variations are the division of the stream into two, one heading east, another heading west, and its continuous flow throughout the year, summer and winter (cf. Ezek. 47:12?). The double direction might be a poetic ploy emerging from the dialectic between summer and winter, as well as between heat[61] and cold and day and night in the previous verses (cf. vv. 6–7).[62]

Despite the apparent dissimilarities within the textual material, the three passages agree in combining the river with the New Zion. The temple source in Ezekiel and the living waters in Zechariah well up *after* the great desolation, as part of YHWH's recreation of Zion. Likewise in Joel, water flows *after* God's final judgement against the hostile nations in the valley of Jehoshaphat. Ezekiel and Joel even accentuate that the river will bring back fertility to the areas desolated by the enemies.[63]

The temple and the foreigners

A notable disagreement can be observed concerning foreigners' relation to the new temple. Ezekiel 44:4–9 displays huge scepticism towards foreigners, and some verses in Isaiah and Zechariah indicate a similar attitude. Before a closer look at this negative position, we shall first examine *Isaiah 56:1–8*. This unit concerns the foreigners, who have already joined themselves to YHWH. The passage therefore reflects a consideration about who, living within the boundaries of the restored nation, is allowed to enter the temple. The foreigners are referred to as בן־הנכר in v. 3 and בני הנכר

THE NEW ZION

in v. 6.[64] Verse 3 assures them that YHWH will not separate them from his people. On the contrary, the foreigners keeping the Sabbath, serving YHWH and observing the covenant will have access to the temple.[65] This means that individual conversion to YHWH and the keeping of his commandments (Sabbath and covenant) replace ethnicity as the proper precondition.[66] After the fulfilment of these conditions, YHWH will bring the righteous foreigners to his holy mountain. Here, they will be joyful in his house of prayer and their sacrifices will be accepted by him. Consequently, the new temple will be called 'a house of prayer for all peoples'. Verse 8 sets this universalistic perspective within a broader context: just as YHWH gathered the outcasts of Israel residing in the worldwide Diaspora and brought them to Zion, his holy mountain, he now gathers and adds even more to their number. In sum, not only the people returning from exile but also the foreigners living within the boundaries of the nation will gather in the new temple.

Ezekiel 44:4–9 contends the opposite view. Individuals already dwelling in the land are the focus of YHWH's utterance. According to v. 9, these include 'every foreigner [בן־הנכר; cf. Isa. 56:3] who is among the people of Israel'.[67] In connection with Ezekiel's vision of the glory of YHWH filling the temple, the prophet is strictly instructed to mark those who may be admitted to the temple and all those who must be excluded. This motif is further highlighted in vv. 7–9, which render an accusation against the house of Israel for breaking the covenant with all their abominations – that is, they allowed foreigners (בני הנכר; cf. Isa. 56:6), uncircumcised in heart and flesh (ערלי לב וערלי בשר), to come into the temple and profane its sanctity. Even worse, they appointed foreigners to keep charge of the sacred offerings. Therefore, YHWH now prohibits any uncircumcised foreigner from entering the sanctuary.[68] The prohibition of uncircumcised attendance constitutes one of several attempts in Ezekiel's vision of the new temple to ensure the sacred glory of YHWH.[69] As we may recall, the idolatry and defilement of the temple resulted in YHWH's abandonment (cf. Ezek. 8–11). This accident must not recur (cf. Ezra 9–10; Neh. 13).

The negative assessment of the uncircumcised (ערלי לב וערלי בשר) appears in one minor text within Isaiah 40–55. In *Isaiah 52:1*, Zion and Jerusalem, the holy city, is urged to put on her beautiful garments, because the uncircumcised and the unclean (ערל וטמא) will never enter the city again. It is quite surprising to discover such a statement by this prophet, therefore Westermann refuses to believe that the uncircumcised are to be barred from the holy domain as such.[70] To him, due to the context of the verse, the uncircumcised stand for the enemies of Israel who destroyed Zion and forced the people into exile (cf. Isa. 52:2–3), not for the foreigners in general. In contrast, Blenkinsopp and Childs argue that the particular reference to 'the holy city' (עיר הקדש) presupposes the condition of the return of YHWH to Zion (cf. Isa. 52:7–10).[71] In so far as this proposal is correct, the reasoning in Isaiah 40–55 is in line with Ezekiel: when the holiness of

YHWH returns (Ezek. 43:1–9), the city and the temple will become holy and are not to be entered by the uncircumcised (Ezek. 44:4–9).

Zechariah 14:21 – the concluding verse of Zechariah – briefly states: 'and there shall no longer be Canaanites[72] in the house of YHWH Sebaoth on that day'. This proclamation is rather odd, because Zechariah 14:16–21 announces that all the surviving nations of the world will go up to God's mountain to celebrate the Sukkoth festival (see below). However, a text-critical problem remains regarding the translation of the Hebrew word כנעני, which in most cases is to be translated as 'Canaanite', although it likewise can be translated as 'trader' (cf. Isa. 23:8).[73] Petersen and Conrad prefer 'trader', in so far as the abolition of trading makes sense as a means to ensure the holiness of the temple (cf. Jer. 17:21–2; Neh. 13:15–22). Nevertheless, we should maintain that a reading of 'Canaanites' is indeed plausibly referring to a neighbour difficult to tolerate.[74]

In sum, it appears that there is no consensus in the texts concerning the new temple and the foreigners. Most clearly in the case of Isaiah 56 and Ezekiel 44, there are contrasting views. On the one hand, Isaiah 56 contends openness to foreigners; an openness also indicated by the vision of the foreign nations going up to Zion (see below). On the other hand, Ezekiel prohibits foreigners to enter the temple in order to protect the holiness of YHWH. Ezekiel's view is further supported by the fact that the temple in his visions constitutes the centre of the twelve tribes of Israel, not the world at large (cf. Ezek. 47–8).

The worldwide pilgrimage to Zion

Visions of the many nations peacefully going up to Zion form an apparent counter-motif to the attack of the approaching enemy army. This vision appears primarily within Isaiah, although hints to it have been found in Jeremiah (cf. Jer. 3:17), Micah, Haggai and Zechariah. Unquestionably, the most famous passage is *Isaiah 2:2–4*, which occurs in an almost identical version in Micah 4:1–3.[75] In the last days (אחרית הימים, cf. Hos. 3:5), the nature of Zion will change dramatically. The mountain of YHWH's house will be established as the highest of the mountains and raised above the hills. This topographical description recalls the reference to the very high mountain in Ezekiel 40:2. To this mountain, nations will stream and many people will come. The arriving peoples are referred to as גוים and עמים – Hebrew terms also designating the approaching enemies.[76] Verse 3b–d forms a chiastic structure, which emphasizes the movements from and towards Zion and highlights the central matter of the passage:

לכו ונעלה אֶל־הַר־יהוה אֶל־בית אלהי יעקב

Come, let us go up to the mountain of YHWH, to the house of the God of Jacob; (Isaiah 2:3b)

THE NEW ZION

וירנו מדרכיו ונלכה בארחתיו

that he may teach us his ways and that we may walk in his paths.
(Isaiah 2:3c)

כי מציון תצא תורה ודבר־יהוה מירושלם

For out of Zion shall go forth instruction, and the word of YHWH
from Jerusalem. (2:3d)

The poetic structure indicates a circularity in its double use of the preposition
'to' (אל) in v. 3b's ascending peoples to the mountain of the temple, opposed
to the preposition 'from' (מן) in v. 3d's movement of the *torah* and the
word of YHWH to the world. Verse 3b highlights that the peoples come
voluntarily, due to the exhortative encouragement to go up to the mountain.
The reason for the pilgrimage is to be taught the ways of YHWH and walk
in his paths. That is what YHWH's *torah* and word are all about: knowing the will of God and living according to it.[77] The stream of *torah* will
'go forth' (יצא), indicating a thematic parallelism with the stream of the
river from Zion (cf. Ezek. 47:1; Joel 4:18; Zech. 14:8). As the river streams
from Zion, providing fertility and life to the waste and desolate region, the
instruction of YHWH goes out from the holy mountain to the people thirsty
for wisdom. Moreover, according to v. 4, the gathering on Zion includes
an act of judgement, where YHWH will judge between the nations.[78] As
noted in chapter 7, the judgement announced in Joel 4 involves a brutal
slaughter of the neighbouring nations. In contrast, Isaiah 2:4 portrays the
divine judgement as a peace treaty with peoples beating their weapons into
farm implements (unlike Joel 4:10).

In the proclamation of the New Zion in *Isaiah 60:1–22*, the migration
of peoples also plays a significant role. In the following, we shall pay attention to two topics in this text: the light on Zion (vv. 1–3, 19–20), and the
nations bringing their wealth to the place (vv. 4–9, 11–15). The light
metaphor is significant, because it forms a decisive contrast to the dark
Day of YHWH. According to Isaiah 5:30 and Joel 2:2, darkness covers
the land on that day; it is a day of clouds and thick darkness (ערפל, חשך).
The exact same words are used to describe the situation in Isaiah 60:1–3,
where darkness and thick darkness cover the earth and the peoples. Yet
in the midst of this darkness, caused by the destruction of the aggressive
enemies, Zion will arise and shine. Her light has come, and the glory of
YHWH has risen upon her. She will become a bright spot in the darkness,
and nations and foreign kings will come into the light.[79] According to an
even more magnificent picture presented in vv. 19–20, the sun and the moon
will no longer be the primary sources of light, because YHWH himself will
be an everlasting light for the city. A similar intensification of the light was
presented in Isaiah 30:26, introducing YHWH's slaughter of the enemies.
In short, light as a metaphor for salvation forms the starkest contrast to

177

THE ZION MOTIFS: BETWEEN JUDGEMENT AND SALVATION

the darkness of judgement.[80] Because of this, the New Zion will not remain in darkness but be bathed in light.

In contrast to Isaiah 2:2–4, the nations serve a different purpose in Isaiah 60:1–22, in so far as they, on the one hand, carry gifts to Zion as part of the glorification of the restored city and temple, and, on the other hand, accompany the people of Israel returning from the Diaspora.[81] According to v. 4, all gather to come to the city, and the sons and daughters of Zion will come from far away. Therefore, according to v. 5, Zion will rejoice because of the 'abundance of the sea' and the 'wealth of nations' being brought to her. Although many interpreters translate המון ים and חיל גוים in similar ways,[82] we should for a moment consider a different translation. In other texts, the term המון refers to 'thunder' or 'roar' – for instance, in Isaiah 17:12 about the nations thundering like the sea (and attacking Zion). Furthermore, the term חיל designates the enemy army in Joel 2:11. These observations suggest that 'the thundering of sea' and 'the army of nations' could also serve as plausible translations. Thus, v. 5's deliberate ambiguity, expressed by the city's dread (פחד) at the sight, implies that once the nations came as enemies, thundering and gathering as an army, but now they come as servants bringing wealth. The gifts include gold, frankincense and animals to bring to the altar and glorify the sanctuary (vv. 6–7). In vv. 8–9, the ships of Tarshish will bring the children of Zion with silver and gold in their hands to exalt YHWH. Because of this continuous flow of treasures, the gates of the city will always be open so that the army of the nations may enter (cf. v. 11; unlike Isa. 54:11–17).

The nations in Isaiah 60:1–22 are described as servants, and those who do not serve Zion will perish. The exaltation of Zion at the expense of the foreign nations continues in vv. 13–15. The sanctuary will be glorified, and in the city will gather those who formerly despised it, and they will call it 'the City of YHWH, the Zion of the Holy One of Israel' (עיר יהוה ציון קדוש ישראל). In this way, the nations serve a twofold purpose: they take part in the recreation of Zion by bringing gifts, and they recreate its sovereign position by recognizing it as a sacred place from which light and prosperity stream.[83] As in Isaiah 62:4, the city undergoes a change from being desolate, hated and with no one passing through (cf. Ezek. 33:28) to being an eternal source of pride and joy. As an ultimate state of peace, violence, devastation or destruction will not be heard within the borders of the land (v. 18; cf. Isa. 2:4).

The Book of Isaiah concludes in the same vein, although the situation in *Isaiah 66:18–24* appears to be slightly different. According to v. 18, YHWH comes to gather (קבץ) all nations and tongues, and they will come and see his glory. This image recalls the passages of Isaiah 2:2–4 and 60:1–3, even though it is YHWH himself who gathers the nations. Verses 19–20 also present a new element: the survivors (of the huge act of judgement in vv. 15–16?) are sent to the nations that have not heard of YHWH or seen his glory. Here, they will preach – that is, do missionary work – among the peoples of the world. This mission will cause a migration of foreign nations bringing the kindred of the exiled Israel (cf. Isa. 60:4) as an offering to YHWH on his holy mountain. Zion will become the centre of a worldwide sacrificial cult. Interestingly, v. 21 states that YHWH will take 'some of them' (מהם) as priests and as Levites. Some of 'whom'? Two options seem available: this may refer to the Israelite missionaries in vv. 18–19 (notice the mentioning of מהם in v. 19);[84] or to the nations/Diaspora-Israelites ('your brothers'; cf. v. 20) coming from far away. In any case, according to Isaiah 56:1–8, it is foreign peoples serving in the sanctuary, which underlines the international status of the temple. Therefore, the temple becomes the centre of the world, and its priests are being recruited from among all nations. Thus, v. 23 can summarize that all flesh will unceasingly come and worship before YHWH. The temple represents life and blessing, while death and abhorrence are found outside the temple.[85] Indeed, v. 24 imagines a scenario later known as hell: the fire which will never be extinguished; a reality that exists outside the presence of YHWH on Zion.[86]

In sum, Isaiah presents different scenarios of the worldwide pilgrimage: the peoples thirsting for wisdom voluntarily seeking the instruction of YHWH on his holy mountain (Isa. 2:2–4); the nations contributing to the glorification of the New Zion by pilgrimage and bringing gifts (Isa. 60:1–22); and, finally, YHWH sending preachers to invite all nations of the world to partake in the sacrificial cult on his holy mountain (Isa. 66:18–24). The pilgrimage of the nations is a central matter of three other texts, which include Haggai 2:6–9, Zechariah 8:20–3 and Zechariah 14:16–21.

In *Haggai 2:6–9*, the bringing of gifts is not an act of free will. As YHWH shakes the heavens and the earth, he will shake all nations so that they will bring their treasures.[87] Because the silver and gold is the rightful property of YHWH, the treasures will fill the temple with luxury. The glory of the new temple will become even greater than that of the former destroyed by the enemies. Due to the context, the 'glory' (כבוד) refers to rich interior and architecture rather than the presence of YHWH.[88] As in Isaiah 2:4 and 60:18, the temple becomes the place where peace will be restored.

The scenario in *Zechariah 8:20–3* appears to be remarkably similar to that of Isaiah 2:2–4: peoples and the inhabitants of many cities will gather saying 'Come, let us go' (נלכה הלוך; cf. Isa. 2:3: לכו ונעלה).[89] The instructions from Zion are not mentioned; instead, the peoples will seek (בקש) YHWH Sebaoth (cf. Jer. 50:4; Hos. 3:5) to entreat him.[90] According to v. 23, men from nations of every language (cf. Isa. 66:18) will even take hold of a Jew, grasping his garments and following him to Zion.

In *Zechariah 14:16–21*, the remnant of the nations surviving the great battle in the previous section of the chapter will come to Jerusalem and worship YHWH as king (cf. Isa. 66:18). This suggests that the recognition of the sovereign power of YHWH is the author's primary concern. That submission and worship will take place year by year on Sukkoth, one of

THE ZION MOTIFS: BETWEEN JUDGEMENT AND SALVATION

the three major pilgrimage festivals. Verses 17–19 concern the punishment for not participating in the worship of YHWH, including plagues and absence of rain. Verses 20–1 conclude with a detailed description of the magnificence of the sacrificial cult.

Although Wildberger identified the worldwide pilgrimage to Zion as an original component of the alleged Zion tradition, which was employed in the vision of Isaiah 2:2–4 as early as the time of Isaiah ben Amos,[91] it is striking that the pilgrimage of the nations, according to the material just examined, is considered to be an eschatological event.[92] In contrast to Wildberger, I would suggest that the proper context of Isaiah 2:2–4 and similar texts examined above is the idyllic future following the experience of desolation, exile and restoration, rather than Judah during the Assyrian crisis.[93] Based on our examination of the six texts, the purposes of the pilgrimage can be divided into three categories: first, the voluntary search for YHWH and his *torah* (Isa. 2:2–4; Zech. 8:20–3); second, the bringing of gifts (Isa. 60:1–22; Hag. 2:6–9); and third, the festival in the temple on the holy mountain of YHWH (Isa. 66:18–24; Zech. 14:16–21).[94] In addition, it is noteworthy that the gathering of the foreign nations corresponds to the reunification of the two kingdoms, Israel and Judah. From a national perspective, Israel and Judah again are joined together under a Davidic monarch; and from an international perspective, all the nations of the world gather around the sanctuary on Zion under the rule of YHWH as visions of a new Solomonic era come to fruition (cf. 1 Kgs 10:1–10, 24–5; 2 Chron. 9:1–12, 23–4).[95]

The peace between man and the animals

Anticipations of the New Zion with regard to political independency and the re-establishing of the temple have appeared to be more or less realistic. In *Isaiah 11:6–9*, however, a marvellous and exceptional vision points to a completely different situation, when peace will be restored between man and beast.[96] The wolf lives with the lamb, the lion eats straw, and the nursing child plays over the hole of the asp. According to v. 9, this wonderful scenario takes place on the holy mountain of YHWH.[97] The text brings to mind the primeval state of humanity portrayed in the Book of Genesis: the picture of man living in harmony with the animals in the Garden of Eden, and the statement in v. 8 about the nursing child and the serpent between whom enmity was set in Genesis 3:15.[98] As a result of the peace depicted in vv. 6–8, there will be tenderness and no destruction on the mountain of YHWH (v. 9). In so far as the myth of the fall of man is presupposed in this vision, Zion is the place where the original state between man and the animals will become re-established. Additionally, the peace encompasses a restoration of the disrupted relationship between God and man indicated in the knowledge of YHWH (דעה את־יהוה) filling the earth. This 'knowledge'

180

THE NEW ZION

may refer to the divine instructions streaming from Zion (cf. Isa. 2:2–4), although it may also allude to YHWH's main accusation against his people in Isaiah 1:3: 'Israel does not know' (ישראל לא ידע). Isaiah 11:6–9, thus, reinstates man in his original position living wisely and in harmony with God and the animals.

A close parallel exists in *Hosea 2:20[18]* where YHWH makes a covenant (ברית) for Israel[99] with the wild animals, the birds of the air and the creeping creatures of the ground (cf. Gen. 1:26; 9:9–10).[100] It is interesting that the second half of the verse accounts that YHWH will break the weapons to ensure safety in the land. Here, we may recall the destruction of the weapons in Isaiah 2:4 and the abolition of violence in Isaiah 11:9 and 60:18. Thus, peace with the animals and abolition of all war should be regarded as parallel expressions, pointing to the same matter. This is indeed the case in Ezekiel, even though the wild animals suffer a different fate. In *Ezekiel 34:25–8*, YHWH makes a covenant of peace (ברית שלום) with his people, entailing the extinction of the wild animals. As mentioned in chapter 8, the wild animals constitute an imminent danger in Ezekiel as one of four deadly acts of judgement (Ezek. 14:21).[101] As in Hosea 2:20, the covenant is made so that the people may live securely. It contains a promise of blessing and prosperity as well as concerning the people of YHWH dwelling around his divine hill (סביבות גבעתי)! Verse 28 reiterates the idea that the inhabitants will not be devoured by the animals of the land and they will not be booty for the foreign nations again. In sum, there seems to be a close relationship between peace with the animals and political peace.

The great feast on the holy mountain

To conclude the examination of the New Zion, we shall look at one of the most astonishing texts of the Old Testament. In *Isaiah 25:6–10a*,[102] YHWH will make a feast for all peoples on his mountain. This feast constitutes a close parallel to the pilgrimage of peoples as portrayed in Zechariah 14:16–21, with its reference to the Sukkoth festival and the different kinds of cooking utensils (vv. 20–1). Isaiah 25:7–8 adds the new and surprising element: on this mountain, YHWH will destroy the shroud (לוט) that has been cast over all peoples, as well as the sheet (מסכה) spread over the nations. What does the term 'shroud' refer to? Within the Old Testament, the term לוט does not occur in this sense elsewhere than in this verse. Gesenius, apparently, understands the shroud to be congruent with the darkness covering the peoples, in so far as Isaiah 60:2 is mentioned in brackets.[103] The other term מסכה does not provide any greater elucidation, although the term in Isaiah 28:20 designates a bedcover. Then what function does it serve? Some interpreters posit that it is the cover that prevents one from seeing God face to face (cf. Exod. 34:33; 2 Cor. 3:12–18); other interpreters propose that it is the piece of cloth covering the head in time of mourning (cf. 2 Sam. 15:30, Jer. 14:3–4).[104] The latter proposal makes good sense within the context of the passage, since YHWH in v. 8 will wipe away the tears from all faces. The mourning shroud will be destroyed, and death will be abolished forever. On Zion, sorrow and death will be no more. YHWH not only takes away the disgrace of his people from all the earth, but is also revealed as the master of life and death.

This wonderful scenario gives rise to the final praise in vv. 9–10a. The glorification of God is overwhelming: 'this is our God; we have waited for him, so that he might save us'. For the hand of YHWH – his power and strength – rests on this mountain!

Summing up: the New Zion

Anticipations of the New Zion encompass a realistic restoration of the desolate city and a repopulation of its ruined places. Nevertheless, the descriptions rapidly turn into mythological scenarios, including walls of precious stones and the fire of YHWH forming a ring around the city. Furthermore, it is remarkable that the New Zion includes a reunification of the two kingdoms: the northern kingdom of Israel and the southern kingdom of Judah. Although an account of their conflict is absent within the prophetic literature as such, there is firm belief in the reconciliation of the two kingdoms. Jeremiah and Ezekiel even link this reunification with the gathering under the rule of one king – a new Davidic figure – as the political leader of the new and restored empire.

Isaiah, Ezekiel and Zechariah anticipate a new temple on Zion, while it is uncertain whether Jeremiah expects a temple or not. From the new city or from the sanctuary, a source of life will flow providing fertility to the surrounding areas, which enemies had destroyed and burned down. Concerning access to the temple, opposing views are presented. Ezekiel, on the one hand, prohibits foreigners from entering in order to protect the glory of YHWH; to be sure, the temple in the book of this prophet is only meant to be the holy centre for the twelve tribes of Israel. Isaiah 56 and Zechariah, on the other hand, accept and even prompt the presence of foreigners, yet nations that do not serve Zion will perish (Isa. 60). A similar universalistic perspective occurs in the visions of the worldwide pilgrimage to Zion. The nations come for different reasons, including hearing the divine instructions flowing from Zion, bringing gifts and participating in the cultic festivals serving YHWH.

Eventually, Zion is the place where man and the people will be reinstated in their proper position towards God. The ideal relationship with God, which sin has disrupted (cf. Gen. 3), is restored, and the earth is filled with 'a knowledge of YHWH' (Isa. 11:9). In addition, man and animal live in harmony, death is abolished and sorrow will be no more.

THE NEW ZION

In sum, the New Zion becomes the centre of everything: a national centre for Israel and Judah under the rule of a Davidic monarch; a religious centre with a new temple and its life-giving source; an international centre to which nations will stream to hear the word of YHWH and praise him as their God and king; and, finally, a cosmic centre filled with life, light, eternal blessing and peace.

Notes

1 In general, the term היכל is translated into 'palace', 'temple' and 'middle area' (cf. Gesenius 1921: 179; Ottosson 1978: 383). This semantic variety may derive from the fact that the palace and temple at a time existed as one integrated institution (cf. Ottosson 1978: 'Since a temple is often considered a god's dwelling-place, the distinction between palace and temple is only minor'). Nevertheless, the crux of the matter appears to be whether the foundation of a new היכל refers to a restoration of the Davidic monarchy or to a restoration of the temple as a religious institution. Since Isa. 40–66 hardly is concerned with any future king, but, on the contrary, focuses intensely on the temple institution, the latter translation seems most plausible; cf. NRSV; Westermann 1987: 152; Childs 2001: 345; Blenkinsopp 2002: 243.

2 Notice the use of 'to found' (יסד) which relates to a terminology of creation, that is, YHWH laid the foundations of the earth (cf. Isa. 48:13; 51:13, 16; Zech. 12:1; and several psalms, e.g. Pss 24:2; 104:5); see further in Schreiner 1963: 167–8, who, however, asserts that 'Zwar erteilt [Jahwe] nach Is 44:28 die Weisung, daß der Tempel "aufs neue gegründet werde". Aber nirgends wird geäußert, daß Jahwe selber es zu tun gedächte.'

3 Childs 2001: 353: 'The address to the "deep" resonates with the notes of the drying up of the floods at the Red Sea (Ex. 15:5; Neh. 9:11). Elsewhere, in Isa. 51:9ff., the redemptive events of creation, exodus, and deliverance from Babylonian captivity are fused as moments within the one divine purpose, all sharing the selfsame content of overcoming chaos.' See also Berges 2011: 103: 'The restoration of the ruins and the drying up of deep waters are the two aspects of one and the same divine act.'

4 Westermann 1987: 157.

5 An imagery heavily used in the vision of the New Jerusalem in Rev. 21:11–12; Dow 2011: 239: 'The author of Revelation paints a picture of the New Jerusalem taken mainly from the glorious-future-of-Zion scenarios of the Old Testament prophets.'

6 Childs 2001: 430 intriguingly asks: 'Is this an echo from First Isaiah of a past time when God employed an enemy to wield its weapons against Israel (10:5)?'

7 Cf. Westermann 1987: 276. 'Your children' is maintained by NRSV; Childs 2001: 425; Blenkinsopp 2002: 358.

8 See further, for instance, in Baumann 2003; Mandolfo 2007: 29–54.

9 NRSV has 'so shall your builders marry you'.

10 Cf. Childs 2001: 512: '[T. D.] Anderson argues that the image of sons returning to their mother and the image of Zion as bride are combined in the idea of the sons who represent the returning people also being the bridegroom of Zion . . . Nevertheless, the explanation remains strained even with this appeal to the flexibility of Isaiah's imagery. No fully satisfactory solution has as yet emerged.'

11 Blenkinsopp 2003: 233. However, is 'to be united' not semantically too far away from 'beherrschen, besitzen' or 'zur Frau nehmen, heiraten' (cf. Gesenius

THE ZION MOTIFS: BETWEEN JUDGEMENT AND SALVATION

1921: 106)? Childs 2001: 508 has 'marry'; Westermann 1987: 372 renders, like in Isa. 54:13, בָּנַיִךְ into 'your builders'; yet it does not make any difference.

12 Childs 2001: 510, 513.

13 Westermann 1987: 379.

14 Blenkinsopp 2003: 244.

15 Cf. Allen 2008: 339: 'Towns destroyed by divine judgment (cf. 2:15; 4:7, 26, 29; 9:11) would rise again.'

16 Fischer 2005b: 135.

17 This rather odd expression occurs in Jer. 50:7, too, where it stands in apposition to YHWH; YHWH *is* the abode of righteousness (NRSV: 'the true pasture'). Likewise in Jer. 25:30, YHWH roars *from* his holy habitation *against* his fold (עַל־נָוֵהוּ); Allen 2008: 351 emphasizes that the notion of righteousness reminds us of the righteous Zion in Isa. 1:21, 26.

18 For this view, see Fischer 2005b: 166: 'In jedem Fall bezieht sich "darin" auf das in V 23 erwähnte "Land".' Cf. also Lundbom 2004: 456: '[righteous pasture] is normally the "pasture" in which sheep graze, but in certain cases is applied metaphorically to the land given to Israel as an inheritance from Yahweh (10:25; 23:3; 50:19) . . . the "righteous pasture" here is Jerusalem.'

19 Allen 2008: 354: 'There is a hint of reversal since the 587 disaster had, earlier in the book, been presented as taking a toll on humans and animals (Jer. 7:20; 9:10[9]; 21:6; cf. 32:43; 33:10).'

20 Fischer 2005b: 169.

21 For a treatment of this passage with regard to the topography and archaeology, see Simons 1952: 231–3.

22 Allen 2008: 359.

23 Carroll 1986: 618.

24 This, however, depends on how one understands the indefinite הִ. Carroll 1986: 633; Jones 1992: 420; Lundbom 2004: 528 propose 'earth' according to LXX's *gēn* (cf. NRSV); Allen 2008: 372 has 'things'. Fischer 2005b: 255 maintains the indefinite 'sie/es' but suggests to interpret it either as the plan of YHWH, as the earth or as Jerusalem. According to Fischer, the ambiguity may be deliberate.

25 Joyce 2009: 207.

26 Cf. for instance Andersen & Freedman 1989: 913–14.

27 This may, however, be two sides of the same coin (cf. Gese 1974: 121). In Nathan's prophecy to David, YHWH's promise to build a house is closely linked with his support of the Davidic monarchy (2 Sam. 7:11–17).

28 Several options are listed in Wolff 1977: 355, including the Davidic dynasty, the desolated Judah, the fallen empire of David and Solomon, and Jerusalem.

29 See further in Andersen & Freedman 1989: 924–6.

30 Meyers & Meyers 2010: 157.

31 Due to this hope for reconciliation between the northern and southern kingdoms (as well as the gathering of the Diaspora), Isa. 11:11–16 is often regarded as late exilic or post-exilic; see Childs 2001: 104–5.

32 Fischer 2005a: 196.

33 Allen 2008: 346.

34 Cf. Hjelm 2004: 10: 'Combining themes of Ephraim as firstborn and the mountain of Ephraim with themes of movement to Zion, 31.1–20 offers a fulfilment of attempts at reconciliation, with which Hezekiah had been so unsuccessful (2 Chron. 30.6–12).' According to Hjelm, however, Samaria is only regarded as a profane vineyard. In addition, Jeremiah sets a contrast between 'a Samaria of the past and a Zion of the future'.

35 See further in Block 1998: 297.

THE NEW ZION

36 Cf. Allen 2008: 259: 'Although the text speaks in individual terms, the reader should not imagine a single messianic figure. The king stands for the new regime or as the inaugurator of a fresh branch of the royal line.'

37 Cf. Sweeney 2007: 317: 'The links between Isa. 11:1–16 and Jer. 23:1–8 appear especially in vv. 5–6, although they tend to be thematic rather than lexical.' For a general comparison of Isa. 11 and Jer. 23, see this fascinating article by Sweeney, in which he argues for a more nuanced view on Jeremiah's assessment of the Davidic monarchy and his relation to the Isaianic tradition than scholars have usually had.

38 Cf. Allen 2008: 378–9: 'The arcing between cosmic time on the one hand and crown and cult on the other in terms of covenant supplies an argument for the permanence of the latter two.'

39 For this interpretation, see Lust 1994: 43–4.

40 Lundbom 2004: 545; Allen 2008: 379. Fischer 2005b: 238 also supports the latter interpretation, although he underlines that, due to the ambiguity, both readings are plausible.

41 Joyce 2009: 210 asserts that 'the issue of the restoration of monarchy is overshadowed here by the affirmation of renewed unity'.

42 Nevertheless, Zimmerli 1983: 275–6 asserts that vv. 15–19 and vv. 21–4a have different concerns. Whereas vv. 15–19 as a pre-exilic oracle merely anticipate a reunification of the kingdoms (cf. Jer. 3:6–18; 30–1), vv. 21–4a reflect the time after 587 BCE: 'Here there is no longer expected "reunification" of the two kingdoms, both of which have now disappeared, but rather the gracious divine protection of the newly gathered people from a new schism.'

43 Hjelm 2004: 252: 'The envisioned return is not a return to a restored pre-exilic Israel, fighting for independence or being under the vassalage of foreign rulers. The return is a recapture of a long-vanished past, a golden age of unity coming into being, as is Israel's people in Ezekiel's pesher-like closure in a prediction of everlasting unity under a Davidic "prince".'

44 According to Joyce 2009: 198, with the exception of Numbers, 'prince' (נשׂיא) is used most times in Ezekiel within the Old Testament as such: 'In the use of *nāśî* in Ezekiel's future expectation we encounter a dialectical critique of monarchy, allowing it a place within the divinely ordained polity, but only when radically subordinated to the will of God and to the real needs and interests of the community of the people of God.' Cf. Tuell 2009: 240: 'the language here referring to the re-established king is modest'.

45 Cf. Joyce 2009: 138 who notices that vv. 22–4 pick up and rework some of the vocabulary of vv. 1–21.

46 As Block 1997: 551 observes, only here in Ezek. 17:22–4, and not in Ezek. 34:23–4 and 37:21–8, are the motifs of Davidic monarchy and Zion brought together.

47 The same idea is revealed, for instance, in Isa. 11:10: 'On that day the root of Jesse shall stand as a signal to the peoples; the nations shall inquire of him, and his dwelling shall be glorious.'

48 Following BHS; cf. the footnote in NRSV.

49 For this view, see Jeremias 1983: 35; Landy 2011: 50. For an alternative proposal, which sees the verb עלה in an agricultural sense as 'growing up' or 'increasing/flourishing', see Dearman 2010: 105–6.

50 Jeremias 1983: 57 considers ואת דוד מלכם and באחרית הימים to be later additions and proposes omitting them (cf. footnote in BHS).

51 Jones 1992: 103; Fischer 2005a: 194–5.

52 Cf. Allen 2008: 58: 'the eschatological tradition of a new and glorious Jerusalem . . . would mean that Yahweh's ark-linked presence was released to pervade the city'.

THE ZION MOTIFS: BETWEEN JUDGEMENT AND SALVATION

53 Zimmerli 1983: 347.
54 See, for instance, Tuell 2009: 284.
55 For a short review, see Hayes 1963: 423; Kraus 1986: 80–1; Hoppe 2000: 25–6; Joyce 2009: 236; Tuell 2009: 331–4.
56 In addition, Isa. 33:21 accounts for a place of broad rivers and streams. Despite this reference to an abundance of water, the parallel appears to be too vague.
57 For a detailed overview of geographical matters, see Block 1998: 693–5.
58 Cf. Barton 2001: 109, who, however, asserts that 'the Wadi Shittim cannot be identified with any certainty, and it might (like the valley of Jehoshaphat) be a mythical or imaginary area, "the brook of the acacias", acacia wood being regarded as particularly valuable and used in the manufacture of Temple furniture'. Cf. Crenshaw 1995: 200.
59 Wolff 1977: 73 translates נחל השטים into 'valley of the acacias', a particularly dry area.
60 Or 'waters of life'; cf. Meyers & Meyers 2009: 435.
61 Reading אור as heat.
62 Petersen 1995: 146.
63 Notice that the river here forms an antithetic parallelism with the motif of return. Just as the desert blooms when the redeemed exiles return *to* Zion (cf. Isa. 35:1–10), the surrounding land is filled with prosperity by the river flowing *from* Zion (cf. Isa. 2:2–4; see below).
64 Cf. Childs 2001: 457, these foreigners are described as belonging to a class of proselytes.
65 According to Isa. 60:10, foreigners will build the walls of the city.
66 Westermann 1987: 314.
67 For a list of proposals of who these foreigners are, see Block 1998: 622–3.
68 See Deut. 23:2–9 for similar restrictions.
69 Cf. Joyce 2009: 231–2: 'The concern here is the typically priestly one of preserving holiness and proper separation, a theme highlighted later in this chapter in the priestly task of teaching the people the difference between the holy (*qōḏeš*) and the common (*ḥōl*), the unclean (*ṭāmē'*) and the clean (*ṭāhôr*) (44:23; cf. 42:20).'
70 Westermann 1987: 316.
71 Blenkinsopp 2002: 340, although he still regards the uncircumcised as 'foreign conquerors'. Cf. Childs 2001: 405: 'Jerusalem is to become the holy city, a dwelling that reflects the nature of God's holiness. For that reason, the uncircumcised and unclean will not be allowed in the city to profane the name of God . . . Israel, which was once oppressed and exploited by foreigners, will find in a purified city the environment in which to come to know God.'
72 Cf. the footnote of NRSV; the translation has 'trader'; see comments below.
73 Cf. Gesenius 1921: 353, who in this case reads 'Händler im Tempel'. Apparently, the Canaanites were renowned for their activities in seafaring and trade; see Lemche 1991.
74 Cf. Meyers & Meyers 2009: 489–92: 'The idea of business transactions taking place in the Temple seems too far afield from the themes and claims of Second Zech., especially when the message carried by the use of "Canaanites" as such . . . would be significantly more appropriate to the context . . . Canaanites will no longer be in Yahweh's house, because that which defines "Canaanite" – a culture in tension with Yahwism – will no longer exist.'
75 For a critical discussion concerning the literary dependency between the two text passages, see, for instance, Wildberger 1991: 83–5; Williamson 2006: 166–71, 178–9.
76 Cf. Isa. 5:26; Ezek. 23:24; 38:6, 9, 15; Zech. 12:2–3; 14:2.

THE NEW ZION

77 Scholars usually understand *torah* here in a very broad sense as referring to 'instruction'; cf. Levenson 1985: 126; Wildberger 1991: 82. However, Ingrid Hjelm has mounted the case that *torah* here refers to the law given on Mount Sinai. Due to the significance of the term 'the mountain of YHWH', she claims that 'intertextually, the term forms a continuum between the Israelites who leave Sinai, "the mountain of Yahweh, walk for three days with the ark of the covenant . . . to seek a resting place" . . . on their way to "the place about which Yahweh has said: 'I will give it to you'" . . . This place, Isaiah implicitly claims, they found, when they urged each other to go up to "the Mountain of Yahweh"' (Hjelm 2004: 255). Although sympathetic to a canonical approach to determine the meaning of *torah* in Isaiah (cf. Hjelm and scholars before her), Childs is far from convinced of seeing the *torah* as a reference to the Mosaic Torah; see Childs 2001: 30.

78 Nevertheless, it is striking that the motif of divine kingship often connected to the holy mountain is muted and apparently replaced by the motif of the divine *torah*; see Hoppe 2000: 66.

79 The light also occurs in the small epilogue in Isa. 2:5, where the house of Jacob is urged to walk in the light of YHWH (אור יהוה).

80 Cf. Childs 2001: 496.

81 Cf. Berges 2012: 77: 'They do not come in order to learn Torah (cf. 2.2–4) but in order to return the living children of Zion who are among them, along with precious gifts (60.4–9; cf. 29.18ff.).'

82 NRSV: 'the abundance of the sea' and 'the wealth of the nations'; cf. Westermann 1987: 354; Childs 2001: 491; Blenkinsopp 2003: 204: 'the sea's abundance' and 'the wealth of nations'.

83 Cf. Westermann 1987: 361.

84 Blenkinsopp 2003: 315.

85 Cf. Childs 2001: 542: 'In spite of God's new heavens and earth, the exaltation of Zion, and the entrance of the nations to the worship of God, there remain those outside the realm of God's salvation.'

86 Antti Laato interprets this verse in light of Isa. 36–7: 'Those peoples which will not come to worship in Jerusalem – as predicted in 2:2–4 – will be annihilated like the Assyrian soldiers before Jerusalem. The loyal inhabitants of Jerusalem can come to see the dead bodies of these rebels just as in the time of Hezekiah the inhabitants of Jerusalem (= the promised remnant) came to see the dead bodies of the Assyrian soldiers' (Laato 1998: 116–17).

87 See Meadowcroft 2006: 164–5, who proposes that Haggai takes up this judgement-motif from Jeremiah and Ezekiel: 'Yet, unlike his predecessors, who also use the term to foreshadow the coming judgement against Israel, Haggai has re-directed the metaphor. Now it heralds a gathering of the nations into Israel.'

88 Petersen 1984: 68.

89 Williamson 2006: 177.

90 Neither Zion nor the temple is mentioned; Jerusalem, though, is in v. 22.

91 Wildberger 1957: 62–81. Wildberger regards Isa. 2:2–4 as a compilation of the mythopoetic imagery already encompassed in the alleged Zion tradition, that is, the stream enjoying the city of God (Ps 46:4–5[3–4]); the praise reaching to the ends of the earth (Ps 48:10[9]); and the destruction of weapons (Ps 76:3[2]). For a critical review of Wildberger, see Williamson 2008: 142–3.

92 Childs 2001: 29.

93 Cf. the opinion of many recent interpreters dating the final redaction congruent with Second Isaiah or in the Persian period; see Childs 2001: 28–9.

94 For a list of parallels in ancient Sumerian hymns, see Weinfeld 1983: 111–12.

THE ZION MOTIFS: BETWEEN JUDGEMENT AND SALVATION

95 Cf. Dow 2011: 63.
96 The question, however, remains if the ancient authors have thought in the same way. Does the peace between man and the animals seem less 'realistic' and obtainable than the unification of Israel and Judah, the gathering of all nations and a worldwide peace?
97 Verses 6–8 and 9 constitute one text unit due to the parallel allusion in Isa. 65:25 linking the peace with the animals (v. 25a) and the reference to the holy mountain (v. 25b); see Childs 2001: 99, 101–2.
98 Childs 2001: 104 downplays such allusions: 'Although there are occasional hints in the primordial history of Genesis that the alienation from God also produced enmity between man and beast (3:15; 9:2ff.), this concept was never fully developed and only infrequently shimmers behind the text. Rather, the portrayal of universal peace in this chapter is set within an eschatological context . . . and is an expansion of the picture of the future harmony among the peoples who flow to the holy mountain.'
99 BHS reads 'for them' (בהם); NRSV changes it into 'for you'.
100 For a thorough study of this 'cosmic covenant' concept, see Murray 1992.
101 Cf. Joyce 2009: 198: '[the banishment of wild animals] is part of the reversal of the former situation, for wild animals had been a mode of judgement'.
102 The feast in Isa. 25:6–8 has often been regarded as the latter part of a ritual of coronation, succeeding Isa. 24:21–3. This is, however, difficult to prove, therefore we shall treat the text passage as a discrete text unit; cf. Blenkinsopp 2000: 358.
103 Gesenius 1921: 381: 'Verhüllung, Schleier'.
104 The latter position is supported by Kaiser 1974: 162; Blenkinsopp 2000: 359. See also Childs 2001: 184–5: 'Some have suggested that [the covering] refers to spiritual blindness, but more fitting in the present context of a festival would be to see the veil of mourning replaced by a garment of celebration.'

CONCLUSION

In line with recent synchronic studies (especially A. Laato, I. Hjelm, C. Körting and L. Dow), this investigation has challenged tradition-historical interpretations of Zion. The Zion motif has mainly been seen as having a simple and clearly defined content – an inviolable city – which has been adopted and used differently by Old Testament authors. This study, however, presents the Zion motif as a theological theme associated with a wide range of sub-motifs, events and characteristics. In contrast to a general reading of the prophets' visions about Zion as based on and interpreted in light of the Psalms, this study has attempted an examination of the prophetic literature in its own right. If one reads the prophets solely in search of historical traces of the alleged Zion tradition and its basic motifs, as they were defined in Germany in the decades following the Second World War (Rohland, von Rad), one fails to see that two opposing images of Zion exist side by side within the prophetic corpus (cf. Körting's criticism).

Due to descriptive surveys primarily of the prophetic books, it became clear that basically there are two main perceptions of Zion, which stand in structural tension with each other: Zion as the last bastion and Zion as a place which is destroyed and rebuilt. Because of this observation, I chose to operate with two Zion motifs designating the different fates of the place: first, the classical Zion motif designating the inviolable city and YHWH's defeat of the city's enemies (cf. the Zion tradition); second, the dynamic Zion motif designating the dynamic development and transformation of Zion: it is destroyed and abandoned, yet eventually rebuilt and repopulated. Common to both motifs is the attack on the city of foreign enemies. However, whereas, according to the first motif, the city and a faithful remnant are saved, the city is, according to the second motif, totally destroyed and a remnant of survivors is brought into foreign captivity.

The manifold descriptions of the attacking enemies share the idea that YHWH stands behind the attack. It is YHWH who brings the hostile nations to Zion. A group of texts relates the attack to the 'Day of YHWH' or 'on that day': a day of darkness. Several passages state that the enemies

CONCLUSION

will fulfil YHWH's judgement against his people. Furthermore, the enemies are portrayed as powerful, tremendous and invincible.

In the classical Zion motif, the deliverance of Zion and the defeat of the enemies serve several purposes. In *Isaiah*, *Joel* and *Zephaniah*, who interpret the attack as YHWH's judgement against his sinful people, the deliverance is an expression of divine grace: that YHWH on Zion leaves a faithful remnant, who repented in time. Indeed, the trust in and repentance to YHWH are conditions of his salvific intervention. In *Ezekiel 38–9*, *Obadiah*, *Micah 4:11–13* and *Zechariah 12:1–13:1*, the foreign nations are gathered not to judge but to be judged; here, the focus is on the slaughter of the enemies. This slaughter happens either to display the power of YHWH, to gain control of the neighbouring states or as revenge. After deliverance from enemies, the outpouring of a spirit cleanses the sins of the surviving people and they live on in a strengthened, politically independent and prosperous Zion, with YHWH as its king.

We divided the dynamic Zion motif into three stages: destruction and exile, the return and the New Zion. This basic structure shapes parts of Isaiah, Jeremiah, Ezekiel, Micah and Zechariah.

The destruction is predominant in Jeremiah, where it implicitly stands in tension with the classical Zion motif as composed in Isaiah. While YHWH, according to the classical Zion motif, explicitly leaves Zion as an invulnerable place, his decision of final destruction in Jeremiah will not be changed. This final judgement means that the city and land will be made desolate and empty of inhabitants. While the classical Zion motif contains a remnant of 'returners' on Zion, no one returns in Jeremiah, and only by YHWH's mercy, a small remnant of survivors (the good figs) is brought into exile. Common to Jeremiah, Ezekiel and Micah is their assertion of a close relation between the sinful deeds of the people of YHWH and the total destruction of their city as a righteous punishment. In addition, Jeremiah and Ezekiel appear to interpret the catastrophe as a fulfilment of the covenantal curses, contained in the Pentateuch.

The exile is portrayed as foreign captivity, from which the people are eventually redeemed, and as a process of self-loathing where the people recognize their guilt. The people's self-recognition results in divine forgiveness, their sins are washed away and they will return as an entirely new people.

In the return to Zion, it is crucial that both YHWH and his exiled people return. However, since the term 'return' (שׁוּב) also designates the people's spiritual conversion to God, their repentance to YHWH and return to Zion are two sides of the same coin. YHWH is portrayed several times as a shepherd gathering his people, leading them out of exile and bringing them home to their pastures. It is an amazing feature that the return of the exiled is described in the same terms and images as was the calling of the enemies to destroy Zion.

CONCLUSION

Imageries of the New Zion move between a realistic anticipation of restoration and repopulation, and a virtual Zion as a new centre, which encompasses political and religious functions in the form of a national-political centre of a reunified Israelite people under the rule of a Davidic king, a cultic centre with a life-giving source, an international centre to which foreign nations come to worship, and a cosmic centre where the people dwell in peace with God and where death has been abolished.

It is significant to observe that similar terms and language are employed to describe features in the two motifs. Several sub-motifs are constantly contrasted and turned upside down. The language that expresses YHWH's summoning of the enemies is also the language of the people's return. The language of restoration mirrors that of destruction. More importantly, the classical Zion motif of Isaiah (chapter 7) and the dynamic Zion motif of Jeremiah (chapter 8) form an antithesis: Isaiah portrays inviolability, Jeremiah portrays total destruction; Isaiah expects a faithful remnant, Jeremiah laments that no one returns; Isaiah anticipates a cleansed remnant on Mount Zion, Jeremiah anticipates a new people emerging out of foreign captivity. The language of inviolability mirrors that of destruction.

The classical and dynamic Zion motifs thus share a common cluster of sub-motifs, which can be applied in either a positive or a negative way. The two overall narratives – stories of inviolability and defeat – derive from a common source of language, images and ideas. This observation indeed underlines the literary character of the motifs and explains the abundance of intertextual links. Rather than accurately reflecting historical episodes within the history of Israel, the motifs are literary devices, which treat central theological themes.[1]

In connection with this, it is a surprising discovery that YHWH stands behind all of these events. He directs the enemies; he saves or destroys his city; he leaves a remnant on Zion or he brings a few survivors into exile. Furthermore, YHWH is the one who eventually redeems the exiled and gathers them from foreign lands. YHWH rebuilds and repopulates the new city and calls for peaceful nations to come. He abolishes death on his holy mountain. Because of this, we have not only encountered two different motifs of Zion's fate, but in fact two different *theologies*: two different ways in which YHWH judges and saves his people – either by leaving a remnant of 'returners', who are spared and cleansed while all others perish; or by destroying everything and allowing a flock of survivors to be purged, when in foreign captivity, before allowing them to return to a new Zion.

In sum, the classical and dynamic Zion motifs offer two trajectories that highlight some important differences in the prophets' perception of the fate of Zion between divine judgement and divine salvation.

CONCLUSION

Note

1 The acknowledgement of the literary nature of the Old Testament writings may have significant consequences, for instance, for the dating of biblical texts. Noticing the similarities between Isaiah's portrait of King Hezekiah (Isa. 36–7) and Jeremiah's portrait of King Zedekiah (Jer. 37), S. De Jong and K. A. D Smelik have argued that the Hezekiah story is based on the Zedekiah story and not the other way around. If so, the righteous figure of Hezekiah is a counterpart of both King Ahaz and Judah's last king, who were unfaithful and experienced YHWH's wrath; cf. Hjelm 2004: 103–4.

BIBLIOGRAPHY

Albrektson, B. 1963. *Studies in the Text and Theology of the Book of Lamentations. With a Critical Edition of the Peshitta Text*. Lund: CWK Gleerup.

Allen, L. C. 1976. *The Books of Joel, Obadiah, Jonah, and Micah*. Grand Rapids, MI: Eerdmans.

Allen, L. C. 2008. *Jeremiah. A Commentary*. Louisville, KY: Westminster John Knox Press.

Amesz, J. G. 2004. 'A God of Vengeance? Comparing YHWH's Dealings with Judah and Babylon in the Book of Jeremiah'. In *Reading the Book of Jeremiah. A Search for Coherence*, M. Kessler (ed.), 99–116. Winona Lake, IN: Eisenbrauns.

Andersen, F. I. 2001. *Habakkuk. A New Translation with Introduction and Commentary*. New York: Doubleday.

Andersen, F. I. & D. N. Freedman 1980. *Hosea. A New Translation with Introduction and Commentary*. New York: Doubleday.

Andersen, F. I. & D. N. Freedman 1989. *Amos. A New Translation with Introduction and Commentary*. New York: Doubleday.

Baltzer, D. 1971. *Ezekiel und Deuterojesaja*. Berlin: Walter de Gruyter.

Barstad, H. 1989. *A Way in the Wilderness. The Second Exodus in the Message of Second Isaiah*. Manchester: Manchester University Press.

Barstad, H. 1997. *The Babylonian Captivity in the Book of Isaiah. 'Exilic' Judah and the Provenance of Isaiah 40–55*. Oslo: Novus forlag.

Barth, H. 1977. *Die Jesaja-Worte in der Josiazeit. Israel und Assur als Thema einer produktiven Neuinterpretation der Jesajaüberlieferung*. Neukirchen-Vluyn: Neukirchener Verlag.

Barton, J. 2001. *Joel and Obadiah. A Commentary*. Louisville, KY: Westminster John Knox Press.

Barton, J. 2012. *The Theology of the Book of Amos*. Cambridge: Cambridge University Press.

Baumann, G. 2003. *Love and Violence. Marriage as Metaphor for the Relationship between YHWH and Israel in the Prophetic Books*. Collegeville, MN: Liturgical Press.

Berges, U. F. 2000. '"Ich bin der Mann, der Elend sah" (Klgl 3,1). Zionstheologie als Weg aus der Krise'. *Biblische Zeitschrift* 44(1): 1–20.

Berges, U. F. 2011. 'Zion and the Kingship of Yhwh in Isaiah 40–55'. In *Enlarge the Site of Your Tent.' The City as Unifying Theme in Isaiah*, A. L. H. M. van Wieringen & A. van der Woude (eds), 95–119. Leiden: Brill.

BIBLIOGRAPHY

Berges, U. F. 2012. *Isaiah. The Prophet and His Book*, P. Sumpter (trans.). Sheffield: Sheffield Phoenix Press.

Berlin, A. 1994. *Zephaniah. A New Translation with Introduction and Commentary*. New York: Doubleday.

Berlin, A. 2002. *Lamentations. A Commentary*. Louisville, KY: Westminster John Knox Press.

Beuken, W. A. M. 2003. *Jesaja 1–12*, U. Berges (trans.). Freiburg: Herder.

Blenkinsopp, J. 2000. *Isaiah 1–39. A New Translation with Introduction and Commentary*. New Haven, CT and London: Yale University Press.

Blenkinsopp, J. 2002. *Isaiah 40–55. A New Translation with Introduction and Commentary*. New Haven, CT and London: Yale University Press.

Blenkinsopp, J. 2003. *Isaiah 56–66. A New Translation with Introduction and Commentary*. New York: Doubleday.

Block, D. I. 1997. *The Book of Ezekiel. Chapters 1–24*. Grand Rapids, MI: Eerdmans.

Block, D. I. 1998. *The Book of Ezekiel. Chapters 25–48*. Grand Rapids, MI: Eerdmans.

Block, D. I. 2000. 'Divine Abandonment: Ezekiel's Adaption of an Ancient Near Eastern Motif'. In *The Book of Ezekiel. Theological and Anthropological Perspectives*, M. S. Odell & J. T. Strong (eds), 15–42. Atlanta: Society of Biblical Literature.

Boadt, L. 2007. 'Do Jeremiah and Ezekiel Share a Common View of the Exile?'. In *Uprooting and Planting. Essays on Jeremiah for Leslie Allen*, J. Goldingay (ed.), 14–31. London: T&T Clark International.

Bolin, T. M. 2003. 'The Making of the Holy City: On the Foundations of Jerusalem in the Hebrew Bible'. In *Jerusalem in Ancient History and Tradition*, T. L. Thompson (ed.), 171–96. London and New York: T&T Clark International.

Campbell, A. F. 2005. *2 Samuel*. Grand Rapids, MI: Eerdmans.

Carroll, R. P. 1986. *The Book of Jeremiah. A Commentary*. London: SCM Press.

Cazelles, H. 1984. 'Zephaniah, Jeremiah, and the Scythians in Palestine'. In *A Prophet to the Nations. Essays in Jeremiah Studies*, L. G. Perdue & B. W. Kovacs (eds), L. G. Perdue (trans.), 129–49. Winona Lake, IN: Eisenbrauns.

Childs, B. S. 1959. 'The Enemy from the North and the Chaos Tradition'. *Journal of Biblical Literature* 78: 187–98.

Childs, B. S. 1967. *Isaiah and the Assyrian Crisis*. London: SCM Press.

Childs, B. S. 1979. *Introduction to the Old Testament as Scripture*. Philadelphia, PA: Fortress Press.

Childs, B. S. 2001. *Isaiah*. Louisville, KY: Westminster John Knox Press.

Christensen, D. L. 2009. *Nahum. A New Translation with Introduction and Commentary*. New Haven, CT and London: Yale University Press.

Clements, R. E. 1980. *Isaiah and the Deliverance of Jerusalem. A Study of Interpretation of Prophecy in the Old Testament*. Sheffield: JSOT Press.

Clements, R. E. 1982. 'The Ezekiel Tradition: Prophecy in a Time of Crisis'. In *Israel's Prophetic Tradition. Essays in Honour of Peter R. Ackroyd*, R. Coggins, A. Phillips & M. Knibb (eds), 119–36. Cambridge: Cambridge University Press.

Clements, R. E. 2011. *Jerusalem and the Nations*. Sheffield: Sheffield Phoenix Press.

Clifford, R. J. 1972. *The Cosmic Mountain in Canaan and the Old Testament*. Cambridge, MA: Harvard University Press.

Coggins, R. J. 2000. *Joel and Amos*. Sheffield: Sheffield Academic Press.

Conrad, E. W. 1999. *Zechariah*. Sheffield: Sheffield Academic Press.

BIBLIOGRAPHY

Conroy, C. 1983. *1–2 Samuel, 1–2 Kings with an Excursus on Davidic Dynasty and Holy City Zion*. Wilmington: Michael Glazier, Inc.

Crenshaw, J. L. 1995. *Joel. A New Translation with Introduction and Commentary*. New York: Doubleday.

Dahood, M. 1963. *Psalms I*. New York: Doubleday.

Davies, P. R. 2008. *Memories of Ancient Israel. An Introduction to Biblical History —Ancient and Modern*. Louisville, KY: Westminster John Knox Press.

Dearman, J. A. 2010. *The Book of Hosea*. Grand Rapids, MI: Eerdmans.

Dekker, J. 2007. *Zion's Rock-Solid Foundations. An Exegetical Study of the Zion Text in Isaiah 28:16*. Leiden: Brill.

Dobbs-Allsopp, F. W. 2004. 'R(az/ais)ing Zion in Lamentations 2'. In *David and Zion. Biblical Studies in Honor of J.J.M. Roberts*, B. F. Batto & K. L. Roberts (eds), 21–68. Winona Lake, IN: Eisenbrauns.

Dow, L. K. F. 2011. *Images of Zion. Biblical Antecedents for the New Jerusalem*. Sheffield: Sheffield Phoenix Press.

Eidevall, G. 1993. 'Lions and Birds as Literature. Some Notes on Isaiah 31 and Hosea 11'. *Scandinavian Journal of Old Testament* 7: 78–87.

Eidevall, G. 2009. *Prophecy and Propaganda. Images of Enemies in the Book of Isaiah*. Winona Lake, IN: Eisenbrauns.

Emmerson, G. I. 1984. *Hosea. An Israelite Prophet in Judean Perspective*. Sheffield: JSOT Press.

Fabry, H.-J. 2004. 'שׁוּב'. In *Theological Dictionary of the Old Testament*, vol. 14, G. J. Botterweck, H. Ringgren & H.-J. Fabry (eds), D. W. Stott (trans.), 461–522. Grand Rapids, MI: Eerdmans.

Ferry, J. 2008. *Isaïe: 'Comme les mots d'un livre scellé . . .'* Paris: Cerf.

Fischer, G. 2005a. *Jeremia 1–25*. Freiburg: Herder.

Fischer, G. 2005b. *Jeremia 26–52*. Freiburg: Herder.

Fischer, I. 2008. 'World Peace and "Holy War"—Two Sides of the Same Theological Concept. "YHWH as Sole Divine Power" (A Canonical-Intertextual Reading of Isaiah 2:1–5, Joel 4:9–21, and Micah 4:1–5)'. In *Isaiah's Vision of Peace in Biblical and Modern International Relations. Swords into Plowshares*, R. Cohen & R. Westbrook (eds), 151–65. New York: Palgrave Macmillan.

Fleer, D. 1983. 'Exegesis of Joel 2:1–11'. *Restoration Quarterly* 26: 149–60.

Fohrer, G. 1971. 'Zion-Jerusalem in the Old Testament'. In *Theological Dictionary of the New Testament*, vol. 7, G. Friedrich (ed.), G. W. Bromiley (trans.), 293–319. Grand Rapids, MI: Eerdmans.

Follis, E. R. 1992. 'Zion, Daughter of'. In *Anchor Bible Dictionary*, vol. 6, D. N. Freedman (ed.), 1103. New York: Doubleday.

Garrett, D. A. 1985. 'The Structure of Joel'. *Journal of the Evangelical Theological Society* 28(3): 289–97.

Gese, H. 1974. 'Der Davidsbund und die Zionserwählung'. In his *Vom Sinai zum Zion. Alttestamentliche Beiträge zur biblischen Theologie*, 113–29. Munich: Chr. Kaiser Verlag.

Gesenius, W. 1921. *Hebräisches und Aramäisches Handwörterbuch*. Leipzig: Verlag von F. C. Vogel.

Goldingay, J. 2007. 'Jeremiah and the Superpower'. In *Uprooting and Planting. Essays on Jeremiah for Leslie Allen*, J. Goldingay (ed.), 59–77. London: T&T Clark International.

BIBLIOGRAPHY

Gunkel, H. & J. Begrich. 1933. *Einleitung in die Psalmen. Die Gattungen der religiösen Lyrik Israels*. Göttingen: Vandenhoeck & Ruprecht.

Hasel, G. F. 1974. *The Remnant. The History and Theology of the Remnant Idea from Genesis to Isaiah*. Berrien Springs, MI: Andrew University Press.

Hausmann, J. 1987. *Israels Rest. Studien zum Selbstverständnis der nachexilischen Gemeinde*. Stuttgart: W. Kohlhammer.

Hayes, J. H. 1963. 'The Tradition of Zion's Inviolability'. *Journal of Biblical Literature* 82: 419–26.

Hertzberg, H. W. 1964. *I & II Samuel. A Commentary*. London: SCM Press.

Hill, J. 1999. *Friend or Foe? The Figure of Babylon in the Book of Jeremiah MT*. Leiden: Brill.

Hillers, D. R. 1992. *Lamentations. A New Translation with Introduction and Commentary*. New York: Doubleday.

Hjelm, I. 2004. *Jerusalem's Rise to Sovereignty. Zion and Gerizim in Competition*. London and New York: T&T Clark International.

Hjelm, I. forthcoming. 'Samaritan Literature in the Roman Period'. In *Oxford Companion to the Literatures of the Roman Period*, D. L. Selden & P. Vasunia (eds). Oxford: Oxford University Press.

Høgenhaven, J. 1988. *Gott und Volk bei Jesaja. Eine Untersuchung zur biblischen Theologie*. Leiden: Brill.

Hoppe, L. J. 2000. *The Holy City. Jerusalem in the Theology of the Old Testament*. Collegeville, MN: The Liturgical Press.

Irsigler, H. 2002. *Zefanja*. Freiburg: Herder.

Jenson, P. P. 2008. *Obadiah, Jonah, Micah. A Theological Commentary*. London: T&T Clark.

Jeppesen, K. 1987. *Græder ikke saa saare. Studier i Mikabogens sigte*. Århus: Aarhus Universitetsforlag.

Jeremias, Jö. 1971. 'Lade und Zion. Zur Entstehung der Ziontradition'. In *Probleme biblischer Theologie. Gerhard von Rad zum 70. Geburtstag*, H. W. Wolff (ed.), 183–98. Munich: Chr. Kaiser Verlag.

Jeremias, Jö. 1983. *Der Prophet Hosea*. Göttingen: Vandenhoeck & Ruprecht.

Jeremias, Joh. 1919. *Der Gottesberg. Ein Beitrag zum Verständnis der biblischen Symbolsprache*. Gütersloh: Verlag von C. Bertelsmann.

Jones, D. R. 1992. *Jeremiah*. Grand Rapids, MI: Eerdmans.

de Jong, M. J. 2011. 'From Legitimate King to Protected City. The Development of Isaiah 7:1–17'. In *'Enlarge the Site of Your Tent.' The City as Unifying Theme in Isaiah*, A. L. H. M. van Wieringen & A. van der Woude (eds), 21–48. Leiden: Brill.

Joyce, P. M. 2009. *Ezekiel. A Commentary*. London: T&T Clark International.

Kaiser, O. 1974. *Isaiah 13–39. A Commentary*, R. A. Wilson (trans.). London: SCM Press.

Kaiser, O. 1983. *Isaiah 1–12. A Commentary*, J. Bowden (trans.). London: SCM Press.

Kessler, M. 2003. *Battle of the Gods: The God of Israel Versus Marduk of Babylon. A Literary/Theological Interpretation of Jeremiah 50–51*. Assen: Royal Van Gorcum.

Kiesow, K. 1979. *Exodustexte im Jesajabuch. Literarkritische und motivgeschichtliche Analysen*. Göttingen: Fribourg.

Klein, G. L. 2008. *Zechariah*. Nashville: B&H Publishing Group.

Körting, C. 2006. *Zion in den Psalmen*. Tübingen: Mohr Siebeck.

BIBLIOGRAPHY

Kraus, H.-J. 1986. *Theology of the Psalms*, K. Crim (trans.). Minneapolis, MN: Augsburg Publishing House.

Kraus, H.-J. 1988. *Psalms 1–59. A Commentary*, H. C. Oswald (trans.). Minneapolis: Augsburg Publishing House.

Kraus, H.-J. 1989. *Psalms 60–150. A Commentary*, H. C. Oswald (trans.). Minneapolis, MN: Augsburg Fortress.

Laato, A. 1998. *'About Zion I will not be silent.' The Book of Isaiah as an Ideological Unity*. Stockholm: Almquist & Wiksell International.

Landy, F. 2011. *Hosea*. Sheffield: Sheffield Phoenix Press.

Lemche, N. P. 1991. *The Canaanites and their Land. The Tradition of the Canaanites*. Sheffield: JSOT Press.

Lemche, N. P. 2008. *The Old Testament between Theology and History. A Critical Survey*. Louisville, KY: Westminster John Knox Press.

Levenson, J. D. 1976. *Theology of the Program of Restoration of Ezekiel 40–48*. Missoula, MT: Scholars Press.

Levenson, J. D. 1985. *Sinai and Zion. An Entry into the Jewish Bible*. San Francisco, CA: HarperSanFrancisco.

Levenson, J. D. 1992. 'Zion Traditions'. In *Anchor Bible Dictionary*, vol. 6, D. N. Freedman (ed.), 1098–1102. New York: Doubleday.

Levine, L. I. 2002. *Jerusalem. Portrait of the City in the Second Temple Period (538 BCE–70 CE)*. Philadelphia, PA: Jewish Publication Society.

Lim, B. H. 2010. *The 'Way of the Lord' in the Book of Isaiah*. New York and London: T&T Clark.

Lisowsky, G. 1993. *Konkordanz zum hebräischen Alten Testament*. Stuttgart: Deutsche Bibelgesellschaft.

Lund, Ø. 2007. *Way Metaphors and Way Topics in Isa 40–55*. Tübingen: Mohr Siebeck.

Lundbom, J. R. 1999. *Jeremiah 1–20. A New Translation with Introduction and Commentary*. New York: Doubleday.

Lundbom, J. R. 2004. *Jeremiah 21–36. A New Translation with Introduction and Commentary*. New York: Doubleday.

Lundbom, J. R. 2006. *Jeremiah 37–52. A New Translation with Introduction and Commentary*. New York: Doubleday.

Lust, J. 1994. 'The Diverse Text Forms of Jeremiah and History Writing with Jer. 33 as a Test Case'. *Journal of Northwest Semitic Languages* 20: 31–48.

Lutz, H.-M. 1968. *Jahwe, Jerusalem und die Völker. Zur Vorgeschichte von Sach 12,1–8 und 14,1–5*. Neukirchen-Vluyn: Neukirchener Verlag.

Maier, M. P. 2010. 'Israel und die Völker auf dem Weg zum Gottesberg: Komposition und Intention der ersten Korachpsalmensammlung (Ps 42–49)'. In *The Compositions of the Book of Psalms*, E. Zenger (ed.), 653–65. Leuven: Peeters.

Mandolfo, C. R. 2007. *Daughter Zion Talks Back to the Prophets. A Dialogical Theology of the Book of Lamentations*. Atlanta, GA: Society of Biblical Literature.

Marrs, R. R. 2004. ' "Back to the Future": Zion in the Book of Micah'. In *David and Zion. Biblical Studies in Honor of J.J.M. Roberts*, B. F. Batto & K. L. Roberts (eds), 77–96. Winona Lake, IN: Eisenbrauns.

Martens, K. 2001. 'With a Strong Hand and an Outstretched Arm'. In *Scandinavian Journal of Old Testament* 15(1): 123–41.

Mason, R. 1994. *Zephaniah, Habakkuk, Joel*. Sheffield: JSOT Press.

BIBLIOGRAPHY

Mathews, C. R. 1995. *Defending Zion. Edom's Desolation and Jacob's Restoration (Isaiah 34–35) in Context*. Berlin/New York: Walter de Gruyter.

McCarter, Jr., P. K. 1984. *II Samuel. A New Translation with Introduction, Notes and Commentary*. New York: Doubleday.

McConville, G. 1992. 'Jerusalem in the Old Testament'. In *Jerusalem Past and Present in the Purposes of God*, P. W. L. Walker (ed.), 21–51. Cambridge: Tyndale House.

Meadowcroft, T. 2006. *Haggai. Readings*. Sheffield: Sheffield Phoenix Press.

Mettinger, T. N. D. 1982. *The Dethronement of Sabaoth. Studies in the Shem and Kabod Theologies*, F. H. Cryer (trans.). Lund: CWK Gleerup.

Meyers, C. L. & E. M. Meyers 1992. 'Jerusalem and Zion after the Exile: the Evidence of First Zechariah'. In *'Sha`arei Talmon' Studies in the Bible, Qumran, and the Ancient Near East. Presented to Shemaryahu Talmon*, M. Fishbane & E. Tov (eds), 121–35. Winona Lake, IN: Eisenbrauns.

Meyers, C. L. & E. M. Meyers 2009. *Zechariah 9–14. A New Translation with Introduction and Commentary*. New Haven, CT and London: Yale University Press.

Meyers, C. L. & E. M. Meyers 2010. *Haggai, Zechariah 1–8. A New Translation with Introduction and Commentary*. New Haven, CT and London: Yale University Press.

Miller II, R. D. 2010. 'The Origin of the Zion Hymns'. In *The Compositions of the Book of Psalms*, E. Zenger (ed.), 667–75. Leuven: Peeters.

Mowinckel, S. 1922. *Psalmenstudien II. Das Thronbesteigungsfest Jahwäs und der Ursprung der Eschatologie*. Kristiania.

Murray, R. 1992. *The Cosmic Covenant. Biblical Themes of Justice, Peace and the Integrity of Creation*. London: Sheed & Ward.

Nielsen, K. & J. Strange 1988. *Ezekiels Bog fortolket*. Copenhagen: Det Danske Bibelselskab.

Noth, M. 1950. 'Jerusalem und die israelitische Tradition'. *Oudtestamentische Studiën* 8: 28–46.

Ollenburger, B. C. 1987. *Zion, the City of the Great King. A Theological Symbol of the Jerusalem Cult*. Sheffield: Sheffield Academic Press.

Otto, E. 2003. 'צִיּוֹן'. In *Theological Dictionary of the Old Testament*, vol. 12, G. J. Botterweck, H. Ringgren & H.-J. Fabry (eds), D. W. Stott (trans.), 333–65. Grand Rapids, MI: Eerdmans.

Ottosson, M. 1978. 'הֵיכָל'. In *Theological Dictionary of the Old Testament*, vol. 3, G. J. Botterweck & H. Ringgren (eds), J. T. Willis & D. E. Green (trans.), 382–8. Grand Rapids, MI: Eerdmans.

Paul, S. M. 1991. *A Commentary on the Book of Amos*. Minneapolis, MN: Fortress Press.

Petersen, D. L. 1984. *Haggai and Zechariah 1–8. A Commentary*. London: SCM Press.

Petersen, D. L. 1995. *Zechariah 9–14 and Malachi. A Commentary*. Louisville, KY: Westminster John Knox Press.

Petersen, D. L. 2002. *The Prophetic Literature. An Introduction*. Louisville, KY: Westminster John Knox Press.

Pope, M. H. 1977. *Song of Songs. A New Translation with Introduction and Commentary*. New York: Doubleday & Company, Inc.

BIBLIOGRAPHY

Porteous, N. W. 1961. 'Jerusalem-Zion: the Growth of a Symbol'. In *Verbannung und Heimkehr. Beiträge zur Geschichte und Theologie Israels im 6. und 5. Jahrhundert v. Chr. Festschrift für Wilhelm Rudolph*, A. Kuschke (ed.), 235–52. Tübingen: J. C. B. Mohr (Paul Siebeck).

Poulsen, F. 2011. *En redegørelse for Zionmotivet i profetlitteraturen*. Copenhagen University: Afdeling for Bibelsk Eksegese, Det Teologiske Fakultet.

Poulsen, F. 2012. 'Eksodusbegivenheden i Deuterojesaja: Genskrivning eller overskrivning?' In *Bibelske genskrivninger*, J. Høgenhaven & M. Müller (eds), 89–109. Copenhagen: Museum Tusculanums Forlag.

Raabe, P. R. 1996. *Obadiah. A New Translation with Introduction and Commentary*. New York: Doubleday.

von Rad, G. 1958. 'Die Stadt auf dem Berge'. In his *Gesammelte Studien zum Alten Testament. Band I*, 214–24. Munich: Chr. Kaiser Verlag.

von Rad, G. 1962. *Old Testament Theology. The Theology of Israel's Historical Traditions*, vol. 1., D. M. G. Stalker (trans.). Edinburgh: Oliver & Boyd.

von Rad, G. 1965. *Old Testament Theology. The Theology of Israel's Prophetic Traditions*, vol. 2, D. M. G. Stalker (trans.). Edinburgh: Oliver & Boyd.

Renkema, J. 2003. *Obadiah*. Leuven: Peeters.

Renz, T. 1999. 'The Use of the Zion Tradition in the Book of Ezekiel'. In *Zion, City of Our God*, R. S. Hess & G. J. Wenham (eds), 77–103. Grand Rapids, MI: Eerdmans.

Riede, P. 2009. *Ich mache dich zur festen Stadt. Zum Prophetenbild von Jeremia 1,18f und 15,20*. Würzburg: Echter Verlag.

Riesner, R. & S. Kreuzer 2000. 'Jerusalem/Zion. A) Altes Testament und Frühjudentum'. In *Theologisches Begriffslexikon zum Neuen Testament*, vol. 2, L. Coenen & K. Haacker (eds), 1038–42. Wuppertal: Neukirchener Theologie.

Roberts, J. J. M. 1973. 'The Davidic Origin of the Zion Tradition'. *Journal of Biblical Literature* 92: 329–44.

Roberts, J. J. M. 1982. 'Zion in the Theology of the Davidic-Solomonic Empire'. In *Studies in the Period of David and Solomon and Other Essays*, T. Ishida (ed.), 93–108. Tokyo: Yamakawa-Shuppansha.

Roberts, J. J. M. 1991. *Nahum, Habakkuk, and Zephaniah. A Commentary*. Louisville, KY: Westminster John Knox Press.

Roberts, J. J. M. 2003. 'Solomon's Jerusalem and the Zion Tradition'. In *Jerusalem in Bible and Archaeology. The First Temple Period*, A. G. Vaughn & A. E. Killebrew (eds), 163–70. Atlanta, GA: Society of Biblical Literature.

Rohland, E. 1956. *Die Bedeutung der Erwählungstraditionen Israels für die Eschatologie der alttestamentlichen Propheten*. Dissertation, University of Heidelberg.

Rowley, H. H. 1962. 'The Early Prophecies of Jeremiah in their Setting'. *Bulletin of John Ryland's Library* 45: 198–234.

Rudnig, T. A. 2007. ' "Ist denn Jahwe nicht auf dem Zion?" (Jer. 8,19). Gottes Gegenwart im Heiligtum'. *Zeitschrift für Theologie und Kirche* 104: 267–86.

Sasson, J. M. 1990. *Jonah. A New Translation with Introduction, Commentary, and Interpretation*. New York: Doubleday.

Scharling, C. H. 1890. 'Zions Bjerg og Davids Stad. Topographiske Studier'. In *Indbydelsesskrift til Kjøbenhavns Universitets Aarsfest til Erindring om Kirkens Reformation*, 1–46. Copenhagen: J. H. Schultz.

Schmid, H. 1955. 'Jahwe und die Kulttraditionen von Jerusalem'. *Zeitschrift für die alttestamentliche Wissenschaft* 67: 168–98.

BIBLIOGRAPHY

Schmitt, H. C. 2004. '"Reue Gottes" im Joelbuch und in Exodus 32–34'. In *Schriftprophetie. Festschrift für Jörg Jeremias zum 65. Geburtstag*, F. Hartenstein, J. Krispenz & A. Schart (eds), 297–305. Neukirchen-Vluyn: Neukirchener Verlag.

Schreiner, J. 1963. *Sion-Jerusalem Jahwehs Königssitz. Theologie der heiligen Stadt im Alten Testament*. Munich: Kösel-Verlag.

Schweitzer, S. J. 2007. *Reading Utopia in Chronicles*. New York: T&T Clark.

Seitz, C. R. 1991. *Zion's Final Destiny. The Development of the Book of Isaiah. A Reassessment of Isaiah 36–39*. Minneapolis, MN: Fortress Press.

Simons, S. J. 1952. *Jerusalem in the Old Testament. Researches and Theories*. Leiden: Brill.

Smith, M. S. 1995. 'Myth and Mythmaking in Canaan and Ancient Israel'. In *Civilizations of the Ancient Near East*, vol. 3, J. M. Sasson (ed.), 2031–41. New York: Charles Scribner's Sons.

Snaith, J. G. 1993. *Song of Songs*. Grand Rapids, MI: Eerdmans.

Son, K. 2005. *Zion Symbolism in Hebrews. Hebrews 12:18–24 as a Hermeneutical Key to the Epistle*. Milton Keynes: Paternoster.

Stolz, F. 1970. *Strukturen und Figuren im Kult von Jerusalem. Studien zur altorientalischen, vor- und frühisraelitischen Religion*. Berlin: Walter de Gruyter.

Stolz, F. 1976. 'Zion'. In *Theologisches Handwörterbuch zum Alten Testament*, vol. 2, E. Jenni (ed.), 543–51. Munich: Chr. Kaiser Verlag.

Strange, J. 2007. *Jerusalem. Jødedom, kristendom, islam*. Copenhagen: Forlaget Multivers.

Strazicich, J. 2007. *Joel's Use of Scripture and the Scripture's Use of Joel. Appropriation and Resignification in Second Temple Judaism and Early Christianity*. Leiden: Brill.

Strong, J. T. 1996. 'Joel 2:1–2, 12–17'. *Interpretation* 50(1): 51–4.

Strong, J. T. 2000. 'God's *Kābôd*: The Presence of Yahweh in the Book of Ezekiel'. In *The Book of Ezekiel. Theological and Anthropological Perspectives*, M. S. Odell & J. T. Strong (eds), 69–95. Atlanta, GA: Society of Biblical Literature.

Stulman, L. 2005. *Jeremiah*. Nashville, TN: Abingdon Press.

Sweeney, M. A. 2003. *Zephaniah. A Commentary*. Minneapolis, MN: Fortress Press.

Sweeney, M. A. 2007. 'Jeremiah's Reflection on the Isaian Royal Promise: Jeremiah 23:1–8 in Context'. In *Uprooting and Planting. Essays on Jeremiah for Leslie Allen*, J. Goldingay (ed.), 308–21. London: T&T Clark International.

Sweeney, M. A. 2012. *Tanak. A Theological and Critical Introduction to the Jewish Bible*. Minneapolis, MN: Fortress Press.

Tan, K. H. 1997. *The Zion Traditions and the Aims of Jesus*. Cambridge: Cambridge University Press.

Thompson, T. L. 1999. *The Bible in History. How Writers Create a Past*. London: Jonathan Cape.

Thompson, T. L. 2003. 'Holy War at the Center of Biblical Theology: *Shalom* and the Cleansing of Jerusalem'. In *Jerusalem in Ancient History and Tradition*, T. L. Thompson (ed.), 223–57. London and New York: T&T Clark International.

Thompson, T. L. 2005. *The Messiah Myth. The Near Eastern Roots of Jesus and David*. New York: Basic Books.

Tiemeyer, L.-S. 2011. *For the Comfort of Zion. The Geographical and Theological Location of Isaiah 40–55*. Leiden: Brill.

200

BIBLIOGRAPHY

Tuell, S. S. 2000. 'Divine Presence and Absence in Ezekiel's Prophecy'. In *The Book of Ezekiel. Theological and Anthropological Perspectives*, M. S. Odell & J. T. Strong (eds), 97–116. Atlanta, GA: Society of Biblical Literature.

Tuell, S. S. 2009. *Ezekiel*. Peabody, MA: Hendrickson Publishers.

Vlaardingerbroek, J. 1999. *Zephaniah*. Leuven: Peeters.

Wanke, G. 1966. *Die Zionstheologie der Korachiten – in ihrem traditionsgeschichtlichen Zusammenhang*. Berlin: Verlag Alfred Töpelmann.

Watts, J. D. W. 2005. *Isaiah 34–66 (Revised Edition)*. Nashville, TN: Thomas Nelson.

Webb, B. G. 1990. 'Zion in Transformation. A Literary Approach to Isaiah'. In *The Bible in Three Dimensions. Essays in Celebration of Forty Years of Biblical Studies in the University of Sheffield*, D. J. A. Clines, S. E. Fowl & S. E. Porter (eds), 65–84. Sheffield: Sheffield University Press.

Weinfeld, M. 1983. 'Zion and Jerusalem as Religious and Political Capital: Ideology and Utopia'. In *The Poet and the Historian. Essays in Literary and Historical Biblical Criticism*, R. E. Friedman (ed.), 75–115. Chico, CA: Scholars Press.

Wessel, W. J. 2006. 'Zion, Beautiful City of God – Zion Theology in the Book of Jeremiah'. *Verbum et Ecclesia* 27: 729–48.

Westermann, C. 1987. *Isaiah 40–66*, D. M. G. Stalker (trans.). London: SCM Press Ltd.

Whitelam, K. W. 1996. *The Invention of Ancient Israel. The Silencing of Palestinian History*. London: Routledge.

van Wieringen, A. L. H. M. 2011. 'The Diseased King and the Diseased City (Isaiah 36–39) as a Reader-Oriented Link Between Isaiah 1–39 and Isaiah 40–66'. In *'Enlarge the Site of Your Tent.' The City as Unifying Theme in Isaiah*, A. L. H. M. van Wieringen & A. van der Woude (eds), 81–93. Leiden: Brill.

Wildberger, H. 1957. 'Die Völkerwallfahrt zum Zion. Jes. ii 1–5'. *Vetus Testamentum* 7: 62–81.

Wildberger, H. 1991. *Isaiah 1–12. A Commentary*, T. H. Trapp (trans.). Minneapolis, MN: Fortress Press.

Wildberger, H. 1997. *Isaiah 13–27. A Continental Commentary*, T. H. Trapp (trans.). Minneapolis, MN: Fortress Press.

Wildberger, H. 2002. *Isaiah 28–39. A Continental Commentary*, T. H. Trapp (trans.). Minneapolis, MN: Fortress Press.

Williams, T. F. 1997. 'פקד'. In *New International Dictionary of Old Testament Theology & Exegesis*, vol. 3, W. A. VanGemeren (ed.), 657–63. Carlisle: Paternoster Press.

Williamson, H. G. M. 2006. *A Critical and Exegetical Commentary on Isaiah 1–27*, vol.1. London: T&T Clark.

Williamson, H. G. M. 2008. 'Swords into Plowshares. The Development and Implementation of a Vision'. In *Isaiah's Vision of Peace in Biblical and Modern International Relations. Swords into Plowshares*, R. Cohen & R. Westbrook (eds), 139–49. New York: Palgrave Macmillan.

Willis, J. T. 2004. 'David and Zion in the Theology of the Deuteronomistic History: Theological Ideas in 2 Samuel 5–7'. In *David and Zion. Biblical Studies in Honor of J.J.M. Roberts*, B. F. Batto & K. L. Roberts (eds), 125–40. Winona Lake, IN: Eisenbrauns.

BIBLIOGRAPHY

Wischnowsky, M. 2001. *Tochter Zion. Aufnahme und Überwindung der Stadtklage in den Prophetenschriften des Alten Testaments*. Neukirchen-Vluyn: Neukirchener Verlag.

Wolff, H. W. 1977. *Joel and Amos. A Commentary on the Books of the Prophets Joel and Amos*, W. Janzen, S. D. McBride & C. A. Muenchow (trans.). Philadelphia, PA: Fortress Press.

Wolff, H. W. 1986. *Obadiah and Jonah. A Commentary*, M. Kohl (trans.). Minneapolis, MN: Augsburg Publishing House.

Wolff, H. W. 1990. *Micah. A Commentary*, G. Stansell (trans.). Minneapolis, MN: Augsburg Fortress.

Zimmerli, W. 1979. *Ezekiel 1. A Commentary on the Book of the Prophet Ezekiel, Chapters 1–24*, R. E. Clements (trans.). Philadelphia, PA: Fortress Press.

Zimmerli, W. 1983. *Ezekiel 2. A Commentary on the Book of the Prophet Ezekiel, Chapters 25–48*. J. D. Martin (trans.). Philadelphia, PA: Fortress Press.

INDEX OF SCRIPTURE

Genesis
Book of	19n76
1	164
1:2	138
1:26	181
2:10–14	173
3	182
3:15	180, 188n98
14	72n10
14:17–24	65
22:1–19	65
22:14	65

Exodus
Book of	165, 181
15:1–18	65
15:5	183n3
15:17	65
17:6	148
19	81
40:34	162n54

Leviticus
Book of	73n24, 133, 138, 163n72
18:24–28	142n64
26:27–9	125
26:29	132
26:33–39	141n42

Deuteronomy
Book of	8, 17n34, 19n64, 54, 58, 64–66, 69, 72n15, 140n15
8:53–7	140n16
28	138
28:53–7	132
30:1–10	161n36
30:15	127
30:19	126

Joshua
Book of	66, 72n15

Judges
Book of	66

1 Samuel
Book of	76n19

2 Samuel
Book of	76n19
5	73n23
5:6–8	66
5:7	64

1 Kings
Book of	7, 33n26, 76n19, 147
12:21	170

2 Kings
Book of	7, 33n26, 76n19
8:1	64
8:13	72n11
19:21	64
19:31	64
25	29

1 Chronicles
Book of	7, 33n26, 64–65, 73n17, 76n19, 165
11:5	64
21	66, 67

2 Chronicles
Book of	7, 33n26, 64–65, 73n17, 76n19
3:1	67
5:2	64

INDEX OF SCRIPTURE

9:1–12	180	2:4	53, 166
16:8	143n67	4	13, 106, 108, 113, 120n98
20	120n97	5:3	13
23–4	180	5:8–24	83
30:6–12	184n34	5:25–30	26, 48, 52, 53,
36:21	140n21		81–84, 94, 115n15,
			138, 157, 177
Ezra		6:1–9	122–24
Book of	64, 65, 66, 73n28	6:11–13	13, 29, 122
9–10	175	7	4, 27, 33n25, 33n26, 191
47:1–12	173	7:1–9	95–96, 99
		7–8	28
Nehemiah		8	82–85, 86n8, 125
Book of	64, 65, 66, 73n28	8:7	82, 84, 93, 101
13	175, 176	8:10	46, 125
		9	119n79
Psalms		10:12	92–94, 112
Book of	1–9, 11–13, 16n26,	10:20–23	99
	17n34, 18n57, 20n87, 55,	10:24–34	91
	64, 67–70, 74nn41, 44,	10:27	150
	75n51, 118n67, 189	11:1–5	170
2	67, 85	11:1–16	184n31, 185n37, 185n47
46	3–7, 11, 16n27, 18n57,	11:6–9	180–81, 182
	67–68, 85, 119n79, 173	11:13	169
48	3–7, 11, 16n27, 18n57,	12:6	13
	42n16, 67–68, 85, 119n79	13	81
76	3–7, 11, 16n27, 18n57,	14:1–4a	31
	67–68, 85	14:24–7	92–93, 109, 116nn25, 26
84	12	14:30a	119n78, 121n117
95:3	67	16:1	13
99:2	2	17:12–14	26, 85, 90–91, 178
102	12, 68	25:6–10a	181, 188n102
110	67	28:14–18	9, 95, 120n98
126	68, 75n52	28:20	181
132:13	2, 67	29:1–8	1, 4, 85, 89–91, 92,
137	68		94, 108, 111, 123
		30:15–17	96, 104, 126
Song of Songs		30:26–33	93, 94, 116nn34,
Book of	19n76, 69–70		35, 140n13
		30:27–33	26, 93, 116n35, 127
Isaiah		31:4–9	94–95, 104, 112
Book of	3, 5, 7–13, 25–35	31:6	99, 104, 130
1	101, 109, 117n53, 181	33	47, 107, 111, 119n70,
1:4–9	88–89, 98		186n55
1:8–9	123, 133	34–35	55, 116n38, 121n104
1–12	92	35	29, 119n69
1:21–8	101, 109, 136	35:1–10	144–47, 150, 151, 157,
1–35	96		159n5, 160n11, 168
1–39	9, 15n19, 18–19n62,	36–7	27, 28, 52, 82–83, 96, 98,
	21n90, 25, 29, 86n15		105, 130, 187n86, 192n1
2:2–4	172, 176–78, 179,	37:14–38	97–98
	180, 181, 187n91	37:30–32	99, 111, 112, 130

INDEX OF SCRIPTURE

37:33–5	123	26:1–6	128
39–40	29, 66, 122	26–52	37
40:1–11	146–47	29:10–20	130–31
40–55	15n9, 15n13, 25,	30:3	149–50
	29–30, 51n29, 144,	30:18	166
	146–50, 152, 154, 156,	31	150–51
	158, 160n27, 161n35,	31:21–2	151
	162n51, 165–66, 169,	31:23–5	166
	175–76	31:27–8	167
43:14–21	147–48	31:31–4	169, 170, 173
44:26–8	164, 168, 172	31:38–40	167
48:20–21	148	33:1–11	167–68
49:9–13	148	33:14–26	170–71
51:3	75n64	50:4–5	169
52:1	175	50–51	38, 40–41, 52, 149,
52:7–10	148–49		151–52, 184n17
54:11–17	30, 148–49, 165	56–66	9, 30, 34–35n44,
56	176, 179, 182		34nn42, 43, 49, 172
56:1–8	174–75		
56–66	9, 15n9, 25, 30, 49,	**Lamentations**	
	172, 174, 176	Book of	13, 69–70, 75n62, 63,
60:1–22	165, 177–78, 180,		163n66
	181, 182, 186n65		
62:1–12	165–66	**Ezekiel**	
64:9–10	13, 29, 122	Book of	44–51, 63n51, 82, 84,
66:18–24	178–79, 180		102, 112, 162n51, 185n46
		1–3	46–48, 147, 162n57
Jeremiah		1–39	119n84, 94
Book of	37, 42n16, 82, 84–85,	5:5–17	132
	90, 141n25, 168–69	6:8–10	133–34
1–25	37, 123, 129–30, 151	7:21–7	134–35
3:16–17	173	11	51n28, 147
3:18	169–70	14:21–3	134, 146
4–10	38, 42n20, 48, 53	17:22–4	171
4:23–6	138–39, 159n8	20:33–44	152–53
4:26	159n8	25–32	48
6:19	122–24, 139n5	33–7	48
7:30–8:3	125–26	33:21–9	133
8:19	161n32	34:11–16	153–54
9:10–15[11–16]	124–25	34:23–4	171
12:7–12	126	36:33–8	168
17:19–27	128–29	38–9, 48	53
18:7–12	128	39:11–16	125
19:3–9	125	40–48, 48	49
19:8	163n76	44:4–9	175–76
19:12	140n13	47:1–12	174
21:4–10	126–27		
22:4–5	141n30	**Daniel**	
23, 149	185n37	Book of	64, 66
23:1–8	170		
24:1–10	128–29	**Hosea**	
25:4–7	127–28	Book of	52, 54, 56, 60, 172, 181

205

INDEX OF SCRIPTURE

Joel
Book of — 52–54, 55, 60, 61n7, 62n18
2:1–11 — 79–81, 82, 84–85, 177, 178, 190
2:12–4:21 — 104–7, 108, 109, 112, 113, 114, 120nn87, 89, 129, 137, 153–54
3:18 — 174
4:16 — 53, 61n7, 62n18, 107

Amos
Book of — 10, 12, 54, 55, 56, 60
9:11–15 — 168–69

Obadiah
Book of — 54–55, 60, 62nn18, 19, 109, 112, 113–14, 190
15–21 — 107–8

Jonah
Book of — 52, 55, 60

Micah
Book of — 1, 13, 55–57, 61, 71
1:8–16 — 135–36
2:3–4 — 136
2:8–10 — 136
3:9 — 1, 57
3:9–4:5 — 57–58
3:9–12 — 136
4:11–13 — 109, 112, 113, 114, 135–37, 154, 158, 162n58, 176, 190

Nahum
Book of — 52, 57, 60

Habakkuk
Book of — 57, 60, 84, 87n19

Zephaniah
Book of — 57–58, 61, 81, 112, 113–14
3:1–20 — 109–11, 136, 190

Haggai
Book of — 58, 59, 60, 63n42, 43, 44, 152, 176, 187n87
1:3–6 — 155
1:12–17 — 155–56
2:6–9 — 179
8:14–15 — 155

Zechariah
Book of — 16n27, 58–60, 61, 63nn49, 54, 76n66, 122, 172–73, 182, 186n74
1–8 — 58–59
1:12–17 — 155–56, 157
2:4b–5 — 169
2:10–17 — 156–57
8:1–8 — 157
8:14–15 — 155, 157
8:20–23 — 179
9–11 — 59
10:8–10 — 157, 163n76
12:1–13:1 — 112–14, 190
12–14 — 60, 82–85, 106
14:1–5 — 137, 157–58
14:8 — 173, 174
14:16–21 — 175, 176, 179–80, 181

Malachi
Book of — 60

206

INDEX OF NAMES

Allen, Leslie 41n5, 42n24, 53, 61n12, 121n106, 128, 139n6, 140nn20, 22, 141n37, 161n37, 162n47, 167, 184n19, 185n36, 38, 185n52

Barstad, Hans 161n33
Barton, J. 119n85, 121n102, 186n58
Berges, Ulrich F. 25, 34nn35, 43, 118n67, 161n32, 183n3
Berlin, Adele 13, 69, 121n116
Blenkinsopp, J. 118n64, 165, 166, 175
Block, Daniel 45, 51n34, 162n55
Boadt, Lawrence 49n2
Bolin, T. M. 72nn9, 10, 73n28

Carroll, R. P. 42n29, 139nn5, 6, 141nn31, 37, 162n45
Childs, B. S. 33nn20, 30, 42n20, 90, 116nn25, 38, 117nn45, 47, 118nn61, 64, 159nn4, 5, 6, 160nn21, 24, 25, 26, 175, 183n2, 187n85, 188nn98, 104
Clements, Ronald E. 5, 16–17n32, 33n28
Clifford, Richard J. 4–5
Coggin, Richard James 62n17
Conrad, E. W. 176
Crenshaw, J. L. 106, 120n89

Dahood, Mitchell 74n44
Dekker, Jaap 9
Dobbs-Allsopp, F. W. 75n62
Dow, Lois 2, 10, 42n28, 65, 72n10, 15, 76n66, 141n42, 183n5, 189

Eideval, G. 115n19

Fabry, Heinz-Josef 160n15
Fischer, Georg 167, 170, 184n18

Fleer, David 86n3
Fohrer, Georg 14n10

Gese, Hartmut 4, 15n21
Gesenius, Wilhelm 146, 157, 163n76
Gunkel, Hermann 74n39

Hayes, John H. 4, 94, 96
Hjelm, Ingrid 7, 9, 11, 12, 15n16, 19n64, 33n25, 65, 74n45, 79, 86n8, 140n15, 184n34, 185n43, 189
Hoppe, Leslie 9, 20n87, 21n90, 32n19, 34nn36, 42, 45, 65, 68, 75n51, 115n9, 117n41, 118n67, 120n86

Irsigler, Hubert 110–11
Isaiah ben Amos 180

Jenson, Philip Peter 120n101, 121n106, 142nn58, 64, 143nn67, 68
Jeppesen, Knud 56, 135, 136
Jeremias, Johannes 2, 14–15n11
Jeremias, Jörg 4, 61n5, 74n41
Jones, Douglas 42n16, 123
Joyce, P. M. 50n21, 119n80, 142n44, 162n51, 185nn41, 44, 186n69, 188n101

Kaiser, Otto 27, 90, 115n10, 117n45, 160n9
Keil, Carl F. 87n23
Körting, Corinna 11, 12, 13, 68–69, 74–75n48, 75nn50, 52, 189
Kraus, H.-J. 74nn43, 46

Laato, Antti 9, 18–19n62, 25, 33–34n31, 33n22, 34–35n44, 34nn32, 33, 115n6, 116nn34, 35, 117n53, 139n1, 187n86, 189

207

INDEX OF NAMES

Levenson, Jon D. 8, 42–43n31
Lundbom, Jack 37, 141n37, 161n44, 184n18
Lutz, Hanns-Martin 4, 16n27, 76n66, 86n15, 95, 96

Marrs, Rick R. 56, 62n34, 162n58
Mason, Rex 57
McCarter, Jr., P. K. 66, 73n22
McConville, Gordon 7, 35n45, 140n22
Meadowcroft, T. 187n87
Mettinger, Tryggve 50n20
Meyers, C. L. 20n87, 21n92, 63nn43, 44, 49, 54, 121n119, 162–63n65, 163nn67, 70, 169, 186n74
Meyers, E. M. 20n87, 21n92, 63nn43, 44, 49, 54, 121n119, 162–63n65, 163nn67, 70, 169, 186n74
Mowinckel, Sigmund 2–3, 8, 9

Ollenburger, Ben C. 9, 12, 17n38, 20n80, 61n2, 74n40, 117n50
Otto, Eckart 14n10
Ottosson 183n1

Petersen, David L. 52, 121nn122, 123, 176
Pope, M. H. 75n55

Renkema, Johan 62n25
Renz, Thomas 44–45
Roberts, J. J. M. 5, 6, 17nn33, 34, 20n78, 34, 63n37
Rohland, Edzard 3, 5–6, 7, 79, 189

Schreiner, Josef 4, 15n22, 74n41, 183n2
Seitz, Christopher 117–18n57
Stolz, Fritz 4
Strong, John T. 45, 50n11, 120n87
Stulman, Louis 37, 41n12, 139n11
Sweeney, M. A. 121n112, 185n37

Tan, K. H. 11, 19n77, 20n79
Thompson, T. L. 73n24, 139–40n12, 160n11
Tuell, Steven 45, 49, 50nn7, 26, 51n31, 134, 142nn46, 47, 162n49

von Rad, Gerhard 3, 7, 8, 12, 15nn18, 19, 26, 37, 189

Wanke, Gunther 4, 8, 11, 16n26, 17n38
Warren, Charles 66
Watts, J. D. W. 159n2
Webb, Barry 20n85, 21n2
Wessel, W. J. 42n31
Westermann, C. 165, 166, 175
Wildberger, Hans 3, 12, 90, 96, 114n3, 115–16n23, 117n44, 118n59, 119n72, 180, 187n91
Wolff, Hans Walter 54, 62n24, 80, 106, 108, 120nn94, 97, 136, 142–43n66, 142n61, 162n61

Zimmerli, Walther 44, 50n5, 51n30, 87n19, 119n75, 142nn45, 47, 185n42

INDEX OF SUBJECTS

About Zion I Will Not Be Silent (Laato) 9
Abram/Abraham 65, 133
acknowledgement 102–4, 105, 107
Ahaz, King 27–28, 33nn22, 25, 26, 99, 192n1
ambiguity 33n25, 91, 92, 94, 110, 111, 158–59, 160n28
Amos 54, 60, 168–69
animal metaphors 52, 59, 125, 180–81, 188n98, 100; jackals, imagery of 70, 124, 138, 145–46
Ariel 27, 89, 94, 115n6
Ark of the Covenant 173, 187n77
ark-traditions 6, 9, 14n10, 66
Assyrian siege, 701 BCE 4, 5–6, 16–17n32, 17, 18–19n62, 25, 28, 33n22, 26, 34n35, 57, 71, 84, 96–98, 116n26, 130, 134

Baal, mountain of 5, 38
Baals 37, 74n44, 124
Babylon 46, 56, 58, 68, 84, 116n26; fall of Jerusalem 126, 127, 128; return from captivity in 147–49, 151, 159nn5, 7, 161n37
Babylonians 29, 38, 39, 40, 48
battle of the nations motif 11, 16n26, 37 *see also* defeat; enemy attack
before-after theme 59, 157
birth imagery 26, 30
Book of the Twelve 10, 52–63
booth imagery 54, 60, 99, 118n67, 168

Canaanite traditions 4–7, 38, 186n74
cannibalism 125, 140n16
canonical approach 10

captivity 37–40, 47, 49, 129; return from in Babylon 147–49, 151, 159nn5, 7, 161n37
Chaldeans 82, 84, 126, 130, 151–52
city of David 19n76, 64–65, 73n17
classical Zion motif 71–72, 101; battle against the nations 79, 98; in Ezekiel 49, 138; four basic motifs 173, 189–91; in Isaiah 32, 102, 130–31; in Jeremiah 36, 37, 122–24, 130–32, 138, 152; in Joel 53, 60, 129; in Psalms 70; in Zechariah 60–61; in Zephaniah 58, 61
cloud imagery 82, 100, 153
comfort 26, 29, 58, 69, 75n64, 146–47, 148, 156
consolation 146–47
The Cosmic Mountain in Canaan and the Old Testament (Clifford) 4
covenants 8–9, 37, 52, 125, 138; broken 37, 39, 41n12, 139n11, 175; with David 8; in Ezekiel 47; Sinai 8–9, 39
cultic tradition 2–4
cup metaphor 112, 120n101, 121n102
Cyrus, King 141n25, 37, 160n27, 164–65

Daniel 66
Darius, King 58, 59
dating 7–9, 10, 58–59; post-exilic period 4, 7, 8, 9, 14n10, 17n33, 18–19n62, 42n20, 54, 60, 63n49, 139n1; pre-exilic period 4, 14n10
daughter Zion motif 13, 21n92, 25, 57–58, 139n5; in Isaiah 29–30; in Jeremiah 36, 41n5, 122–24; in Micah 56, 109

INDEX OF SUBJECTS

David: booth of 54, 60; chosen by
YHWH 3, 5; covenant with 8;
dating issues 7; moves ark 3, 4, 6;
siege of Jerusalem 6, 66
Davidic monarchy 8, 14n10, 66,
95–96, 98, 117n45, 168, 170, 180,
183n1, 185n37, 191
Davidic-Solomonic age 5, 6, 15n22,
17n33, 34, 169, 173, 185n43
Day of YHWH 15n13, 52, 55,
61, 79–81, 99, 137, 189–90;
deliverance and 106, 107; enemy
attack as 82–83, 91
decision, theology of 27
defeat of Zion 5, 8, 26, 122–43, 191;
of chaotic floods 5, 6; in Ezekiel
132–35; fall of Jerusalem 124–27;
in Jeremiah 122–32; in Micah
135–37; possible prevention of
destruction 127–29; Topheth 94,
101, 125, 140n13; in Zechariah 137
see also desolation of Zion; exile
deliverance 88–121; conditions for
94–96; in Ezekiel 102–4, 113–14;
faith and 95–96; in Isaiah 88–102,
113–14; in Joel 104–7; in Micah
109, 114; in Obadiah 107–8,
113–14; purging of Zion 100–101,
106, 109, 112, 113, 114; remnant
of Israel 98–100; in Zechariah
112–13; in Zephaniah 109–11, 114
'Der Davidsbund und die
Zionserwählung' (Gese) 4
desolation of Zion 46–47, 60, 70, 98,
126, 129, 133; in Ezekiel 46; in
Isaiah 26, 29, 31–32; in Jeremiah
36–40, 122–24, 151; return to
Zion and 150–56, 158–59 see also
defeat of Zion
Deuteronomistic tradition 8, 17n34,
19n64, 54, 65, 69, 140n15,
141n43
Diaspora 148, 161n35, 166, 172, 175,
178–79, 184n31
Die Bedeutung der
Erwählungstraditionen Israels für die
Eschatologie der alttestamentlichen
Propheten (Rohland) 3, 5–6
'Die völkerwallfahrt zum Zion'
(Wildberger) 3
Die Zionstheologie der Korachiten
(Wanke) 4

divine plan 27, 41, 109; in Isaiah 91–93,
96, 99, 102–3, 115n14, 116n25
dramatic scenario 25, 28, 39, 62n34,
79–80, 85, 91–93
dynamic Zion motif 70–71, 189–91;
in Ezekiel 44, 47, 48, 49, 138, 159;
in Jeremiah 32, 37, 40, 129, 138;
in Micah 56–57, 61; three stages
138, 153; in Zechariah 59, 60, 61

earthquake imagery 38, 81, 84, 85,
89, 103
Edom (Esau) 55, 107–8, 113–14,
120n101, 145, 168
El, mountain of 5, 17n39
El Elyon cult 3, 4
enemy: judgement of 92, 106–7,
110–11, 113–14; from north 38,
42n20, 48, 54, 74n44, 80, 84,
91–92, 105; as shepherds 123,
126, 139n6; YHWH's sudden
intervention 89–91
enemy attack 4, 8, 26, 38, 71–72,
79–87; as Day of YHWH 82–83,
189–90; invincible army 84; in Joel
79–81; locust army 79–80, 86n3;
mythological characteristics of
enemy 38, 42n20; return to Zion
and 159; YHWH summons and
leads army 26, 37, 81–82, 85, 94,
134–35, 138
Ephraim 39, 55, 58, 170, 184n34
Esau, Mount 55, 108 see also Edom
(Esau)
eschatological perspective 3, 8–9,
15n19, 16n32, 20n79, 25, 45n44,
115n5, 166, 180, 185n52, 188n98
exile 14n10, 38, 122–43; fall of
Jerusalem 124–27; good and bad
figs 130–31; as limited 130–31;
self-loathing during 47, 138, 153,
155, 190; seventy-year period 137,
138, 141n37, 156; in Zechariah 59,
63n54 see also defeat of Zion;
return to Zion
Exodus traditions 3, 54, 65, 148, 152
Ezekiel 10, 44–51, 71, 82–83; avoids
Zion as term 13, 19n76, 44–45, 49,
50n5, 173; defeat of Zion 132–35;
deliverance in 102–4, 113–14; fall
of Jerusalem 125–26; motifs, events
and characteristics associated with

210

INDEX OF SUBJECTS

Zion 46–49; remnant of Israel in
47, 132–34; return to Zion 152–54;
six main parts 48–49; twelve tribes
of Israel 48, 51n34, 176, 182
Ezra 66–67

faith: as a condition of salvation 4,
28–29, 34–35n44, 160n21;
deliverance and 95–96, 106
figs, good and bad 123, 129–31
fire imagery 82, 94, 100, 112
fleeing motif 122–23, 151–52
foreigners 49; brought to Zion 30–31;
new temple and 174–75; as servants
of Zion 178; uncircumcised as
175–76, 186n71; YHWH destroys
53
fountain imagery 60, 113, 114, 164

Garden of Eden 29, 47, 168, 173, 180
gathering of people 48, 111, 151–52
Genesis 65, 180
glory of YHWH 29, 45, 46, 147, 153,
162n54, 177, 182
Gog 48, 82, 83, 113, 119n80, 125
Der Gottesberg (Jeremias) 2
grace 8, 47, 105, 131, 134

Habakkuk 57
Haggai 58, 59, 179
Hellenistic period 7, 9, 10
heritage, people as 53, 105, 106, 126,
140n22
Hezekiah account 16n32, 18n51,
19n62, 27–29, 33n22, 34n34, 67,
192n1; in 2 Kings 64–65; Day of
YHWH 82–83; deliverance of Zion
and 96–98, 104, 117–18n57,
117n53; prayer to God 97–98;
reconciliation theme 184n34; water
channel 66, 73n23
highest mountain motif 2, 5, 47,
171–72, 176
historical approaches 2, 5, 12, 46, 54
historical books 13, 64–67
The Holy City (Hoppe) 9
Holy Way 29, 144–46
Hosea 52, 172

idolatry 54, 60, 69, 71, 124–25;
abolition of 94, 95, 128; in Ezekiel
46; in Jeremiah 37–39

Images of Zion (Dow) 2, 10
inhabitants of Zion 20n78, 21n90, 25
inviolability of Zion 1–8, 16–17n32,
66, 191; fall of Jerusalem missing
from Isaiah 29, 34n34; prophet
as inviolable 40, 41, 42n28;
in Zechariah 60, 112–14
Isaiah 9–10, 25–76, 190; Ahaz
account 27–28, 33nn22, 25, 26, 99,
192n1; ambiguity in 33n25, 91, 92,
94, 110, 111, 158–59, 160n28;
classical Zion motif 32; daughter
Zion motif 29–30; decisive turn in
105, 106; deliverance in 88–102,
113–14; enemy attack 81–82;
Exodus motif 34–35n44; feast on
holy mountain 181–82; Hezekiah
account 27–28, 64, 192n1; Holy
Way 29, 144–46; Jerusalem's fall
missing from 29, 34n34; between
man and the animals 180–81;
motifs, events and characteristics
associated with Zion 26–31;
rebuilding of city and temple
(40–55) 25; remnant of Israel
19n62, 26, 28–29, 31–32, 33n26,
57, 63n39, 70–71, 89, 97–100,
101, 102, 107, 108, 114; return to
Zion 29, 146–50; structure 25,
34n43, 35n46, 88–89; two main
perceptions of Zion 31–32;
universalism in 30–31, 166, 175,
182; Zion as term in 25–26
see also Assyrian siege, 701 BCE
Isaiah and the Deliverance of
Jerusalem (Clements) 5
Isaiah of Jerusalem 3, 15n22
Jacob, house of 55, 108, 113
'Jahwe und die kulttraditionen von
Jerusalem' (Schmid) 3
Jebusites 4, 6, 65–66
Jehoshaphat, valley of 53, 61n7,
106–7, 120n97, 174
Jeremiah 10, 13, 36–43, 71, 82–83;
broken covenant in 37, 39, 41n12;
defeat of Zion 122–32; destruction
of Jerusalem in 37, 38–40; fall of
Jerusalem 124–27; messages of
judgement and salvation 36; motifs,
events and characteristics associated
with Zion 37–40; motifs turned
upside down 167; movement from

211

INDEX OF SUBJECTS

judgement to redemption 37, 39–41; remnant of Israel 40, 123, 150; return to Zion 38, 149–52; reunification of Israel and Judah 39; structure 37; temple sermon 40; Zion as term in 36–37

Jeremiah (prophet) 40, 41

Jerusalem: Assyrian siege, 701 BCE 5–6, 16–17n32, 17, 130, 134; Babylonian invasion 29; as city of David 19n76, 64–65, 73n17; cosmic topography 10, 19n76, 20n78, 48, 50n26; as daughter 58; David moves ark to 3, 4, 6; destruction of in Jeremiah 37, 38–40; fall of 124–27; fall of missing from Isaiah 29, 34n34; not synonymous with Zion 12–13; pre-Israelite 6; religious importance of 3; 'YHWH is There' 49; in Zechariah 112–14

'Jerusalem und die israelitische Tradition' (Noth) 3

Jerusalem's Rise to Sovereignty (Hjelm) 9

'Jerusalem-Zion: the Growth of a Symbol' (Porteous) 4

Joel 52–54, 129, 190; deliverance in 104–7; enemy attack in 79–81

Jonah 55

Joseph, house of 59, 108, 113, 157

Joshua 66

Judah 13, 48, 54, 58, 71; reunification with Israel 39, 41, 52, 55, 59, 164, 166–67, 169–72, 180, 182, 185n42; in Zechariah 112–14

judgement 27, 37, 63n49; Day of YHWH 15n13, 52, 55, 61, 79–83, 81–83, 91, 106, 107, 115n14, 137, 189–90; of the enemies 92, 106–7, 110–11, 113–14; enemy attack as 27; gleaning motif 122–23; of political leaders 45, 89, 108, 109–11, 136–37; spirit of 100; in valley of Jehoshaphat 53, 61n7, 106–7, 120n97, 174; in Zechariah 112–14 *see also* defeat of Zion

Judges 66

'Lade und Zion' (Jeremias) 4

Lamentations 69–70, 75n62

last bastion 12, 70, 88–89, 189; in Isaiah 26, 28–29, 31–32; in Jeremiah 37, 40–41; in Obadiah 55

Levites 170–71, 173, 179

light imagery 30, 94, 177–78, 187n79

lion imagery 95, 116–17n40, 146

logic of retribution 125, 138, 139–40n12, 156

Malachi 60

Melchizedek 65

Micah 55–57, 61, 71, 190; deliverance in 109, 114; ploughed field 135–37; return to Zion 154; Zion as poetic synonym 13

Moriah, Mount 65

Moses 148

Moses, song of 65

motifs, events and characteristics associated with Zion: Ezekiel 46–49; Isaiah 26–31; Jeremiah 37–40

Mount Zion: as cosmic mountain 1–2, 4–6, 20n78; as highest mountain 2, 5, 176

mountain cults 14–15n11

mountains 2–3; in Canaanite, Hittite, and Hurrian religions 4–5; cosmic 1–2, 4–6, 20n78

mourning 25, 29, 37, 69–70, 113, 182

Nahum 57

Nebuchadrezzar/Nebuchadnezzar, King 38–39, 84, 71, 126, 141n25

Nehemiah 66–67

New Exodus 148, 152, 161n35

New Year festival 2–3, 9, 15n13

New Zion 15n13, 76n66, 138–39, 164–88, 183n2, 190–91; feast on holy mountain 181–82; in Jeremiah 35n45, 38–39; new temple on 172–73; peace between man and the animals 180–81; rebuilding and repopulation 164–69; temple and the foreigners 174–75; temple source 173–74; worldwide pilgrimage to 176–80

north, kingdoms of 38, 42n20, 48, 54, 74n44, 80, 84, 91–92, 105

Obadiah 54–55, 190; deliverance in 107–8, 113–14

offerings, cultic 48, 53

Old Testament Theology (von Rad) 3

Olives, Mount of 60

212

INDEX OF SUBJECTS

parallelism 69, 118n64, 158, 177, 186n63
pasture metaphor 41n5, 47, 111, 121n117, 139nn5, 6, 152, 184nn17, 18, 190
patronage 140n12, 142n46
peace 4, 48, 53, 180–81
peace, hope for 30–31
Pentateuch 65, 66, 138, 162n49
Persian period 7, 9, 10
pilgrimage motif 3, 5, 11, 179–80
plant metaphors 47, 99–100
political leaders 45, 89, 108, 109–11, 136–37, 185n44
poor, theology of 111, 114, 160n11
pre-Israelite cult 3–4, 6, 14n10, 15n16, 17n33, 18n44, 66
priestly concerns 44, 58, 105, 106, 136, 170, 186n69; Levites 170–71, 173, 179
prophecy-fulfilment-motif 125
prophets: minor 52–63, 82; as secondary source 1, 8
protection 6, 9, 14n10, 26, 93, 137; animal metaphors 95; as classical Zion motif 37, 49; of prophet 40, 41
Psalms 67–69, 85; dating issues 7–9, 8; New Year festival 2–3; as primary source of Zion theology 1, 8; Zion psalms 3–6, 9, 67–68, 74n39
purification: in Ezekiel 47; in Isaiah 18n62, 34n39, 152; in Jeremiah 131, 152; in Micah 56–57; self-loathing 47, 138, 153, 155, 190

redaction scholarship 1, 54, 58
remnant of Israel 70–71, 118n59, 191; in Ezekiel 47, 132–34; good and bad figs image 123, 129–31; in Isaiah 19n62, 26, 28–29, 31–32, 33n26, 57, 63n39, 70–71, 89, 97–100, 101, 102, 107, 108, 114; in Jeremiah 40, 123, 150; in Joel 113; Shearjashub 28, 99, 118n61; in Zecharaiah 60, 63n54; in Zephaniah 57–58, 60, 109–11
repentance 50n21, 53, 66, 95, 99, 128–29; inner transformation 104–5, 146
repopulation of Zion 70–71; in Ezekiel 47; in Isaiah 29–30, 31; in Jeremiah 39

restoration of Zion 70–71, 138; in Isaiah 29–30; in Jeremiah 39
retribution 39, 135, 136; logic of 125, 138, 139–40n12, 140n15, 156
return to Zion 25, 144–63, 158–60; from captivity in Babylon 147–49, 151, 159nn5, 7, 161n37; in Ezekiel 152–54, 158; in Isaiah 29, 146–49, 158; in Jeremiah 38, 138, 149–52, 158; in Micah 154, 158; spiritual and physical 158–59; YHWH's 45, 64n43, 148–49, 155–59, 161n35, 162–63n65, 190; in Zechariah 155–58
reunification of Israel and Judah 55, 59, 164, 169–72, 180, 182, 185nn42, 43; in Amos 52; in Jeremiah 39, 41
river imagery 68, 145, 148, 173–74
river of Zion motif 4, 5, 11
rod and staff 91, 93, 115n19
root image 92, 99, 100, 102, 111, 114, 138, 170, 185n47
royal psalms 3

Salem 65, 72n10
salvation: in Ezekiel 48; faith as condition for 4, 28–29, 34–35n44, 160n21; light metaphor 30, 94, 177–78, 187n79; return as consequence of 130, 155 see also last bastion; repopulation of Zion; restoration of Zion; return to Zion
salvific themes 2, 13, 27–38, 57–58; Assyrian siege and 9, 28; YHWH's interventions 126, 147, 150–51, 155, 157, 190
Samaria 56, 184n34
Samaria, Mount 54, 62n15
Samarian Gerizim 9, 50n24, 65
scholarly literature 1–2; circularity 11–12; historical approaches 2, 5, 12; historical-critical 1, 5, 12, 29, 46, 58, 130; methodological issues 10–11; survey of 2–10
self-loathing 47, 138, 153, 155, 190
Sennacherib 6, 16–17n32, 28, 34n35, 71, 96–98
shepherd metaphors 47, 116n30, 162n58; enemy attackers 123, 126, 139n6; for YHWH 149–50, 153–54, 157–58, 162n58, 170–71, 190
shroud metaphor 181–82

213

INDEX OF SUBJECTS

Sinai, Mount 8
Sinai and Zion (Levenson) 8–9
Sinim (Syene) 148
Sion-Jerusalem Jahwes Königssitz
(Schreiner) 4
Sodom and Gomorrah 26, 89, 98
Solomon 5, 65
sons of Zion 52, 53, 67, 69, 105
spirit 100, 106, 113, 120n94
stone metaphor 112, 117n45
*Strukturen und Figuren im Kult von
Jerusalem* (Stolz) 4
sub-motifs 12, 13–14, 189, 191
Sukkoth festival 176, 179–80, 181
synchronic approaches 8, 10, 189

temple 8–9, 30, 39, 183n1; abandoned
by YHWH 46–47, 50n20; in Ezekiel
46–47, 147; on New Zion 172–73;
profanation of 46, 135, 153;
rebuilding of 25, 58, 63n43, 168;
source of river 173–74
temple ideology 6, 14n10, 40
temple psalms 8
theological motifs 2, 11, 12, 70
threshing-floor metaphors 67, 109,
114, 121n107
Topheth 94, 101, 125, 140n13
topography 10, 19n76, 20n78, 48,
50n26, 51n27
torah of YHWH 57, 124, 187n77, 78
'The Tradition of Zion's Inviolability'
(Hayes) 4
trumpet image 52, 53, 79, 82, 105, 123

Ugarit tablets 3, 4, 5, 6, 17n39
uncircumcised 175–76, 186n71
uncleanness 58, 135, 142n63, 175,
186nn69, 71
utopian imagery 30–31, 68

vineyard image 37, 70, 88, 99, 126,
140n20
Völkerkampf-motif 6, 16nn26, 27, 28,
29, 17n41, 20n80; in Psalms 68,
72, 85 *see also* enemy attack

Wadi Shittim 174, 186n58
waters: defeat of 5, 6, 26, 63n37,
183n3; enemy attackers compared
with 26, 82, 84, 87n24; river
imagery 4, 5, 11, 68, 148, 173–74

way imagery 149, 161n35; Holy Way
29, 144–46
weak and needy: return to Zion 150,
160nn11, 24; Zion as refuge for 26,
34n35, 93, 109–11, 114, 121n117
wedding metaphor 165–66,
183–84n11, 183n10
wilderness narrative 70–71, 160n9,
162n51; in Isaiah 26, 29, 75n64,
100, 122, 144–49, 152, 158; in
Jeremiah 124, 126, 131

YHWH: abandons temple 46–47,
50n20; enthronement 2, 9, 15n13;
glory of 29, 45, 46, 147, 153,
162n54, 177, 182; heritage 37, 53,
70, 105, 106, 126, 140n22;
individual relationship to 106;
knowledge of 180–81; presence and
protection 6, 9, 14n10, 26, 74n43,
100–101; return to Zion 45, 64n43,
148–49, 155–59, 161n35,
162–63n65, 190; as shepherd
149–50, 153–54, 157–58, 162n58,
170–71, 190; summons and leads
army 26, 37, 81–82, 85, 94,
134–35, 138; torah of 57, 124,
187n77, 78; vengeance of 36,
39–40, 145, 151–52; whistles for
enemy 81–82, 157–58; wrath of 4,
26–27, 37, 48, 156
YHWH Sebaoth 89, 91, 93, 98, 112,
157, 176, 179; as term 2, 44, 63n43

Zaphon, Mount 5, 6, 17n39, 38,
74n33
Zechariah 58–60, 190; classical Zion
motif 60–61; deliverance in 112–13;
fountain imagery 60, 113, 114;
inviolability of Zion 60, 112–14;
remnant of Israel 60, 63n54;
return to Zion 155–58; three major
parts 58
Zedekiah, King 131, 192n1
Zephaniah 57–58, 190; deliverance in
109–11, 114
Zion: as centre of world 8, 14n10,
20n78, 47–48, 60, 102, 108, 128,
132, 158, 172, 179, 182–83, 191;
chosen by YHWH 2, 3, 5, 19n77,
20n78, 65; as city of festivals
93–94, 101, 179–80, 181, 188n104;

214

INDEX OF SUBJECTS

defined 13; dual role 2, 27, 36, 56–57, 70–71, 76n66; Ezekiel avoids term 13, 19n76, 44–45, 49, 50n5, 173; glory of 30, 147; as heavenly 49, 51n31; as holy mountain 2, 5, 13, 15n18, 26, 30, 31, 47–48, 67–68, 107–8, 152–53, 166, 175, 179–82; inhabitants 20n78, 21n90, 25, 34n45; inviolability 1–8; as last bastion 12, 26, 28–29, 31–32, 37, 40–41, 70, 88–89, 189; motifs, events and characteristics associated with 26–31; not synonymous with Jerusalem 12–13; as place 11, 120n97; as place of permanent safety 93, 96, 102, 117n50; poetic imagery 11, 13, 43n31, 159n1, 177, 187n91; purging of 100–101, 106, 109, 112, 113, 114; as refuge for needy 26, 34n35, 93, 109–11, 114, 121n117, 145, 160n11; as sinful city 2, 44, 76n66, 115n6; *Sitz-im-Leben* of 5, 8, 19n64; as symbol 9; as term in Amos 54; as term in BHS 19n76; as term in

Isaiah 25–26; as term in Jeremiah 36; as term in Joel 52–53; as term in Micah 55–56; as term in Obadiah 54–55; as term in Zephaniah 57–58; as theological motif 2, 11, 12; topography 20n78, 21n90, 91; two main perceptions of 31; as woman 30–31; as YHWH's special dwelling 2, 19n77 *see also* classical Zion motif; defeat of Zion; dynamic Zion motif; restoration of Zion; return to Zion; Zion, Mount

Zion, the City of the Great King (Ollenburger) 9

Zion in den Psalmen (Körting) 9

Zion motif: defining 11–13

Zion theology: in Psalms 67–68 *see also* Zion tradition

Zion tradition 28–29; characteristics of 5–6; consensus 5; as Israelite tradition 6; in Jeremiah 40; not evident in Old Testament 7–8; as plural concept 11, 20nn79, 80; protection claim 46

Zion's Rock-Solid Foundations (Dekker) 9

eBooks
from Taylor & Francis
Helping you to choose the right eBooks for your Library

Add to your library's digital collection today with Taylor & Francis eBooks. We have over 50,000 eBooks in the Humanities, Social Sciences, Behavioural Sciences, Built Environment and Law, from leading imprints, including Routledge, Focal Press and Psychology Press.

Choose from a range of subject packages or create your own!

Benefits for you
- Free MARC records
- COUNTER-compliant usage statistics
- Flexible purchase and pricing options
- 70% approx of our eBooks are now DRM-free.

Benefits for your user
- Off-site, anytime access via Athens or referring URL
- Print or copy pages or chapters
- Full content search
- Bookmark, highlight and annotate text
- Access to thousands of pages of quality research at the click of a button.

ORDER YOUR FREE INSTITUTIONAL TRIAL TODAY

Free Trials Available

We offer free trials to qualifying academic, corporate and government customers.

eCollections
Choose from 20 different subject eCollections, including:

- Asian Studies
- Economics
- Health Studies
- Law
- Middle East Studies

eFocus
We have 16 cutting-edge interdisciplinary collections, including:

- Development Studies
- The Environment
- Islam
- Korea
- Urban Studies

For more information, pricing enquiries or to order a free trial, please contact your local sales team:
UK/Rest of World: **online.sales@tandf.co.uk**
USA/Canada/Latin America: **e-reference@taylorandfrancis.com**
East/Southeast Asia: **martin.jack@tandf.com.sg**
India: **journalsales@tandfindia.com**

www.tandfebooks.com